STIGMA CITIES

■ STIGMA CITIES ■

The Reputation and History of
Birmingham, San Francisco, and Las Vegas

JONATHAN FOSTER

UNIVERSITY OF OKLAHOMA PRESS : NORMAN

Publication of this book is made possible through
the generosity of Edith Kinney Gaylord.

Some ideas and information in this volume have been previously published in "Stigma Cities: Las Vegas and Birmingham in the National Newspaper Media, 1945–2000," *Nevada Historical Society Quarterly* 50, no. 4 (Winter 2007): 297–324, and are used here by permission.

Library of Congress Cataloging-in-Publication Data

Name: Foster, Jonathan, 1972– author.

Title: Stigma cities : the reputation and history of Birmingham, San Francisco, and Las Vegas / Jonathan Foster.

Description: Norman : University of Oklahoma Press, 2018. | Includes bibliographical references and index.

Identifiers: LCCN 2017058759 | ISBN 978-0-8061-6071-9 (hardcover : alk. paper)

Subjects: LCSH: Birmingham (Ala.)—History. | San Francisco (Calif.)—History. | Las Vegas (Nev.)—History. | Stigma (Social psychology)—United States. | Cities and towns—Social aspects—United States.

Classification: LCC HT123 .F7175 2018 | DDC 307.760973—dc23

LC record available at https://lccn.loc.gov/2017058759

The paper in this book meets the guidelines for permanence and durability of the Committee on Production Guidelines for Book Longevity of the Council on Library Resources, Inc. ∞

For Marianne, Nora, and Sadie

Contents

Illustrations

Preface

I grew up in Birmingham, Alabama, in the 1970s and '80s. Looking back, it was in many ways a wonderful place to be a kid. What kid wouldn't love a city of steel mill smokestacks lighting the night with fire under the watchful eye of the *Vulcan* statue, a fifty-foot-tall Roman god of the forge. I vividly recall the smell of those foundries and the colors of the city. Now it seems the colors are what most inform my recollection of the place. I remember always looking to see *Vulcan's* green light held aloft in the night sky from his perch atop Red Mountain. We all knew the story of how, for earlier generations, the light's color had literally meant life or death—red light signified a traffic fatality that day, and green meant everyone was safe.[1] Even though that practice had long passed by the '70s, I still glanced up with a kid's morbid anticipation each time we drove down I-65—just in case. Farther down the road, after exiting onto I-59 and heading west for a few miles, I sought out the flames of U.S. Steel's smokestacks. Their color, too, meant life or death in Birmingham. My granddad once worked there, and I knew that a fiery orange glow over the Fairfield Works meant jobs, money, and survival. These colors, green, red, and orange, all meant Birmingham to me.

But to the outside world, as I was well aware at even an early age, other colors defined my city. Birmingham was a city that many locals and outsiders alike believed was ruined by the oppression and violence of hate between white and black. Now I know it's likely that most of the outsiders never actually spent very much time in Birmingham. Their recollections, unlike mine, were not based on firsthand experience in the city. Instead, their ideas of Birmingham emerged from television, newspaper images, articles, and various other forms of media. The events and characteristics conveyed by these media representations helped to form and perpetuate Birmingham's stigmatized identity as a racially intolerant and violent place.

Growing up, I was always aware of racial tension and division in Birmingham. One couldn't help but know of the city's history of racial segregation, violence, and oppression. So, as enthralled as I was with Birmingham, I realized that it had problems, and I was bothered by that knowledge. My city's past wasn't so great. In fact, it was horrific. With education and maturity, a sense of shame came to accompany my realizations. I didn't like being associated with and judged by my city's stigma.

I was also bothered that Birmingham's reputation rested on its past rather than its present. I understood that the city was stigmatized because of historical characteristics and events that were increasingly viewed as outside the American mainstream of values—or at least outside what Americans convinced themselves were their mainstream values. But why did that reputation live on, and what did its perseverance mean for the city and its people? Did other cities undergo similar experiences? That curiosity and those questions eventually formed the basis of this book.

While it is perhaps one of the most obvious examples, Birmingham is, I have found, only one of many cities to be seen as distant from what Americans consider normal and acceptable. The stigmatization of urban places has occurred with some regularity in twentieth- and twenty-first-century America. In addition to Birmingham, this historical process has also played out in San Francisco, California, and Las Vegas, Nevada. Like Birmingham, both of those cities have developed reputations as being outside America's perceived norms during the twentieth century—San Francisco as a gay mecca and Las Vegas as Sin City.

Acknowledgments

I have often heard that the historian's work is a solitary endeavor. It is an occupation defined by lonely hours in archives or in front of computer monitors, sifting through the literary remnants of bygone years and lives once lived. I disagree. While this book might be the product of long hours, it is not the product of merely one individual's effort.

No work of history can be a solitary endeavor. Behind every such book, there is an army of kind and professional benefactors. In writing this book, I have received support from too many people to recall in ways that reignited my faith in the generosity of humankind. I could have never completed *Stigma Cities* without their assistance. Whatever insight this book possesses is attributable entirely to their support. Likewise, all deficiencies and inaccuracies are of my own doing. For, had I asked the correct questions, I would have undoubtedly received thorough help and generous support that would have led to conclusions that are more accurate.

This book began as my doctoral dissertation. I was lucky to establish a tremendous dissertation committee comprising David Wrobel, Eugene Moehring, Thomas Wright, and John Tuman. Without their guidance, the questions that form this book's foundation would not have been adequately addressed. I am extremely grateful for David Wrobel's assistance and perseverance over the past few years in inspiring me to complete the revision of that dissertation for

publication. Long after any professional responsibility as my dissertation committee chair has passed, David continues to remind me to not let the everyday
tasks of academia stand in the way of scholarly production. He should know, as
he remains one of the busiest and most productive scholars I have ever known.
I am lucky to have benefited from his expert advice, assistance, and motivation.

I would also be remiss if I failed to mention several of my colleagues at Great
Basin College. Specifically, Danny Gonzales and Laurie Walsh provided encour-
agement and support over the past several years as I attempted to gain tenure
while balancing teaching, service, and scholarly production.

I must also thank the graduate school and department of history at the University of Nevada, Las Vegas, for their support of my work while at the dissertation
stage. Through fellowships and assistantships, they made my dream of graduate
education—and in the process, this book—a reality.

This book's existence is also due to the staff at the University of Oklahoma
Press. I am forever indebted to the press for the professionalism of its editors and
staff. Of particular note, Kent Calder's patience and expertise is rivaled only by
his ability to answer this author's inane questions with tact and professionalism.
Thank you, Kent, for guiding me through this process. I also owe thanks to
Stephanie Evans for expertly ushering me through the final stages of this book's
production and to Abby Graves for her skillful copyediting.

Numerous archivists, librarians, and academics have helped me to locate
material and hone my ideas. While I wish it were possible to remember them
all, it would be inexcusable to not single out and thank Jim Baggett and Don
Veasey at the Birmingham Public Library, Christina Moretta at the San Francisco
Public Library, and Su Kim Chung and Delores Brownlee at the University of
Nevada, Las Vegas, Library Special Collections as well as the staffs of the Delta
Flight Museum's archives in Atlanta and the Birmingham Civil Rights Institute.

Most important, my family has made possible my life as an academic and, by
extension, this book. I will never forget how my parents, Kaye and Lavon, worked
so hard and always without complaint to provide a good life and opportunities
for my sisters and me. Likewise, my in-laws, Sissel and Rolf, have never failed
to encourage my work. And then there is my lovely wife, Marianne, and my
daughters, Nora and Sadie. I cannot thank them enough for supporting me,
inspiring me, and making me laugh every single day. They are far more important
to me than writing any book or teaching any class. Without those things, I could
survive just fine. Without my wife and daughters, I would be forever lost.

STIGMA CITIES

1

Imagining Place

This book is guided by the belief that ideas, with respect to their impact on places, rival the more obvious physical and economic contexts.[1] I believe this to be evident in the role that reputation plays in shaping the historical trajectories of cities. Cities, as significant and easily identifiable places, lend themselves easily to reputation-based identification by the public. In particular, the stigmatization of a place for being abnormal or even deviant often creates a reputation-based identity that can be impactful and long lived. People quite simply define a city by what they know about its historical characteristics. This shapes how people and institutions interact with the city. Such stigmatization is also complex in that its effect might not be universally bad for a place, nor is it necessarily permanent. Some places have benefited from notoriety that their own residents purposefully helped to create and exerted a great effort to maintain over time. Others have long suffered under disreputable identities to such a degree that residents have become hypersensitive and reactionary regarding any association or activity that might draw attention to their city's seeming abnormality. Still others have experienced onetime stigmas that become more acceptable and even profitable with shifts in society's norms over time. As this book suggests and as the historical interaction between a city and it image supports, sometimes it is good to be different, and sometimes it is not.

In examining stigmatization's complex historical influence on urban places, *Stigma Cities* looks to Birmingham's reputation as a racist city, San Francisco's as a gay mecca, and Las Vegas's as a sinful city. Each case study explores the stigma's historical formation, perseverance, and significance over time. While these case studies serve the purpose of illuminating the process and significance of these places' stigmatization, they are by no means comprehensive. The list of stigmatized cities is long and continues to grow. I chose these specific cities simply because I am most familiar with them and because they all experienced powerful stigmatization during the twentieth century. These three cases also represent three distinct manners in which urban stigmatization has played out. Birmingham shows the distinctly negative impact of stigmatization. There, a previously celebrated city was stigmatized due to a shift in cultural norms away from one of that city's characteristics. San Francisco shows how a formerly stigmatizing attribute can ultimately exert a positive influence on the city as cultural norms shift toward acceptance of that trait. Finally, Las Vegas offers a prime example of a city that, with its growth into a major American metropolitan area, seeks to enter the mainstream while simultaneously maintaining, on some level, its stigmatizing but lucrative abnormality. The histories of all three cities provide valuable insight for other places that have been stigmatized in the past or are experiencing the effects of similar transformation in the present. Hopefully the result is a history that explains stigmatization of place as a powerful, complex, and varied process linked directly to a city's wider historical and cultural context.

This process of urban stigmatization can emerge from any number of historical events or characteristics deemed different or counter to the contextual norms and attitudes of a particular time. This stigmatization can form almost instantaneously as the result of a city's association with a spectacular abnormal event, or it can grow gradually as numerous suggestive smaller events that are dutifully reported over time accumulate. Once entrenched, the stigmatization can be long lived and influential but is not necessarily permanent. While mass media news, popular entertainment, and even politics often serve as primary perpetuators of stigma, economic concerns and shifting societal values can ease the longevity and impact of such an identity. Or they can make it worse.

These case studies also show the influence of stigmatization and the consistent flux of urban reputations. Birmingham's reputation as a "magic city" of industrial progress grew in concert with the city's development as a center of racial oppression and violence. Throughout the late nineteenth and first half of the twentieth centuries, in a time when industrialization was prized and racism largely accepted or ignored, Birmingham's positive image as the forward-looking steel center of the New South held sway. Yet, in the changing context of the mid-twentieth century—and helped along by the local power structure's violent reaction to the civil rights demonstrations of 1963—Birmingham found itself recast as a national pariah. Since that time, its outsider status has remained strong as national opposition to racism has grown and shifting economic conditions have rendered industrial cities somewhat passé. Birmingham has subsequently experienced long-term negative consequences related to its infamy. Even today, when the city has long since moved beyond its pre-1963 violent racism, one can readily observe the continued influence of stigmatization on residents. In recent years, as the city has moved toward embracing its historic role in changing American racial norms, each attempt to honor Birmingham's civil rights history has awakened deep-seated anxiety in some residents. These Birminghamians believe that to publicly remember or celebrate the city's place in history is to revisit the city's troubled past. Such a past, they argue, might be better left ignored because remembrance could fuel the public's equation of the city with the violent and now unacceptable racism of its past.[2] They have subsequently expressed reticence with public acts of remembrance such as the naming of landmarks in honor of civil rights activists, the development of the Civil Rights Institute, and most recently, the city's successful campaign to have the areas associated with the 1963 demonstrations declared a national historic monument.

San Francisco's stigmatization as a gay mecca again shows the evolution of a stigma's influence over time due to changing contextual values. The city's reputation as a gay center or destination, which was layered on top of a preexisting reputation as an exotic city, has been politicized and used to show the city as abnormally liberal, radical, or even un-American. More recently, this gay-friendly notoriety has lost much of its bite. That is because gay Americans have fought for and made great strides toward obtaining a greater degree of acceptance and equality. As the perceptual center of gay America, key battles of that fight were centered in San Francisco and led by locals. As those battles joined with others to bear fruit on a national scale, San Francisco remained the reputational center of American homosexuality. With the widespread normalization of homosexuality, the impact of the divisive and dystopian rhetoric of the "values crowd" lessened while new voices promoting lifestyle tourism grew stronger. By the late twentieth and early twenty-first centuries, the gay mecca identity benefited the tourism industry of a city that has always been perceived as a bit exotic, radical, and just outside supposed mainstream American norms. As the previously taboo became acceptable, the place where it has seemingly always been commonplace became even more of a destination.

Finally, in Las Vegas, the Sin City image has served variously as the engine of the city's economy, a divisive force among city residents, and an obstacle to development. Recently some of the roadblocks to the city's mainstream acceptance have lessened because of changing national attitudes toward gambling as well as the tireless efforts of locals. Las Vegas now paradoxically attempts to be simultaneously mainstream and risqué. Americans likewise continue to both abhor and love the city to varying degrees. There is consequently a long history of values-based condemnation of the city existing alongside ever-increasing rates of visitation and urban growth. Las Vegas, as the nation's preeminent Sin City, has been held at arms length historically by those who control many of what are considered the true markers of a city's success. Only recently, for example, have major-league sports such as the National Football League (NFL) and National Hockey League (NHL) embraced the city. Such an embrace, even if heavily resisted and late in coming, might signify either a changing context or the power of economic concerns in overwriting values-based ostracism.

These three cities and their residents serve as case studies for this book because they offer insight into the nature and significance of place stigmatization. Each city developed and maintained a widely held identity in the twentieth century that has continued to evolve and influence the city's trajectory in the twenty-first century. In each case, politicians, the media, intellectuals, and other purveyors of popular culture have made use of the city's stained identity long after the events that created that identity. Because of this tendency, conversations regarding each city often refer to that city's stigmatized trait regardless of whether the issue under discussion relates to the stigma or not. The public is readily aware of these cities' reputations. This is true whether it is one politician labeling another a "San Francisco Democrat," an advertisement for Las Vegas promising, "What Happens Here, Stays Here," or a journalist employing the label *Bombingham* to link Birmingham's present to its past.[3] Yet the identities and their effects are not fixed and unmalleable. These cities' histories show us that attitudes and contexts, while always important, have a tendency to change over time. They also show us that actions matter.

In the latter regard, it is important to remember the significance of local residents' agency in the formation and perpetuation of place stigmatization. As historical actors, locals obviously engaged in actions and activities that brought about the initial stigmatization. Yet their importance did not end there. Over the years, the continued actions and attitudes of locals contributed to the maintenance and evolution of their city's stigmatization. Whether hiding from the past to avoid reminding a nation of a city's historical role or projecting an in-your-face defiance of norms in the name of equality or profit, these cities' residents and leaders have played and continue to play significant roles in the stigmatization process.

It is also important to note that in regard to how they have viewed their cities throughout history, Americans cannot be simply cast as anti-urban or pro-urban. Since the earliest days of European settlement in North America, locals have held widely varying ideas about their cities. At any time, the urbanite, small town resident, or farmer could apply his or her ideal of America to its cities in a favorable light just as easily as in a negative light (or perhaps in both lights simultaneously). Thus Thomas Jefferson could posit, "The mob of the great cities add just so much to the support of pure government as sores do to the human body," while J. Hector St. John de Crevecoeur, writing as the "American Farmer," alluded to the superiority of America's "fair cities."[4] In the end, it all becomes a matter of values and needs. In other words, the social context has largely determined how Americans have viewed their cities at any one time.

Yet the social context, in combination with past events, also allows the public to place a city in the appropriate conceptual category and lock it away there for long periods of time. For example, in the antiracism context of post–civil rights movement America, it became easy to conceptually lock Birmingham away in the untouchable box of racism. That box remains secure as associations with racism grow ever more unacceptable. Likewise Las Vegas, and all that goes on there, long sat hidden in the box labeled *sin*, only to be brought out and enjoyed when no one could see. San Francisco, once locked away like Birmingham, now joins Las Vegas in enjoying the light of day more often as the acceptability of homosexual demonization has lessened, albeit far too slowly and incompletely. Today, as homosexuality and gaming become more mainstream, those cities are less frequently locked away in their roles, but they remain uncomfortable for some.

Research and Theoretical Grounding

Although primarily a work of history, this book relies on interdisciplinary ideas. In order to understand the formation, perseverance, and influence of stigmatization and public opinion, even when such phenomena are rooted in historical events and circumstances, one must cast a broad net both in terms of research and theoretical grounding. Subsequently, this book rests on a plethora of popular and scholarly sources while unashamedly borrowing from numerous concepts and theories developed in sociology, psychology, and media studies to explain the characteristics of historical stigmatization.

In exploring these cities' reputations and their historical influences, I have consulted sources ranging from Twitter to scholarly monographs and include just about everything in between. Although heterogeneous, these sources were not chosen randomly. In drawing on social media and online comments on news articles, for example, I have attempted to gauge the popular sentiment and interest relative to various events. In consulting newspapers, television news, and online news, I seek to understand both what is being projected and how its characteristics perpetuate and otherwise influence stigmatization. I rely heavily on the *New York Times* and network news broadcasts because these are as close to national media voices as exist in the United States. Similarly, local newspapers, television news, and news websites provide a glimpse, if incomplete, of local issues and attitudes. Oral histories and interviews are used to gain insight into events and, more important, attitudes concerning those events. Finally, scholarly sources are used when available to provide theoretical grounding as well as other scholars' interpretations of the various histories associated with the events under discussion. All these sources were examined with the intent of providing a more comprehensive history of how these cities gained their reputations, how those reputations have survived and evolved over time, and how those reputations have influenced these cities' trajectories.

Scholars in the fields of psychology and sociology have produced a strong body of work on the subject of stigmatization. In particular, the pioneering works of Erving Goffman and Irwin Katz have contributed to understanding stigma as an important and complex social process.[5] From these and other social scientists, a definition and a framework present themselves, offering historians an exciting and potentially invaluable new way of looking at the influence of the perception of place over time.

The word *stigma* itself dates back to ancient Greek origins. In its original usage, a stigma represented a defacing mark, burn, or cut that was applied to an individual with the intention of instantly identifying a person as being "different." Beginning in early Christian times, *stigma* expanded on this with a dual meaning. On one level, the word referred to outward signs of physical disability and, by relation, bodily deviance. At the same time, many early Christians saw a connection between physical eruptions of the skin and an individual's proximity to holy grace.

More recently, society has adopted a more complex and abstract usage of the word. *Stigma* now as commonly refers to a suspected or confirmed association with a known deviant activity as it does with the outward appearance of any physical "abnormality." While still important in revealing some stigmas, physical markings are no longer required for all. Further, an action that a population might stigmatize in one culture or era might find complete acceptance in another. Acceptance and rejection might also change over time. In sum, stigmatization has emerged as a social construct, ever changing and relative to the cultural mores of its respective era and setting.[6]

Goffman offers the consensus definition of modern stigma as "an attribute that is deeply discrediting" and that leaves wider society with the impression that an individual "is not quite human."[7] These attributes, while varying over time and place, normally discredit the stigmatized while confirming the "usualness" of others.[8] Goffman further argues that modern stigmatization takes on one of three main variations: physical "abominations of the body," perceptual "blemishes of the character," and stereotypical "tribal stigmas."[9]

The concepts of *character blemish* and *tribal stigma* are particularly relevant for a historical understanding of the stigmatization of place. Character blemishes result from direct actions that are perceived to be outside societal norms. These deviations might include criminal acts, manifestations of mental or physical infirmities, or any other acts that are perceived to be contrary to normal expectations. Tribal stigmatization, by contrast, characterizes individuals as deviant simply because of their association with a larger group that is considered abnormal.[10] Thus an outsider, having never met a particular Birminghamian, might cast the individual as a racist simply because prevailing stereotypes are built on the city's history of racial intolerance. At the same time, a San Franciscan or Las Vegan might enjoy a reputation as being individualistic, which rests merely on the public's frontier-rooted notions of the West as the nation's most individualistic region. At the same time, someone from a distant location who is influenced by Las Vegas's frequent objectification of women might actually believe that former Las Vegas mayor Jan Jones was a showgirl or an exotic dancer before taking office simply because she was a female residing in Las Vegas.[11] Or politicians like former governor Richard Lamm of Colorado might even believe his unsupported and offhand remark that "one of eight women under 45 in Las Vegas is a prostitute."[12]

Media coverage can perpetuate the stigmatization process. Once place-based stereotypes are created by observable characteristics or spectacular events that reside outside the perceived national norms, they gain and retain popularity as journalists refer to those sensational events of the past, although they often have no bearing on current activities or characteristics. Further, as with people, popular stereotypes of regions in which cities reside provide easy intellectual references for journalists to employ. The local place, therefore, easily assumes the identity of both the abnormal event and its wider geographic and cultural placement.[13]

Beyond content, the changing nature of the mass media over the last two centuries has also influenced perceptions of place. Once the telegraph broke the link between transportation and communication, the speed and reach of the media embarked on an exponential trajectory that continues unimpeded. As Daniel Czitrom argues, this break "opened the age of electronic media" and helped change the world as people knew it.[14] In relatively rapid succession, movies, radio, television, and the Internet flooded through this opening to propel humanity headlong into the communication age. Along the way, demarcation lines between culture and the media and between fact and fiction became increasingly blurred. Today the term *popular culture* is almost synonymous with these new and ever-more-available mediums of communication. At the same time, people who are afloat in the torrent of information have trouble distinguishing between fake and real news while communication-savvy opinion setters consistently act as though a message's reception is more important than its accuracy.[15] Information overload, it seems, does not always lead to the widespread dissemination of accurate opinions about the world in which we live.

Once the message has been received, regardless of its accuracy or the process of its dissemination, the public does not always act in a strictly uniform manner toward stigmatized places. While many outsiders react negatively to the stigmatized, that is not always the case. Often, even though the public views a person or place as being deviant in certain ways, a level of pity or curiosity in the unusual or even a tendency to pull for the underdog leads outsiders to cast the stigmatized in an improved light. This inconsistency results from an ambivalence that is central to the relativism of the stigmatization process. An individual or society may harbor feelings of both love and hate for a person, group, or place at the same time. Depending on the accepted cultural mores of a time and setting, a degree of oscillation between emotions often presents itself in greater society's dealings with "others."[16]

Although it is a complex and varied process, there is hope of finding meaningful patterns within the history of place stigmatization. One can see among the myriad scattered actions and reactions the ever-present influence of historical context on beliefs and individual actions concerning stigmatized cities. This process first illuminates the way in which ideas that are born of historical events can influence people and then reproduce themselves in subsequent generations. People's dispositions develop relative to and are influenced by their historical placement in society and culture.[17]

The relevance of such a disposition resides in the portrayal, perseverance, and eventual evolution of a person's perception of a place and this perception's influence. Social interactions—including through the media, in person, and in academia—almost constantly reinforce accepted ideas of a locality. Ultimately, as in the case of Birmingham's relation to violent racism, San Francisco's to homosexuality, and Las Vegas's to sin, the reputation becomes the unquestioned reality. Journalists write of racial problems when covering an abortion clinic bombing in Birmingham; presidents associate corporate trips to Las Vegas with wasteful hedonism; and the promoters of "traditional family values" equate San Francisco with homosexuality.[18] Through such suggestions and reinforcements in the media, people, to borrow the words of Carl Becker, "fashion a history" of "past times and distant places," which informs their everyday routines, lives, and opinions.[19]

Obviously, the prevalence of such perceptions coincides with stereotyping. In the 1920s social commentator Walter Lippman expanded the definition of the word *stereotype*—a word once meaning only a method of printing from solid plate—to include attitudes and beliefs. *Stereotype* has since taken strong root in the English language and American culture and is central to the stigmatization of place. Lippman argued that stereotypes are a necessary part of life in the modern age. Quite simply, the amount of news available to the individual increased dramatically during the latter half of the nineteenth century and exponentially throughout the twentieth century. With increases in population, dispersal, technology, and events, journalists could not hope to explain in detail the backgrounds of all events, just as the reading public could not dream of consuming such explanations in their entirety. People sought easily recallable characterizations to make sense of the world's happenings. Lippman understood this and used the word *stereotype* to describe the role of preconceived notions in society:

> But modern life is hurried and multifarious, above all physical distance separates men who are often in vital contact with each other, such as employer and employee, official and voter. There is neither time nor opportunity for intimate acquaintance. Instead we notice a trait which marks a well-known type, and fill in the rest of the picture by means of

the stereotypes we carry about in our heads. He is an agitator. That much we notice, or are told. Well, an agitator is this sort of person, and so *he* is this sort of person. He is an intellectual. He is a plutocrat. He is a foreigner. He is a "South European." He is from Back Bay. He is a Harvard Man.

After giving his definition of *stereotype*, Lippman expands upon its ubiquitous and necessary existence:

> The subtlest and most pervasive of all influences are those which create and maintain the repertory of stereotypes. We are told about the world before we see it. We imagine most things before we experience them. And those preconceptions, unless education has made us acutely aware, govern deeply the whole process of perception. . . . Were there no practical uniformities in the environment, there would be no economy and only error in the human habit of accepting foresight for sight. But there are uniformities sufficiently accurate, and the need of economizing attention is so inevitable, that the abandonment of all stereotypes for a wholly innocent approach to experience would impoverish human life.[20]

One can see that stereotypes, as defined by Lippmann, were a required element of understanding. Individuals were well aware of their use of stereotypes and of the inaccuracies therein. Because of this, people tended to cling to their generalizations "lightly" and "to modify them gladly." Whether or not the stereotype became dangerous depended upon the preconception's "character" and the "gullibility" with which the individual embraced it.[21]

While the stereotype may have found self-reflective acceptance in the 1920s, certain types of stereotypes had definitely fallen out of favor by the century's latter decades. A growing self-awareness of racism and inequality brought about by the civil rights and other social movements of the post–World War II period helped usher in the demise of the widely accepted overt racial stereotype. That is not to say that such stereotypes, or the racism on which they were often based, disappeared instantaneously and completely. Rather, their grossest forms became taboo in popular forms of media and discourse as people embraced the norms of a changing society. Racial stereotypes most likely remain privately held and publicly flouted in less recognizable forms. For example, politicians might operate according to the assumption that African American citizens cannot obtain true equality without the help of government institutions.[22] While perhaps well intentioned, this course of action reveals a paternalistic stereotype held by the politician in regard to racial self-sufficiency. But at least mainstream newspapers and magazines no longer employ such overtly stereotypical headlines as "The Coolies and the Negro," "Negroes Also Have Feelings," and "The Negro Point of View."[23]

Despite the long-overdue condemnation and reduction of such intolerant stereotypes, Lippman's explanation of generalizations remains cogent to some degree. With the technology and availability of communication improving at unimaginable rates, the need for mental shortcuts in understanding one's world has grown incredibly. If one could not employ generalizations of some sort, one certainly could not make sense of a world gone mad with twenty-four-hour cable news, fake news, social media, and saturation-level advertising for every conceivable product known to humanity. Generalizations subsequently continue to serve an important informational function in modern society by reducing the required amounts of data needed to form a conclusion. In so doing, the generalization reduces the amount of effort needed for information processing to a manageable level.[24] Unfortunately, such generalizations are not always accurate and are frequently biased.

Stereotypes have subsequently never vanished. Instead, their use remains strong and perhaps a bit more ominous as people have lost a degree of self-awareness concerning them. Although self-proclaimed sensitive and tolerant individuals of the late twentieth and early twenty-first century might never have considered the deliberate use of stereotypes to describe a race of people, they continued to do so unwittingly about place.[25] In effect, the vanquishing of the racist stereotype has opened the door for widespread and dangerous use of other preconceptions. The removal of the most blatant and damaging stereotypes has allowed society to feel a false sense of accomplishment in the belief that all stereotypes have been revealed and rightfully condemned. In this context, a place-based stereotype with the seeming backing of history might go largely undetected. Society has, therefore, failed to heed Lippman's warning about the dangers of stereotypes; indeed, it has fallen into the very gullibility of which he warned.[26]

In examining the role of the media in perpetuating stigmatizing stereotypes, one can look to the framework of a conservative media as put forth by Noam Chomsky and Edward Herman. Their Propaganda Model of News Media suggests that the media operates in the interest of and at the whim of society's elite and that it is in the best interest of those elites to have a stable society. Such stability is threatened by a society that widely considers freedom of the press and expression to be cornerstones of its existence. In such a society, people often wittingly or unwittingly use the media as a tool to suppress dissent. This suppression, and the stability it brings about, is accomplished, according to Chomsky and Herman, through a series of media filters that strain out unacceptably inciting aspects of coverage.[27]

The framework of Chomsky and Herman's Propaganda Model is not without merit. By looking at the media from an institutional vantage point, one can easily find a conservative tendency in the manner of news coverage. That is not to say that journalists themselves are politically conservative—study after study has revealed a marked liberal leaning among journalists—but rather that they operate conservatively within the confines of what is acceptable news coverage.[28] Further, the uniformity with which nonnews forms of popular media and discourse—such as films, television programs, novels, and political comments—fall back on the accepted stereotypes of Las Vegas, Birmingham, and San Francisco implies that such a conservative tendency is widespread.

All these ideas and cross-disciplinary examinations of stigmatization can help to advance our understanding of the past. In the case of stigmatized places, it becomes apparent that the historical situations in which people live—including people with the power to set opinions—have shaped their perceptions. As a result, the images of these places that are presented tend to be those that people expect regardless of the events that cause media coverage. Market forces and professional considerations play heavily into this perseverance of established ideas. A journalist, editor, or politician has no reason to rock the boat and possibly upset advertisers, subscribers, or prospective voters on a merely contextual issue such as location.[29] The most efficient move is to invoke the established norm of the place in which the event has occurred, then move along and explore the event. Many likely do this without conscious thought or purpose if the generalization about the place's historical identity is deeply entrenched. This reliance on established stereotypes of place, even if unwitting, distorts the message by implying false relationships between current events, characteristics, and a place's past.

Unfortunately, too few historians have looked at the influence of stigmatization on places and people over time. Beyond the work of Howard M. Solomon, few have been willing to advocate the centrality of ruined identities to their subject material. Solomon argued that the stigmatization of groups throughout history is central to understanding both the cultures in which they existed and the groups themselves. Unfortunately, he did not apply these ideas or the historical study of stigma to understanding the identities of cities or places.[30] If the historiographical net is broadened, there is a relatively extensive body of work on city images relative to urban decline, design, and planning. Key works in the literature include Peter Hall's *Cities of Tomorrow: An Intellectual History of Urban Planning and Design in the Twentieth Century*; William Sharpe and Leonard Wallock's *Visions of the Modern City*; Eric Avila's *Popular Culture in the Age of White Flight: Fear and Fantasy in Suburban Los Angeles*; Robert Beauregard's *Voices of Decline: The Postwar Fate of U.S. Cities*; and Steve Macek's *Urban Nightmares: The Media, the Right, and the Moral Panic over the City*.[31]

Exciting work on stigmatization of place has emerged recently in disciplines other than history. Sociologists have looked at the process and influence of what they have termed *territorial stigmatization* in a number of insightful urban-centered studies. They have placed much emphasis on understanding the development of the public's conceptualization of certain areas as *ghettos* and how that stigmatized characterization affects residents. Some scholars such as Loïc Wacquant have even placed this issue in political and transnational context. His pathbreaking *Urban Outcasts: A Comparative Sociology of Advanced Marginality* compares the stigmatization of the urban ghetto in the United States with that of France's working-class *banilieus*. Wacquant finds a strong marginalization of both areas often driven by state-centered policies and directives. Further, he argues that the stigmatized American ghetto model, which is based to a significant degree on racial segregation and oppression, has been projected to explain urban marginality on an international scale. This includes, as he illustrates, the misuse of the ghetto model to explain the very different reality of the French outer city.[32] Others such as sociologists Lynn Hancock and Gerry Mooney along with geographers Tom Slater and Ntsiki Anderson have also found significant, if varied, territorial stigmatization in England's urban centers. Whether brought about by racial or activity-related stereotypes, territorial stigmatization is seen by all as a socially and politically powerful instrument in modern society.[33]

That is not to say, however, that a place's reputation, or even the influence of that reputation, is written in stone. Instead, while it can be exceedingly difficult for a place to fully shed its stigma once established, it is entirely possible that the wider society might alter its view of the stigmatizing characteristic or experience a change in values. Just as a contextual change in societal values might contribute to a city's stigmatization, a similar change could also improve an already-stigmatized city's ruined reputation. In this regard, a city might remain exactly as it was yet become acceptable. Its residents could even benefit from doubling down on and exaggerating the event or characteristic for which they were once shamed. As is indicated by the lessening impact of Las Vegas's and San Francisco's stigmatization, this might be the most likely way for a city to escape the negative influences of stigmatization.

Thus stigmatization can play a significant if variable role in the historical trajectory of a place. It is deserving of additional historical inquiry. The chapters that follow attempt to answer a few of the historical questions related to this important social phenomenon. Chapter 2 will examine the history of Birmingham and the development of its reputation as a center of racial violence by the mid-twentieth century. Chapter 3 will build upon this by discussing the perpetuation and influence of that stigmatized identity on Birmingham's historical course since the civil rights movement. Chapter 4 will take the reader to San Francisco as it highlights the city's longtime perceptual placement as one of the nation's most exotic and cosmopolitan urban areas. This identity provided a fertile ground for the development of San Francisco as the nation's gay mecca. Chapter 5 details the link of this identity with historical on-the-ground action as the city became a center of the gay rights movement, the fight against AIDS, and sexual-identity tourism. From San Francisco, the book moves to its final case study of Las Vegas. Chapter 6 looks at the environmental and social influences of Las Vegas's development as the nation's Sin City. Chapter 7 delves into the challenges and opportunities presented by its stigma as modern Las Vegas attempts to be both deviant and more mainstream at the same time.

All these chapters argue from a historical perspective that what people think of places has a direct influence on what places become and how people behave regarding those places. But these thoughts also occur in the wider context of shifting societal values. As we journey through the information age, these mental constructions deserve equal consideration alongside the physical structures and institutions that are so often viewed as the defining characteristics of place. In the end, and with regard to history, reputation matters.

2

Not Always a Pariah

Birmingham's Journey from Magic City to Bombingham

Birmingham, Alabama, claimed its share of popularity in the late nineteenth and early twentieth centuries. Founded in 1871 at the rare confluence of iron ore, limestone, and coal, the city had all the natural resources to develop into a giant of iron manufacturing. It was a New South city par excellence—a technological wonder showcasing the industrial might of the United States of America. As such, Birmingham seemed the local antithesis to a southern region that was so often perceived as being agricultural, lazy, and backward.[1]

Early on, boosters liked to associate Birmingham with this ideal of the New South. The booming young town seemingly turned its back on the South's troubled agrarian past and embraced modern industrialism wholeheartedly. As blast furnaces and factories dotted the local landscape by 1885, boosters who prophesied a southern rival to northern industrial centers seemed destined to be right.[2] The town's population growth (from 3,086 in 1880 to 26,178 in 1890, an astonishing 748 percent) further supported their optimistic outlook. In addition, approximately twenty thousand people resided immediately beyond the city limits in 1890. By 1910 Birmingham had become the largest city in the state and a force to be reckoned with regionally, claiming a population of 138,685 people.[3]

Yet in many regards, this burgeoning New South city proved to be not so new after all. Slaveholding interests had actually conceptualized an industrial center at Birmingham in 1859. Their plans called for an industrial slave center that would help move the South into the industrial future while preserving the status quo of antebellum labor and race relations. Although the Civil War intervened to render this plan impossible, the city that emerged soon afterward illustrated the New South's continuity with the Old South. Many of the city's founders and early industrialists, for example, shared a common planter or upper-class background. These men represented the elite of the antebellum period with their business, labor, and racial philosophies formed along the lines of plantation society. In Birmingham these owners and their progeny initiated a system that embraced African American convict labor and actively sought to keep labor divided along racial lines for decades. The city's industrialists further traveled the path of the Old South by choosing to rely upon labor-intensive methods of production over recent technological innovations that were simultaneously being utilized by northern industry. The divided labor force was, after all, cheap and readily available while the latest innovative technology required a considerable capital outlay.[4] In some regards, the booming town came to resemble what one historian aptly described as "an overgrown iron plantation."[5]

Birmingham's racially centered labor system matured in the twentieth century's first three decades. In 1910 African Americans held 75 percent of steel mill and iron furnace jobs. But African American employment in the industry fell to 54 percent by 1930 as unionized whites entered the city's industrial workforce in large numbers. Jobs within the plants also exhibited an increased stratification of white and black work. Skilled positions tended to go to white workers while black workers remained mired in unskilled, dangerous, and labor-intensive duties. Labor organization strengthened this separation as unionized white workers exercised their newfound influence on management to enforce job discrimination.[6] That is not to say that Birmingham unions never organized African American workers. Between 1901 and 1908, for example, the United Mine Workers (UMW) added six thousand African American workers to its rolls. The city's white workers nevertheless always organized at a higher rate than its black workers did.[7] This is likely due to intimidation, the frequent and violent enforcement of established racial boundaries, and plain old discrimination against African American workers. In early twentieth-century Birmingham, African American workers' fear of being seen as stirring up trouble was entirely justifiable.

Labor divisions and expectations even influenced the development and direction of public education as Birmingham entered the twentieth century. On the surface, Birmingham leaders seemed to take a progressive step in regard to the public education of its African American population. With the opening of

BIRMINGHAM INDUSTRIAL DISTRICT c.1950

Birmingham Industrial District, Birmingham, Jefferson County, Alabama, ca. 1968.
Library of Congress, Prints and Photographs Division, HAER AL-105.

Industrial High School in 1901, the city became the first in the Southeast to offer publicly supported secondary education for its black residents.[8]

Historian Horace Bond theorizes that ulterior motives prompted Birmingham's city leaders to this seemingly radical action during such a racially oppressive period. As a new and rapidly growing industrial center, the city needed a stable labor force. In his work *Negro Education in Alabama: A Study in Cotton and Steel*, Bond proposes that city leaders supported the new school because local industrialists favored the industrial education of the black workforce. This argument credits education as a tool of social stability. Because local African Americans would have the necessary qualifications to assume skilled positions, increased education would reduce the probability of walkouts by white labor. Adding to the logic of Bond's conclusion is the obvious notion that increased education equals increased worker productivity.[9]

While local industrialists certainly hoped to leverage a skilled African American labor pool against strike-prone white employees, local African American leaders also contributed to the establishment of public secondary education for their children. On June 9, 1900, black leaders petitioned the educational board for the establishment of a black high school. This desire for increased tutelage conformed to southern African Americans' high regard for education in the post–Civil War South. After they were long denied education under slavery, freedmen realized that socioeconomic advancement required the formation of schools. These men and women often, and sometimes begrudgingly, accepted segregated institutions because any integration into the white system seemed impossible at the time. This aura of impossibility grew in part from the prevalent opinion among whites that African Americans should not receive any education much less education alongside their own white children. As historian Howard Rabinowitz postulates, the establishment of certain segregated institutions following Reconstruction actually offered a relative improvement for the black population. Although black schools certainly lacked equality with white institutions, they did offer educational inclusion in place of the black population's former exclusion from education.[10]

Birmingham's board of education did not approve the black citizens' request for a publicly supported high school out of hand. After a contentious and heated debate, dissenters acceded to the high school's formation only after board president Samuel Ullman's direct and forceful intervention in favor of the idea. Even then, board members clashed over the school's funding. While a monthly tuition rate of $1.50 for residents and $2.50 for nonresidents—intended to help cover structural costs—persuaded finance committee president Burghard Steiner to approve of the venture, tension rose regarding the payment of instructors. Board member H. B. Gray proposed that the city not pay the new school's teachers at all. In place of a city salary, he preferred leaving the educators to draw what remittance was possible from the tuition plan. Opposed by Ullman, this motion failed, and the city assumed the instructors' salaries. Ullman's open support for black education and vocational training—low-key yet present for several years previous—ultimately contributed to the progressive reformer's loss of his esteemed position. The city's board of aldermen refused to reelect the longtime board president later that same year. Regardless of whether the call for a black high school would have failed without Ullman's support, the fact remains that Birmingham's black population played a significant role in bringing the issue to the board's attention. The city's African Americans of the time rightly looked upon the school's institution with a sense of accomplishment.[11]

This seeming success for African American residents in public secondary education convinced some in national media outlets that Parker High—formerly known as Industrial High School—represented a prime example of racial cooperation. With a new multistory brick building completed in 1924 and the largest enrollment of any black high school nationwide, Parker High School was cited in national publications as evidence of Birmingham's foresight and leadership in providing the opportunity of secondary education, albeit industrial in scope, for its black citizens. From *School Day* to the *Christian Science Monitor*, these publications lavished praise upon this burgeoning educational experiment of the Deep South's Birmingham.[12] But by this time, Birmingham had grown accustomed to being praised as a trendsetter.

It should be noted that as progressive as this school was, it was still very much a part of the de jure racial segregation that defined almost all racial interactions in the city. By 1901 Jim Crow ordinances segregated the city's public transportation, lavatories, and fountains on the basis of race. Also, Birmingham's African American residents were barred outright from using seventeen public playgrounds, most hotels and restaurants, the zoo, and the library. Even though African Americans were allowed to patronize most stores, they faced discrimination in terms of service. For example, many clothing stores did not allow African Americans to try on apparel or shoes and prohibited them from returning merchandise.[13] Such segregation was not, however, the main focus of media attention on Birmingham during this early period. Instead, the city's national reputation benefitted from such things as the creation of the high school and the city's roaring growth and industrialization.

Early on, the national press seldom shied away from singing the praises of this new and seemingly different southern town. By 1887 the *New York Times*, in a review of A. J. McClure's *The Great South*, joined with the author in championing the industrial center as a southern trendsetter. Relying heavily on Birmingham's centrality to the state's tenfold increase in iron output from sixty thousand to six hundred thousand tons annually over the city's brief existence, the *Times* agreed that this "new Pittsburgh of the South," gave Pennsylvania "good cause to be anxious."[14] This piece followed similar accolades printed only months earlier in the *Louisville Courier-Journal*. In an article reprinted nationally, the *Courier* wrote that Birmingham was in the process of "converting Alabama from a poor and listless farming territory into a rich, active, and prosperous community, with diversified interests, a mixed and vigorous population, and an entirely new character."[15] The *Times* had also taken approving note of locals' preference for calling Birmingham "the Magic City" by this time.[16] The nickname, coined by local developer Col. James R. Powell of the Elyton Land Company in 1872, was oft repeated by both locals and outsiders in the decades to come.[17]

From the mid-1880s to well into the 1930s the national press continued to bestow praise on this "new character" that Birmingham provided the South. This character of industrial success was often presented as progressive and good. It was a formerly impoverished area that was turning from the past to grab hold of one of the most technologically advanced industries of the day and, in so doing, improving its situation markedly. Time after time, additional comparisons to Pittsburgh appeared alongside such language as *pride, show, boom, busy, prosperity, riches, public spirit, leading, miracle, wonder,* and *throbbing* in descriptions of this atypical southern city.[18]

In addition to being cast as a leading example to its regional neighbors, Birmingham was also placed in a favorable national context by writers. At times, the city took on a decidedly patriotic identity, such as in 1887 when the *New York Times* printed that "no man . . . who care[s] for national development and national progress," could look away from Birmingham's example.[19] Another piece placed Birmingham among the few southern cities that "promote a harmony of feeling and interests with the rest of the country."[20] As war with Spain broke out in 1898, the trend of using Birmingham as an example of patriotism and progress continued. The proposed war production in the city's steel mills was said to be an "example of increasing national unity," "higher patriotism," and "true progress."[21] At the same time, a universal principle of disassociating Birmingham from other "drunken," "dry" (alcohol free), and "sleepy" towns of the South permeated national articles describing the city.[22]

This trend continued through the first two decades of the twentieth century. In 1910 the *Times* called attention to the fact that the booming metropolis had "quadrupled" in population, from 38,417 to 132,685, over the course of the preceding decade.[23] The 1920s also kicked off with an article that highlighted Birmingham's progress. *Times* journalist Charles A. Selden found that Birmingham, while leading the South in industrial production, had also taken a central role in improving conditions for southern African Americans. The piece praised *Birmingham News* editor Frank Glass for lending support to black suffrage for "high class Negroes."[24] Five years later *Times* journalist Frank Bohn praised the industrial might of Birmingham in climbing its way to third in national iron production. Such industrial production was in large part responsible for Bohn's characterization of the New South as the "most fascinating part of present-day America."[25]

That is not to say, however, that all press coverage of early Birmingham was favorable. Beginning in the first decade of the twentieth century and increasing steadily alongside this stream of positive press, coverage could be found of a more distressing characteristic of the city's regional placement. In 1900 and 1901 the *New York Times* ran two small pieces that alluded to the nature of race relations in Alabama. These pieces portrayed Birmingham as a setting for racially charged activity but not as an irredeemably bigoted place outright. First, in December 1900, the newspaper reported that members of the Alabama Democratic Executive Committee had gathered in Birmingham to arrange for a ballot measure to be presented to the voting public the following April. This measure—which was in line with the contemporary currents of southern progressivism—called for the state constitution to be rewritten, in the words of the *New York Times*, to exclude the "ignorant negro vote." It would also ensure that no former Confederate soldier would find his vote in jeopardy.[26]

The following September a second piece addressing the proposed constitution appeared, revealing that certain leaders of the state's African American population had met in Birmingham and agreed not to oppose the disenfranchisement due to a lack of political power. Instead, they would seek other avenues to test the legality of the new constitution's provisions following its approval.[27]

In December of that year a far more disturbing article mentioned, without condemnation, the forced deportation of African American mill workers from their homes in Birmingham to newly opened iron plants in Nova Scotia. Former Sloss-Sheffield Furnace superintendent J. H. Means, who had been named general manager of Nova Scotia's Dominion Coal and Iron Company, sought to acquire a stable, cheap, and experienced labor supply for his new assignment. The article mentioned that Means overcame worker "opposition" to the forced migration and succeeded in departing with "three carloads of Alabama negroes" and their "wives and daughters" from Birmingham. No mention was made of the fate of any sons they might have had or of any working agreement or contract between Means and the northward-bound residents.[28]

The 1910s witnessed much of the same in regard to the coverage of race relations in Birmingham. The city was mentioned in one article on the wider southern rivalry between Jewish immigrants and black merchants and in an editorial on the decline of lynching in the South—with only cursory mention of Birmingham—by Booker T. Washington. The story of a man arrested for inciting black laborers to strike in a mining community some thirty miles north of the city also appeared in April 1917.[29] Of these, the latter piece on the inciter proved the most revealing as it made no connection between the racial antagonisms at the mine and the treatment of black workers in its parent iron industry in Birmingham. Instead, the averted racial strike was presented as an isolated event.[30]

Coverage of race in the Birmingham area during the 1920s reflected a decidedly violent turn. The year 1927 seemed to mark the peak of coverage of increased violence toward Birmingham-area African Americans as five separate articles in the *New York Times* focused on a rash of floggings and other physical acts of violence perpetrated by local bands of the Ku Klux Klan (KKK).[31] The KKK, having reemerged in the 1910s, had spread nationwide before retreating somewhat in the mid-1920s. In 1927 it remained strong in Alabama, and brutal instances of KKK violence occurred around Birmingham during this time. The circumstances behind the violence varied from individual to individual. Arthur Hitt, for example, was removed from his house by a band of masked Klansmen after having refused to sell a tract of his land to a white man. After a severe beating, Hitt agreed to sell the land for a price far below its market value. In another instance, Eston Murchenson of the Birmingham suburb of Bessemer was forcefully removed from a car in which "two strange girls" had offered him a ride. Murchenson was then whipped by a gang of assailants. He claimed that the white girls had set him up by giving him the ride, which had provided the motive for the beating. Even women were subject to the attacks, as was the case with Bertha E. Slay. A band of both males and females entered Slay's home, tied her husband and sister to a bed, and forced her out into the home's front yard. Once in the yard, Slay was tied to a barrel and whipped viciously with an automobile fan belt. News reports failed to mention the reason behind this brutal attack. A similar lack of motive marked a series of attacks on local resident James Bolton. In January, Bolton was lured outside his home, at which time he was bound, taken to a deserted road, and severely whipped. The following June, Bolton was once again tricked into opening his door for an individual who claimed to need help for a sick girl. Bolton was then "beaten unmercifully with a large strap" as his home was set ablaze.[32]

Despite this rash of race-related violence in the Birmingham area in 1927 and the national attention it garnered, the city itself was not labeled as violently bigoted by the national press. Instead, articles linked the attacks more broadly to the South or to the state of Alabama. This is evident in the titles of the stories devoted to the floggings. In each instance, either the "South" or "Alabama" appeared as the geographical setting.[33] A closer reading reveals that Birmingham was treated as distinctly different and more tolerant than outlying areas in regard to this violence and racism. In one instance readers learned that Birmingham newspapers had joined with several in Georgia in going "after the Klan with gloves off." Although perhaps slow to do this, the *Birmingham News*'s stance against the Klan placed the city, in the eyes of the *Times* journalists, far ahead of comparable areas in Florida and Tennessee where floggings were carried out brazenly and almost without notice.[34]

Just as Birmingham maintained its progressive industrial reputation despite the spate of racial violence of the 1920s, the tribulations of the Great Depression proved to be no match for the image of the Magic City. Still, economically and socially, the Great Depression decimated local industry in Birmingham. Already substandard, conditions for black workers and their families grew exponentially worse as unemployment and hunger gripped the town. White residents fared little better. In some instances, out-of-work men could be seen daily hitching rides out of town on railway freight cars to the countryside. There, they would gather berries and other available food before hitching a ride back into town later in the day. Occasionally one might even be seen holding tightly to a wayward goat he had been lucky enough to rustle.[35] The devastation of the local area prompted Franklin Roosevelt to ultimately proclaim Birmingham the "worst hit" city in the nation.[36]

Despite the crush of the Great Depression, Birmingham kicked off the 1930s with a portrayal in the national media to which its residents had over the years grown accustomed. On July 6, 1930, the *New York Times*' Anne O'Hare McCormick published a lengthy feature article focusing on the "Industrial Capitals" of the South. At first glance, Birmingham's success among the region's young industrial centers jumped out at the reader. The caption beneath a large portrait of the city's skyline on the article's first page announced the city as the "First Forge of Steel Civilization in the Cotton Country." McCormick's piece then went on to distinguish Birmingham from the rest of the state and the South. The author was surprised by an amount of "vigor" in Birmingham that "one does not expect in Alabama." It was, after all, a state that "suggests the languor of the lower South." No mention was made of race relations, segregation, or the growing economic crisis.[37]

Articles such as McCormick's seemed to place the city on a pedestal, exalting its progress as exceptional. When this was not the case and an article lumped the city in with the rest of the region, characterizing it with the backwardness that founded many readers' perceptions of the South, residents quickly voiced their displeasure. For example, in 1933 Birmingham resident Eugene R. Lyde Jr.

informed the nation through a *Times* letter to the editor that his city was not "agrarian" or "backwoods." Responding to a recent article that relied on several generalizations of the local level of advancement based on stereotypes of the wider South, Lyde took great offense at the conceptualizations that "Northerners" tended to hold of their southern neighbors. In particular, he sought to inform readers that Birmingham was a successful, substantial city complete with skyscraping hotels and electric streetcars.[38]

This defensive attitude could also be seen on a statewide scale by 1934 with regard to portrayals of race relations. In the midst of the sensational Scottsboro trial, in which nine African American teenagers were accused of rape, and the mass of media attention that the trial cast on the nature of race and society in the state, many felt unfairly criticized by a northern region that they saw as equally discriminatory. Popular Birmingham journalist John Temple Graves II complained bitterly in a *New York Times* letter to the editor that the labeling of the entire state as racist was unfair and that the characterization of Alabama governor Bibb Graves as the "Klan Governor" was insulting. While racial intolerance obviously existed in the state, Graves argued that it also existed in the North and that levels of intolerance within Alabama varied greatly. Further, he implied that even if some rural parts of Alabama were violently bigoted, his beloved Birmingham certainly was not.[39]

These defensive editorials by Birmingham residents in the early to mid-1930s suggest that the nation was taking a closer look at the racial situation in the Birmingham area and was perhaps taking an increased general interest in the nature of race relations in America. Both assumptions are correct to an extent. In the mid-1930s, the coverage of racial violence in the Birmingham area had increased. To a large extent, as these examples have shown, the articles centered on mob violence toward blacks, agitation by outsiders, and locals' denials of racial issues. In most cases the media continued to project the racial problem onto the entire state or region. A specific media focus on Birmingham's race relations or outright condemnations of the city as a center of racial segregation were not evident during this period. Yet this 1930s increase in coverage of racial topics was indicative of a cultural process that was gradually occurring in American society in regard to the acknowledgment of racial inequality. Ultimately, in the decades to come and as a result of this cultural shift concerning the acceptability of racism, Birmingham emerged as the symbol of unacceptable intolerance.

A few very limited examples of increased awareness of and shifting cultural views toward racial inequality in Birmingham can be found coming from somewhat unlikely sources during the 1920s. President Warren Harding's speech in Birmingham's Woodrow Wilson Park on October 26, 1921, offers one such example. Uncharacteristically for a man who won his election by promoting a return to "normalcy," Harding astounded the local crowd by advocating political and economic opportunity for the South's African Americans. Harding's remarks, although stressing that an "amalgamation" of the races through social equality was beyond consideration, were daring enough to shock and draw sound condemnations from locals and southern Democratic senators.[40]

After Harding's untimely death in 1923, Calvin Coolidge lent support to the race issue. In both 1923 and 1925 he unsuccessfully called for the creation of a Negro Industrial Commission that could foster better understanding and cooperation among the races. He also voiced support for a federal antilynching law and named the nation's first African American ambassador. Whether such actions by Harding and Coolidge were mere lip service to the northern African American voting bloc or examples of at least some racial sensitivity remains contested.[41] Regardless, their limited support for improvement in race relations signifies an increased, albeit insufficient public awareness of racial inequality during the 1920s.

The basis of this increased awareness can be found in the historical context in which Harding and Coolidge formulated their policies on race. As mentioned earlier, the nation was in the midst of a resurgence of the Ku Klux Klan. The Klan, by its mid-'20s heyday, could claim millions of members nationwide.[42] Although more adaptive to such local issues as immigration, vice, and anti-Catholicism, which allowed for its phenomenal growth in membership, the Klan still held white supremacy as its central belief.[43] In the resultant racialized environment, lynchings, floggings, murders, and abductions skyrocketed across the South, as did press coverage of such occurrences.

Awareness of racial inequality continued to slowly increase during the 1930s. The actions of Eleanor Roosevelt helped this process along. Roosevelt, as a true racial liberal, occasionally forced the president's hand by exposing racial injustice through her actions. One prime example of this occurred at Birmingham's 1938 Southern Conference for Human Welfare when she refused to abide by the legally prescribed segregated seating at the city's Municipal Auditorium. Much to the shock of her hosts and, one would imagine, the president, Roosevelt placed her chair in the center of the isle dividing Birmingham blacks from whites. Likewise, Chief of Staff Harold Ickes fought hard for increased equality and inclusion in New Deal programs for African Americans. Yet his actions often met defeat as the economic and political necessity of retaining the support of conservative southern Democrats in Congress won out over any competing attempt to improve conditions for blacks. For example, Ickes found himself forced to compromise the antidiscrimination measures of Public Works Administration projects in many southern states.[44]

A few New Deal program heads nevertheless managed to implement surprisingly progressive policies with regard to race. Among these, Aubrey Williams of the National Youth Administration (NYA) and Will Alexander of the Farm Securities Administration (FSA) stand out. Williams's NYA employed approximately three hundred thousand black teens and paid them the same wages as whites. The FSA likewise provided loans to a number of black farmers that equaled the overall percentage of black farmers in the nation.[45]

Thus one can see the seeds of racial consciousness developing in the federal government during the 1920s and '30s. In the 1920s this consciousness—at least as manifested by Republican presidents—tended to be in reaction to a wave of intolerance and violence linked to the resurgence of the Ku Klux Klan. In the 1930s any racial awareness of the New Deal administration often came from below the president and at times conflicted with his own political concerns. That such pleas emanated from his subordinates and his wife during this period is not surprising when one looks at one final aspect of the wider historical context of the 1930s and early '40s. This was, after all, the era of the rise of "-isms."

It was during World War II that Americans began to publicly acknowledge on a large scale that racism was a significant problem and to condemn it. During this era, in the context of growing awareness of the racial atrocities committed under Nazism, the American media began to cast racism as un-American. First, the use of the term *racism* in the American media and its linking to Nazism spread quickly in the 1930s. The first instance of this and the earliest use of the term that I have found in the pages of the *New York Times* appeared on June 17, 1935. That day the *Times* quoted League of Nations high commissioner for Palestine James G. MacDonald as saying that the "racism and statism" of Nazi Germany were "unacceptable to Jews, . . . Catholics and Protestants."[46] By 1938 readers in both Los Angeles and Chicago could find articles in their respective newspapers frequently employing the term and concept. Again, the pieces tied racism to Nazism or Fascism without fail. The *Chicago Tribune* chose to highlight Jewish author Henry Bernstein's refusal of the Order of Saint Maurice and Lazare, which was awarded to him by Benito Mussolini himself. The *Tribune* quoted Bernstein as basing his stance on the Italian Fascists' "racism of recent invention" and their related persecutions of law-abiding Italian citizens.[47] The *Los Angeles Times* introduced the term to its West Coast audience about a month later. In an article addressing the eighth National Eucharist Congress meeting in New Orleans, the *Times* reporter focused on the Catholics' distrust of the various "-isms" that were floating around contemporary society. The piece quoted Monseigneur Francis J. Haas of Catholic University affirming, "The spread of Communism, Fascism, and racism . . . proposes a weltanschauung, a philosophy of life totally at variance with fundamental Christian concepts."[48]

Throughout the last years of the 1930s and during the war years that followed, there was a steady stream of articles relating racism to the enemies of America and democracy. Thus were the American people provided with a specific term under which to place systematic intolerance. More important, this term and the practices it encompassed were often linked to insidious, anti-American ideologies. While racism itself had existed on the North American continent for centuries by this time and was inherent in many of America's institutions, it had seldom been characterized so distinctly and certainly as dangerously un-American.

In the aftermath of the war and with the revolutionary upheaval of the civil rights movement, the extent of racism and racial oppression in America was fully and publicly acknowledged, questioned, and eventually adjusted. Such a shift was visible in the immediate postwar years in many ways. During this time, as evidenced by the United Nations' Universal Declaration of Human Rights (1948), intellectuals seemed intent on stressing the universality of humans. In part as a reaction to the atrocities of Nazism, this philosophy held that all people shared basic fundamental rights as humans regardless of perceived variations.[49] In the United States such a belief eventually helped fuel the civil rights movement. The resultant shift against outwardly expressed bigotry in the wake of the civil rights movement's victory, while not entirely complete in practice, proved powerful. Although racism and various forms of inequality and discrimination remain embedded in institutions and practices, the American cultural sphere has shifted to such a degree as to render anyone associated with the old explicit acts and expressions of racism irrelevant and dangerously abnormal. The same goes for cities, where the stigma of racism in the post–civil rights movement era was both difficult to shake and hugely significant.

Bombingham

Against this shifting and increasingly sensitized cultural backdrop, the racial inequality built into Birmingham's labor force and social system began to manifest itself in active unrest immediately following World War II. As this occurred, the national media increasingly took note of the city's segregation, racialized inequalities, and violence and categorized them as severely problematic. Widespread publicity of race-related violence, such as the rash of bombings that took place during the 1940s, 1950s, and into the 1960s, earned the city the derisive moniker of *Bombingham*.[50]

As context for the emergence of Bombingham, the Magic City did not seem quite as magical in the late 1940s and through the 1950s. Industrial relocation to the city had slowed dramatically by 1948 and 1949, and many began to see a "civic and economic malaise" defining the city. To make matters worse, the rash of racial bombings and a more widespread knowledge of Birmingham's strictly segregated nature led to comparisons between the city and Johannesburg, South Africa.[51]

Still, with a population of 326,037 in 1950, Birmingham was Alabama's largest city and closely trailed Atlanta—its "great rival" against whom residents tended to measure success—with its 331,314 people.[52] Yet in the coming decades, the competition between the two cities proved to be a mismatch. The more cosmopolitan and economically diversified Atlanta, often referred to as "the city too busy to hate," left Birmingham far behind in growth and in national perception.[53] By 1970 Atlanta claimed 496,973 people to Birmingham's 300,910.[54] The Georgia city had by then clearly surpassed Birmingham in the race to become the region's leading city. Many Birminghamians charged that Atlanta had used vaguely "unfair tactics" to gain this title.[55] Perhaps in attributing blame for Birmingham's demise as the region's Magic City, those residents should have considered local racial tensions and the image of the city that such tensions provided the world when they exploded. Atlanta avoided this characterization and, ultimately, stigmatization.

In reality, Birmingham proved itself a violently racist place, deserving of the Bombingham moniker during the immediate postwar decades. Between 1945 and 1963, dozens of racially motivated bombings occurred in the city. These bombings reflected great unease among the area's most violent segregationists. Typically, they occurred as a postwar housing crisis forced African Americans to encroach upon neighborhoods zoned for white occupancy or as white supremacists attempted to terrorize African American activists into acquiescence to the established system of race-based subordination.[56]

Real estate–related bombings occurred with great frequency as established neighborhoods transitioned from white to African American occupancy. It is not surprising that the racial transition of neighborhoods led to racial violence when one looks at the role race had played in housing for decades prior to Birmingham's emergence as Bombingham. Racial zoning of residential areas in Birmingham dates to 1925. That year the city's zoning commission established a racial zoning boundary at the Graymont–College Hills neighborhood. This neighborhood bordered one of the largest African American neighborhoods in the city. Over the next three decades, the city refined its zoning ordinance in ways that failed to keep pace with African American population growth. As the African American population increased rapidly, racial zoning boundaries drawn during the 1920s were not substantively redrawn. For example, between 1926 and 1949, only two entire blocks and parts of three others were rezoned as A-2 for single-family African American residency. While more area was rezoned as B-2 for African American multifamily residency, those areas, too, remained woefully inadequate to meet increased demand.[57]

As African Americans suffered from an acute shortage of housing, racial residential zoning of neighborhoods became a hot topic for African Americans and white supremacists. In need of living space, African Americans began attempting to buy, and in some cases obtained, real estate in white-zoned neighborhoods. White supremacists intent on maintaining the racial status quo frequently launched bombing attacks on such houses. This drew the involvement of the National Association for the Advancement of Colored People (NAACP), which challenged the zoning ordinance in court, with local attorney Arthur Shores arguing the cases. As Shores pointed out, Birmingham's zoning ordinance was in blatant conflict with the United States Supreme Court's decision in *Buchanan v. Warley*. That 1917 decision held that the sale of real estate to individuals could not be prohibited on the basis of race.[58]

It took three legal challenges before Shores and the NAACP obtained victory. As a result of the first two, fines were issued in 1945 and 1946, and the zoning ordinance was adjusted in small ways to resolve the specific conditions of the complaints. The third case, filed by Shores in 1949 and argued with NAACP attorney Thurgood Marshall's assistance, resulted in a U.S. District Court ruling that Birmingham's racial zoning ordinances were unconstitutional. This ruling was upheld by the U.S. Fifth Circuit Court of Appeals in December 1949, and a writ of certiorari was refused by the U.S. Supreme Court in May 1951.[59]

As this was all ongoing in 1949, the city government addressed the issue. While commissioner of public improvements James Morgan was concerned over the zoning ordinance's constitutionality and its lack of African American residential areas, fellow commissioner Eugene "Bull" Connor took a hardline stance on zoning. Intent on maintaining existing racial zoning, Connor proposed Ordinance 709-F. This ordinance, written by Tennessee Coal and Iron attorney James Simpson, who was widely regarded as Connor's mentor, provided for the arrest of both whites and African Americans who violated zoning ordinances.[60]

So in response to the housing shortage and legal challenges over the constitutionality of racial zoning, the city passed an ordinance that could be used to jail African Americans for buying property in white neighborhoods while doing nothing to increase the size of areas zoned for African American occupancy. After the passage of Ordinance 709-F, Connor claimed that such authorization of police enforcement of the existing zoning ordinance was necessary because, as he said, "We're going to have bloodshed in this town. . . . The white people are not going to stand for" the transition of the city's neighborhoods from white to African American.[61] Connor's predicted violence was, in fact, already occurring. One local neighborhood is still widely referred to as Dynamite Hill because of the rash of terroristic bombings that accompanied its late-1940s shift from white to middle-class African American residency.[62]

Alongside housing, white supremacists' concerns over individuals challenging the status quo of racial inequality also drove violence. This was most clearly evident in the repeated attacks on Birmingham minister and civil rights activist Fred Shuttlesworth. During the postwar period, Reverend Shuttlesworth was the driving force behind the movement for racial equality in Birmingham. Ever persistent, even in the face of great personal danger, Shuttlesworth often fought singlehandedly for racial equality throughout the 1940s, '50s, and '60s. As a result, he experienced the white supremacists' dynamite on more than one occasion.

Although he is often overlooked, Fred Shuttlesworth ranks among the nation's most historically significant civil rights activists. Without him, Birmingham likely would not have experienced the fateful demonstrations of 1963. Without those demonstrations, the Civil Rights Act of 1964 would have been longer in coming.[63] Shuttlesworth, it can be argued, played a central role in changing the nation and securing a long-overdue victory for human rights.

Judging by his early life, Shuttlesworth did not seem destined to become a Baptist minister and civil rights leader. Born as Freddie Lee Robinson in 1922 to Alberta Robinson and her boyfriend, Vetter Green, he did not receive the name Shuttlesworth until his mother married William Nathan Shuttlesworth in 1927. By that time, the family had moved from Fred's birthplace in Mount Meigs, Alabama, to the Birmingham suburb of Oxmoor. Remaining in this vicinity

Group of locals viewing the bomb-damaged home
of Arthur Shores, NAACP attorney, Birmingham, Alabama.
Photograph by Marion S. Trikosko. Library of Congress, Prints and Photographs Division,
U.S. News & World Report Magazine Collection, LC-DIG-ppmsca-03194.

until his early adulthood, Shuttlesworth graduated from Homewood's Rosedale
High School in 1940. Later that same year he was arrested for bootlegging and
sentenced to two years' probation.[64]

Shuttlesworth's life seems to have settled somewhat beginning with his marriage to Ruby Lynnette Keeler in October 1941. Soon thereafter, a daughter was
born, and the family relocated to Mobile, Alabama, where Fred found employment as a truck driver and within a few months began preaching occasionally at
the Corinthian Baptist Church. He also began to pursue postsecondary education
at this time, enrolling at the Cedar Grove Academy Bible College. The next few
years proved eventful as Shuttlesworth fathered a second daughter and a son,
moved to Selma, continued his education at Selma University and then Alabama
State University, and became an ordained Baptist minister. Soon he was named
minister of Selma's First Baptist Church. After two rather rocky years in this
position, the Shuttlesworth family moved to Birmingham in 1953 where he
assumed duties as the pastor of Bethel Baptist Church.[65]

It was in his role as pastor of Bethel Baptist Church that Shuttlesworth shook
up established race relations in Birmingham. There, Shuttlesworth took on an

increasingly active role in challenging the city's established race relations. At Bethel he promoted an increased civic-mindedness among his congregation and became involved in local issues such as police brutality, voter registration, and school desegregation. This, as one biographer has argued, opened the door for Shuttlesworth's entrance into civil rights activism and illustrated a marked difference between his Birmingham and Selma ministries.[66]

In Birmingham, Shuttlesworth's challenging of the racial status quo often placed him at odds with the local government and gained him a well-deserved reputation as the city's foremost activist for civil rights. By 1955 it seems that Shuttlesworth had fully embraced civil rights activism. He became active in the local chapter of the NAACP, and by June 1955, he petitioned the city of Birmingham to hire African American police officers. Six months later, during the Montgomery bus boycott, he traveled to that city and participated in meetings of the Montgomery Improvement Association. He also supported his former Selma University classmate Autherine Lucy's bid to desegregate the University of Alabama. As a show of support, he accompanied Lucy and her attorney, Arthur Shores, to the Tuscaloosa campus as she attempted to enroll on February 29, 1956.[67]

By early 1956 Shuttlesworth had also assumed the office of membership chairman of the Birmingham branch of the NAACP. As was his custom by then, he embraced this leadership role with gusto, actively seeking to increase the local organization's membership and activism. However, his leadership role with the local NAACP proved short lived as Alabama attorney general John Patterson managed to have the NAACP declared illegal within state boundaries. Patterson accomplished this by exploiting a little-known statute that required all foreign-owned organizations to register as foreign corporations and pay certain fees in order to operate within the state. The Alabama government viewed any organization founded and headquartered outside the state as foreign. As the NAACP had neither successfully registered nor paid the fee, it was deemed to be operating illegally in Alabama. On June 1, 1956, Judge Walter B. Jones agreed with Patterson's argument and issued an injunction against the NAACP operating in Alabama. He further fined the organization $100,000, ordered that all membership lists and records be turned over, and placed an eight-year ban on any NAACP activity in the state.[68]

Shuttlesworth reacted to the NAACP ban by creating a new Birmingham-based civil rights organization. Driven by the belief that existing organizations were too conservative in their actions, Shuttlesworth convened a meeting of fellow ministers and laypeople to plan a new, more activist organization. The group members agreed that such an organization was required and that it might even

Bethel Baptist Church, Birmingham, Alabama. From 1953 to 1961,
the Reverend Fred Lee Shuttlesworth was the pastor.
Library of Congress, Prints and Photographs Division, HABS AL-977.

be necessary for some of them to go to jail for the cause. Before the meeting's conclusion, the new organization was named the Alabama Christian Movement for Human Rights (ACMHR). On June 5, Shuttlesworth was elected president of the new organization by acclamation of almost a thousand people who attended a mass rally at the Sardis Baptist Church to announce the ACMHR's formation.[69]

As head of the ACMHR, Shuttlesworth continued to throw caution aside and act tirelessly for racial equality in Birmingham. By July he was pushing for the end of segregated mass transit in the city and the hiring of African American bus drivers. The next month, his ACMHR filed suit against Birmingham for excluding African Americans from taking civil service exams. Then, following the U.S. Supreme Court's ruling against segregated bussing in Montgomery, Shuttlesworth announced that the ACMHR would ignore local ordinances segregating bussing in Birmingham. By the end of December, twenty-six ACMHR activists had been arrested for refusing to acknowledge segregated seating on city busses.

Under Shuttlesworth's leadership, the ACMHR continued to act and push for racial reform at a breakneck pace—often too fast for some of Birmingham's

Fred Shuttlesworth after the attempted desegregation
of Birmingham's Phillips High School, 1957.
Birmingham, Alabama, Public Library Archives.

African American ministers. Approval of the ACMHR and of Shuttlesworth's
activism was not universal. Reverend Luke Beard, for example, implored Shuttlesworth to call off the June 5 mass meeting announcing the ACMHR's formation.
Others such as Reverends G. W. McMurray and M. W. Witt cautioned that
there were enough organizations already in existence in Birmingham and that
Shuttlesworth and others should "think sanely" about the path they were taking.[70]

Such warnings were not heeded. Shuttlesworth's activism did not dissipate in
the years that followed. If anything, the pace quickened as the ACMHR expanded
its sights to school and retail desegregation. Showing his personal commitment
to the struggle, Shuttlesworth attempted to desegregate Birmingham's all-white
Phillips High School on the morning of September 9, 1957, by enrolling his own
daughters. For his efforts, a crowd of segregationists who had gathered outside

Bomb-damaged trailers at the Gaston Motel, Birmingham, Alabama, May 14, 1963.
Photograph by Marion S. Trikosko. Library of Congress, Prints and Photographs Division,
U.S. News & World Report Magazine Collection, LC-DIG-ppmsca-04293.

the school beat him with chains and baseball bats. Bruised and concussed but undeterred, Shuttlesworth continued to fight for desegregation and increasingly sought mass involvement in ACMHR actions, boycotts, and demonstrations.[71]

As the 1960s dawned, Shuttlesworth's activism in Birmingham was paying dividends and attracting attention both within the community and outside. The ACMHR's actions had succeeded in desegregating bussing and bus terminals, and as a result of the decision in *Shuttlesworth v. Birmingham*, city parks had been desegregated. However, this progress was incomplete and in some cases fleeting. Following park desegregation, for example, the city simply shut down the public parks. After eight years of ACMHR action, Birmingham remained as racially segregated as ever.[72] Further, violence directed at those who challenged the status quo had only intensified.

Shuttlesworth's unceasing actions and increased prominence brought him to the attention of the city's more violent segregationists. For example, on Christmas Day 1956 segregationists bombed the Bethel Baptist Church parsonage in which Shuttlesworth resided. Shuttlesworth, who was in the house when the fifteen sticks of dynamite exploded, survived unscathed. He credited his good fortune to divine intervention and interpreted it as a sign that he was meant to continue leading the Birmingham movement. This he did, and Bethel Baptist Church went on to experience two additional bombings in 1958 and 1963, adding to Birmingham's reputation as Bombingham.[73]

Press Coverage of Bombingham

The violence perpetrated against Shuttlesworth and his church was far from irregular by 1960. Furthermore, the nation was beginning to take note of the violent reprisals against other dissidents in the city. The stigmatization of Birmingham as a city plagued by racial violence took a decisive step forward on April 12, 1960. That day, Birmingham residents reacted with shocked outrage at an exposé appearing in the *New York Times*. The front-page headline read, "Fear and Hatred Grip Birmingham." *Times* reporter Harrison E. Salisbury had produced a two-page indictment of the city's race relations. Salisbury wrote of a "brooding Birmingham" on the verge of outright racial conflict. It was a cowering city, he observed, a place where "no one talks freely" out of fear of violence and retribution. His article revealed that every aspect of life within the city was strictly segregated. He named Commissioner Bull Connor as the brutal enforcer of the racial status quo. Salisbury detailed the wrath individuals encountered in the rare cases when they spoke or acted out against the norm. As proof, he offered the example of one student who participated in a public "prayer for freedom." Later that evening, "seven hooded men" arrived at the youth's house armed with "iron pipes, clubs, and leather blackjacks into which razor blades had been sunk." When they left, the youth, his sister, and his mother lay severely beaten, the mother with crushed hands, a broken leg, and a severely lacerated scalp.[74]

Salisbury followed up his "Fear and Hatred" article the next day with an equally damning front-page article. This time, he set his sights on the entire state of Alabama, claiming that the "corrosive impact" of racism, anti-Semitism, and segregation was disintegrating the state's social and political structure. Often using Birmingham as an example and referring to Connor by name, he wrote of the police terrorizing citizens on a regular basis and turning a blind eye to acts of racial violence committed against blacks and white sympathizers. Salisbury emphasized his points by providing a campaign advertisement for John G. Crommelin, the Birmingham-based candidate for the U.S. Senate. Crommelin's ad championed him as "The Whiteman's Candidate" who pledged to

> ATTACK and EXPOSE the Anti-Defamation League of B'nai B'rth (ADL), the malarial-mosquito of integration and real hidden enemy of White Christian Alabamians, THIS MUST BE DONE.

The ADL (all Jew) is the mosquito; the NAACP (Jew controlled Negro) is the germ.[75]

Neither Bull Connor nor his fellow commissioners should have been surprised at the media's negative portrayal of their city in 1960. The *New York Times* had increasingly addressed racism and racial violence in Birmingham during the 1950s. Local segregation alone had served as the basis for sixteen stories in the paper over the decade's course.[76] Additional stories dealt with white-on-black violence, racially motivated bombings, and intolerance among white citizens.[77] The increasing frequency of such articles in a major newspaper with great agenda-setting power mirrored the nation's growing awareness of racial tension as the civil rights movement moved into higher gear. Yet Salisbury's piece was the most prominent indictment of the city as a whole by a national newspaper on the basis of local racism. As such, it was an important step in constructing the city's racist stigma in the public's mind.

The local reaction to the Salisbury articles has been fittingly described by local attorney and one-time mayor David Vann as "violent."[78] The Birmingham press immediately and directly attacked Salisbury's criticisms in the days following his articles' appearances. The *Birmingham News* led off its April 14 issue with the scathing title "*N.Y. Times* Slanders Our City—Can This Be Birmingham?" before reprinting the "Fear and Hatred" article word for word as it had appeared in the *Times*. The editor's note immediately beneath the title informed Birmingham readers that the *News* was reprinting this article "as an example of what is being written and printed about us."[79] The next day *News* editors continued the strategy, reprinting Salisbury's second article as an example of an unfair attack on the city. This time, however, the Birmingham paper got in a jab at the *Times'* famous slogan while questioning the accuracy of the piece. The local paper's front page that day read, "'All the News That's Fit to Print'?—*N.Y. Times* Continues Attack."[80] The *Post-Herald* likewise informed its readers of Salisbury's take on the city in articles printed on April 14 and 15. Here, labeling the *Times* piece a "race hate story" that "shakes" all of Alabama, *Post-Herald* editors also reprinted the *Times* pieces in full so that Birmingham residents might know how they were being "presented to millions of our neighbors."[81]

The editorial pages also joined in the reaction to Salisbury's pieces. In the *Post-Herald* longtime editorialist John Temple Graves II characterized the articles as "an almost total lie" and blamed Salisbury's opinions on his northern "birth, upbringing, and education in Minnesota." The acerbic Graves concluded that Minnesota had always been the "most South-hating of the states." In Graves's opinion, through the *New York Times*, the Minnesotan had dealt Birmingham a "bitter hurt." While "God might forgive him" for this "cruel . . . body blow," Graves concluded, "we never shall."[82]

Birmingham News editors, only the day before, had outdone even Graves with the publication of perhaps the most outraged editorial ever to grace their paper's pages. Labeling the *Times* piece a "Grave Disservice," the editorial described Salisbury's reporting as "shoddy," "vicious," "malicious," "bigoted," "noxiously false," and "distorted." The editorial went on to accuse the *Times* of "libeling" and "slandering" the city through "journalistic demagoguery." This slander—portrayed as the latest in a long line of "South-baiting" journalism by northern reporters—deserved response because it called out Birmingham specifically and was printed in a paper whose "readership is one of the most influential segments of America." As such, the *News* editors felt that the article threatened to inflict "economic damage" on the city."[83]

The Jefferson County Grand Jury obviously agreed with the *News*' accusation of malicious damage to the city's reputation. Meeting at the Bessemer courthouse at the time of the articles' publication, the grand jury indicted Salisbury for criminal libel.[84] Bull Connor and his fellow commissioners also shared in the opinion of the grand jury and the local newspapers that the Salisbury articles had inflicted great damage on both their reputation and the image of their city. On May 1, 1960, Connor, his fellow commissioners, and the city's business-oriented Committee of 100 and chamber of commerce wrote to the *Times*, demanding a public retraction of Salisbury's stories.[85]

After receiving no reply for five days, Connor's attorneys filed suit against the newspaper in the United States District Court of the Northern District of Alabama. The complaint alleged that through Salisbury's article, the *Times* sought to "defame" Connor "falsely and maliciously." His attorneys went on to claim that Connor had been subjected to "public contempt, ridicule, shame, and disgrace." For this, Connor sought damages of $500,000.[86] In the months that followed, Connor's case was combined with the identical complaints of fellow commissioners James W. Morgan, James "Jabo" Waggoner, Jess Lanier, Herman Thompson, Raymond Parsons, and Joe Lindsey.[87]

Theophilus Eugene Connor et al. v. the New York Times et al. dragged on for approximately six years. In 1964 Connor and his coplaintiffs received a favorable ruling in district court. The jury found that Salisbury's statements in the articles were "made with actual malice." They were not, however, "motivated by personal ill will" or "the intent to do the plaintiff harm." The jury then awarded Connor

$40,000 in compensatory damages and nothing in punitive damages. However, in late 1966 the United States Court of Appeals for the Fifth District reversed the jury's verdict.[88]

Throughout the months preceding the court action and during the trial itself, the plaintiffs' displeasure at the *Times'* portrayal of their city was as evident as their anger over its portrayals of themselves. In fact, of the nine original plaintiffs, only Connor had been mentioned directly in the Salisbury articles. Throughout the legal proceedings, Connor seemed intent on showing that Birmingham was not the incredibly racist place that Salisbury had made it out to be. In answer to pretrial depositions by defense attorneys, Connor frequently protested statements such as one about "Birmingham being like Johannesburg" and claimed that the article caused a "great wave of feeling . . . throughout the state and the nation" against his city. The city further, according to Connor, "had very little disorder, agitation, or demonstration" before the appearance of Salisbury's piece.[89]

From attorney T. Eric Embry's opening remarks onward, the defense's strategy was to clearly show that the article was not about Connor at all but rather about Birmingham. As Embry pointed out, in both of Salisbury's articles, there were only three mentions of Connor and no mentions of the other plaintiffs. Instead, Salisbury had merely carried out an ordinary news assignment to go down to several southern cities, investigate, and report on the impact of the sit-in movement on local race relations. If his reports were libelous simply because they provided an unfortunate image of the city, then all citizens' rights to criticize conditions in "your town and in your community" would be compromised.[90]

The plaintiffs' team attempted to sway the Birmingham jury by casting Salisbury as an ignorant outsider who was biased against the South and intent on meddling with local customs. Attorney Jim Simpson repeatedly referred to Salisbury as a "New Yorker." Over Embry's objections, he told the jury, "No New Yorker can readily measure the climate of Birmingham." Throughout his cross-examination of Salisbury, Simpson questioned the writer's knowledge of the South and his opinion of it. In doing so, he revealed to the jury a man who had never lived in the South, had visited Birmingham only for the few days it took to research the articles, and knew little about southern ways. In his closing statement, Simpson related Salisbury's journey into the South to northerners' Civil War forays that were intended to disrupt southern life. Although he was armed only with a pen, Simpson argued, Salisbury had come with just as definite a purpose as the Union soldiers of the past. Salisbury and the *New York Times*, the jury was told, came to spread "propaganda" and end segregation.[91]

While the trial lingered on and the plaintiffs and defense debated southern identity, slander, and the invasion of Birmingham by pen-wielding Yankees, additional media coverage solidified Birmingham's image as a racist, violent, and intolerant city. In response to the Salisbury article and the libel suit, CBS decided to film a segment of *CBS Reports* in Birmingham early in 1961.[92] Titled "Who Speaks for Birmingham?" and eventually airing nationally on the night of May 18, 1961, the program further exposed the city's racial intolerance and violence while also deeming it representative of regional southern racism. The narrator, respected television journalist and Louisiana native Howard K. Smith, announced that Birmingham was "the largest segregated city in the South." Further, he characterized the local *Birmingham Post-Herald* as the "voice of the segregated South." As for the question raised in the program's title, Smith contended that the violent and uncooperative Bull Connor had "emerged as the voice of Birmingham."[93]

If such media representations had not yet established Birmingham's social deviance from the rest of the United States to an adequate degree, coverage of local events in 1963 ensured the city's future stigmatization. It is interesting to note that Smith wished his documentary to be even more critical of the city and its leaders. Having witnessed local violence firsthand while producing the documentary, Smith felt the need to make a more forceful condemnation of local authorities. This condemnation included a biting radio program that Smith recorded while in Birmingham, and he attempted to conclude the documentary with the popular warning attributed to Edmund Burke: "The only thing necessary for the triumph of evil is that good men should do nothing." CBS's denial of this request led Smith to resign from the network.[94]

Two years later, in May 1963, Bull Connor's position as the "voice of Birmingham" was challenged. That month, civil rights demonstrations overwhelmed the city. Again, Reverend Fred Shuttlesworth and his ACMHR played a central role in bringing about these long-overdue mass demonstrations against racial inequality. Shuttlesworth invited Martin Luther King Jr. and the Southern Christian Leadership Conference (SCLC) to come to the city to help organize and lead the demonstrations. Shuttlesworth realized that following the failure to desegregate Albany, Georgia, the preceding year, the SCLC and King needed a major victory to maintain the movement's momentum. He also understood the significance that such a victory could have if it took place in what was widely perceived as the nation's most violently segregated city. As he later reflected:

The SCLC needed something and we needed something, so I said, "Birmingham is where it's at gentlemen. I assure you, if you come to Birmingham,

Martin Luther King, David Abernathy, Fred Shuttlesworth (*back to camera*), and other activists in parking lot of Gaston Motel, Birmingham, Alabama, 1963.
Birmingham, Alabama, Public Library Archives.

we will not only gain prestige but really shake the country. If you win Birmingham, as Birmingham goes, so goes the nation." So we invited Dr. King and the SCLC into Birmingham to confront segregation in a massively nonviolent war, with our bodies and souls.[95]

Other African Americans in Birmingham—and others with knowledge of the city—held similar ideas about the city's image. Wyatt Tee Walker, the executive director of the SCLC, characterized Birmingham as the "baddest city of the South."[96] Local African Americans were afraid and hesitant to speak or act out. This was evident as members of the SCLC arrived in 1963 and attempted to lead large-scale demonstrations. Local African American business leader A. G. Gaston later recalled that at first, "few blacks in Birmingham volunteered to fill Bull Connor's jail cells."[97] Activist and organizer James Bevel echoed Gaston's observation, recalling that initially only ten to twelve people would show up each day for the planned marches.[98] This lack of participation, driven by fear of economic and violent reprisal, led Bevel and other organizers to call on local schoolchildren to participate. This tactic paid off because the children, unlike their parents, did not have jobs to lose. The children did, however, share the adults' fears of Birmingham and its authorities. As young marcher Patricia Harris indicated, "I was afraid of getting hurt, but I still was willing to march to have justice done."[99]

Soon, as more and more people marched for equality, public safety commissioner Bull Connor initiated the wholesale arrest of demonstrators. The city's jail space was overfilled, and hundreds of arrested protestors were confined at the state fairgrounds' livestock pavilion. The demonstrations soon turned violent when Bull Connor's police force employed his much-vaunted armored tank, dogs, and water cannon.[100] As the tank rolled and dogs attacked, the national media captured it all in both words and images. Articles concerning the demonstrations subsequently gained more prominent placement in the *New York Times*. In the month between April 15 and May 15 alone, some twenty-three articles dealing with the protests were deemed worthy of front-page placement.[101] The most powerful among these appeared on May 4 with an accompanying image of a police dog violently biting the abdomen of a young protester as a uniformed Birmingham police officer held the boy in place.[102] This image, along with others like it, undoubtedly strengthened the national perception of Birmingham as a violent center of racism. In addition to this coverage were the *New York Times'* twenty-eight articles focusing on the tragic bombing of the Sixteenth Street Baptist Church on September 16, 1963. With such events and their coverage, Birmingham's stigma was solidly entrenched and available for future media use as events warranted.[103] There could be no doubt at that point, either in the United States or around the world, that Birmingham most definitely had a racial problem. On a macro scale, the question then seemed to become whether or not racial conditions in the city represented those of the nation as a whole.

In regard to this question, one can see how contextual world events of the post–World War II era had an influence in shaping the nation's acceptance of Birmingham's stigmatization. Aware of the contradiction between racism and American democracy's supposed egalitarianism, the public and government sought to rationalize the image they held of themselves and projected to the Cold War–era world. This led some parts of the nation to form their identities in opposition to other parts that were seen as deviantly racist. Actions of the United States government contributed to this process. Cold War–influenced concern over the United States' international image prompted the government to purposefully label the South, and violently racist areas within it such as Birmingham, as deviant from the national norm.[104]

At a time when the United States actively sought to export its influence, governmental system, and economic theory abroad, internationally publicized instances of racial violence proved embarrassing. The Soviet Union made great propagandistic use of racist events and images "such as those flowing out of Birmingham" in extolling capitalism's inherent inequality. This particularly threatened the United States' democratic image in the newly independent nations of Africa. To quell the success of the Soviet propaganda campaign, the United States government initiated one of its own. In addition to characterizing southern areas as abnormal within the American system, the campaign championed instances of federal intervention in such wayward areas. This intervention stood as proof that the nation emphasized equality even in seemingly backward areas. The media's portrayal of Birmingham thus took on a degree of official sanction. The South, with its brutal and uncompromising Bull Connors, assumed the role of repository for the nation's sin. As an isolated and deviant exception to the national norm, the nation rationalized that the racial oppression in that city was an anomaly in a democratic system. Viewing the oppression as an anomaly helped to reconcile its continued existence in a post–World War II era in which overt racism had become increasingly viewed as un-American. The Soviets' propaganda, it could be argued, was a purposefully misleading generalization meant to hurt the United States as a whole whereas Birmingham's existence as a racist anomaly provided a reference point against which rest of the nation could form its own racially progressive identity.[105]

Interestingly, the protests and reactionary violence that helped create this worldwide image of Birmingham occurred in a very limited section of the city's geographic area. The famed events of May 1963 and the Sixteenth Street Baptist Church bombing in September of the same year all occurred within a three- to four-block area in the city's central district. Each day during the protests, the demonstrators often assembled at the Sixteenth Street Baptist Church located at Sixteenth Street North and Sixth Avenue North. They would then set out for the city hall, located between Sixth and Seventh Avenues on Twentieth Street. Often they would advance no farther than the Kelly Ingram Park, which borders both Sixteenth and Seventeenth Streets on Sixth Avenue. Here, less than a block from where they had embarked, Connor stopped the marchers daily with excessive force. Thus, in a geographic sense, less than a full city block defined an entire city's abnormally violent race relations for the world.[106] As will be seen, the same can also be said regarding the urban geography of the stigmas associated with San Francisco and Las Vegas. There, the events or characteristics associated with the relatively small areas of the Castro district or the Strip played very large roles in defining the cities' reputations to the world.

Such geographic considerations aside, the changing media portrayal of Birmingham and the resulting national and international stigmas were not solely consequences of the sensational and racially charged events that occurred in the city during the civil rights movement. In order for this coverage to occur and for the nation to condemn the actions that were portrayed so dramatically, there first had to be a shift in the very way that America viewed racial oppression and inequality. This shift had begun decades earlier and culminated with the tragic bomb blast on Birmingham's Sixteenth Street in 1963. In the postwar decades, racism took on un-American connotations that allowed for the stigmatization of people and places associated with it. When Birmingham had been at the forefront of industrial production in an era before the widespread development of this racial sensitivity, it had been easy for citizens who were concerned more with celebrating industrial progress to overlook the city's oppressed workforce, racial violence, and segregation. To them, early Birmingham was the city of the American dream; it was the Magic City of growth and prosperity. Many found themselves excluded from that dream. However, as more Americans gained a racial conscience, beginning with the linkage of racism with Fascism in the 1930s, blacks' exclusion and the progress-based defense of Birmingham's apartheid-like system grew more difficult to maintain. Ultimately, the violent anti–civil rights outbursts of the early 1960s proved to be a slap in the face to the nation's more highly developed sensitivity. With the sting of this slap, Birmingham, Alabama, made the mental journey from Magic City to Bombingham. This shift from pacesetter to pariah thus occurred in tandem with a cultural paradigm shift regarding racial consciousness. As the next chapter will show, it subsequently proved devastating and incredibly difficult to surmount as the racist stigma emerged as one of the most crushing in the last decades of the twentieth century.

3

Remembering Bombingham

Race and Anxiety in Post–Civil Rights Movement Birmingham

The banner looked to be about six feet tall and maybe eight feet wide. Two National Organization for Women activists held tightly to its support poles, stretching it taut so that all onlookers that day in Birmingham might see its message. It read simply, "Bombingham Alabama! 1963–1998 Never Again!"[1] Thirty-five years earlier, civil rights demonstrators had marched through the streets of Washington, D.C., under a similar sign. Its words read, "No More Birminghams," above an enlarged image of the bombed-out Sixteenth Street Baptist Church.[2]

The two signs, although separated by three and a half decades, drew their power from the ability to link tragic events to a specific location and a cause. In the case of the former banner, the specter of Bombingham was raised to affirm the tragedy of a recent deadly bombing at an abortion clinic on the city's south side. The latter sign employed the horrific image of the church bombing as a symbol of why the nation must change and what it must avoid in the future. Both reveal the degree to which the city itself was stigmatized by racist and violent resistance to the currents of social change.

These protest signs are but two of many examples in recent decades of how the events of 1963 defined the city and its image. This lingering perception of the city has, in turn, influenced the post–civil rights era trajectory of Birmingham. The media's continual association of Birmingham with the violence of 1963 has

Congress of Racial Equality (CORE) conducts march in memory of those killed in
Birmingham bombings, All Souls Church, Washington, D.C., September 22, 1963.
Activists march under a "No More Birminghams" sign.
Photograph by Thomas J. O'Halloran. Library of Congress, Prints and Photographs Division,
U.S. News & World Report Magazine Collection, LC-DIG-ppmsca-04298.

caused many locals to be hypersensitive to any event that might threaten to
bring forth the demons of that past. The perpetuation of Birmingham's post-1963
stigma and local sensitivity to it can partly be traced to three distinct forms of
media coverage throughout the 1970s, '80s, and '90s: the acknowledgement of
civil rights–related anniversaries in the city, the long delay of trials for crimes
committed during civil rights demonstrations, and the connection of the city's
past to unrelated events in its present. Thus Birmingham's violent history has
remained firmly attached to its contemporary identity regardless of any progress
the city has made in race relations.

The violent racism of Birmingham's past is regularly thrust into the national
spotlight through the recognition of anniversaries of civil rights–era events.
Highlighting the anniversary of a spectacular event every decade or so makes
for dramatic television. At times this seems almost as compelling as live coverage
of the event itself.

September 15, 1983, marked one such anniversary for the city. On that day,
twenty years had passed since a bomb had ripped through the lower levels of

the Sixteenth Street Baptist Church, forever linking the city with the senseless killing of four young girls. This anniversary was not to be missed by the national press as both television and print media recalled the two-decade-old tragedy and commented on the city's violently divisive history. On *ABC Evening News* Peter Jennings and Charles Murphy treated viewers to a four-minute-long segment that highlighted the city's violence and segregation while prominently invoking the words of segregationist governor George C. Wallace.[3]

The anniversary-driven recollections did not stop with the church bombing. Approximately two months later, a new round of Birmingham evocations occurred as the media acknowledged the twentieth anniversary of President John F. Kennedy's assassination. Dan Rather's guests on the *CBS Evening News*, for example, offered commentary on what they saw as the greatest challenges facing the president during his tragically short administration, which included the violent racism of Birmingham along with the Bay of Pigs episode, the Cuban Missile Crisis, and the desire to explore space.[4]

Such recollections continued each time a ten-year milestone offered a new opportunity for news editors to fill time and recall a sensational event from the nation's past. In 1993 the church bombing once again appeared in the nation's news broadcasts, reminding Americans that thirty years had passed since Birmingham had flown into a racial rage. As Tom Brokaw put it, this "was one the most infamous events of the bloody civil rights movement." It was a "story out of America's violent past"; it was the story of "the Birmingham bombing." This was a story that occurred in a place where "so much remains to be done" despite how much progress has been made. Reporter Bob Dotson made sure to point out that while Birmingham had elected a black mayor and black city council members and although its police force numbers consisted of over 50 percent blacks and was headed by a black chief in the years since the bombing, the economic power remained in the hands of whites. With fewer than six black-owned businesses per hundred thousand blacks in its population, the city ranked at the bottom of the nation in terms of black-owned businesses. In fact, he claimed, it ranked even lower in this category than it had on that deadly day in 1963.[5]

Yet another anniversary presented itself on May 12, 2001, as the nation recalled the freedom rides of forty years earlier. Once again Birmingham served as the backdrop for news reports. The *ABC Evening News* briefly recalled the event, focusing on the commemoration that had taken place in Birmingham the previous day. With help from violent images of that 1961 day when the freedom riders rode into the Birmingham bus station, the news managed to once again link twenty-first-century Birmingham both visually and audibly to its racist past of forty years earlier.[6]

Beyond anniversaries, newsworthy events continued to grow out of the violence of 1963 in the decades that followed through ongoing attempts to bring the perpetrators of the Sixteenth Street bombing to justice. This process turned into a decades-long endeavor that has proven rife with negative publicity for Birmingham.

On February 18, 1976, for example, the national news reported that Alabama attorney general Bill Baxley was reopening the criminal investigation into the tragic bombing. Walter Cronkite revisited the events of September 15, 1963, on the *CBS Evening News* and informed the American public that an FBI agent had named nine people who were potentially involved in the unsolved bombing that had left four dead and twenty-three wounded.[7] When indictments and court proceedings followed the next year, the national news embraced the story with a vengeance. From the day of Robert Chambliss's indictment on September 27, 1977, through his conviction on November 18, ABC, NBC, and CBS broadcast sixteen segments on their evening news shows dealing with the trial.[8] Each one evoked memories of the events and images of Birmingham in 1963. For example, on November 14, while standing in front of an image of the damaged church, NBC's David Brinkley spoke of the seventy-three-year-old hardware clerk's trial opening and recalled the city's deadly violence some fourteen years earlier.[9] Four days later, in a segment relaying Chambliss's conviction and life sentence, both prosecuting and defending attorneys stressed how the attitudes of city residents had changed since 1963. Prosecutor Bill Baxley claimed that changed attitudes toward race in the city had allowed the conviction to occur and would enable him to bring forth more indictments against Chambliss's coconspirators in the days to come. Defense attorney Art Haynes Jr. also claimed that Birminghamians' attitudes had changed. Yet he saw this change as damaging to his client's chances. As Haynes put it, "The people of this community . . . wanted and hoped for [the case] to be solved," which put his client in a "difficult position." Birmingham's citizens wanted the past put behind them once and for all. As the mother of Carol Robertson—one of the young girls slain by the bombing—put it as she left the courtroom: "Things are better. Things are looking up."[10]

Although things might have been looking up that day in 1977, it took another twenty-two years for additional indictments to be brought against the coconspirators whom Baxley had talked so enthusiastically about prosecuting in the afterglow of Chambliss's conviction. The indictments and eventual trials of Bobby

Frank Cherry and Thomas Blanton Jr. would once again prove to be too enticing for the national media to pass up. After a litany of delays, competency hearings, and even a made-for-television movie, a Birmingham jury ultimately convicted the two men who were by then elderly. Ultimately, for their barbaric actions in 1963, they found themselves sentenced to life imprisonment.[11] While justice was finally served, the coverage of these events once again thrust Birmingham's past into the present light of national and international attention.[12]

The *New York Times* broke the story of the new indictments with a front-page story on May 15, 2000. *Times* reporter Robert Slack wrote that the Birmingham bombing held special significance in the history of the civil rights movement "because of the randomness of its violence, the sacredness of its target and the innocence of its victims." He went on to write that Birmingham experienced the "most violent resistance" of the movement and that the bombing had both turned the nation against southern segregation while it "emboldened" leaders of the movement to increase their efforts.[13]

On the same day that Slack's piece announced the indictments, the *New York Times* also ran an editorial dealing with the recent developments in the 1963 bombing. In "Alabama's Long Search for Justice," the *Times'* editors lauded the "new breed of southern prosecutors" who were willing to reopen civil rights–era cases. These prosecutors were atoning for the actions of the past and bringing about the "promise of a new southern justice." Yet this new justice would not have been required if it had not been for the old leaders—the George Wallaces and J. Edgar Hoovers—who condoned racial violence by standing in the way of the legal system. The *Times* condemned these people as having allowed the perpetrators of such crimes as the Sixteenth Street Baptist Church bombing to go unpunished for far too long. This was, after all, "the most heinous crime of the civil rights era."[14] Additional front-page articles in the *Times* during the trial referred to "Birmingham's '63 Nightmare" and "the Shame of 1963" in their titles.[15]

The *New York Times* was far from the only national media outlet whose attention perked up at the new developments in the old court case. Coverage of the indictments and trials that followed ran the gamut from print to radio to television. On the morning of May 2, 2001, Blanton's conviction led off as the top story on CBS's *The Early Show*. The segment featured an overview of the bombing and prosecution and interviews with U.S. Attorney Doug Jones and Blanton's defense attorney, John Rollins, as well as local civil rights activist Reverend Abraham Woods. In a telling exchange, interviewer Mark Strassmann asserted that Rollins felt the conviction only occurred because the "community . . . felt guilty and wanted to blame someone." Rollins, far from disagreeing with that synopsis, admitted that he had expected a conviction "because of where we were." Woods added that the decision was proof that the people of Birmingham were "beginning to come to accord with [their] conscience."[16]

Likewise, coverage of Cherry's trial and ultimate conviction kept the image that Birmingham was a bastion of violence and delayed justice very much alive into the twenty-first century. Following Blanton's conviction, National Public Radio (NPR) had reported that Cherry's defense strategy was to be declared mentally incapacitated. On July 16, 2001, this seemingly worked as Birmingham-based circuit judge James Garrett declared the onetime Klansman unfit to stand trial as a result of vascular dementia. In response, Abraham Woods commented, "[The] system seems to have set up a kind of situation where white people can escape when they murder negroes. I feel very sad about that." NPR correspondent Debbie Elliott interpreted this to mean that Woods believed, "Birmingham can't move beyond its racist past until it deals with all the suspects in the notorious Sixteenth Street Baptist Church bombing case."[17]

Eventually Birmingham dealt with Frank Cherry. After Judge Garrett's ruling of incompetency was overturned, Cherry faced his trial. After deliberating for a total of six and a half hours, a jury of six white women, three black men, and three black women returned a verdict of guilty on four counts of murder. The seventy-one-year-old Cherry, now claiming that "the whole bunch lied all the way through this," was led off in shackles to serve a mandatory life sentence.[18]

Unfortunately, Birmingham was not able to "move beyond its racist past" merely by exorcising the demons of Blanton and Cherry. Instead, in a very real sense, the prosecution of the two bombers and the media coverage that it created revived Birmingham's past on a national scale. That is not to criticize the media for covering the trials. Rather, with the possible exception of Debbie Elliot putting words into Abraham Woods's mouth about Birmingham's inability to "move beyond its racist past," the reporting of the prosecutions proved evenhanded and warranted in reference to Birmingham's past.[19] The fact that the past may be damaging to the public's present perception of the city is unavoidable and must be accepted because the events in the present are direct carryovers from those historical actions. This is an example of a way in which the media perpetuates a stigmatized identity in a perfectly legitimate way.

If such negative representations of place always occurred in such a manner— only when events in the present day related directly to the stigmatizing events of the past—then stigmatized identities would likely prove less enduring over time.

Yet, all too often, current events with no ties to the stigmatizing events of the past are placed within the context of that stigma. That is not to say that there is some conspiracy among journalists to slander places such as Birmingham and keep their reputations in tatters. On the contrary, this is often done without conscious effort or ill intent. Over time the stigma assumes such a central part in the city's identity that the mere suggestion of that city triggers the stereotype created by its historical circumstances. Using only a few words related to this stereotype, a journalist can evoke a historical context within which the reader can place current activities. Such shortcuts are required in modern society as it is impossible to adequately research and provide comprehensive historical background material on each place mentioned in news coverage.[20] In the case of Birmingham, for example, coverage of a bombing in the city would most likely include a reference to the proliferation of racially motivated bombings in the city during the civil rights era. This is true even if the bombing has nothing to do with race or civil rights. Simply put, the combination of the words *bombing* and *Birmingham* evokes racism for both the journalist and the public. The mention of Birmingham's violent past thus places the modern-day bombing in a well-worn historical context. In a very real way, the cultural baggage that the journalist and the reader carry limits the way such a bombing can be reported.[21]

This was exactly the case with certain elements of press coverage following a bombing at the All Women, New Woman health-care center by Eric Rudolph on January 29, 1998. With this act, the radical "pro-life" activist secured his place in history as having carried out the first abortion clinic bombing in United States history that resulted in a fatality.[22] He also managed to reassociate Birmingham with its violently explosive past.

The *New York Times* proved commendable in its coverage of this terrible incident. In a series of articles over the following days, journalist Rick Bragg stuck to the issue at hand, impartially relating the circumstances and tragic nature of the bombing. He made no speculative connections between the city's history of bombings and this latest blast.[23] If any fault can be found in the *Times'* coverage, it resides in reporter Kevin Slack's later articles that emphasized the event's and the bomber's "southern" identities.[24]

Print coverage in other large markets lacked the *Times'* tact in dealing with the tragedy. A headline in the *Atlanta Constitution-Journal* read, "Birmingham Clinic Bombing: A City's Past Comes Roaring Back." Reporter Marlon Manuel went on to directly equate the clinic bombing with the city's epidemic of racially motivated blasts between 1945 and 1963. More specifically, he drew a comparison to the Sixteenth Street Baptist Church bombing of September 15, 1963.[25] On the same day, an equally unfair commentary by Clarence Page appeared in the *Chicago Tribune*. Having recently viewed Spike Lee's film *4 Little Girls*, Page drew an eloquent comparison between the racially motivated bombing of the Sixteenth Street Baptist Church and the recent bombing of the abortion clinic. Both, he argued, were motivated by hate. Although this moving article made a valid point, Page's usage of the church bombing and employment of the term *Bombingham* drew from and reinforced the established perception of the city as a violently intolerant place.[26] Although the clinic bombing had nothing to do with racism, press accounts of it refreshed the idea of a racist Birmingham.

Local manifestations of anxiety have also appeared in response to numerous attempts at honoring the roles that the city of Birmingham and various local activists played in the civil rights movement. The resulting controversies have once again centered on perceived damage to the city's contemporary public image. These have most readily revealed themselves during public debate over whether institutions of remembrance should be created or when attempts have been made to honor those who participated locally in the civil rights movement. Likewise, booster campaigns and reactions to other racially sensitive events have exposed significant local concern over the city's image and the publicity of its history. Several of these episodes have also revealed anxiety among some whites in regard to increased African American political power. A look at a few specific instances during the city's post–civil rights decades thus reveals a city that is not fully at peace with its historical identity and is unsure of how to portray its story.

The longest-lasting episode of acute anxiety over remembrance in Birmingham began in 1979. That fall, Mayor David Vann proposed a museum to honor Birmingham's role in the civil rights movement. Having been greatly moved by a recent visit to Jerusalem's Holocaust museum, the mayor realized the power of such institutions in helping a people come to terms with an uncomfortable history. On November 10, Vann gained support of the city council and began the process of planning and drafting organizational documents.[27] The city seemed poised to publicly present the region's history as well as exorcise a few demons and maybe make a few tourist dollars along the way.[28] Yet thirteen years passed before the first patron entered the Birmingham Civil Rights Institute.

Vann hoped that by placing the struggles of its past within a museum, his city could improve its image by highlighting its progress beyond old racial antagonisms and tensions. The city could clearly tell the world, "Look, that's history. That's not today."[29] Yet Vann learned quickly that with regard to the events of

1963, many people preferred to "put it behind us" and "forget about those racial demonstrations."[30] Vann's outlook was especially relevant in 1979 because the city was then embroiled in a fresh upheaval of racial tension that would, in fact, cost Vann his seat as mayor.

On the night of June 22, 1979, Birmingham police officer George Sands arrived on the scene of a Kingston-area convenience store robbery in which a clerk had been shot in the shoulder. Standing over his wounded coworker, another clerk pointed out a green Buick in the store's parking lot, claiming it belonged to the assailant. Sands and his partner then approached the car from the rear and ordered its occupant to remain still. In the confusion that followed, the car's occupant dove downward, and Sands unleashed a barrage of gunfire. When calm returned, twenty-one-year-old Bonita Carter lay mortally wounded in the car's seat, shot three times in the back. Carter, who was black and unarmed, was an acquaintance of the robber, who had ordered her into the car as he ran from the scene in the robbery's immediate aftermath. Officer Sands, who was white and had a documented history of brutality toward suspects, had ignored the shouts of a group of bystanders who yelled that the suspect had fled on foot.[31]

The shooting of Bonita Carter reignited smoldering racial tensions in Birmingham. Waves of protests, cries of racism, and a lack of action by the police department divided the city violently along racial lines. Over the next two weeks, the situation turned even uglier as white groups faced off with black groups nightly in the Kingston area. Late on July 5, riot police were called to the scene as bullets and blows were exchanged between white and black demonstrators. Ten black protestors were arrested, one was injured, and there were claims of police brutality toward black residents. The next day, Reverend E. W. Jarrett stood on the steps of Sixteenth Street Baptist Church alongside SCLC president Abraham Woods, both men's hands filled with spent shotgun shells from the previous night's altercation. The police, Woods pointed out to the inflamed crowd, had arrested only one white protestor during the melee. That night, police arrested eight Ku Klux Klan members for demonstrating in the area in violation of a court order. The next day two white men suspected of being snipers were arrested for pointing shotguns at black pedestrians.[32]

By July 24, demonstrators flooded the streets of the Kingston area demanding justice. When attempting to restore order through a "power sweep," the Birmingham police force found its advances met with rocks, bottles, and at times, gunfire. Ultimately, the police were forced to shoot out overhead streetlights in order to advance into the community under the cover of darkness.[33]

The local print media provided saturation-level coverage of the Bonita Carter shooting and the events that followed. For over a month, one could hardly pick up a Birmingham newspaper without being confronted with some aspect of the tragedy and the ensuing strained race relations. At the height of the tensions, in the month following the June 22 shooting, forty-nine feature articles, twelve editorials, and nineteen letters to the editor appeared in the *Birmingham News* and the *Birmingham Post-Herald*.[34] Interestingly, the black press seemed greatly divided on the issue. The more conservative *Birmingham World* virtually ignored the shooting and controversy, printing mention of it only once in a letter to the editor lambasting a *Post-Herald* article that attempted to humanize Officer Sands.[35] The *Birmingham Times*, by contrast, devoted most of its front page (along with significant portions of its second and third pages) to the shooting and the racial tensions it spawned over the course of the summer. There, one could find such dramatic headlines as "Klan Launches Weekend Kingston Invasion" and "Bonita Is Dead . . . Mayor Does Nothing."[36]

The uproar and racial division spurred by the shooting moved Mayor Vann to quickly authorize a citizens' committee to investigate the shooting. The racial sensitivity of the situation revealed itself early and obviously in the board's equal distribution of black and white members. Chosen by Operation New Birmingham (ONB), the eight members ranged from University of Alabama at Birmingham historian Blaine Brownell to ACMHR president Reverend Edward Garner. While the committee had no power to convict or exonerate those involved, it could, if it so chose, make recommendations to Mayor Vann concerning what action he might take. Vann agreed to listen to such recommendations but steadfastly asserted that the responsibility for dealing with the case ultimately resided with the mayor and police chief.[37] In addressing the committee on its opening day, Vann stressed that "the greatest and primary purpose" for its existence was to supply the public with the facts concerning the case. This, Vann asserted, was a duty of "rather unique importance in this city" because the racially divisive "rumors" about what had occurred could overturn "all the good work" of the previous fifteen years.[38] The committee ultimately found the shootings to be unjustified, but Mayor Vann refused to dismiss either the police chief or Officer Sands. Instead, Sands was reassigned to a desk job until a mental breakdown on July 31 removed him from active duty.[39]

Beyond revealing festering racial tension within Birmingham in the late 1970s, the Bonita Carter incident also revealed a population's concern with its city's image. Newspaper editorials, articles, and letters to the editor by citizens of the city displayed evidence of this concern. The name Bull Connor, for example, made appearances as citizens and reporters saw the events of 1979 raising the ghosts of 1963.[40] Other residents hoped that the biracial citizens' council and the earnest attempts to deal with such a "difficult moment" in the city's history would show the quality of Birmingham's citizens and the "greatness" of a city that had "learned to cope with such tensions."[41] An editorial in the *Birmingham Post-Herald* warned of the danger if authorities did not act quickly and wisely in resolving the aftermath of the Bonita Carter shooting, given the "legacy of our city's racial history."[42] Likewise, the *Birmingham News* editorialized that the racially violent acts erupting in Kingston were "remnants of an era of police dogs and fire hoses of 15 years ago." The *News* editor continued that "Birmingham had come too far" to allow this episode to ruin its racial progress.[43] A week and a half later, as violence increased in the Kingston community, the *Birmingham News* editors directly related the racial upheaval to the city's past and its public image:

> Birmingham has been through this kind of messy business before. We know first hand what the costs are in both social and economic terms and in terms of the individual and the community. The city, despite good and positive changes, still suffers from the reputation garnered by violence and confrontation in the '60s. We have too much that is positive and good going for us to turn back the clocks. . . . So let's cool it. Now—before it's too late.[44]

The next week, the *News* once again warned of the dangerous ground Birmingham was traversing in regard to its national image. This time, editors spoke directly of the "stigma" of racial violence that devastated the city in the aftermath of 1963:

> Many have probably forgotten or are too young to know the trauma that followed in the wake of violence in the '60s. The city's progress came to an abrupt halt and the economy literally shriveled. All efforts to bring new enterprises to the city were for naught. Some Birmingham based firms actually pulled up stakes and departed. They wanted no part of the stigma that resulted from violence in the streets, and even numbers of our sons and daughters fled the city for better opportunities elsewhere.[45]

It is also revealing that Operation New Birmingham took the lead in putting together the citizens' committee hearings into the shootings. ONB, characterizing itself as "Birmingham's unique, privately sponsored civic action organization," had begun as the Birmingham Downtown Improvement Association (BDIA) in

1957. That year, twenty-seven downtown business owners formed the BDIA in response to the local construction of suburban malls and the threat this posed to downtown businesses. In 1963 the BDIA changed its name to Operation New Birmingham and expanded its objectives to include taking an active role in the city's public relations. Specifically, ONB sought to "reshape the city's image, both in the eyes of its own citizens and in the view of the rest of the country."[46] Just as the organization's name implies, it attempted to build a "New Birmingham" from the ashes of the old.

By 1979 ONB had attempted to rehabilitate Birmingham's image among its own citizens and on the national scale through a variety of means. On the local scale, it frequently sponsored pro-Birmingham exhibits at local libraries and museums, speeches at various local venues by political leaders and such famous local products as Jim Nabors of *The Andy Griffith Show* and *Gomer Pyle* fame, and invented the city's own civic pride holiday, Mayor's Day. The organization also launched "positive thinking campaigns" such as the 1967 "A Number One-derful City" essay competition. In an effort to "rebuild self-confidence in their city," local businesspeople advertised the contest on television and radio and in newspapers for the contest, which ultimately drew over twenty-five hundred entries from around the city.[47]

On a national scale, ONB attempted to improve Birmingham's image by publicizing positive aspects of the city. In this regard, one could argue that the organization was a late twentieth-century descendent of the post–Civil War New South booster campaigns in the nineteenth century. For example, in the late 1960s ONB issued numerous press releases through the city's national public relations company, John Moynahan and Company of New York, which highlighted such positive developments as the construction of new high-rise buildings, the arrival of major companies, and the praise the city received from national political figures.[48] In one attempt to distance Birmingham from the violent demonstrations of its past, ONB made sure to publicize a "paint-in" demonstration in which two hundred "rich, poor, black, and white" individuals had come together to paint murals across the city. Including an image of a psychedelic mural featuring the words "Love, Peace, God, Country, [and] Mankind," the press release stated that "in this age of 'ins'—sit-ins, stand-ins, kneel-ins, love-ins—a new kind of 'in' happened this week in Birmingham."[49]

ONB's greatest, or at least most vaunted, success in reshaping Birmingham's national image came in early 1971. Since 1968 the organization had attempted, without success, to get Birmingham named to *Look* magazine's annual list of

"All-America Cities." Finally, in 1970, ONB's Community Affairs Committee submitted a joint application with the Birmingham Area Chamber of Commerce. After reviewing the applications, the declining magazine—this would be its last year of publication—placed Birmingham alongside such other distinctly American towns as Gainesville and Lakeland, Florida; Lumberton and Shelby, North Carolina; Ardmore, Oklahoma; Dallas, Texas; Indianapolis, Indiana; Enfield and Bloomfield, Connecticut; and Fitchburg, Massachusetts.[50]

Following the receipt of this "national honor and coveted award," city business leaders partook in a virtual orgy of self-congratulation. The chamber of commerce's monthly magazine, *Birmingham*, devoted five out of eight feature articles to the award in its March issue and eight out of fourteen total articles in April. Calling the award a "promoter's dream come true," editor Donald A. Brown wrote of the chamber's national campaign that would publicize Birmingham's "All-America" designation through television, print, radio, and press kits. He further urged "every company in the city" to use the March and April issues of *Birmingham* as "national mailing pieces."[51] The chamber also deemed it fitting to place a seal bearing the words "Birmingham All-America City" on the upper-left corner of each magazine's cover for the remainder of the year.

In the April issue, editor Brown took a firm stance on the reason why this award meant so much to Birmingham as to justify a second issue devoted to its receipt. He wrote:

> Becoming an All-America city is stumbling back into the sunshine after being lost in some abandoned mine shaft.... Back in 1963 we were abruptly awakened to learn that our hoop-skirted dreamworld was the fantasy and our secret nightmare was upon us.... There are those who still may think of Birmingham as the Tragic City.... Set them straight with an extra copy of this All-America issue. Spread the word. The Magic is back.[52]

Throughout the pages that followed, the magazine's writers echoed Brown's theme, extolling the great progress Birmingham had made since its darkest point seven years earlier. This was, after all, a city that even prominent locals had declared "dead" in 1963.[53] Now the editor of a respected national magazine was asking to come to Birmingham to present it with a national honor. In the magazine's view, Birmingham was no longer the "doormat" of the "world."[54]

Thus, through the public relations activities of ONB and the chamber of commerce, Birmingham locals had reason to believe that their city had made great strides regarding its image by the mid to late 1970s. Unfortunately, the

Bonita Carter shooting and its violent aftermath threatened to overturn that progress.[55] This is what motivated the editors of local newspapers and the mayor in 1979 to warn against the dangers that the controversy potentially held for the city's reputation.

While Mayor Vann attempted to contain the damage to his city's image by approving the formation of the biracial citizens' committee and implementing procedural changes in police force tactics, he failed miserably at heading off damage to his own reputation. To make matters worse, 1979 was an election year. The outrage caused by the shooting and subsequent violent confrontations sealed Vann's fate. Ironically, Vann, who had been instrumental in the 1963 shift from a commission to a council form of government that removed Bull Connor from office and had long been a proponent of racial equality, lost support of the black community as well as a large number of white liberals. He lost this significant portion of his base because he appeared less than forthcoming with documents requested by the citizens' committee and then declined to fire the officer—whom the district attorney had also failed to indict.[56]

If Vann's handling of the Bonita Carter shooting closed the door on his political career in Birmingham, it swung that same door wide open to his longtime friend and supporter, city council member Richard Arrington. The former zoology professor and head of the recently formed Jefferson County Citizens' Coalition, rode the crescendo of anti-Vann sentiment and used the issue of police brutality to win the election and take his place as the city's first African American mayor in early 1980.[57]

The local media did not seem to catch on to the significant chance that Birmingham might elect its first black mayor until election night results made it readily apparent that the incumbent was not going to be reelected. Articles on the October 9 election day in leading newspapers merely listed the candidates along with brief biographical information and voting instructions. The race pitted incumbent Vann against city council members Richard Arrington, Larry Langford, John Katapodis, local attorney Frank Parsons, grand dragon of the Alabama Knights of the Ku Klux Klan Don Black, and Socialist Workers' representative Mohammed Oliver. In its election day editorial, the *Birmingham News* made no reference to Arrington and Langford—the two serious black contenders—in its endorsement of Vann.[58]

On October 10, as the extent of the heavy turnout became apparent and the initial results rolled in, everything changed. Suddenly the significance of what was occurring dawned on the local press, and race became the central topic of discussion in regard to the mayor's election. The *Birmingham Post-Herald*, now touting Arrington as the man "often predicted to become Birmingham's first black mayor," revealed that the councilman had finished a whopping twenty thousand votes ahead of his closest opponent, Frank Parsons. Sitting mayor Vann had finished an embarrassing fourth behind councilman Katapodis, with 15 percent of the vote compared to Arrington's 45 percent. As no one received over 50 percent of the vote, a runoff between the top two candidates would follow on October 30.[59]

The extent of the racial focus in the *Post-Herald* and the *News* on the day after the election was striking. Every article dealing with the mayoral race, with the exception of two small pieces on fringe candidates in the *Post-Herald*, either centered on or prominently mentioned race.[60] Articles appeared in both papers dissecting the racial breakdown of the vote. Each ultimately concluded that Arrington had pulled the majority of the black vote as well as a small yet significant portion of the white vote that had supported Vann four years earlier. In some black neighborhoods, the newspapers revealed, turnout approached 70 percent. As one Vann supporter put it, over half of Vann's supporters in 1975 had deserted the mayor in favor of Arrington. This supporter reasoned that this turnabout was solely the result of the Bonita Carter shooting: "It just makes you sick to think that just because of Bonita Carter, all of those blacks could turn against him." Arrington supporter state representative Earl Hilliard agreed, stating, "Vann had to have the black vote and he blew it with Bonita Carter."[61]

Editorials followed suit, emphasizing the magnitude of race in the election and the significance of Birmingham's possibly electing a black mayor. The *Birmingham News*, while letting race dominate its postelection coverage, warned its readers against letting race become "the primary focus of the campaign."[62] Both the *News* and the *Post-Herald* cautioned against the "easy temptation" of saying that voting played out on strictly racial lines. Their editorials—in striking opposition to what would come in *New York Times* pieces after the runoff election—stressed Arrington's impressive strength in some predominately white precincts and his failure to dominate some black precincts.[63] In an interesting aside, one Birmingham resident expressed concern over the election's influence on the city's historically battered racial image. Karen Robinson, in a *Birmingham News* letter to the editor, looked on the mayoral campaign of KKK leader Don Black with great regret. In summary, she concluded that his candidacy had damaged the "fine reputation" that the people of Birmingham and Alabama had worked so hard to rebuild after the publicity of the 1960s had labeled it "racist."[64]

On a day threatening rain, the turnout for the October 30 runoff election surpassed all expectations as 71 percent of the city's black voters and 66 percent of its white voters cast their ballots. After campaigning on improving the city's economy and fighting crime in black areas, Arrington defeated Parsons by a margin of 52 percent to 48 percent. That evening, in his acceptance speech, Arrington spoke of the significance of his election to the city's image. He claimed that the majority's election of a black man in Birmingham "says more about our city . . . than all the PR we can do and all the things we can say." President Jimmy Carter echoed Arrington's words as he called to congratulate the new mayor shortly thereafter. The president concluded that this was a "great day" for a city whose history was so stained by the racial turmoil of the 1960s.[65]

Local editorials also took on a celebratory tone, their authors feeling that Arrington's election must reveal to the world once and for all the progress that Birmingham had made since 1963. The *Post-Herald* called his election a "symbolic confirmation" of racial progress that was more important than any policy. Under the headline "City Wins Election," the *Birmingham News* wheeled out the old name Magic City in lauding the election as confirmation of a "truly new Birmingham."[66] Residents such as Jacqueline McCarroll agreed, writing that for the first time in her life, she was "really proud of this city." The election, she felt, projected a "new and beautiful image to the rest of this nation and the world." After this, certainly, Birmingham could no longer be "looked upon" as a "non-progressive city" defined by "racial prejudice and unrest."[67]

Not all within the community shared the opinion of the local press and McCarroll that Arrington's election represented progress or a boon for Birmingham's image. The negative responses by citizens in the press revealed that at least some of Birmingham's population could not care less whether the city was viewed as racist. One has to doubt that James Thompson, for instance, ever lost sleep over Birmingham being stigmatized as a racist city. After all, on the day that the city elected its first black mayor, Thompson openly argued for a return to racial segregation in a letter published in the *Birmingham News*. Claiming that both racial majorities and minorities would forever reject each other's cultures, Thompson concluded that the *News* had been terribly wrong in calling for an end to racial polarization during the campaign. The only solution that made sense, in his mind, was a return to "separate but equal."[68] Others such as Vera Jones and an unnamed "white insurance agent" found much to fear in the election of a black mayor. The insurance salesman felt that Arrington would turn out to be a "racist" who would only push issues that were of importance to the black community. Jones, echoing these racially based fears, felt sure that whites would "be left out in the cold."[69]

Such fears remained significant enough throughout Arrington's five terms as mayor to necessitate occasional reference in Arrington's yearly State of the City addresses. When delivering this speech on January 5, 1982, for example, he reminded residents that as mayor, he worked "equally for both blacks and whites." Arrington further elaborated on the racialized nature of his city by stating that in Birmingham, people had an "obligation" to work for a successful multiracial society. This was required more in Birmingham than in other cities, because "no other city in the U.S." had come further in regard to race relations over the past twenty years.[70]

Arrington often returned to race relations and Birmingham's special historical identity in subsequent speeches. In 1983 he spoke of how the "burden of past racial antagonisms rests heavily" upon Birmingham. His hope in the forthcoming election was to prove to "those who watch us so closely" that Birmingham had been successful in "surmounting the burdens of her past."[71] The next year, Arrington was still hoping that the city could overcome race "once and for all as a matter of controversy and concern."[72] Unfortunately, as the new decade broke six years later, Arrington conceded that the city was still undergoing "continuing efforts to heal the wounds of the past."[73]

One way that Arrington felt he could address these "wounds" of Birmingham's history was by adopting Vann's idea of a civil rights museum in the city, albeit belatedly. In 1982 he lent his support to a plan for the institute that was drawn up by a citizens' committee and presented to the city council. Finances, however, put the project on hold. Quite simply, there were no funds available to build the multimillion-dollar project, and the idea of taxation to support an institute that many in the community viewed with suspicion was not a viable option. Thus the project languished for four years until Arrington formed a museum task force in 1986 to study the feasibility of the museum and hopefully get it on track to fruition. Led by Odessa Woolfolk, the director of urban affairs at the University of Alabama at Birmingham, and chamber of commerce president Frank Young III, the task force included a diverse cross section of Birmingham's political and social leadership who were both African American and white, including members of the civil rights movement, radio personalities, and even former mayor David Vann. Many more, however, turned down an offer to serve on the task force. Often, even liberal white businesspeople claimed they wanted no association with what they saw as a very controversial issue with potentially negative connotations for the city. The task force named the proposed museum the Birmingham Civil Rights Institute, had architectural plans created, and issued a mission statement.[74]

Arrington suggested paying for the institute by way of a special bond issue. Over the next four years, the bond issue for the institute was placed on the countywide ballot twice. In both 1986 and 1988 the referendum went down in defeat.[75] These defeats did not merely reflect popular resistance to the establishment of the Civil Rights Institute. As the proposals called for a $5 million tax increase, one has to surmise that the final tally against the measure resulted from both antitax and anti-institute sentiments.[76]

Although it still lacked funding, Mayor Arrington publicly reiterated his support of the project in his 1988 State of the City address. He informed the city that the Civil Rights Institute task force would soon be reporting "to the community" on the planned site where a building was to be placed directly south of the Sixteenth Street Baptist Church and west of Kelly Ingram Park. At this time, Arrington portrayed the institute completely in terms of downtown revitalization and made no mention of history or race relations.[77] This approach changed markedly by the time of his next mention of the institute two years later. In 1990 Arrington used the full weight of the city's history and its damaged public image in supporting the creation of the institute. He spoke of how Birmingham had yet to become the "harmonious, inclusive community" that it must be if the city was ever going to "prosper" and successfully overcome the "perception" of a place that was "not a city of promise, particularly for [the] young minority." Claiming that "no site in the nation" was more important to the civil rights movement than Birmingham, Arrington advised his fellow citizens to take pride in the June 1990 groundbreaking and support the institute. He closed by emphasizing that no "bond funds" would be used in the institute's construction.[78]

Later that same year, the mayor created the Birmingham Civil Rights Institute Board of Directors, employing many of those individuals who had served on the task force. He chose Woolfolk as the institute's first president and, along with the city council, accepted a financing plan that drew money from the city and county government as well as the private sector. The Jefferson County Commission provided the institute with a direct construction grant while the city shifted funds from its sale of the Social Security Building. Despite Arrington's claims to the contrary, additional funding was drawn from bond sources. This bond money came from general revenue bonds issued by Birmingham's Historical Preservation Authority. Additional funding to cover the museum's construction came from corporate donations. When the structure was completed, the city would lease it to the Birmingham Civil Rights Institute.[79]

When the Civil Rights Institute finally opened in 1992, it neither swamped the city with negative press nor increased division along racial lines. National press coverage proved favorable. The *New York Times* praised the institute as an example of how to positively embrace the city's history. By the end of 1993 the center had drawn some 37,470 visitors from forty-four states and thirteen countries. Further, it had expanded its mission to include hosting human rights conferences, sponsoring historical tours of the civil rights district, and conducting educational outreach programs for schoolchildren in addition to holding art exhibits and performances.[80] Instead of looking to history with regret, the Civil Rights Institute celebrated progress and the role that the city and its brave residents had played in changing the world.

Locally, Birmingham basked in the favorable publicity surrounding the institute's opening. The chamber of commerce devoted an article in its *Birmingham* magazine to arguing that, as institute vice president Abraham Woods put it, the institute was a "symbol" to the "nation and world" of how far Birmingham had come since the days of Bull Connor.[81] The black *Birmingham World* likewise wrote that the city was being "praised for its vision" and the institute's "boost" to the "city's image."[82] Arrington credited the institute's opening with bringing "more favorable national and international recognition" to the city than ever before in its history. To him, the press coverage had been "extraordinary."[83] As the local press reported, he felt that the institute was helping the world "look at Birmingham in a new light" as a "forward looking city" that "has confronted and accepted its past."[84]

Unfortunately, this idea of Birmingham having accepted its past proved premature in 1992. Some sixteen years later, in 2008, the reaction to another mayor's proposal revealed that many still harbored misgivings about drawing attention to the events of the 1960s. In this instance, Mayor Larry Langford unintentionally ignited what he considered to be a firestorm of controversy with his suggested renaming of the Birmingham International Airport in honor of local civil rights activist Reverend Fred Shuttlesworth. Langford viewed the renaming as an appropriate honor for the man who was perhaps most responsible for bringing change to Birmingham in the 1960s and who "led Birmingham to . . . become the conscience of the world."[85]

Almost immediately following Langford's announcement, examples of unease and outright opposition emerged in the local media. Where previously

Sculpture dedicated to the foot soldiers of the Birmingham civil rights movement, Kelly Ingram Park, Birmingham, Alabama, February 28, 2010.
Photograph by Carol M. Highsmith. Library of Congress, Prints and Photographs Division, LC-DIG-highsm-05100.

the editorial pages of newspapers had served as a means of airing such public discourse, much of this 2008 discussion played out in a more technologically advanced medium. Specifically, citizens shared their views in the comment sections of online *Birmingham News* articles. This format offered a democratization of the press in that it allowed far more voices to be heard than traditional letters to the editor. Langford viewed this as a negative aspect of the technology, bemoaning that it gave the less tolerant elements of society "the shade to hide their faces behind once again."[86] Certainly, online commenting can loosen the binds of self-censorship often prevalent in open cultural dialogue.[87] It can also attract the basest elements of society on both sides of a topic. Regardless, out of 124 comments that appeared almost instantaneously following a June 28 *News* article reporting that Birmingham Airport Authority board members supported the renaming, only fifteen comments could be classified as positive or neutral relative to the name change. When printed out, the responses amount to thirty typewritten pages of highly emotional commentary.[88] While these comments might not present an absolutely accurate representation of the public's position on the issue, their volume certainly shows the public's interest and concern.

Many commentators felt certain that renaming the airport after Shuttlesworth would reopen the racial wounds of the city's past in the public eye. One individual proposed that the city should "move past this civil rights mess . . . to shed that image of Birmingham."[89] Another obviously agreed, writing that the naming would "only keep us in the past and hold on to the image that so many are ready to leave behind."[90] Others, claiming weariness of having civil rights–related issues "pushed down everyone's throats," perceived the renaming as "embarrassing" for the city.[91] Other commenters proposed allowing the "things" that "happened forty years ago" to be forgotten. This line of reasoning held that there could "never be peace until" Birmingham "quit living in the past and CONSTANTLY rehashing it."[92]

Beyond concerns over reviving a difficult past, the anxiety over race and political power also permeated the posts. References to "racist blacks" and to black politicians honing in on "whitey" revealed mindsets that were tainted by racism and fearful of what they saw as African Americans' dominance over local political power.[93] One commenter made sure to point out that the Birmingham Airport Authority board was composed completely of African Americans who, borrowing a phrase from New Orleans mayor Ray Nagin, wanted to transform Birmingham into a "chocolate city."[94] Others argued that if black city leaders failed to get their way with the renaming, then they would really play the race card and "call in the brothers and sisters" to protest and force the change on area whites.[95]

Mayor Langford took note of this racial hypersensitivity and believed it to extend beyond the reactionary elements of the white community and into local political action. Specifically, he recalled how such sensitivity to perceptions of race and political action influenced African American politicians and the quality of their constituents' lives. In making this case, he pointed to the stark contrast between such wealthy areas of town—the Highway 280 corridor—and the poorer and predominantly black areas—West End and Five Points West.

Some differences in appearance in these areas, he observed, were as much a product of hypersensitivity to perceptions of racial favoritism and use of political power as they were of structural economic inequalities. In his experience as a city council member, journalist, and mayor, Langford claimed to have observed African American council members from these areas refusing to seek available city funds for their constituents. Such refusals, according to Langford, resulted from a fear of public backlash and claims that the appropriations occurred there only because the majority-black city council and mayor wanted to direct tax money to black neighborhoods. Instead, as Langford put it, existing sidewalks were repaired in white areas while other areas had "no sidewalks to repair."[96]

Almost five decades have passed since hatred's dynamite shattered the early morning calm of Birmingham's Sixteenth Street North. Today, as patrons of the Birmingham Civil Rights Institute meander through the facility's permanent exhibition, they inevitably find themselves facing a large window. With quiet gasps of recognition, they realize that the window frames the Sixteenth Street Baptist Church, located directly across the street. The church itself, the site of the infamous bombing, subsequently becomes a part of the exhibition. It is a powerful vision that brings forth the past in a way that few others can. From this enlivened past, the much-worried-about Bombingham fails to filter through the window, fails to permeate the institute, and fails to project the stigma of violent racism upon the city once again. Instead, the institute emphasizes a version of the city's history that promotes humanity's ability to change and one city's role in effecting that change. Yet not all have embraced the city's past as a narrative of progress. As recent debates over the renaming of landmarks attest, some remain ill at ease with the city's history and with the local intersections of race, power, and remembrance.

Recently, however, those who wished to embrace the city's significant role in American history scored a major victory. On January 12, 2017, President Barack Obama designated the Birmingham Civil Rights District a national historical monument. With such a designation, the area will be preserved under the Antiquities Act and fall under the supervision of the National Parks Service.[97] The drive to gain national monument status for the district had been strongly supported by Mayor William Bell, U.S. congresswoman Terri Sewell, the National Trust for Historic Preservation, and perhaps most important, many residents in the local community.[98] As with previous attempts at remembrance, voices of opposition quickly followed. Among the 254 comments in response to a news article announcing the national monument decision on AL.com—a website run by Alabama's largest media conglomerate, which now owns the *Birmingham News*—one could find numerous responses opposing the monument. Some were ridiculously racist: "Reverse discrimination is an ugly thing. King Hussein Obama has only a few more day [*sic*] to promote racial unrest."[99] Other oppositional comments were a bit more thoughtful and directly addressed concerns over Birmingham's image. One reader, for example, bemoaned that this was "just a scab being scraped so the wound can't heal. In Birmingham it's always 1963. Sorry, Folks, that's how the rest of the world sees us. It's the reputation we have made for ourselves."[100] But not all comments were opposed. Interestingly, at least an equal number of posts challenged the negative commenters and voiced support for honoring Birmingham's important place in history. This was perhaps best summed up by a reader with the screen name SteelShield, who replied,

> Some of the posters on here have written: "It's always 1963 in Birmingham."
>
> Is it always 1945 in Hiroshima and Nagasaki?
> Is it always 1863 in Gettysburg?
> Is it always 1941 in Pearl Harbor?
> Is it always 1776 in Philadelphia?
> Is it always 1838 on the trail of tears?
>
> History is part of the fiber of these places and important events in history should be preserved and learned from not forgotten and ignored.[101]

San Francisco is a mad city—inhabited for the most part by perfectly insane people.
Rudyard Kipling, 1891

4

Never Quite American

The Deviantly Exotic Reputation of San Francisco, 1776–1969

Unlike Birmingham, San Francisco had yet to receive the National Civic League's "All-America City" designation as twentieth century drew to its end. In the fifty-one years since the award's creation, the league had not seen fit to label the bayside city as all-American.[1] Likewise, even Las Vegas carried the mantle of *Time* magazine "All-American" city by the mid-1990s though San Francisco did not.[2] As this chapter will argue, it is not surprising that these national publications and award-granting organizations have ignored the city in their proclamations of what is quintessentially American. Instead, the so-called Baghdad by the Bay has, since its induction into the nation, often carried the identity of something exotic and not quite American.[3]

Geographically, modern San Francisco occupies a peninsula defined by the Pacific Ocean, Golden Gate Strait, and San Francisco Bay. It shares this sliver of land with forty hills reaching heights of up to one thousand feet. At only forty-seven square miles in total area, the modern city is spatially cramped. In comparison to Birmingham's 152 square miles and Las Vegas's 113 square miles, it occupies the smallest physical space of any city in this study.[4] Yet, as with Birmingham, even smaller geographical segments of the city have contributed disproportionately to its modern identity. In the late nineteenth and early twentieth centuries, for example, the Barbary Coast vice district had a national reputation as an anything-goes type of town. Later, in the last decades of the twentieth century, the centrally located Castro district helped project the image of San Francisco as a gay mecca. This was due in no small part to the vibrant gay culture in the former working-class Irish neighborhood and the district's role as the seat of the San Francisco gay rights political movement in the late 1970s.[5]

Early San Francisco

In the same year that Thomas Jefferson declared the United States its own sovereign and independent nation, Franciscan monks traveled northward into California from established settlements in Spanish Mexico. Upon reaching one of the greatest natural harbors in the Western Hemisphere, they stopped to construct a small mission on the shore of what is now Yerba Buena Cove. Compatriots of these early travelers also erected a presidio, or fort, at the mouth, or "golden gate," of the harbor. With approximately eight hundred head of cattle, horses, and mules, these missionaries of the faith and the few Spanish cowboys who accompanied them began what would be a largely unprofitable outpost. Over the next few decades, the Spanish eked out a minimal existence at the far-flung settlement while members of the Native population found their numbers depleted by some three-quarters due to the introduction of disease and forced labor at the mission.[6] Nonetheless, these sites were the first European settlements in what would one day become known as the San Francisco Bay Area.

It was not until 1835 that Captain W. A. Richardson, an Englishman working as harbor master for the now independent Mexican government controlling the area, threw up a canvas tent supported by four redwood poles. This would later be remembered as one of the first structures on the site of present-day San Francisco outside the mission. Richardson could have never imagined how prescient the name adopted by the settlement, Yerba Buena, or "good herb," would be 130 years in the future when the hippie movement was centered there, though the mayor of Yerba Buena had changed the town's name to San Francisco on January 30, 1847.[7]

Such associations have colored San Francisco's identity since its earliest days as part of the United States. Although the missionary settlement of the area shares a tenuous chronological association with the most revered date in the nation's founding, the identity of San Francisco has always been tinged with a bit of the exotic. In the modern day, for example, writers of such wildly popular travel guides as Lonely Planet's *San Francisco City Guide* characterize the city as a place of "outcasts among outcasts." Would-be travelers who read such travel guides learn very quickly that from the time the city entered into the United States, it was a preferred place for everyone from "crackpots" to "visionaries," including "Chinese, Irish, African Americans, Australians and Mexicans."[8] Such characterizations of the city throughout its history are not abnormal. On the contrary, one can trace this labeling of San Francisco as something different from the time of its foundation as a Mexican outpost, through its rough-and-tumble emergence as an American port city, and finally into its twentieth-century history of social dissent. As this chapter will show, many perceived San Francisco to be deviantly radical long before it earned a mental placement as the preeminent gay mecca in the nation and even the world.[9] This long history of otherness prepared the perceptual ground in which the gay mecca label and reality took root so firmly.

The Mexican-American War of 1846–48 obviously played a central role in the relationship between the city and the United States. This is, after all, how San Francisco became part of the United States. The belief in Manifest Destiny—the idea that the United States was destined by God to stretch across the North American continent to the Pacific Ocean—was widely held by 1846.[10] While the much-delayed annexation of Texas into the nation and the resultant border dispute with Mexico marked the immediate causes of the war, one should not discount the influence of U.S. designs on California. A U.S. diplomatic mission headed by John Slidell, for example, had gone so far as to attempt to purchase California from the Mexicans for the sum of $25 million in the months leading up to the war. This unsuccessful bid carried the full support and blessing of President James K. Polk. It should come as no surprise that the president was willing to fight when Slidell could not reach an agreement with the Mexicans on either the Texas border dispute or the California question. He had, it should be noted, campaigned on the slogan "Fifty-Four Forty or Fight!" which, although it referred to Polk's willingness to go to war with Britain over Oregon's northern boundary, also revealed the acquisition of California as one of his administration's main goals.[11] Yet, beyond the strong belief in Manifest Destiny, one of the oldest motivations in human history also likely contributed to American designs on California.

A mere nine days before the Treaty of Guadalupe Hidalgo brought hostilities with Mexico to an end and provided the United States with a bargain-basement price on what was to become the southwestern quarter of the nation, James Marshall picked a bit of gold out of the American River near present-day Sacramento. Soon news of this discovery blanketed the United States, spread internationally, and set off what has been called the greatest gold rush in history. Over eighty thousand gold-hungry settlers ventured to the state in 1849, followed by an estimated three hundred thousand by 1854. The great gold rush of 1849 subsequently placed San Francisco on the map, rapidly brought statehood to California, and helped fill the nation's treasury.[12]

History seldom follows such a neat linear trajectory, though. The previous chain of events, for example, ignores many key elements of the story. While news of Marshall's discovery in 1848 set off the gold rush, knowledge of gold in California actually predated the Mexican-American War; two thousand ounces of the precious metal had been shipped to Washington, D.C., from the San Fernando Valley in 1843. Dispatches from the U.S. consul to Monterrey, Thomas O. Larkin, to his Washington superiors that same year, detailing the mineral wealth of California, show an earlier knowledge.[13] And there are also various press reports and rumors linking California, the far West, and gold that predated even the Franciscan monks' founding of their little mission by the bay. The *Pennsylvania Packet* and the *New York Journal*, for instance, wrote in 1772 of the reported "immense" riches and gold mines on the California coast. They claimed, "With very little labor, vast quantities of grains of gold have been found."[14] In 1804 newspapers across the nation ran an editorial of British origin warning of the dangers of Napoleon gaining control of "the gold mines of Mexico and California."[15] By 1819 leading papers were reporting on the vast quantities of gold and silver that "abound in Old and New Mexico." They went on to tell of "immense" gold shipments originating in Santa Fe, while the land of Sonora and California also held great prospective value to Americans.[16] Fifteen years later, while claiming that the United States' mines had the greatest quality gold in all the world, a piece that appeared in both South Carolina's *Southern Patriot* and Massachusetts's *New Bedford Review* referenced the reception of "specimens" of California gold by the Geological Society of Pennsylvania.[17] While many of these claims were directed at what is today southern California and Mexico's Baja California, they set a precedent of associating California and the Pacific Coast area with gold. Then, of course, there are the numerous reports of gold in the San Francisco area in 1842. Many of these refer to a "prolific vein of gold extending nearly twenty miles" that was discovered near the bay of "St. Francisco, in Upper California."[18] Others tend to be more vague but still equate Mexican California with gold.[19]

Simply put, the idea of gold in California did not magically appear in 1848 as the Mexican-American War came to an end. The notion, and proof of the notion, had been floating around for quite some time before Marshall pulled a few glittering grains from the riverbed. But adherence to this story provides a simple, clean-cut narrative for the Americanization of California and, by association, of

San Francisco. As a sole foundation, the story, although it encompasses factual events, becomes mythical in scope. The myth then provides a romantic element to mining and prospecting. Anyone, even an eccentric carpenter like Marshall, could go out and strike it rich on his own, as an individual, without the burden of indebtedness to others or servitude to the corporate overseer. Such romantic founding myths are key to the development of national and local identities. They provide a place with a sense of destiny, accomplishment, and independence.[20] In a way, they give a quick reference point upon which to base and build subsequently arising perceptions of a place as needed by intervening historical events.

Because it was perceived to be an independent activity, mining became a gamble for many who would decide to head west after 1848. By association, San Francisco itself became something of a gamble. It was the center of golden-hued hopes, serving as an entry point and service center for those hoping to hit the jackpot in nature's casino. An article on the European press's coverage of the gold mania emanating from California in 1849 directly linked the search for gold to gambling no less than five times.[21] And European nations had cause to worry. The goldfields lured Americans, Latinos, Asians, Europeans, and every other kind of human who was ever tempted by riches. The influx of foreign-born prospectors brought about by the gold rush was so significant that at least one historian of the era labeled it the instance of "internationalism" that "most boldly" conveyed the "increasingly global nature" of the United States' society in the nineteenth century.[22] Unlike many American cities and regions, San Francisco and northern California thus exhibited a very cosmopolitan character from early on. As Glenna Matthews has pointed out, this cosmopolitanism ultimately became valued for its own sake, and it prompted a regional consciousness that was less hateful and suspicious of the "other" in American society. While suspicion and hate were never completely removed from the equation, a significant portion of San Franciscans—often at odds with other national groups—displayed a live-an-let-live philosophy, according to Matthews. This idea of born-in cosmopolitanism can also be applied to San Franciscans' relative acceptance of their city being labeled the gay mecca in the late twentieth and early twenty-first centuries.[23]

Beyond the cosmopolitan seeds it planted, the California gold rush certainly qualifies historically as a "great event," according to Albert Hurtado. He argues that the gold rush "set a pattern of mineral rushes, industrial mining, and environmental despoliation that has marked the West from the mid-nineteenth century to the present day." Further, he asserts, "The gold rush earthquake set off political, social, and demographic tremors that continue to shake the West and wider world."[24] He could have added that the gold rush also sowed the seeds of San Francisco's radical image, which took firm root with astonishing speed during this period and continued to flower throughout the twentieth century.

It is not difficult to imagine what it was like in this boomtown and the surrounding environs in the era of the gold rush. By 1850 the young city existed as the United States' foremost port on the Pacific and boasted a population that was overwhelmingly male and under forty years of age.[25] As that year drew to an end, one could count 12.2 males to every female in California. In 1852 this ratio had lessened to 5.2 to 1, yet by the dawn of the Civil War, males still outnumbered females at a rate of more than 2 to 1.[26]

This gender imbalance highlights the fact that prospecting, mining, and seafaring—all gambles and harsh physical enterprises—tended to draw from the young unattached male demographic. This demographic is also the most unstable in its almost constant search for excitement and various forms of entertainment. The search for excitement took on added impetus for men who had been out to sea or out in the wilderness panning for gold for extended periods. Gambling held a particular attraction for men who had journeyed to the area with the intention of striking it rich. As one historian has observed, "Gambling remained the principal diversion of the great mass of restless, turbulent, gold-hungry men who almost over night had transformed the once peaceful hamlet of San Francisco into a bawdy, bustling bedlam of mud holes and shanties."[27]

Gambling was everywhere, and there were no real efforts at enforcing state control until the 1870s. In the interim, a person could open a gambling establishment anywhere he or she wanted to set up a table.[28] As early as 1849, the American press began reporting on "The Revolting State of Things" in San Francisco, where would-be miners had "given themselves up to gambling and drinking."[29] Less than a year later, a dispatcher to the *Daily Globe* of Washington, D.C., decided that the whole town had been "converted into one large gambling hall."[30] Yet, despite a propensity by letter writers and journalists to refer to "drinking and gambling" as the "only amusements" and the "prevailing vice," at least one more form of entertainment readily availed itself.[31]

As one might suspect, prostitution also flourished in the early city. Working women arrived literally by the boatload in the early 1850s. Two thousand disembarked in the foggy western port in the first six months of 1850 alone, principally hailing from France, New York City, and New Orleans. The local *Pacific News* ran a feature in October of the same year, highlighting the expected arrival of another nine hundred French ladies of "beauty, amiability, and skill." Unfortunately for many of the miners' expectations, only fifty of the French ladies actually made the trip. Nevertheless, rumor held that San Francisco had at least one prostitute of every national origin plying her wares in its ever-growing vice district by 1852. This district had grown in only a few years to become larger than many of the towns that miners and sailors had left in search of adventure and fortune.[32]

Considering this state of things, New York's *Evening Post*, as early as 1849, referred to the people of San Francisco as "mad, stark mad."[33] They did, after all, choose to live among gambling houses and dens of ill repute that rivaled even "the hells of Paris."[34] This allusion to the "hells of Paris" is a prime and early example of giving the eastern reader a metaphorical foundation upon which to build a stereotypical vision of the distant western city. As journalists and others began to talk about this new and exciting place, they had to come up with proper metaphors or reference points so that their readers might understand the city's nature more readily. One way to do this was to compare the young city with established urban areas as the *Post* writer did by evoking the sinful foreign stereotype of Paris. Another early example of this presents itself in a song written by Caleb Lyon as he prepared to embark on the long journey from New York, around South America, to San Francisco. In an attempt to place San Francisco mentally, Lyon referred to the California city as "the Naples of the West."[35]

Obviously, San Francisco was not the only American destination cast in terms of European sites during the nineteenth century. Promotional literature of the time often talked of western places relative to European ones. For example, one could read of the Rocky Mountains as being America's Alps or the southern California coast as being the American Mediterranean. But, as Marguerite Shaffer points out in *See America First*, such parallels were made considerably less often in the twentieth century as a means of legitimating American places as tourist destinations.[36] Yet San Francisco and its Barbary Coast district retained exotic connotations.

The notorious Barbary Coast vice district emerged early on to meet the needs of a rapidly growing, increasingly cosmopolitan city that was already labeled consistently as something other than purely American. Even the name *Barbary Coast* suggests the foreign shores of the distant Mediterranean. One can find mention of the Barbary Coast district as early as 1867 in the local *San Francisco Bulletin*. There the writer sarcastically expounded on the "honest" miner who eventually drifted to the dens of either Pacific Avenue or the Barbary Coast to take part in the type of illicit "amusement" that "he prefers."[37] While these types of amusement were increasingly coming under attack in the older parts of the

United States, in San Francisco of the gold-rush heyday, they were widely viewed as the normal accompaniments of the gold-dust frontier.[38] Such tacit acceptance was quickly challenged by both city and nation alike as San Francisco grew and the nation became increasingly self-conscious of its bawdier side.

Within two years, knowledge of San Francisco's exotic district had spread eastward. The reading public in New Jersey, for example, learned of how the city's Barbary Coast district was a "haunt" of "Chinamen" and "Mongolians."[39] Later that week, Macon, Georgia, residents also learned of the Barbary Coast's international characteristics. In a more extensive condemnation of foreign immigrants and illicit activities, they were treated to a piece about the smuggling of opium into the area by Chinese immigrants.[40]

Throughout the 1870s the Barbary Coast's name appeared often in the San Francisco press and occasionally across the nation. During this period it was increasingly tied to the hardships and dangers brought about by vice. Myriad stories told of the tragic ruin of young people who had ventured to the city from rural America only to have their dreams torn asunder by the vices of the Barbary Coast.[41] Likewise, in reporting on the assault of a local citizen while visiting San Francisco, the *Arizona Weekly Journal* observed, "It was more dangerous to travel on the Barbary Coast than among the bloodthirsty Apaches."[42] Other pieces, such as one printed in Silver City, Idaho, tied together the danger, vice, and foreign nature of the district. There the writers inquired as to the whereabouts of local citizen Jim Crutcher, who had failed to return from a visit to San Francisco. Friends reported him "nearly being Shang-haied" by Chinese immigrants and then driven to desperation by the dire predictions of a Barbary Coast fortune-teller.[43] It is interesting that by this time the articles no longer faced the necessity of explaining that the Barbary Coast was a center of gambling and illicit sexual activities in San Francisco. Increasingly, as the populace became aware of this, a simple reference to the Barbary Coast sufficed to elicit the mental generalization regarding the area's stained reputation.

This pattern of highlighting the Barbary Coast's vice and danger continued in the press throughout the closing decades of the nineteenth century. During the early years of the twentieth century, however, a marked change in the subject matter of the articles took place. As the Progressive Era gripped the nation, San Francisco's vice district came under increased attack. Thanks to municipal officials who chose to look the other way rather than enforce laws against prostitution or other lewd and obscene behavior, the Barbary Coast survived the reformist impulse unscathed until 1913. The lax attitude toward

the vice district changed markedly that year as state business leaders voiced
their concern to San Francisco mayor James Rolph over the possibility that the
Barbary Coast's notoriety would cast a shadow over the city's Panama-Pacific
Exposition, which was planned for 1915. Having donated millions of dollars to
the exposition, local business leaders pressured the mayor to avoid embarrassing
the city by either cleaning up or shutting down the district. Publisher William
Randolph Hearst then got in on the action in September 1913 by running a series
of front-page exposés on the Barbary Coast. Less than a week after Hearst's last
exposé, the mayor announced that under new policies, the San Francisco Police
would forbid all forms of prostitution as well as dancing by females in saloons
and the serving of drinks by females within the district. While the cleanup that
ensued proved effective both in public relations and in substance, many of the
saloons and brothels survived for at least a few more years. Weakened further by
the enforcement of California's Red-Light Abatement Act, the remaining clubs
ultimately succumbed to police raids in early 1917.[44]

Although the Barbary Coast was one of the most famous vice districts, virtually every major American city had its own vice or red-light district by the turn
of the twentieth century. In New Orleans, one could gain quite a few stories from
a visit to Storeyville. A trip to Chicago's Levee or New York's Tenderloin districts
would also provide discreet excitement to otherwise upstanding citizens. While
the most explicit details of what took place in these districts seldom made it into
the public sphere, knowledge of their existence was widespread among adults.[45]
Historian Neil Shumsky argues that Americans, while viewing red-light vices
such as prostitution as "evil, animal, and unhealthy," accepted them as inevitable
until the earliest decades of the twentieth century. As long as the vice could
be segregated and contained within a physical location for the working-class
segment of the population, middle- to upper-class leaders of American society
saw no need to destroy such a district. In fact, as distasteful as it might have been,
Shumsky points out that many saw the red-light district as a welcome means of
controlling those below them on the social scale. The physical boundaries of the
district helped distinguish where one belonged in society. If a person crossed
the boundary and entered the district, then that person obviously flouted the
established sexual norms and had no place in proper society.[46]

While it is debatable whether red-light districts served as markers of social
belonging—and it is absurd to think that none but the working class ever entered
them—one cannot deny that they housed the unacceptable, segregated other
in American society. While these districts often bordered the central business

districts and conducted business enterprises on a scale that might even have surpassed their city neighbors, they could never be legitimate. Where banking, commerce, and government were respectable American occupations, the equally profitable practices of catering to drinkers, fornicators, and gamblers were not. These weaknesses had to be separated, spoken of in whispered tones, and labeled as the province of the supercharged sexuality of immigrants, the unwashed, and the mentally ill. Thus, Shumsky is correct in assuming that Americans treated the red-light district as a sort of ghetto. They accepted or ignored its existence until it threatened to "spill over" into their own hallowed space.[47]

Something akin to this fear of spilling over underwrote the reform mindset that ultimately closed down the nation's red-light districts. Between the late nineteenth century and the late 1910s, reform movements for public health and morality coalesced in their fight against prostitution and red-light districts. A white slavery panic in the early 1910s—in which media outlets claimed that foreign pimps were kidnapping and forcing young white women of rural origin into prostitution in the nation's cities—added fuel to the fire. It is, however, important to note that urban business interests often resisted attempts to close vice districts. Such districts brought visitors and profit to many local, non-vice-industry establishments. Yet, at times, morality outweighed business concerns, and between 1910 and 1917, nearly every U.S. metropolis commissioned a panel to study the effects of immorality within its city limits.[48]

Ultimately, Americans embraced a policy aimed at more stringent policing of prostitution and mandatory reporting of those infected with venereal disease. Much of this came about as the result of the new American Social Hygiene Association's (ASHA) leadership-recruitment efforts among the medical, scientific, and eugenicist fields.[49] The United States military also contributed to the demise of vice districts. With the leadership of its newly created Committee on Training Camp Activities (CTCA), heavily filled with purity and social health reformers, the military launched an all-out drive against venereal disease and the solicitation of prostitutes. In the end, the CTCA implemented five-mile "pure zones" around military camps in which prostitution was strictly prohibited. Beginning in 1917, it also placed heavy pressure on municipal leaders to close their city's red-light districts under the threat of losing lucrative military bases.[50]

The fact that one of the best-known red-light districts was in San Francisco did not serve the city's reputation during such a period of reform. Throughout the 1910s and '20s, reformers across the nation often traced their own problems with vice back to Barbary Coast origins. In so doing, they further stained the name of San Francisco by association. This was exactly the pattern found when New York City established a commission to investigate the morality of the city's dance halls in 1912. Mrs. Charles Henry Israels's Committee on Amusement and Vacation Resources for Working Girls found much to be alarmed about concerning the risqué styles of dancing that had seemingly swept the city. On January 27, 1912, Israels presented her findings to the city's Welfare Committee with the recommendation of banning such dances as the Shiver, the Bunny Hop, and certain forms of the Turkey Trot. These gasp- and shudder-soliciting dances were said to have originated in San Francisco's notorious Barbary Coast district.[51] Likewise, a New York settlement house operator—listed only by the name Miss de G. Trenholm—proclaimed that this "indecent dancing" stood alongside inefficiency and immodesty in dress as the primary contributing factors to the distressing state of the city's working women in 1912. As Miss de G. Trenholm stated,

> We could not tolerate the bunny hop and turkey trot. What a wildly foolish craze for the young people of the Nation to take up! The women could have stopped it. Why didn't they? I hesitate to think. The turkey trot, I am informed, originated in the vicious dives of the Barbary Coast in San Francisco. I find it quite impossible to comment adequately on the state of things which made it possible for such a dance, with such an origin, to be transplanted into the great drawing rooms of our best people.[52]

While Israels and Trenholm failed to wipe all vestiges of the "indecent" dancing form New York City in 1912, their failure did not stop the emergence of a new anti-dance-hall movement in the city in 1924. This time the reform was aimed at "closed dance halls." These closed dance halls were said to be frequented by "socially undesirable Orientals" and consisted of men who paid young ladies four cents per dance. A study by Mrs. Henry Moskowitz's Commercial Recreation Committee found that 20 percent of the halls permitted "immoral" behavior. Once again, the journalist claimed that this form of dancing was "imported from the Barbary Coast."[53] Additional articles suggested that the best way to deal with this outbreak of immorality in New York City was to reform and ultimately close all Barbary Coast dance halls. At the Barbary Coast they had found that prohibiting women from sitting in dance halls and from smoking in 1917 had helped reduce the amount of dancing until the city ultimately decided to ban women from being paid for public dancing altogether in 1920. While Maria Lambin, who was in charge of the local survey of New York dance halls, conceded, "You can't stop Italians, Poles, Bohemians, and Scandinavians from dancing," she did feel that they could regulate the way they danced after the example of the Barbary Coast.[54]

Thus, during the Progressive Era and the 1920s, reform not only came to the Barbary Coast; the Barbary Coast came to reform. The district had gained such a national reputation for vice that, years later, its example as progenitor of questionable activities often underwrote moral reform thousands of miles away. In this regard, the coast served as an easy repository for the sin of one's home. If the hometown could somehow be shown as the victim and not the creator or instigator, then its central goodness could remain. It was far simpler to throw the blame on an established center of obscenity than to accept that relative standards of morality might exist in one's own city and even among one's own social class. This is exactly what Israels meant when she stood aghast at things of "such origin . . . entering the great drawing rooms of our best people."[55]

Exotic San Francisco

Although lacking the moralizing and anti-dance-hall craze of the previous decades, the 1930s also witnessed San Francisco's portrayal as deviantly exotic and not quite 100 percent American. One interesting example of this can be found in the earliest in-flight airline magazines. Written with the hope of attracting travelers to destinations in cities serviced by the airlines, these articles tended to be overwhelmingly positive in their descriptions. Yet difference is not always portrayed as being blatantly negative.

Western Airlines began operation in 1925 as Western Air Express when the U.S. postmaster general awarded the upstart company an airmail route between Salt Lake City and Los Angeles with a refueling stopover in Las Vegas. A year later, the airline would branch out and carry its first load of human cargo along the same route, becoming the first regularly scheduled passenger service in U.S. history. Over the next few years, Western's routes expanded over more of the West and Midwest, and the number of passengers increased correspondingly. By the time the airline celebrated fifty years of passenger service in 1976, it had expanded its routes to include Anchorage, Honolulu, and Mexico City.[56]

Once it had started carrying people in the 1920s, Western proved innovative in the field of in-flight entertainment. By 1930 the airline had launched the first ever in-flight magazine. Aptly titled *Speed*, the magazine highlighted destination cities along Western's ever-expanding routes in each monthly issue. These articles are valuable for illuminating contemporary perceptions of various American cities.

Most of the early pieces tended to be written by local boosters who had a stake in portraying their city in a positive light. Such biases make certain references and omissions all the more telling.

For instance, many writers tended to describe their cities as quintessentially American. Herbert O. Fischer, for example, the director of aeronautics for the Indianapolis Chamber of Commerce, had no qualms about pronouncing his city "The Typical American City." In a virtual laundry list of what he considered to be American characteristics, Fischer related how Indianapolis was the largest inland city in the nation, was located nearest the U.S. center of population, and had diversified industrial, agricultural, and commercial economic activity as well as the largest number of automobiles in the United States, high homeowner rates, and of course a famous speedway. All this, he concluded, enabled the Midwest metropolis to take its rightful and destined place as the leader of American air transport.[57] Along these lines, in future years he would take to quoting his American-centered city's former slogan: "There is less wobble at the hub."[58]

At least two writers disagreed with Fischer's proclamation of Indianapolis as the typical American city and eventual leader of the airline industry. An anonymous article in the July 1931 edition of *Speed* proclaimed Columbus, Ohio, to be "The American City."[59] A similar piece in the March 1933 edition by resident Oscar Kahan credited Saint Louis, Missouri, as being the "Thoroughly American City."[60] Both of these pieces followed the pattern of the earlier Indianapolis feature by extolling the traits that qualified them as so American. For Saint Louis, this revolved heavily around being the geographic center of the country, a place where "Eastern thrift, Northern energy, Western enterprise, and Southern hospitality" could easily come together. Likewise, it was as if the town had "caught in stone and steel some quality of purposefulness which is typically American."[61] In Columbus, one could look around with nativist pride at the 94 percent of local residents who were born in America. Also, who could argue with it being the largest of the nineteen places named in honor of that Italian explorer who sailed under the Spanish flag so long ago?[62] Certainly, with such intrinsic characteristics, the city must have been exceptionally American.

One would assume that since San Francisco was added to Western's destinations early on and eventually became the airline's corporate headquarters, some local promoter would have staked a claim in *Speed*'s ongoing contest over the most American of American cities. This assumption is, however, false as no one associated with the magazine wrote that San Francisco was typically American. Instead, magazine writers and San Francisco boosters alike chose to emphasize the city's cosmopolitan and exotic characteristics. San Franciscan Richard O. Jones, for example, began his July 1931 feature by exclaiming: "The Paris of America, . . . San Francisco!" He went on to write not of any distinctly American attributes but rather of the "exotic" nature of a place where "Asia meets the Old West." This place of cultural melding (or collision; he is never quite clear) is romantic and wild, harboring "bits of old China" and "bazaars that rival Gay Paree and Tokio."[63]

Herbert O. Warren took a similar tack in his description of places to see and things to do while in San Francisco. Just as Jones began by comparing San Francisco to Paris, Warren saw in her hills a likeness to ancient Rome. He told of a fascinating city, "born of the sea," containing the largest Chinese ethnic settlement outside the Chinese mainland. He then almost begrudgingly admitted that San Francisco was "essentially an American city." That is not to imply, however, that the city does not have its own unique and "old tradition that she's not likely to forget; a tradition of come what may, let's live each day to the fullest."[64]

The irony of San Francisco boosters using San Francisco's Chinese influences and settlements as a promotion tactic should not be lost on readers. Like Birmingham, early San Francisco certainly engaged in its share of discrimination against minorities. In San Francisco that discrimination was often directed at Chinese immigrants. At times, again similar to what occurred so often in Birmingham, such discrimination resulted in violence and death.

Regardless of such irony, it is important but hardly surprising that San Francisco never quite made the grade of the "typical" American city in these earliest air-travel magazines. Writers from the Midwest showed no hesitation in casting their cities in the all-American glow, but San Francisco boosters took an opposite approach. This shows that Bay Area boosters recognized what their city could legitimately be seen as having to offer. They were after tourists and directed their articles wholeheartedly toward this end. Where boosters of Indianapolis, Columbus, and Saint Louis also sought short-term visitors, their pieces revealed a greater interest in making the most of the burgeoning airline industry. While San Francisco boasted of its exotic and unique qualities, the others sought to present themselves as the most convenient and sensible choice through which to move the most Americans in the most efficient manner.

These cities had a distinct profit to be gained from being seen as "normal." San Francisco, on the other hand, had yet to be considered normal and had developed in such a way that any such casting of normality might not be entirely beneficial at that time.

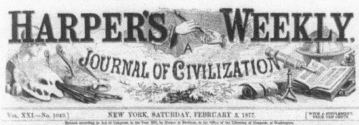

HARPER'S WEEKLY.

A JOURNAL OF CIVILIZATION

Vol. XXI.—No. 1049.]   NEW YORK, SATURDAY, FEBRUARY 3, 1877.   [WITH A SUPPLEMENT.
PRICE TEN CENTS.

Entered according to Act of Congress, in the Year 1877, by Harper & Brothers, in the Office of the Librarian of Congress, at Washington.

Chinese Immigrants at the San Francisco Custom-House, 1877. Wood engraving by P. Frenzeny. This image appeared on the cover of *Harper's Weekly*, February 3, 1877.
Library of Congress, Prints and Photographs Division, LC-USZ62-93673.

The Postwar City

The Japanese attack on Pearl Harbor ushered in significant changes to San Francisco. Population, industrial development, and technological fields certainly blossomed as the government and the private sector entered into an unprecedented union aimed at defeating their common enemy. The war transformed the West and its cities in many ways. As Gerald Nash points out, it brought about a diversification of economic life that both helped dispel attitudes of colonial inferiority and instilled a "new self confidence" that all challenges could be met.[65]

One such challenge that San Franciscans would find themselves meeting in the decades following the war was the growing size and increasingly vocal nature of the city's homosexual community. The origin of this community can be found in the war years alongside Nash's proposed can-do attitude. During the war, San Francisco served as a major mustering point for the military. Subsequently, thousands of gay servicemen were processed out of the military into the city over the length of the conflict. Many from the vast reaches of America found others who were like themselves for the first time in their lives. A sense of community subsequently developed as many of the men chose to remain in San Francisco after leaving the military. These individuals ultimately served as an important boost in the development of San Francisco's distinctive postwar gay community.[66]

The shared experiences and struggles of the war created a stronger sense of community on both the national and local levels.[67] Along with this shared sense of Americanness, the increased interest in a common historical background and the growth of a consensus mindset dominated academia in the 1940s and 1950s.[68] In the aftermath of World War II, San Francisco, a city that had been portrayed throughout its entire existence as exotic and in many regards un-American, found itself in a nation swept along by an ideological tide that promoted consensus. As a result, two possibilities existed. The nation could shift away from years of accumulated thought about the city and stress its Americanness, or it could step up its portrayals of San Francisco as an aberration on the otherwise-consistent canvas of America.

Overall, the latter tack proved to be where the nation was headed in regard to San Francisco. In the postwar years, the more conservative and consensus-loving elements of American society cast San Francisco as radically liberal or just plain strange, beginning with the Beat culture of the 1950s, building with the hippie and student movements of the 1960s, and culminating with the gay-rights advances of the 1970s and '80s. Thus, in the postwar years, San Francisco would remain a stigmatized outcast, often pushed even further away from mainstream America than it had been at any point during its prewar existence.

The first major postwar episode that both drew from and built upon San Francisco's stigmatization presented itself on October 7, 1955. That night, somewhere between 150 and 200 people gathered in a former automotive body shop on Fillmore Street that had recently been reborn as the Six Gallery. The main entertainment consisted of San Francisco poets Philip Lamantia, Michael McClure, Kenneth Rexroth, and an unknown young New Yorker named Allen Ginsberg. Ginsberg's sidekick and one-time Columbia classmate Jack Kerouac refused to read before the crowd, preferring instead to help the crowd and poets gain insight via the multiple jugs of burgundy he brought along for the occasion. So with the mood set and the crowd loose, a bearded Ginsberg shuffled up to the orange crate that served as the poet's podium.[69] And with a howl into that San Francisco night, the poet said that something was terribly wrong with America.

Ginsberg's "Howl" can be traced back to an interesting peyote trip the poet experienced about a year before his debut at the Six Gallery. On October 7, 1954, after consuming an unknown amount of peyote in his apartment, Ginsberg proceeded to watch the Sir Francis Drake Hotel and the Medical Arts Building in San Francisco morph into giant incarnations of Moloch, an ancient Phoenician god.[70] Either scared or inspired or both, he started writing soon thereafter.

With style eerily reminiscent of Walt Whitman's best writing, Ginsberg's finished poem addresses more than the long-forgotten god of the Middle Eastern seafarers that haunted his peyote vision. It lashes out at a nation wasting away under stifling conformity. It speaks of "the best minds" of America "wasted," having been "starving, hysterical naked, . . . looking for an angry fix." He is mad and he wants his generation to be mad that their ideas and lives are being drowned and silenced by strangleholds of a false consensus between society and academia. This America is not the "starry dynamo" that it can be. No, it is an America in which his generation meets face-to-face the "scholars of war . . . waking nightmares . . . horrors through the walls . . . dreams, with drugs . . . and the sirens of Los Alamos."[71] Allen Ginsberg was angry with America, and his anger would be heard far beyond the dusty walls of that old transformed San Francisco body shop.

In expressing his anger, Ginsberg shocked not only the people in the audience but the nation as well. When Lawrence Ferlinghetti published "Howl" in 1956 as installment number four of his City Lights Bookstore's Pocket Poet Series, the poem's provocative content gained notice beyond that of poetry enthusiasts. By

1957 the U.S. government declared the book obscene and had its customs agents confiscate and destroy some 520 copies. San Francisco later charged its publisher with distribution of obscene material. With such major news outlets as *Life* and *Time* magazines providing coverage, Ferlinghetti stood trial that summer. Ultimately, the poet/publisher was acquitted with the judge's ruling that Ginsberg's poem had some redeeming social value and, as a work of art, was thus not to be considered obscene. In the process, however, San Francisco became forever linked with the birth of the Beat movement and the angry dissidence of youth.[72]

By 1958 the popular press had firmly established a link between these Beats and the city of San Francisco. Time and again, articles and interviews tied the writers to the city while highlighting their abnormality. *Time* magazine, for example, crowned Jack Kerouac the "patriarch and prophet" of this movement of "mystics," originating in San Francisco's "smoke filled cellar cafes and cold water flats."[73] The magazine then went on to publish segments of a transcript from a recent television interview of Kerouac by Mike Wallace. The highlights include the author of the recently released *On the Road* proclaiming Beatness a religious movement and at one point flippantly interchanging the words *god* and *tangerine*:

> WALLACE: What do beat mystics believe in?
>
> KEROUAC: Oh, they believe in love. They love children. . . . They love women, they love animals, they love everything. . . . What I believe is that nothing is happening. . . . We're an empty vision—in one mind.
>
> WALLACE: In what mind—the mind of God?
>
> KEROUAC: That's the name we give it. We can give it any name. We can call it tangerine . . . god . . . tangerine. . . . But I do know we are empty phantoms. . . . And yet, all is well.[74]

This was dangerous ground for Kerouac to tread in Cold War–era America. Throughout the 1950s was an ongoing religious revival of sorts that was absolutely anchored to the postwar conflict between communism and capitalism. Beginning in the late 1940s and continuing throughout the 1950s, such evangelists as Billy Graham built huge followings by traversing the nation with revivals that were as heavy on anti-Communist rhetoric as on the supposed word of God. Even President Eisenhower got in on the game, frequently meeting with Graham and becoming the first president to be baptized in the White House. He pronounced at one point, "Our government makes no sense unless it is founded on a deeply felt religious faith."

In 1956, only two years before Kerouac equated God with a tangerine, 96 percent of the American people had cited a specific denominational affiliation in response to the census bureau's questioning of religious preference.[75] That same year, a now-familiar motto appeared via federal law on all U.S. paper currency. The phrase "In God We Trust," although it had appeared on coinage with a few interruptions since the Civil War, now proudly equated America with God on that all-important American icon, the dollar bill. Only a few months previously, Congress had voted to declare the phrase the nation's official motto and to thus place it on all money.[76] Congress had also recently inserted the phrase "under God" into the wording of the pledge of allegiance.[77]

All this was so successful, one historian of the era writes, that religion had become "virtually synonymous with American nationalism."[78] On the other side of the coin, Communism had then become the domain of the atheist. This was the era of Joseph McCarthy, when references to godless Communism were frequent and powerful. Falling outside acceptable religious expectations and norms could be problematic and outright dangerous. Thus, in this hyperreligious environment, Kerouac's unconventional take on God could be viewed as un-American. Subsequently, the link between Kerouac, as king of the Beats, and San Francisco added to the already long-held perception that San Francisco was a different sort of place than the rest of the nation.

By the time the Beats were firmly tied to San Francisco, both the dissidents and the city were increasingly linked to foreign nations. News article after news article carried on the tradition of characterizing San Francisco and its odd residents as foreign and exotic. Readers learned that the San Francisco Beats were like "Francoise Sagan's generation in France, . . . the angry young men of England, and Existentialists on the Continent."[79] Others read that these San Francisco artists possessed the "chi chi of Paris," whatever that might be.[80] One journalist pointed out that the beatniks' style of beard "flourishes not only in San Francisco . . . but in London, Paris, Rome, and other European cities.[81] But then, these "bearded beatnik poets from San Francisco" were very similar to the expatriate of the 1920s "Lost Generation," who "moodily or talkatively spent his time over his coffee, beer, or absinthe at the Dome or Rotunde in Paris."[82]

In San Francisco, the Beat epicenter of North Beach soon housed an establishment even more controversial and risqué than Ginsberg's poetry and Kerouac's stream-of-consciousness writings. In 1964, waitress Carol Doda danced topless atop a piano in the Condor Club located at the corner of Broadway and Columbus. With her dance, San Francisco laid claim to the nation's first topless bar. Soon a large neon likeness of Doda graced the establishment's front, and a number of strip joints lined Broadway. Within five years, Doda had gone bottomless as well and achieved nationwide fame. One could also find Broadway Street characterized as a "Disneyland for Adults" in the pages of the *New York Times*.[83] Attempts to shut down the topless bars from the late 1960s to the mid-1970s drew further national attention. Such well-publicized campaigns only added to San Francisco's deviantly exotic reputation by drawing attention to the city as the originator of topless and totally nude dancing.[84]

As heirs to the beatniks, the student protestors and hippies of the 1960s cemented San Francisco's placement in the minds of many Americans as an abnormal city. Because print coverage of the counterculture tended to portray the city as the center of the movement, San Francisco took on such descriptions as "bizarre," dangerous to "American youth," and drug infested.[85] In one loosely veiled drug reference, a young Hunter S. Thompson equated the city to both the drug culture and counterculture in a special piece on the hippie movement that he wrote for the *New York Times* while writing his first novel. The future author of *Fear and Loathing in Las Vegas* called San Francisco's Haight-Ashbury district "Hashbury, . . . the Capital of the Hippies." He went on to highlight the violence of the Hell's Angels and pronounce that "most of the people . . . [are] involved in some way or another in the drug traffic." In his view, the only people who refused to use LSD and marijuana were police informants and the few others who did not mind being ostracized by the community.[86] Likewise, the *Atlantic*'s Mark Harris ran an eleven-page feature on the hippies of San Francisco. Going into great detail on the history of Haight-Ashbury, Harris concluded that while there may be hippies in other places, the Haight "is certainly the biggest, floweriest, and most psychedelic."[87]

The Early Gay Rights Movement and San Francisco

Although the Stonewall Inn rebellion of 1969 often receives credit for beginning the gay rights movement, it was actually more important in drawing attention to and energizing a long-existing struggle for acceptance and equality. In San Francisco, for example, gay rights organizations had been fighting for recognition for many years by the time New York's Stonewall patrons decided they had had enough. As early as the late 1940s—despite still-recurring police crackdowns—the city had gained a reputation among homosexuals as one of the gayest in the United States.[88] Since at least the 1950s, West Coast gay rights organizations had been working to shift ideas in the wider American public about homosexuality and end discrimination against gays.

The Los Angeles–based One, Inc.; the Daughters of Bilitis; and the Mattachine Society would form the early triumvirate of gay rights activism. This early activism, although conservative by later eras' standards, paved the way for the gay rights gains of the 1970s and beyond. It did this by embracing, first and foremost, a strategy of promoting discourse on homosexuality in the public sphere beyond the tired and overused gay-man-as-danger article. This would be accomplished via each organization's publication of periodicals and constant criticism of the mainstream press over how it portrayed gay Americans.[89]

The Mattachine Society had originated in Los Angeles in 1951 with a leadership comprised of left-wing sympathizers and, in such instances as Henry Hay, Communist Party members. Using organizational skills gained in previous political activities, these organizers implemented a cell-like structure to protect members against exposure. They directed their actions at publicizing the gay lifestyle to prove that it was not all about sex but rather was a distinct community with its own culture and positive values. With such recognition, the Mattachine Society hoped that the straight public would accept homosexuals and that homosexuals themselves could overcome their internalized stigmatization and shame. With acceptance, this shame could be replaced with a pride common to all distinct communities.[90]

Despite the climate of oppression created by the excesses of early 1950s McCarthyism and the homophobic attitudes it fostered, the secretive Mattachine expanded into the San Francisco Bay Area by 1953. From the beginning, the San Francisco foundation differed from its southern California originator. There, local lesbians took a far more active role in both the leadership and rank and file than in the male-dominated cells of Los Angeles. As a result, its membership grew at a greater rate. Also, the San Francisco element took on responsibility for publishing its own magazine, the *Mattachine Review*. This also added to the group's visibility in the gay community, resulting in further increased membership. Ultimately, the San Francisco branch so outgrew its Los Angeles counterpart that by 1956 it became the organization's national headquarters.[91]

In 1955 Del Martin and Phyllis Lyon, following a suggestion from their friend Rose Bramberger, decided to create a social club for lesbians in the San Francisco Bay Area. Such clubs fulfilled an important function for gays and lesbians in the 1950s as socializing in public could often be a dangerous undertaking. Inspired by Pierre Louys's poem "Songs of Bilitis," with its character who lived on the Isle of Lesbos, the group chose the name Daughters of Bilitis (DOB) for their new organization and elected Del Martin as president and Lyon as treasurer.

The DOB then held its first official meeting on October 19, 1955, at the home of Marcia Foster. Although they were intended to be an avenue for socializing, the group's weekly meetings would invariably turn toward problems that women faced because of their lesbianism.[92]

By late 1955 Martin, Lyon, and other early members decided to take the club in a more political direction. Having recently become aware of the Mattachine Society's presence in San Francisco, they decided to pattern the DOB's transformation on this pace-setting forerunner. The DOB statement of purpose proclaimed four goals for the organization: "Education of the variant, . . . education of the public, . . . participation in research, . . . and investigation in the penal code." In October 1956 the DOB began its attempt to educate both lesbians and the general public with its publication of a two-hundred-copy run of what became the nation's first large-scale-distribution lesbian periodical, the *Ladder*.[93] From there, the DOB would go on to become the premier lesbian rights organization in the nation. Within two years and with help from *One Magazine* and the Mattachine Society, it would have chapters in New York City, Los Angeles, and Rhode Island. Soon chapters spread farther to include Boston, Chicago, Cleveland, Denver, Detroit, New Orleans, Philadelphia, Portland, and San Diego.[94]

Over the course of the next decade, the local DOB and the Mattachine Society worked tirelessly to gain positive exposure for the gay community and break down stereotypes and bigotry by educating people about the community's true nature. Such education was certainly needed during this period in San Francisco as municipal authorities' antigay activities seemed to reach an all-time high. For example, in 1959, after Mayor George Christopher's opponent in the upcoming election, Russ Woolden, accused the mayor of being soft on homosexuals, Christopher's police force cracked down on gay bars citywide. Woolden, in his attacks on Christopher, claimed that homosexuality and such newly arrived advocacy groups as the Mattachine Society and the DOB would "subvert public morals and change our entire societal structure to the point that homosexual activities will be regarded as normal and harmless. . . . Organized homosexuality in San Francisco is a menace that must be faced today."[95]

Ultimately, Christopher won reelection over Woolden, and the DOB and the Mattachine Society found their stature among the city's gay population greatly increased thanks to the publicity generated by Christopher's campaign and the crackdowns on gay establishments. Then, in 1964, their tireless efforts to educate the public on homosexuality paid dividends on a national scale. That year *Life* magazine published an article titled "Homosexuality in America," which was monumental in providing a new representation of gay life and helped establish for the American public the idea that San Francisco was an exceptionally gay-tolerant city.[96]

Many in the gay rights movement and at least one historian have credited the publication of "Homosexuality in America" and the "media spectacle" that accompanied it as a watershed moment in which many gays decided to migrate to California.[97] At the very least, it represented a very important moment for the representation of gays. For the first time, the mainstream media portrayed gays as a community with all the relative interests and problems that plague other recognizable social groups. Missing was the characterization of homosexuals as sick, deviant, or dangerous that had dominated American discourse on homosexuality for decades. Interest in the topic also proved great as the issue sold out within two days in San Francisco and Los Angeles. Nationwide it sold a very impressive 7.5 million copies, and it went on to be published in *Life*'s international edition.[98]

In providing a sense of legitimacy and normality to San Francisco's gay community, the *Life* article confirmed for much of the American public San Francisco's exotic nature and deviant ways. By the late 1960s, homosexuality still retained a strong stigma in American society. One could still find homosexuality listed alongside such disorders as schizophrenia, paranoia, and depression in the American Psychiatric Association's *Diagnostic and Statistical Manual of Psychological Disorders*. Likewise, one could still find instances of names being placed on lists as questionable and untrustworthy citizens. The state of Florida, for example, had unveiled a list of 123 teachers suspected of being homosexual only three years before the *Life* article. This list was the result of a three-year $500,000 investigation that was originally aimed at rooting out Communism in the state government and university system. The pamphlet report produced by the commission was declared obscene and removed from circulation by the state government because it displayed two men kissing and contained "erotic" terms.[99]

Psychologists, psychiatrists, and police officers meanwhile went on attempting to "cure" and punish homosexuals by a variety of means. These included marriage, shock therapy, group counseling, simple repression of desires, and arrest.[100] Even in San Francisco, individuals could find themselves under police surveillance and subject to detainment for merely attending suspected gay functions. Such was the case with local attorneys Evander C. Smith and Herbert Donaldson on January 1, 1965. The two found themselves arrested and charged with a variety of crimes in return for questioning the police department's right to harass and photograph partygoers as they entered a suspected gay New Years party at San Francisco's California Hall.[101]

In the context of such attitudes, the homosexual characteristic of postwar San Francisco, combined with the already existing prewar perception of the city as being exotic and not quite American, solidified the city's outcast identity. With images of hippies roaming high and naked through city streets and *Life*'s exposé on the local gay community, the American public received merely the latest confirmation that something was not quite normal about the City by the Bay. Since the time of city's entrance into the United States, this had been the pattern. From boisterous and vice-ridden boomtown of the gold rush to hippie capital, San Francisco had never really fit comfortably in the box that American culture prescribed for its urban areas. Perched on the West Coast, shrouded in fog, with its port-induced cosmopolitanism, it could never be Indianapolis, with its claim to the center of American population, or Columbus, with its boast of a 97 percent American-born population. No, San Francisco was different from these "typical American" cities in many ways, and by the 1960s the people of America were well aware of it. In the coming three decades, this awareness of the exotic West Coast port would culminate in the physical and mental creation of the nation's gay mecca.

Battlefield by the Bay

San Francisco's Emergence, Trials, and Acceptance as America's Gay Mecca

Although Dan White's San Francisco may never have claimed the prestigious "All-America" title, by late 1978 the clean-cut young city supervisor was no stranger to the title personally. In fact, just the year before, "all-American" was the phrase that friends and the media alike turned to when asked to describe the former firefighter, policeman, paratrooper, baseball player, and father. Having recently rescued a young girl from the thirteenth floor of a burning building, White had parlayed his heroism and wholesomeness into a successful run for local political office in 1977. Often with the support of local police officers, White had campaigned door to door throughout his working-class and immigrant district of southern San Francisco. Along the way, the prospective city supervisor and his volunteers handed out fliers that stressed his desire to "eradicate the malignancies" that "shamed" San Francisco "throughout the nation." White was, he assured voters, the most conservative of the area's residents, and if elected, he would root out the "social deviates" and promote traditional values.[1]

Another successful candidate for the board of supervisors that year likely fit squarely into White's concept of "social deviates." If White was the quintessentially all-American supervisor, then Harvey Milk must certainly have represented everything the conservative establishment of the late 1970s opposed and feared. Milk was, after all, an unapologetic uncloseted gay man with political ambition.

Harvey Milk campaigns for seat on San Francisco Board of Supervisors, 1975.
Harvey Milk Archives—Scott Smith Collection (GLC-0033),
LGBTQIA Center, San Francisco Public Library.

His ultimate election marked the first time in United States history that an openly gay man had obtained an elected office of this importance.[2] Over the year that followed, the very different men, Milk and White, assumed key roles in a battle of cultural change that ultimately cemented San Francisco's place as the nation's most widely perceived gay mecca.

By the 1970s San Francisco possessed a reputation as the epicenter of the nation's gay population. National perceptions of homosexuality had developed in the previous thirty-plus years to ensure its treatment as deviant and threatening by many in the self-proclaimed American mainstream. As the previous chapter suggests, a public discourse over homosexuality in the 1950s and early '60s linked the sexual orientation to disloyalty, deviance, and mental illness.[3] With its roots in the 1940s as a military muster and discharge center leading to its distinctly large gay population, San Francisco was positioned to emerge as an important center of the American gay population. In the aftermath of World War II, heavy-handedness by local authorities and a need for community led to the creation and spread of such influential gay rights organizations as the Mattachine Society and the Daughters of Bilitis in San Francisco.[4] The publicity these groups gained as they coalesced in San Francisco contributed to the city's wider reputation for deviance. The gay mecca identity subsequently found strong roots in a city that was already considered un-American by many.

As a city that had been viewed as somewhat exotic and vice ridden from its very entrance into the United States, San Francisco served as a reasonable place for "normal" Americans to deposit such strangeness as homosexuality. It was, after all, a city that many Americans had characterized as a "Sodom by the sea" as early as the late nineteenth century.[5] While the open acknowledgement of a gay San Francisco in the groundbreaking 1964 article "Homosexuality in America" helped to legitimize homosexuality as an alternative orientation, it also served to "out" San Francisco as an epicenter of gayness.[6] By 1971 even the president of the United States allowed the stigma of homosexuality to shape his view of the city. That year Richard Nixon, while discussing the issue of homosexuality in America, told aides John Ehrlichman and H. R. Halderman, "I can't shake hands with anybody from San Francisco."[7]

Yet, during this decade, the discrimination against and oppression of gay Americans seemed to be easing dramatically. Acknowledgement of homosexuality no longer resulted in the automatic firing from government positions and questioning of loyalty that so often occurred in the fifties. Both the American Psychological and American Psychiatric Associations removed homosexuality from their lists of psychological disorders in 1973.[8] Gay Americans likewise took on increased visibility in the early 1970s as they fought successfully for ordinances and statutes forbidding discrimination against homosexuals in the workplace. At the same time, activists worked to decriminalize homosexual acts on the state level nationwide. Their efforts bore fruit as nine states updated their sexual laws to ease restrictions on private, consensual homosexual acts by 1974. Before 1970 only one state had viewed sex acts between adult homosexuals as legal. By 1975 an additional thirty-four measures repealing such laws appeared on ballots nationwide. Ultimately, five states repealed their sodomy laws that year alone, bringing the total number of states to decriminalize private homosexual acts to thirteen.[9]

Many Americans, however, remained uncomfortable with homosexuality. According to the Field Institute's California poll conducted in 1977, only 31 percent of Californian respondents felt that homosexuals should be accepted in society and protected against discrimination. Only 43 percent could be classified as "minimally tolerant" of homosexuality. The state, according to the poll's comments, stood "sharply divided" on the issue.[10] This sharp divide had revealed itself two years earlier through the fight over the state's "sexual bill of rights." In 1975, after lopsided passage in the assembly, the state senate had required a tie-breaking vote by Lieutenant Governor Mervyn Dymally to abolish the 103-year-old ban on anal and oral sex. After Governor Jerry Brown signed the statute, a group calling itself the Coalition of Christian Citizens attempted to bring the statute up for a referendum vote. Ultimately it failed to gain the required 350,000 signatures.[11]

This reaction by a part of the Christian Right in 1975 was not an anomaly. In fact, one can view it as an early example of a much wider reaction against the increased visibility of gay Americans and the significant granting of homosexual rights in the early 1970s. This process, as we will see, culminated in 1978 as San Francisco activists and officials fought the oppressively homophobic State Proposition 6. When this battle ended, the connection between San Francisco and homosexuality became more evident than ever before. Subsequently, the successful resistance to Proposition 6 opened the way for the city to emerge full force as the nation's proud gay mecca.[12]

The Short and Lively Career of Harvey Milk

Few could have guessed that the young son of Bill and Minerva Milk would grow up to become one of the most powerful openly gay political leaders in American history. This young man who would ultimately be the cause of large amounts of tension, heartache, and worried pontification on the part of the supposed protectors of America's cultural and moral values did not seem all that threatening early on. Milk was, after all, a young man who finished high school a year early, loved sports, professed conservative political positions while earning a degree in education from the State University of New York at Albany, and went on to serve with distinction as a deep-sea diver in the United States Navy.[13]

Following his discharge from the navy in 1955, Milk seemed destined for success, excelling in his work in the insurance industry and then in the financial sector. His early conservative political leanings still revealed themselves at this time as, while employed by the Wall Street financial firm of Bache & Company, Milk campaigned for Barry Goldwater's 1964 presidential bid. Yet his boss sensed that Milk was not to be a permanent Wall Street fixture. When he looked at the young financial analyst, he saw a man with wanderlust in his eyes and some sort of inner trouble.[14]

Milk's inner trouble might well have stemmed from being gay in a nation that did not accept gay people. Beginning when he was a young teen taking unsupervised visits downtown and continuing through his university, navy, and Wall Street years, Milk had surreptitiously engaged in affairs with other men. At least once, at the age of seventeen, he had been temporarily detained by authorities on suspicion of such activities in a neighborhood park.[15] Always having at least one steady boyfriend hidden away, he lived in constant fear of exposure. Exposure in those days often meant jail or, at the very least, public disgrace and loss of employment. It also meant being labeled psychologically ill, a stigma that included subjection to various often-painful "cures."[16]

By the late 1960s Milk had walked away from his Wall Street job and landed in San Francisco's financial district. There, once again working as a financial analyst, Milk continued to lead his double life and prospered financially. Yet his political views gradually shifted as he found himself running with a company of theater actors and producers. For the first time, as biographer Randy Shilts notes, Milk's hair touched the top of his ears. Something was going on in the mind of Harvey Milk.[17]

That something burst forth on the morning of April 29, 1970, when Milk, enraged by Nixon's "incursion" into Cambodia and the subsequent widening of the Vietnam War, joined a group of antiwar protesters on his lunch break. The news cameras caught it all as the square-looking Milk jumped down into the protesters, pulled out his Bank of America credit card, and cut it in half. Milk's statement about corporate backing of the war for profit got him fired later that day after his antics were brought to the attention of his bosses. The years that followed found Milk's hair and beard growing even longer as he returned to New York City to produce theater and then traveled around California with his partner, Scott Smith. Milk would later recall this time as the best of his life.[18]

As all good times eventually end, Milk and Smith found themselves dangerously low on funds by 1972. That year the couple invested the last of their savings in an old Victorian home in a run-down neighborhood of San Francisco. Rent was cheap in the working-class Castro district, and a few gay bars had recently opened. The two lived upstairs in their new house and decided to make a living by opening a camera shop downstairs. Selling cameras quickly became an afterthought at Castro Cameras as Milk rapidly transformed the store into a welcome center for visitors and gay newcomers. By 1973, when Milk decided to make his first foray into politics by running for a seat on the city's board of supervisors, the camera store served as the unofficial city hall of an increasingly gay Castro district.[19]

Milk's first campaign opened his eyes to both his love of politics and the divided nature of San Francisco's gay community. Although he had built a reputation and following among newly arrived gays in the Castro, many in the old guard of the city's gay community refused to support him. Primary among these was Jim Foster, the leader of San Francisco's gay Democrats and a speaker at the 1972 Democratic Convention. Foster, along with the gay Golden Gate Democratic Club and the Alice B. Toklas Democratic Club, resented Milk because he was too brash, too new on the scene, and overly ambitious. In their opinions, gays needed more mainstream candidates who would start out by seeking lower offices rather than one of the powerful city supervisor positions. Their complaints, unwanted advice, and lack of endorsement served only to antagonize the candidate as Milk was never one to proceed with caution. Without the support of the gay political infrastructure and having to campaign citywide for his seat, Milk lost that first race handily.[20]

The Democratic clubs' cautioning of Milk is understandable. While political newcomers are often cautioned to be less brash out of deference to established officials or simply because they have yet to pay their dues, Milk represented what was unfortunately a very controversial issue. It was a time of anxiety over "outing" and public backlash against vocal gays. Many gays in San Francisco, for example, remained closeted to their families, workplaces, and friends. One has only to look at the Billy Sipple incident to see the dangers that too much public exposure presented to many gay Americans in the mid-1970s.

On September 22, 1975, Sipple, a former marine and one of Harvey Milk's campaign workers, joined a crowd outside San Francisco's Saint Francis Hotel, awaiting the exit of President Gerald Ford. As President Ford approached, Sarah Jane Moore raised a gun and fired one shot in his direction. Sipple, upon seeing the gun, grabbed Moore's arm. His quick reaction deflected the aim of her first shot and likely saved the president's life by preventing additional fire. As a result of his quick reaction, Sipple gained nationwide notoriety. However, within two days newspapers began characterizing him as being active in San Francisco's gay community. Milk, a friend of Sipple's, then charged that President Ford had delayed thanking the hero because of Sipple's sexual orientation. When asked by a reporter whether he realized the "enormous . . . national ramifications" of a gay man saving the president, Sipple replied that the personal "ramifications" were also "enormous." His mother and much of his family back in Detroit learned of his sexual orientation for the first time from the news reports. She then disowned her son, who eventually turned to alcohol. He died in 1989, having never reunited with his family.[21] Such widely publicized occurrences both added to the perceptual link between San Francisco and homosexuality and no doubt contributed to many people's reticence, which Milk's candidacy sought to bring into the public spotlight.

That year Milk went on to lose his second race for supervisor.[22] He then ran for the California legislature against Art Agnos in 1976. This race proved doubly troubling as San Francisco's mayor George Moscone had recently appointed Milk to an important seat on the city's board of permits and appeals. At the time, this caused quite a stir in the city's gay community because it was the highest municipal position ever held by one of their own. Be that as it may, it was not enough for the ever-ambitious Milk, who sensed a political opportunity. Only five weeks into his new job—after four weeks of hinting at his intention—Milk declared himself a candidate for the assembly. An angry Mayor Moscone—who fervently supported Agnos—responded by making his own announcement hours later that Milk had been replaced on the city board of permits and appeals.[23] Milk's campaign literature portrayed him as a groundbreaking, independent-minded "up-front gay" who was concerned with the rights of both homosexual and heterosexual San Franciscans. Agnos's campaign similarly addressed the sexual orientation issue directly, portraying the supervisor as "the first straight candidate to speak out for gay rights."[24] Milk ultimately lost to Agnos.

The name recognition and political skills that Milk gained from this string of unsuccessful campaigns came into play when he declared himself a candidate for city supervisor once again in 1977. As was his norm, Milk threw himself into the race heart and soul. He campaigned tirelessly, traversing his district, handing out flyers, shaking hands, and appearing before any group that would listen to him. He further embarked on a mobilization of the gay community to act as human billboards, keeping his name in constant view alongside busy roadways. Although resentment from more moderate-minded gay leaders continued, Milk now had the support of the rank and file of a more highly developed gay community in the Castro and Tenderloin districts who were willing to work for his election. In his previous campaigns and during his short stint on the board of appeals, he had proven himself capable and sincere in his intention to bring San Francisco gays out of the closet and into the political mainstream. But most important, for the first time in 1977, San Franciscans elected city supervisors by district rather than by citywide vote. This allowed Milk to run in the heavily gay Castro district where he lived rather than having to draw votes from all areas of the city.[25]

On the night of November 8, 1977, when the votes were counted, Harvey Milk made history and helped to solidify San Francisco's association with homosexuality. The election results revealed that he had beaten his nearest opponent by a

Harvey Milk leaning against Castro Street sign, 1977.
Harvey Milk Archives—Scott Smith Collection (GLC-0121),
LGBTQIA Center, San Francisco Public Library.

two-to-one margin. Spontaneous celebrations broke out in front of Milk's Castro Camera. Many of those gathered watched with rapt pride as Milk came forth to address the crowd. As he spoke, casting this victory as a sign of hope for all oppressed minorities, shouts of "Milk for Mayor" echoed in the background.[26] Although Milk would not live to be a serious candidate for that office, neither the city of San Francisco nor its image would ever be the same after his short stint as supervisor.

The national media took notice of what happened that night in San Francisco. A major U.S. city had elected an openly gay man to one of its highest offices. The *New York Times* had already laid the groundwork for Milk's election in a piece appearing the day before titled "A Walk on San Francisco's Gay Side." In this article, journalist Herbert Gold revealed how local heterosexuals accepted the growing political influence of gays in this city whose national "reputation has the city crowded with homosexuals." He went on to detail how the energetic gay community had organized itself and demanded inclusion in the political process in a city "best known for innovations in lifestyles." Supervisor Harvey Milk assumed a prominent role in the article as the "hard-line" leader of a gay population, demanding representation in government by other gays.[27] The day following the election, Milk became one of a few local supervisors or council members elected that year to be acknowledged nationally. That morning the *New York Times* printed a piece titled "Homosexual on Board Cites Role as Pioneer." The five-paragraph article devoted four paragraphs to Milk's homosexuality and one to Ella Hill Hutch, who had become the city's first ever black supervisor.[28]

One has to question why the election of the city's first black supervisor did not merit the attention paid to the election of its first gay supervisor. Most obviously, Hutch was not the first black citizen elected to a high city position in American history. Beyond this, the election of an African American did not play off and strengthen the established stereotype of San Francisco. The election of Harvey Milk did so in a spectacular way. The fact that a gay man was elected to one of the highest positions in the city supported the stereotypes of the abnormal and increasingly gay city. Yet, most important, Milk's election came at a time when gay rights and equality were hot topics on the national scene.

Just as gay Americans had made great gains in securing their rights and sexual freedoms on the state level in the early 1970s, the mid to late 1970s witnessed much progress at city and county levels. By the time of Milk's 1977 campaign, activists had secured gay rights ordinances and measures in approximately three dozen various localities. Traversing the national geography from Portland to Miami, these ordinances sparked powerful reactions from so-called values-oriented opponents.[29] These opponents quickly coalesced into a variety of organizations aimed at repealing any ordinance or statute that could be seen as providing equality under the law for gay Americans.

Perhaps the most vocal and, for a time, most powerful of these reactionary organizations was headed by former beauty queen, singer, and Florida orange juice spokesperson Anita Bryant.[30] Since her days as Miss Oklahoma and then as a pop singer with a couple of top-ten hits in the late 1950s and early '60s, Bryant had relocated to Florida and gained employment as a spokesperson for the Florida Citrus Commission. She added to her high profile with multiple television commercials for Minute Maid Orange Juice as well as by singing the national anthem at the 1969 Super Bowl and the "Battle Hymn of the Republic" at President Lyndon Johnson's funeral in 1973. In the meantime, Bryant had become increasingly critical of the growing visibility and demands of homosexuals in the United States.[31]

On the morning of January 18, 1977, Bryant stood and watched in disbelief as Florida's Dade County Commission voted five to three to prohibit discrimination against gays in housing, public accommodation, and the workplace. As a Southern Baptist mother, Bryant could not fathom raising her children in a world where gays, whom she considered "sinful," enjoyed equal rights with straight people. The flabbergasted Bryant claimed that she would not "take this sitting down." She would not stand idly by and accept an ordinance that "condones immorality and discriminates against my children's right to grow up in a healthy, decent society."[32] Thus, basing her action on both her own religious beliefs and a professed concern for the welfare of children, Bryant launched the Save Our Children campaign.

Thanks to her celebrity, Bryant's Save Our Children escapade drew heavy media coverage. Her comments increasingly took up national news airtime as the campaign drew on. For example, on March 27, 1977, she made national headlines for criticizing the Carter administration for meeting with gay rights proponents.[33] In the aftermath of this criticism, administration officials felt compelled to appear on news television programs such as CBS's *Face the Nation* to explain their activities in an attempt at damage control. Throughout 1977 Bryant's campaign and her stance against homosexuality were covered on the nightly news by ABC, CBS, and NBC no fewer than seventeen times.[34] In 1978 her organization's nationwide efforts against gay rights in such places as Wichita, Portland, Saint Paul, and across California received an additional eight appearances on the nation's nightly news broadcasts.[35]

Back in Miami, Bryant campaigned tirelessly and successfully to repeal the Dade County ordinance. Religious and conservative political figures from around the nation journeyed to southern Florida to join Bryant's Save Our Children campaign. Ministers such as Jerry Falwell became prominent in the fight, sending out mailers that depicted gays as perverts hell-bent on molesting children and corrupting society.[36] To Bryant and those who accepted her call, homosexuals sought to ruin the nation by "recruiting" its youth into a deviant lifestyle and using them as sexual playthings.[37] In light of such public stances and media coverage, Bryant's well-publicized activities could not help but stir up antigay feelings across the nation and reveal the antigay stance as a potentially powerful political strategy. According to poll data from the time, a substantial segment of the American population was swayed by her belief that gays should not be allowed equal admittance to all occupations. A nationwide Harris Survey released in July 1977 stated that 55 percent of respondents felt that homosexuals should not be allowed to work as teachers. An additional 63 percent opposed their employment as counselors for young people. Occupations that the majority of respondents felt that homosexual Americans had the right to hold included artist (86 percent), factory worker (85 percent), and store clerk (80 percent).[38]

With such numbers in mind, Bryant's Save the Children campaign presented an ambitious Republican state senator from California with what he believed to be a golden opportunity. John V. Briggs had long set his sights on positions beyond his seat in the California statehouse. Having already made an unsuccessful run at the governorship, the legislator from Fullerton needed to attach himself to a spectacular cause, which would hopefully propel him into higher office. That cause, Briggs believed, revealed itself to be what he interpreted as an increasingly adamant reaction against gay rights. Following Bryant's lead and proclaiming California's children to be in dire threat of recruitment into the gay lifestyle, Briggs pitted "normal" California against what he cast as the dangerous "San Francisco influence."[39]

Briggs rushed to Dade County to take an active role in Anita Bryant's campaign. While there, he took every opportunity to be photographed alongside Bryant, pass out leaflets, and pontificate about the dangers that homosexuality posed for American society. An exuberant Briggs confided to reporter Randy Shilts that this cause would be his ticket to the governorship. Ironically, Briggs had no idea that Shilts, with whom he spoke so candidly, was San Francisco's first openly gay journalist at a major media outlet.[40]

Once safely back in California, Briggs launched the California Save Our Children political action committee in an attempt to get a constitutional amendment passed on the ballot in the November 1978 general election. The wording of the initiative measure, as prepared by the state attorney general, is as follows:

School Teachers—Homosexual Acts of Conduct. Initiative Statute

Prohibits hiring, and requires dismissal by school district board of any probationary or permanent teacher, teacher's aide, school administrator or counselor who has engaged in a public homosexual act described in Penal Code, sections 286 or 288a, or who has engaged in advocating, soliciting, imposing, encouraging or promoting of private or public homosexual acts directed at, or likely to come to the attention of school children and/ or other employees.[41]

In explanation of what exactly constituted a "public homosexual act" in violation of penal code sections 286 and 288a, the full measure that would appear on the ballot provided this clarification:

> "Public homosexual activity" means the commission of an act defined in subdivision (a) of Section 286 of the Penal Code, or in subdivision (a) of Section 288a of the Penal Code, upon any other person of the same sex, which is not discreet and not practiced in private, whether or not such act, at the time of its commission, constituted a crime.[42]

Thus the initiative placed extraordinarily vague requirements on what might constitute a termination-worthy display of homosexuality.

With the politically influential Briggs serving as the initiative committee's chairperson, the initiative quickly gained adequate statewide support to assure its placement on the ballot. This process was certainly helped along when the popular Reverend Louis Sheldon of Fullerton preached the morality of the measure from the pulpit.[43] Secretary of State March Fong Eu certified the measure on May 31 with the comment that it had gained far more than the required number of signatures.[44] The battle over California Proposition 6, or the Briggs Initiative as it became known, subsequently rocked San Francisco and the state to its core. In the months leading up to the election, San Francisco supervisor Harvey Milk emerged in opposition to Briggs as the spokesperson against the proposition's passage. The fight became one perceived to be between the values of gay San Francisco—and to a lesser degree Los Angeles—versus the more conservatively mainstream values of suburban, small-town, and rural California.

Months before Briggs began pushing his initiative, and in the light of Anita Bryant's stirrings in southern Florida, San Francisco advocates of gay rights had attempted to head off what they saw as the impending attempts to codify workplace discrimination against California homosexuals. On January 11, San Francisco's assemblyman Art Agnos, with the support of the recently elected Milk and numerous gay rights advocates, sponsored a bill in the California legislature that would ban workplace discrimination based on sexual orientation. Agnos and all involved agreed that the bill had no chance of gaining passage in that election year. The assemblyman felt that his fellow legislators were too tied to the "myth" of a voter backlash against anyone supporting gay rights. While neither Agnos nor supporters of the bill harbored any illusion that this backlash would be overcome and the measure would pass, they felt that it was important to make the attempt for "educational purposes" because they felt that a substantial attack on the rights of gay Californians was in the offing.[45]

Almost immediately following the defeat of the Agnos measure, Milk succeeded in keeping the issue in the public eye by proposing a gay rights ordinance in San Francisco. By early February, Milk had solicited the endorsements of United States congressmen Phillip Burton of California's sixth district and John L. Burton of the state's fifth district.[46] In addition, speaker of the California assembly Leo T. McCarthy, assembly majority whip Agnos, and assemblyman Willie Brown came out in support of the ordinance. Brown personally contacted San Francisco supervisor Dan White, the leader of the opposition against the ordinance, and asked for his support in helping to end "discrimination of all types."[47]

By this time, San Francisco's place in the ongoing culture war over homosexual rights had found increased coverage in the national press. With the emergence of Anita Bryant's crusade against gay rights in the preceding year, San Francisco's name in relation to homosexuality appeared far more often than it had in the past. In 1977 the *New York Times* printed nine feature columns and editorial letters that specifically linked homosexuality to San Francisco.[48] In the preceding six years of the decade, the *Times* had linked San Francisco directly to homosexuality on only seven occasions: once in 1976, once in 1975, once in 1972, twice in 1971, and twice and 1970.[49] It is worth noting that, A. M. Rosenthal took over as the *New York Times* executive editor in 1977, and he has been criticized for his treatment of gay employees and the gay community during his twelve-year tenure there.[50] *Newsweek* also got in the game in 1977, publishing a feature piece on the increased political power and openness of San Francisco homosexuals. This was the first time *Newsweek* had ever published an article directly linking the city with homosexuality.[51]

Not to be outdone, the television news media also highlighted San Francisco's ties to homosexuality in 1977. In a story about the attempt to repeal Miami's gay rights employment and housing ordinance, ABC News focused on the campaign tactics of Anita Bryant's Save Our Children organization in pushing for the ordinance's repeal. Specifically, the news segment revolved around a Save Our Children television ad that equated the future of Miami's Orange Bowl parade with images of San Francisco's annual gay pride parade. The message was clear: if Miami voters failed to repeal the ordinance, the city would end up as another San Francisco.[52]

Men in drag celebrate Gay Freedom Day, 1976, in San Francisco.
Harvey Milk Archives—Scott Smith Collection (GLC-0129),
LGBTQIA Center, San Francisco Public Library.

The trend toward increased linkage of the city to homosexuality in the national press continued into the tumultuous year of 1978. On March 8 the *New York Times* saw fit to reprint a column by San Francisco's Herb Caen. Fed up with all the moral pronouncements against the "Sodom and Gomorrah West" being espoused by self-proclaimed upholders of American virtue, Caen lashed out at the antigay activism sweeping the nation. Specifically, he called out Anita Bryant's claim that God had placed a yearlong drought on California because of the large number of homosexuals living openly in San Francisco. Instead, he claimed that with the election of Harvey Milk as the first gay supervisor, the rain had returned to its normal levels. This, Caen observed, was "the first normal happening in old Baghdad by the Bay since the earthquake of 1906."[53] Likewise, a feature piece on the city's Gay Freedom Day parade appearing in the *Times* on June 26 explicitly linked the fight for gay rights, the Briggs Initiative, and San Francisco's identity as a "gay haven." As *Times* reporter Les Ledbetter wrote, "San Francisco's reputation as a haven for homosexuals has grown in the past year" thanks to Milk's election and the fight for the city's gay rights ordinance.[54]

On the television airwaves, Walter Cronkite's *CBS Evening News* also alluded to that reputation in 1978. On March 27, Cronkite, along with CBS reporter Don Kladstrup, told a nationwide audience how San Francisco's openness toward gays had led the nation's first openly gay politician to push for a local gay rights ordinance. This, Kladstrup noted, came at a time when other cities were repealing gay rights laws. Although opposition leader Dan White was also interviewed, the segment pointed out that a repeat of events such as Florida's Dade County backlash was highly unlikely in San Francisco.[55]

Initially it appeared as though CBS had correctly portrayed the situation in San Francisco. On April 3, Milk succeeded in getting his gay rights ordinance passed by his fellow supervisors. Approved by a vote of ten to one, Milk's ordinance went further than any other had to that date. It stated that no discrimination whatsoever on the basis of sexual orientation could occur within the limits of San Francisco regarding employment, housing, or any public accommodations. Dan White stood alone as the only supervisor to vote against the ordinance.[56]

Then, over the summer and fall of 1978, the national backlash against the granting of gay rights threatened to void the San Francisco ordinance by sweeping the Briggs Amendment to an easy victory in November. Polls conducted shortly after the initiative secured a spot on the ballot showed that 61 percent of registered California voters favored the amendment's passage.[57] In light of such numbers, Briggs said he was likely to become "America's newest and biggest folk hero—someone who will make a good candidate against (Senator) Alan Cranston in 1980."[58]

Slowly but steadily, however, Briggs saw his hopes of replacing Democrat Alan Cranston in the United States Senate slip away along with his proposition's substantial lead in the polls. By the election's eve, local newspapers reported that the outcome was too close to call.[59] This swing resulted largely from the highly organized response led by San Francisco's gay community, a growing political weariness of the ambitious Briggs, and a series of well-publicized debates between Briggs and Milk.

Publicity-grabbing antics also played a role in drawing attention to the discriminatory nature of the proposition. Many opponents of the measure felt that if they could put a human face on homosexuality, many people's consciences—even those of supposedly conservative rural dwellers and suburbanites—simply would not allow them to cast a yes vote. One such instance was Frank Vel's long walk. Vel felt that the anti–Proposition 6 campaign focused too heavily on the urban areas of San Francisco and Los Angeles while ignoring the small towns and rural areas of the state. Vel argued that these people should not be cast aside as assumed Briggs supporters. Instead, he reasoned, if they had the chance to meet an openly gay man, talk to him, and read about him in their newspapers, they might find some common ground. Thus Vel quit his job in advertising and embarked on a twelve-hundred-mile walk through lightly populated areas of California from the Mexican border to the Oregon state line. Advance troops of activists would arrive in an area before Vel and set up interviews with local media outlets. Along the way, Vel received quite a bit of press, developed a loyal following, and probably changed a few minds in his attempt to bridge the longstanding urban-rural divide of American history.[60]

Additional ploys aimed at increasing publicity occurred regularly. Taking issue with the assumption underwriting the Briggs Amendment—that somehow gays were so different as to be easily spotted and removed from educational institutions—a San Francisco man claimed he had once, before embracing his own homosexuality, dated Briggs's daughter. It seemed that the state senator had somehow missed a gay intrusion into his own home and family life! Opponents of Proposition 6 also distributed "Homosexual Identity Cards" in San Francisco neighborhoods. Cardholders were instructed to check the appropriate box beside either "Camp Briggs" or "Camp Bryant" as their preferred destination once the measure passed and they were ordered to report for concentration camps.[61] Such bold actions kept the measure in the media and in view of the public.

The issue also appeared before the national public in the days leading up to the vote. Walter Cronkite's *CBS Evening News* brought Proposition 6 into American homes on the night of October 26. The three-minute CBS segment discussed the nature of the ordinance, the claims of its author, and the tightening of the polls. Reporter Barry Peterson, in interviewing "No on Six" spokesperson Sallye Fiske in San Francisco, relayed the theme that instead of being merely a homosexual issue, this fight was for the human rights of free speech, fair employment, and privacy.[62]

The anti–Proposition 6 stance also gained momentum heading into the final weeks of the campaign from the actions of political figures. Although hesitant at first, multiple California and national political leaders voiced opposition to the measure. Former California governor Ronald Reagan spoke out against it as did numerous Republican members of California's state legislature. Briggs promptly accused Reagan of being part of the questionable "Hollywood crowd." He could not claim the same about former president Gerald Ford and President Jimmy Carter, who also urged the public to vote no. Quite a few influential California organizations and personalities shared the politicians' concerns as the proposition received more and more publicity. Among these, the California Teachers Association, the state's American Federation of Labor and Congress of Industrial Organizations (AFL-CIO), and Hollywood stars ranging from Carol Burnett to James Garner all condemned the discriminatory measure.[63]

On a more local scale, virtually all San Francisco's official bodies and major organizations came out in strong opposition to Proposition 6. Those vocally condemning Briggs's efforts included San Francisco's mayor, Catholic and Episcopal bishops, the San Francisco Board of Education, the *San Francisco Chronicle*, the *San Francisco Examiner*, and the Bay Area chapter of the National Lawyers Guild. Even Dan White, the primary opponent to Milk's gay rights ordinance, joined with his fellow supervisors in passing a unanimous resolution against the amendment.[64]

Yet, much to Milk's chagrin, the opposition to Briggs's measure was not unanimous in San Francisco. The San Francisco Chamber of Commerce stood as the only major San Francisco institution to refuse Milk's calls for a condemnation of the measure outright. Disregarding personal pleas from Milk, the chamber settled on a "no position" stance on the initiative. This incensed Milk, who, in a biting letter, accused chamber president William E. Dauer of being unable to recognize a "basic human rights issue." He further laid out the following "line-up" to inform the chamber members of whom they stood alongside in refusing to oppose the initiative:

Yes on 6	No on 6
Briggs	The Downtown Association
Ku Klux Klan	The Commonwealth Club
Nazi Party	The *Examiner*
	The *Chronicle*
	Archbishop Quinn
	Bishop Meyers
	Senator Hayakawa
	Senator Cranston
	Mayor Moscone
	Ronald Reagan
	All Eleven Supervisors
	and on and on[65]

Interestingly, Milk's listing of the Nazi Party was not pure hyperbole. A group of neo-Nazis calling themselves the Nationalist Socialist White People's Party had offered their support in a letter to the Briggs Initiative campaign.[66]

In reality, Briggs had a few more supporters than Milk credited him with. Although most politicians and organizations increasingly deserted his cause as the November election drew near, he maintained strong support in rural areas, in suburban enclaves such as Orange County, and with members of some fundamentalist Protestant denominations. Reverend Ray Batema of the Central Pomona Baptist Church served as cochair (alongside Briggs) of the Citizens for Decency and Morality—an organization formed after the initiative received a spot on the ballot in order to see it through to Election Day success. Adopting a quotation from the biblical story of Sodom as the philosophy of the campaign, Batema and Briggs urged their supporters, "Go find me ten righteous men" opposed to homosexuality.[67] It is telling that they looked to the story of Sodom for inspiration on how to wage a battle that was, by that time, often equating gays with San Francisco and equating San Francisco with Sodom.[68] One has to wonder whether they felt it was impossible, as was the case with Abraham in his search in Sodom, to find what they considered ten righteous men in San Francisco.[69]

Obviously, not all Christians agreed with the Citizens for Decency and its stand on gay rights. While Southern Baptists in Orange County campaigned for the measure and condemned President Carter's and other politicians' opposition to it, Catholic and Episcopal leaders in San Francisco spoke out forcefully against the initiative. Likewise, letters to the editor in Los Angeles newspapers in the days leading up to the election found people divided on where exactly the Christian faith came down on the employment rights of homosexuals. Interestingly, the San Francisco editorial pages carried no letters that voiced worries about the effect that all this discussion was having on San Francisco's image.[70]

The death knell for Proposition 6 came in a series of highly publicized debates between Briggs and Milk. Increasingly, Milk became more comfortable in the debate format and began to reveal Briggs's politically ambitious nature, cast him as hateful, and expose the absurdity of his claims. Finally, in a desperate ploy, Briggs challenged Milk to a debate over Proposition 6 in his home setting of Orange County in an event sponsored by his Citizens for Decency coalition. To Briggs's surprise, Milk accepted the invitation, figuring that if Briggs could talk in favor of the proposition from the steps of San Francisco City Hall, then he could certainly debate the issue before an unfriendly crowd on Briggs's own turf.[71]

The debate that followed proved to be a mortal blow for the Briggs Amendment. Milk doggedly stuck to prepared talking points that stressed the discrimination inherent to Proposition 6 as a human rights issue rather than a gay rights issue. As his notes indicated, "Proposition 6 . . . is a misguided, confused, dangerous,

Street signs at the corner of Castro and Eighteenth Streets
read Sodom and Gomorrah, 1974.
Harvey Milk Archives—Scott Smith Collection
(GLC-0112), LGBTQIA Center, San Francisco Public Library.

deceitful, frightening, and un-American attack on basic human rights." Milk
further drove home the point that as virtually every political leader, educator,
religious leader, and law enforcement officer had attested over the course of the
campaign, the proposition was "completely unnecessary" because enforceable
laws already existed for the protection of children. In reality, the entire affair was
nothing more than "a self serving politician dreaming up a moral crusade to ride
to power."[72] Those tuned in to the broadcast were also treated to the recurrent jeers
and threats against Milk made by audience members. One attendee later stated,
"That was when I realized Milk was right—he was going to get shot some day."[73]

Well-attended, televised around the state, and covered heavily in the California
press, the debates cast Briggs and his supporters in a very bad light while Milk's
performance garnered respect. Congratulatory letters to Milk commonly referred

to his debate presence as "fantastic," "magnificent," and "excellent." Some of the individuals using such accolades claimed not to have supported Milk or his causes in the past. In the light of the debates, however, they assured their total support on this issue and even their votes in the future. One individual went so far as to say that that his city of San Francisco was very lucky to have Milk representing it, and hopefully he would long stand as "a beacon of tolerance."[74]

When election results began to roll in on the night of November 8, it became apparent that for the first time since Anita Bryant had assumed leadership of the anti–gay rights drive almost two years prior, an attempt to roll back the rights of homosexuals was going down in stunning defeat.[75] While polls only months earlier had suggested an easy win for the proposition, the polls that really mattered told another story on the morning of November 9. Statewide, 59 percent of those voting cast their ballots against the Briggs Initiative.[76] In San Francisco the defeat was overwhelming with 75 percent voting against the measure.[77]

As thousands of celebrants jammed San Francisco's Market Square that night in celebration of Proposition 6's defeat, a stunned Milk addressed the crowd. He urged those present to take heart from this victory and to go out and proudly proclaim their sexual orientation to all who would listen.[78] Their victory had shown that straights and gays could work together to defeat bigotry and that when gays acted openly and together in their interest, striking change could come about. Sadly, Milk had little time left to enjoy the defining victory of his life.

Milk's position of power, his outspoken nature, and his untiring efforts to defeat Proposition 6 placed the city supervisor at the dangerous forefront of America's culture wars. Throughout his term as supervisor, he had often faced death threats and what can only be described as horribly bigoted hate mail. These letters dripped with an almost inconceivable hatred, fear, and quite frankly, ignorance concerning homosexuality. Such letters streamed in and were overwhelmingly from people outside San Francisco. Some approached incoherence while revealing a violent hatred of gays and a level of mental disturbance warranting professional help. In this category, one can find letters such as those by an individual who chose to sign no name, which were postmarked in Seattle and addressed to the "San Francisco Board of Stupid Visors c/o *Cocksucker* Harvey Milk." Perhaps out of touch with reality, the writer seemed to be under the illusion that Milk was running for governor and detested the fact that "cocksuckers" like Milk were "now very welcomed anywhere in California."[79]

Other letters appeared far more ominous precisely because of the writers' obvious coherence. Among these, one can find evidence of the unease generated by Milk's run for the supervisor's office and the near panic following his election. An anonymous letter to Bay Area state senator Milton Marks threatened defeat at reelection time in return for support of Milk's candidacy. Having written in the margins of a campaign letter from Marks, the anonymous Milk opponent asked if the Senator was a "fruit" himself.[80]

Additional mail, while equally vulgar and hate filled, directly projected Milk's homosexuality onto the city of San Francisco. Standing out among these are a person calling him- or herself "Nguen Rene Phuc Q from Alameda" and the more anonymous "a guy from Iowa." The Phuq Q letter—addressed to "Harvey Milk, Supervisor, Chief Faggot, Asshole Reamer, and Lesbian Lover"—makes a direct comparison between San Francisco and the biblical cities of Sodom and Gomorrah while claiming that Milk's political career might turn the entire nation into a "hotbed for queers."[81] The "guy from Iowa" likewise used a profanity-laced tirade to inform Milk that he would come to San Francisco, what he now realized to be a "cesspool of inequity," and physically put an end to Milk's actions, except that it would mean dirtying his "hands on filth."[82]

Judging from such hate mail, one can hardly blame Milk for being convinced that he would die an untimely and violent death. As the 1970s drew on and Milk's political career blossomed, he had increasingly related this morbid idea to his closest friends. Famously, after recording a message for Mayor George Moscone, stating who he wished to take over his supervisor's seat in the likely event of his death, Milk philosophically stated, "If a bullet should enter my brain, let that bullet destroy every closet door."[83]

When "that bullet" entered his brain on the morning of November 27, 1978, it did not come from those who had threatened Milk in his unsettling flow of hate mail. That bullet—a special hollow-point shell specifically chosen to inflict the most gruesome damage—came from Milk's board-of-supervisors antithesis, the seemingly "all-American" Dan White.[84] After assassinating Mayor Moscone, White calmly walked into Milk's office, leveled his former service revolver, and extinguished the life of America's leading gay politician. Unfortunately, the bullets fired that day did not destroy all closet doors. They did, however, contribute to San Francisco's perceptual place as the nation's gay capital. As sensational violent events so often do, the tragic death of Harvey Milk drew ever more national media attention to the place that Milk called home. Such coverage of events at the end of the 1970s—of which Milk's death was by far the most tragic—fixed San Francisco's reputation once and for all as the perceptual center of the debate over homosexuality in America. In the decades that followed, the city itself would prove far more accepting of the label than it had been in the past.

Throughout this chaotic period, San Franciscans displayed far less interest in how the controversial events happening around them influenced the image of their city than the residents of Birmingham had during and in the aftermath of the civil rights movement. In this case, unlike in Birmingham in 1960, there were no lawsuits filed by city leaders against media outlets for portraying the city and its officials in a derogatory manner. Likewise, newspaper readers of the day would not find an editorial bemoaning the smearing of San Francisco's image as they would in Birmingham whenever some spectacular event with racial underpinnings reached the national media. One of the few instances of local reaction manifested itself in the previously discussed Herb Caen editorial to the *New York Times*. But even in that instance, Caen was not finding fault with San Francisco being labeled as gay friendly but rather with Anita Bryant's belief that being gay friendly was a bad thing.[85] When pointed comments by Briggs, Bryant, and other antigay activists attempted to smear the city with homosexual references, little if any concern was evidenced in the local media from residents or editors. To their credit, the people of San Francisco in 1978 simply did not seem to mind their city being cast as exceptionally tolerant to homosexuality. Even the majority of the hate mail directed at Milk during the fight over the Briggs Initiative originated in places outside San Francisco. While much of it cast San Francisco as deviantly homosexual, not a single letter condemned Milk for any adverse impact he might be having on the city's national image.

San Franciscans exhibited little concern over the image of their city in print outlets well into the 1980s. In stark contrast to Birmingham, where the allusions to past racism and violence often sparked a flurry of letter writing, editorial pages of major San Francisco newspapers proved strikingly silent. For example, nationally publicized tension between gay residents and the local police force in 1982 went by without a local letter to the editor. Similar silence followed Jeanne Kirkpatrick's infamous use of the label "San Francisco Democrat" in her 1984 Republican National Convention speech.[86] Even the renaming of San Francisco landmarks in honor of Milk failed to provoke the outcry heard in Birmingham over similar honors that were afforded to civil rights leaders. In San Francisco today one can find schools, a branch of the public library, a federal building, and a recreation center all bearing Milk's name. In 1997 the corner of Market and Castro Streets was named Harvey Milk Plaza and marked by the installation of a giant rainbow flag because that was the site where thousands gathered following his assassination.[87] In all fairness, however, a deadly and frightening issue had emerged on the San Francisco scene by the mid-1980s.

AIDS and San Francisco

As the 1980s dawned, things were looking up for San Francisco's gay community. Thanks to the monumental strides made by Harvey Milk and other long-working activists, San Francisco's gay population enjoyed openness, acceptance, and even political power that were unimaginable in other American cities. Over the previous few years, a strong community had developed in which they could live openly without excessive anxiety. The gay community's support had propelled an openly gay man to one of the highest seats in municipal government. Thanks largely to Harvey Milk's efforts and the gay community's consolidation and cooperation, the city instituted a strong and far-reaching gay rights ordinance. Further, the mobilization of San Francisco's gay population proved central in defeating the homophobic Briggs Initiative and dealing a strong blow to nationwide efforts aimed at rolling back gay rights. Even following the tragedy of Milk's assassination, gays managed to preserve their recent political gains. Newly seated Mayor Dianne Feinstein, in a rare instance of cooperation with her gay constituents, facilitated this through the appointment of Harry Britt—another gay man—as the slain supervisor's replacement. At the same time, Cleve Jones emerged and assumed Milk's place as the city's foremost gay rights activist and organizer. Having led the White Night riot following Dan White's light sentencing of six years for killing Milk and the mayor, the militant yet media-savvy Jones stood as the perfect spokesman for Harvey Milk's legacy and for gay San Franciscans' rise in the 1970s.[88]

Thus by 1981 San Francisco beckoned like never before to gay Americans who sought to live openly. By that time, approximately five thousand gay men heeded the call and chose to move to San Francisco each year. Hundreds of thousands more embraced the city temporarily as they arrived in June for the Gay Freedom Day parade. For many, it was a good time to be gay in a city that seemingly refused to bow to traditional cultural restraints and pressures. Yet, in the coming years, the spread of a formerly unknown disease would bring these good times to a crashing halt.[89]

When a few young and otherwise healthy gay men in San Francisco and New York City began appearing with rare cases of the Kaposi's sarcoma, various forms of pneumonia, and devastated immune systems in 1981, no one in the health field understood initially that they were witnessing the American emergence of a deadly pandemic. While later theories would posit that the Human Immuno-deficiency Virus (HIV) and the Acquired Immunodeficiency Syndrome (AIDS) that it can lead to originated much earlier in the remote reaches of sub-Saharan Africa, in the early 1980s it only seemed apparent that a deadly malady had appeared from within the ranks of the nation's gay population.[90]

AIDS hit San Francisco hard. Only a few years after its 1981 appearance, many in the gay community knew multiple people who were afflicted with or had died from the disease. For example, gay activist and writer Dennis Altman was stopped on Castro Street in the spring of 1984 by a friend who informed him of the loss of a shared acquaintance, the fifth such loss to the disease that year.[91] To Cleve Jones, it seemed that by 1984 doctors were diagnosing another current or former associate with AIDS every day. The mental strain proved tremendous as he watched friends die and worried about his own risk of contracting the disease due to past behavior. At one point, Cleve—the city's most renowned gay activist of the time—considered abandoning San Francisco for the seemingly safer confines of Hawaii.[92] San Francisco was losing its appeal.

The proliferation of AIDS also brought changes to San Francisco's vibrant and open gay culture. In one example, gay bathhouses came under attack by public health officials as transmission points for the disease. Long a fixture in San Francisco and New York City, the gay bathhouses served as places where sexual inhibitions fell away and gratification came easily and often anonymously. As early as 1982, San Francisco public health officials realized that sexual behavior at the bathhouses contributed to the spread of the disease and launched educational efforts aimed at informing the clientele of unsafe practices. Efforts for the additional regulation and closure of bathhouses proved far more controversial. On October 9, 1984, amid much opposition from the gay community, the San Francisco Health Department ordered the closure of fourteen bathhouses within the city limits. The Harvey Milk Gay Democratic Club stood as the only pre-dominantly gay organization to support the closure. Others such as the Golden Gate Business Association, the San Francisco AIDS Foundation, the Bay Area Physicians for Human Rights, and the Bay Area Lawyers for Individual Freedom held press conferences that challenged the closures as attacks on the liberties of gay San Franciscans. With the support of these organizations, owners of the bathhouses quickly filed legal proceedings to keep the establishments open. Ultimately, on November 28, Judge Roy Wonder ruled that bathhouses could reopen if they allowed monitors to survey the premises every ten minutes for illicit sexual behavior, removed doors, and closed private rooms. Any violation of these provisions warranted immediate closure. Most of the houses that reopened and attempted to live up to these strictures quickly succumbed as business decreased dramatically.[93]

In attempting to shut down the bathhouses, the San Francisco Health Department served as a pacesetter for other municipalities. New York City, for example, quickly followed suit. There, however, the measure proved far less controversial, and resistance from the gay community was minimal relative to what it had been in San Francisco. In this regard, one can see evidence of how politically strong San Francisco's gay community was compared to New York City's.[94] One can also see how politicians tended to panic and implement reactionary measures based on the misguided notion that AIDS was a gay disease.

In the earliest years, one could easily perceptually equate the disease's emergence with San Francisco. The media and population alike, after all, widely recognized the city as the national center of the gay community. The cognitive link was fostered by health officials' and the popular media's early characterizations of the disease as gay-centered and by reports of its impact on San Francisco. If San Francisco existed as the nation's gay mecca, then it made sense that the new gay disease must be centered there.

Examples of the disease being cast as gay include health scientists' original naming of it as Gay-Related Immune Deficiency (GRID).[95] In the popular press, one could commonly find the disease referred to as the "gay plague."[96] As instances of infection outside the gay population mounted, the classification of the disease shifted from GRID to AIDS. By late 1982 the popular press commonly employed the AIDS acronym.[97] Yet the media continued to equate the disease with gay men and, increasingly, with San Francisco. In one representative instance of this, a front-page *Boston Globe* article from 1983 related how San Francisco's rescue workers lived in constant fear of catching the "mysterious" and "deadly" disease of the city's homosexual population.[98] A scan of period newspapers reveals a tendency for the words *AIDS, homosexuality,* and *San Francisco* to appear together in newspaper articles during the first half of the 1980s.[99]

A similar pattern existed in early television news coverage of AIDS. Beginning in 1983 and 1984, network newscasts often equated AIDS with San Francisco. Segments such as *NBC Nightly News'* "AIDS" featured correspondents reporting on the "deadly disease" caused by "promiscuous homosexual activity" while standing in front of gay establishments in San Francisco. Other national newscasts highlighted the closure of gay bars, the opening of AIDS clinics, and the fear that the city's health workers and police officers felt. Other topics that reinforced the relation of San Francisco to AIDS in the national arena explored the frequency of AIDS and prevalence of anxiety among the city's gay population.[100] The net result was to cast the city as not only abnormally homosexual but also dangerously so.

Much of this linkage resulted from the simple fact that the disease first ravaged the gay population and that San Francisco, due to its large number of homosexual men, sustained a disproportionate number of infections compared to other cities. While New York may have had more total AIDS cases, those cases were spread out over a much larger total population. By 1986 no city matched San Francisco's 2,250 confirmed cases and 1,275 deaths out of a total population of approximately 650,000. Further narrowing the impact and linking homosexuality, San Francisco, and AIDS, a whopping 97 percent of the city's AIDS cases by 1986 were among the gay population.[101]

Unfortunately, such coverage led to homophobic opinions among the public in regard to AIDS and San Francisco. In one representative example in 1985, opponents of a gay rights ordinance in Houston told the *New York Times* that the ordinance's passage would turn their city into "another San Francisco" and thus expose its residents to AIDS.[102]

Similar public perceptions of AIDS and San Francisco shifted gradually over time. As the disease's impact on the heterosexual community became more well known over the next decade, the gay stigma associated with it eased. In turn, the idea of San Francisco as an AIDS-ridden city ceased to be a major theme of AIDS coverage and conversation. During the 1990s the discussion of AIDS also became increasingly mainstream and often centered on the worldwide spread of the disease. AIDS in Africa and Southeast Asia became particularly frequent topics in the media.[103]

Beyond this recognition of the wider threat of AIDS, celebrity attention to the crisis also helped shift the perceptual AIDS epicenter away from San Francisco. While much of the celebrity focus on the disease in the early 1990s addressed the topic locally within the United States, by the early 2000s, the emphasis had shifted markedly to developing nations. African nations in particular seemed to take on the central perceptual placement in the battle against AIDS. As the *Economist* noted in 2005, "Domestic AIDS is passé."[104] Unfortunately, while San Francisco and other American domestic centers were distanced from the AIDS stigma, people with the disease continued to face stigmatization in the United States and abroad.

Gay Tourism and Wedding Vows

Evidence of lessening negative influences on San Francisco's reputation as a gay mecca can be found in the success of the city's gay tourism industry in the 1990s and 2000s. By 2008, gay tourism had developed into a major worldwide enterprise with San Francisco as its premier destination. Anthropologist Alyssa Howe has labeled this a form of "identity and homeland tourism" that, very similar to a religious pilgrimage, shapes and influences both the life of the traveler and the nature of the population visited. In regard to San Francisco, Howe argues, major gay travel to the city since the 1980s has helped San Franciscans retain the tolerant and nonconformist identity they had carried since the days of the gold rush. Likewise, visitors have their lives validated in ways that they could never experience in hometowns that do not share San Francisco's gay community, acceptance, or history.[105]

Regardless of motivations, statistics for gay tourism reveal that it is a phenomenon worth exploration by city tourism professionals. According to surveys from the early 2000s, homosexuals were far more likely to travel and possessed more disposable income than their straight counterparts. In turn, American gay and lesbian tourists spent an astonishing $60 billion per year on travel by 2007. Taking note of this, destinations around the world subsequently engaged in a healthy competition for a share of this business.[106] A careful look at the treatment of gay tourism in travel guides and online travel sources reveals several aspects about San Francisco's relationship with its perceptual placement as the nation's premier gay destination at the turn of the twenty-first century.

Mainstream travel guides have come a long way in embracing the industry of gay travel. Some, such as *Fodor's*, have produced guides exclusively devoted to gay tourists.[107] Meanwhile, virtually every major publication from *Frommer's* to *Time Out* contains a section in its city-specific editions on activities of interest for the gay traveler. None, however, highlight homosexuality to the degree that publications centered on San Francisco have. In 1995, for example, a prospective visitor lucky enough to spot *Insight Guides: San Francisco* on the local bookstore's shelf found the face of Harvey Milk smiling out from the book's spine and, inside, an entire feature section devoted to the "gay community."[108] The trend continued, as evidenced by the 2008–2009 edition of Lonely Planet's *San Francisco City Guide*. That guide's historical overview of the city devotes a section to the success of local gays in winning rights and developing one of the world's most vibrant gay communities. It then goes on to devote and entire chapter to "Gay/Lesbian/Bi/Trans SF."[109]

A survey of page numbers devoted to gay and lesbian travel in *Frommer's* travel guides for major United States cities reveals that San Francisco far exceeded the norm in the 2008. *Frommer's San Francisco* provides sixteen pages of resources, either directly or cross-referenced through the "Castro District," for the gay traveler. By contrast, *Frommer's Los Angeles* devotes six pages, *Las Vegas* four pages, and *New York City* five pages. Lonely Planet's *New York City City Guide* seemingly bucks this trend by devoting a full eleven pages to gay travel spots in the nation's largest city. However, a quick scan of Lonely Planet's *San Francisco City Guide* for the same year reveals sixteen pages devoted to gay destinations.[110]

As with print travel guides, websites devoted to gay travel clearly place San Francisco as the top destination city. In the early 2000s, the home page of the now-defunct Gay.com's travel section featured San Francisco more prominently than any other city. Upon opening the page, the would-be traveler was met with links to an article titled "Only in San Francisco" as well as an additional "San Francisco" link under the Featured Destinations menu. The travel page once prominently featured an article titled "The Out Traveler Guides." In this piece, the author explained how to use the site's search engine to find destinations and deals. The well-meaning author wrote: "Go to our destinations page and click on any city (for example, San Francisco)."[111] Once a person followed these instructions, they were rewarded with a fourteen-page bibliographical listing of gay travel articles focusing on San Francisco (Las Vegas had four articles, Los Angeles eleven, Miami eleven, Chicago seven, Key West seven).[112] The site's introduction to the San Francisco page stated blatantly, "San Francisco still reigns as the most gay-friendly, gay-popular and gay-integrated destination in the country, if not the world." In these travel writers' minds, other leading destinations for gay travelers, such as West Hollywood and New York City's Chelsea, could not match up to the experience and ease of acceptance found in San Francisco. There, more than any other destination, one could "find gay women and men throughout the city. They're integrated in the city's political, financial and social life and power structure, and you'll see them living, working, eating and playing quite comfortably, almost all over town."[113]

At least one reader of Gay.com's San Francisco travel page took great offense at the portrayal of the city. This was not because it cast the city as gay friendly but because the reader felt the portrayals disgraced the significance of the location as "where we gained the freedoms we have today." In the comment section following the article, the reader scolded the writers for attempting to sell the Castro district as a place where the "newer generation comes to hook up." Instead, he suggested that the writers should be more in tune with the area's history and more respectful of "Milk, Cleve, Eric and the many other soldiers that paved the way for gay rights."[114] Aside from this critical view of the nature of San Francisco's attraction to homosexuals, there were no condemnations on any of the website's pages concerning the marketing of San Francisco as a gay destination or the effect of such marketing on the city's image.

In line with the lack of condemnation, local businesses seemed to have no problem with highlighting their city as the nation's foremost gay destination. Numerous businesses placed advertisements in the San Francisco sections on Gay.com. These included advertisements for local shows, hotels, and most surprisingly, the San Francisco Convention and Visitors Bureau.[115] A click on the supplied link to the bureau's "Official Visitors' Site for San Francisco," opened an entire section devoted to "Gay Travel." There, the traveler was treated to resources and articles on where to stay, what to do, and how to plan weddings as well as "History, Culture, and Information" about gay San Francisco. In this latter section, the bureau promoted San Francisco as "the Lesbian, Gay, Bisexual, and Transgendered Capital of the World!"[116]

Quite simply, print and Internet travel media reveal that in both gay and straight circles, San Francisco was considered the nation's preeminent gay destination during the first decade of the twenty-first century. This coincided with a 2006 Travel Industry Association survey that ranked San Francisco the number-one gay-friendly destination. Far from displaying grievances with their city's promotion as gay friendly, some San Franciscans expressed anxiety over the idea that other cities might be attempting to overtake their city's spot atop the gay-destination rankings. In the local press, writers and businesspeople espoused worry about the temptations, and in some cases actions, of other cities in attempting to lure away gay tourists. Some, such as Peter Gerhaeuser, then sales and marketing director at San Francisco's Renoir Hotel, admittedly used San Francisco's gay rights history as a tourist draw and lamented that other destinations were increasingly cutting into the city's share of the market.[117]

In relation to gay rights as a tourist draw, the issue of gay marriage also drew much press attention to San Francisco as a result of its attempted legalization in 2004 and again in 2008. The state supreme court struck down the legalization in 2004. In 2008, San Franciscans faced a situation eerily reminiscent of 1978's fight against Proposition 6, albeit with fortunes reversed this time. In the general election that year, Californians overturned the latest legalization by voting 52.2 percent to 47.8 percent in favor of a state amendment outlawing gay marriage. In San Francisco the vote ran 75.1 percent against and 24.9 percent in favor of the proposition. Eighty-one percent of the city's registered voters turned out.[118]

During both brief periods of legalized gay marriage in San Francisco, members of the local business community and tourist industry acted quickly to promote the city as a gay marriage destination. In one instance the San Francisco Visitors and Convention Bureau joined with the Golden Gate Business Association (the nation's first gay chamber of commerce) in a new advertising program to "remind this high-spending tourist population why it should continue making its pilgrimage to the city." The campaign featured colorful brochures that highlighted the city's important role in the gay rights struggle—from the founding of the Daughters of Bilitis to Harvey Milk's election to the legalization of gay marriage—with the caption "Come Out Here."[119]

Local response to the gay marriage issue and tourism was mixed. A 2004 article in the online version of the *San Francisco Chronicle* received twenty-six comments. None of these comments expressed concern over the effect of legalization on San Francisco's image. Instead, a very evident concern by those commenting was that city leaders were using a potential tourism windfall rather than a real concern over gay rights as the motivation for the attempted legalization. As one commenter on the *Chronicle*'s website wrote, "I guess gay marriage isn't about Adam and Steve, it's about the Benjamins."[120] Even those taking a seemingly antigay stance based their views on the idea that the city's motivation was profit rather than a real concern for rights and said nothing about their concern for San Francisco's image as a gay mecca. This view was summed up by another commenter who wrote, "Gays don't want to admit the real reason Newsom wants gay marriages in SF. Its not about 'rights' at all, it [*sic*] only about money."[121] Thus, for those in favor of and in opposition to legalized gay marriage, the main concern (beyond the disagreement concerning the propriety of such marriages) centered on the motivation for legalization rather than the effect of legalization on the city's image.

San Francisco's historic position in support of gay marriage received validation from the U.S. government on June 26, 2015, when the U.S. Supreme Court's five-to-four ruling in *Oberegfell v. Hodges* declared that the right to same-sex marriage is protected under the U.S. Constitution. Justice Anthony Kennedy's majority statement read, "No longer may this liberty be denied" to the people, for "no union is more profound than marriage." It is, he continued, the "keystone of our social order."[122] For Kennedy and the four other justices who agreed, the issue was certainly about the rights and law rather than any economic motivation. This shows a remarkable shift in the contextual attitudes surrounding San Francisco's reputation as a gay mecca. Whether or not this trend toward increased acceptance and equality will continue or face backlash in the years following the decision remains to be seen.

In 1978 political leaders such as Harvey Milk and those who stood with him bucked a national wave of opposition to preserve the basic human rights of a segment of their city's population. In the process, Milk obtained the legendary status that so often accompanies martyrdom. San Francisco, on the other hand, lived on, and its reputation as the perceptual center of gay America greatly increased. This reputation, in times of trial such as the early years of the AIDS pandemic, often took on negative connotations. At other times, such as during the 1990s and 2000s, it proved profitable. As revealed by the active attempts to play up San Francisco as a gay travel destination based on both its vibrant gay community and its historic role in the gay rights movement, the modern perception of San Francisco as a gay mecca remains one that San Franciscans seem comfortable with. Obviously, in relation to Birmingham and its concerns over reputation, San Francisco differs markedly. As the following chapters will show, San Francisco's placement as the nation's gay mecca—a placement largely emanating from the confines of the Castro district, bears both similarities and marked differences with the history of Las Vegas's Strip-based stigmatization as the nation's Sin City.

6

Sinning in the Desert

The Origins and Development of America's Sin City

Although it is vitally important to the city's economic well-being, the history of Las Vegas's image has received scant scholarly attention. Only recently, with the publication of Larry Gragg's *Bright Light City: Las Vegas in Popular Culture*, have academics begun to focus solely on the role of the city's reputation as an engine of its history. This is opposed to the more common practice of examining the city in relation to its main industries of gambling and entertainment and its resulting characteristics. In such works, valuable as they certainly are, the city's image has taken a back seat or is at most discussed as a contextual by-product of the city's unique qualities. To Hal Rothman, for example, Las Vegas's image is that of a postmodern Detroit—a city that offers high-wage service jobs without the accompanying educational requirements that exclude so many Americans from middle-class earnings in other twenty-first-century cities.[1] This image, purely positive and beneficial, exists because the city was unabashedly structured around gambling and tourism. Likewise, Eugene Moehring's classic study meticulously examines the history of Las Vegas's development as a world-class tourist destination or resort city and draws attention to the centrality of Fremont Street, and later of the Strip, in Americans' conceptualization of the city.[2] However, Moehring's superb examination does not place the sin city image as the primary driver of Las Vegas's history. Again, the image is treated as a side effect of the ever-evolving gaming industry.

I believe, as Larry Gragg has argued, that Las Vegas's image has been a central player in the city's history. Gragg writes that he was attracted to Las Vegas because "it's almost all the things that I am not." Gragg, as a product of small-town America, had a definite image of what Vegas was before he ever visited. This popular image, as he illustrates throughout his book, entices millions of Americans to visit Las Vegas each year.[3] The image is an agent in the history of Las Vegas. Admittedly, it likely would not exist if the city's economic basis were not rooted in gambling. But also, without the careful maintenance of the Sin City reputation, the world-class entertainment center that is today's Las Vegas would have never come to be.

Las Vegas's first hurdle in terms of its image was rooted in its geographic location and climate. Quite simply, the city is located in a desert. And it is not just any desert but one of the driest and hottest locations in continental North America. In the early twentieth century, urban boosters often faced difficulty in selling arid or desert locations to prospective settlers. Americans at this time hardly considered the desert quintessentially "American" and did not exactly covet it as a place to raise crops or livestock, nor was it in the nation's burgeoning industrial sector in which one could search out a living. Unlike a booming Birmingham, the desert-situated Las Vegas could not offer jobs in steel mills as incentive for migration or immigration. Likewise, its desert location and hard alkaline soil did not bode well for a self-supporting homestead or agribusiness. Early boosters faced the dilemma of how to overcome the stigma of their town's desert location in the years following the town's founding in 1905. The remote and arid railroad town struggled against these obstacles early on before prospering from its sunbaked location as America's playground several decades later. Along the way, Las Vegas's image traveled an eventful path from a little-known desert outpost to one of the world's most renowned destinations. Ultimately, in its journey through the twentieth century, Las Vegas emerged as the nation's Sin City—a place where people can go to do things that are deemed unacceptable at home.

When William A. Clark bought the Las Vegas Rancho from Helen J. Stewart, it was not much of a gamble. The year was 1902, and $55,000 seemed like a good deal of money even for two thousand acres of land. But the millionaire senator from Montana—known widely to have the Midas touch—was racing to build a railroad from Salt Lake City to Los Angeles. The railroad would cross this southern Nevada valley that was known for its life-sustaining springs in a vast expanse of inhospitable aridity. As a result of these springs' existence, the valley had long been known as a layover point on the old Spanish Trail leading to southern California. Thanks to Clark, Union Pacific passenger cars soon enough replaced the wagons, carts, and horses of yesteryear. On the meadow ranch he had just purchased, the new town of Las Vegas would ultimately make a rather unspectacular entrance into early twentieth-century America.[4]

About six decades before Clark's purchase, Mormon missionaries had settled the area along the banks of the Las Vegas Creek. Life for the few Latter-Day Saints at the Las Vegas Mission from 1855 to 1858 proved difficult in the extreme. The hot weather and lack of most necessities kept the eleven families and a few single men in a state of uncertainty and privation. It was a place, as early settler Maria Barston wrote, where "luxuries were few" and all "thought common necessities were luxuries."[5] The Native American population proved more interested in the mission's crops than in embracing its teachings on religion and agricultural practices. All too often, the settlers found their precious crops missing. Also, settlers found the place depressing due to its remote location and excessive heat. The discovery of lead ore in 1856, while offering the hope of invigorating the settlement, ultimately led only to increased division within the community and less devotion to agriculture. Finally, most of the settlers received permission from Brigham Young to return to Utah during the winter of 1857–58. By the end of summer in 1858, most Mormon settlers had evacuated the fort.[6] By the time of Clark's arrival, no town stood in the valley of "the meadows," or *las vegas*, as the Spanish had dubbed it long before. Instead, only a few large and widely dispersed ranches—the Las Vegas Spring Ranch, Spring Mountain Ranch, Kiel's Ranch in North Las Vegas, and Stewart's Las Vegas Ranch—struggled for existence against both the harsh climate and, at times, each other.[7]

Before discussing the cultural emergence of Las Vegas as America's adult playground, it helps to first look at the city's natural environment. In examining the characteristics of the local geography and climate, along with attempts to shape perceptions of these attributes, one can see the first instances of concern with local image. Before Las Vegas could worry about its image as Sin City, it had to first deal with the stigma associated with its harsh desert location. Ironically, the perception of this harsh location that early boosters sought to shed ultimately contributed to Las Vegas's success.

A Climate for Sin

Located at the edge of the Mojave Desert and the Great Basin, in close proximity to Death Valley, the site of Clark's purchase was distant, inhospitable, and just plain uncomfortable to anyone who might have the misfortune to live there before the advent of air conditioning. Eventually and against all odds, the site would gain the distinction of housing one of the world's largest arid-climate cities.[8] While the opposite seems to make more sense, the distinct geographic placement and harsh, perceptually foreign climate proved over time to be key factors contributing to Las Vegas's rise to its magnificently risqué postwar form.

Southern Nevada is among the driest and hottest places on earth. Midday high temperatures in the midst of summer can routinely reach 110–113 degrees Fahrenheit, and 100 degrees at midnight is not out of the question. One cannot count on rainfall to alleviate the heat because the yearly average is around 4.5 inches. In all, Las Vegas averages more than two hundred days of sunny weather per year. Unfortunately, it is too hot to venture out in comfort between 10 A.M. and sunset on a good number of those days.[9]

The print media has linked Las Vegas with the desert for as long as the city has existed. As early as 1905, newspapers from other cities referred to Las Vegas and the hostile desert it inhabited. The *San Jose Mercury*, for example, wrote of an unfortunate Japanese minister's son who was "toiling in the desert" at Las Vegas instead of joining his siblings at Stanford University.[10] Likewise, newsworthy events such as mining discoveries or labor strikes often necessitated newspaper coverage that equated the city with the desert. This was the case when the *Philadelphia Inquirer* discussed Las Vegas as a desert town following the discovery of gold at the relatively nearby town of Goldfield in 1905.[11] By the end of the year, the *San Jose Mercury* claimed that railroad laborers who had been lured to Las Vegas by "unscrupulous" recruiters were "starving in the desert."[12] A few months later, when flooding washed out much of the railroad in the Las Vegas area, that previously generic desert became the "Nevada Desert between Caliente and Las Vegas" to newspapers around the nation.[13] This practice continued into the teens and twenties as the *Oregonian* featured travel narratives about southern Nevada's desert characteristics.[14] Likewise, by the time of the 1922 railroad strike, readers from California to Florida learned of train transport halting at such "desert points" as Las Vegas, Nevada.[15] In at least one instance, writers went so far as to label the train shutdown the "Desert Strike."[16]

Because of Americans' unease with the desert, early Las Vegas boosters faced an unenviable task in light of such consistent descriptions. Yet, from the very beginning, local boosters took on the problem with gusto. Chamber of commerce literature from the 1910s reveals an almost paranoid avoidance of reinforcing the city's true desert nature to outsiders. Booklets and pamphlets from 1913 and 1915 employ such titles as "Semi-Tropical Nevada: A Region of Fertile Soil and

Flowing Wells" and "Las Vegas, Nevada: Where Farming Pays." In promoting the Las Vegas valley as a "fertile" land, the pamphlets at best misled prospective migrants concerning the climate and soil and at worst lied outright. One has to wonder what those migrants who took the bait of such claims as "Anything that would grow in Southern California would grow in abundance in Southern Nevada" and "No one ever heard of heat stroke or heat prostration" thought upon arriving.[17] As historian David Wrobel has so clearly pointed out, boosters from the last few decades of the nineteenth century through the 1930s "literally tried to imagine western places into existence through embellished and effusive descriptions." Often, in an age when the productive capacity of the land stood as a crucial selling point, these boosters were not averse to imagining "desolate frontiers" as lands endowed with "agricultural advantages, and devoid of danger and privation."[18] In the case of Las Vegas, one has to hope that some lucky settlers brought enough money for a return trip home or at least enough to travel on to a climate more agreeable for agriculture.

The trend of casting Vegas as something of an agricultural utopia continued through the 1920s, although it adjusted somewhat with news of the massive dam project that was scheduled to begin just east of town in the Colorado River's Black Canyon. A 1924 chamber of commerce pamphlet devoted seven of its eleven pages to the valley's plentiful water, rich soil, and tremendous agricultural potential. The remaining four pages focused on the prospective dam project—which also received title-page placement—as well as important buildings and industry and mining operations. While the chamber used the word *wonderful* to describe the local climate, it seldom employed the term *desert*. Authors of the brochures limited such language to before-and-after illustrations intended to show the agricultural potential of the land. For example, the pamphlet described the "greater portion" of the area as being covered by "stretches of desert." The agricultural "possibilities" of these "stretches" could be easily "unlocked" through cultivation to provide bountiful harvests of whatever a person might want to plant. The pamphlet, featuring a grove of very large fig trees, then asked, "Look much like a desert to you?"[19]

The rationale behind downplaying the young city's arid climate resides in historical perceptions of the desert in American history. Americans have held strong and often varied beliefs about the desert environment. At various times, these perceptions of the desert have run from foreboding, overbearing, unconquerable, and suggestive of death to resource rich, escapist, transformable, and recreational.[20] The Judeo-Christian tradition has also defined the desert over time as a site of temptation and trial, often equating it with untamed wilderness.

Likewise, the Judeo-Christian tradition also promoted the idea that wilderness was wasteful and in need of transformation. Humans were thus tasked with taming the land and transforming the wasted wilderness into something pastoral and productive. One has only to look at the biblical accounts of the Hebrews after their escape from bondage in Egypt or of Jesus's temptation in the desert for early and influential examples of the stigmatization of desert.[21]

With such prevalent negative associations with the desert, early city boosters attempted to avoid casting the city's climate as arid, hot, or otherwise permanently desertlike. Instead, they partook of the contemporary trend of casting the environment as welcoming and promising. Their publications subsequently led one to believe that this land was ripe for transformation into the pastoral and productive. It needed only an adequate number of farmers to turn it into an agricultural wonderland.[22]

As Las Vegas began to sell itself in earnest to the rest of the nation as an entertainment destination in the post–World War II years, the chamber adjusted its representation of the city's desert climate. In 1948, as the valley's water supply was becoming more of a concern, a chamber publication titled "Story of Southern Nevada" no longer attempted to sell Las Vegas as an agricultural paradise. Although it contained a brief section on agriculture, it limited itself to highlighting a number of agricultural enterprises in the Moapa Valley. The only reference to Las Vegas in this section was a picture of a turkey ranch somewhere "near Las Vegas."[23]

As for direct references to the desert climate, the 1948 booklet displayed a tendency that became commonplace with the rise of the tourism-based economy. Throughout the piece, assertions of the dry climate's beneficial qualities counterbalanced its few fleeting references to the desert, which were also offset by references to the modern Hoover Dam and the cool Lake Mead. In one example, the booklet's climate section led off with a photo of an exotic-looking "shifting sand dune" that was said to be in the "Sun drenched Las Vegas valley" but that could have believably resided in the Sahara. The main text of the section made sure to highlight Las Vegas's "year 'round sunshine" unhampered by rain; it emphasized the cooling effect of "aridness." This plentiful sun and dry air could only result in "comfortable living."[24]

In 1947 the Union Pacific Railroad, along with other Las Vegas business leaders and influential citizens, decided that the city needed increased publicity in the hope of drawing more tourists to the area. That year famed publicist Steve Hannagan was hired to sell Las Vegas to the American public as a vacation destination. Hannagan, widely regarded as a promotional genius, had formerly headed publicity campaigns for Sun Valley, Idaho; Miami Beach, Florida; and the Indianapolis 500. With a staff of three photographers and four writers, he began to publicize Las Vegas in a variety of ways. One was to photograph out-of-town visitors entering local resorts and send those pictures—along with such captions as "Having a wonderful time in Las Vegas"—to the visitors' hometown newspapers. The idea was to create envy in the photographed person's neighbors by suggesting that Las Vegas was "the place to go."[25]

At the same time, under Hannagan's lead, the Las Vegas News Bureau, as it came to be known, stressed Las Vegas's proximity to a plethora of natural and man-made wonders. These included Lake Mead, Zion National Park, and Death Valley. Thus, the constant sun and warm climate became beneficial to the tourist who was interested in partaking of the area's natural wonders.[26] What boosters formerly viewed as a desert worthy of avoidance became one of the area's strongest selling points.

By 1954 at least some of the chamber's booster material ceased having special sections under the heading "Climate." In some, such as "Las Vegas, This Is Our City," the local aridity was used as a selling point for tourism. Under the "Vital Statistics" heading, a single paragraph addressed the city's desert climate. Primarily it stressed the 219 sunny and fifty partly cloudy days as opposed to only sixty-six days with predominant cloud cover. This was placed under an average low temperature of a warm 51.5 degrees Fahrenheit, 15 percent humidity, and less than 0.56 inches of rain for the entire year of 1956. All this combined, in the chamber of commerce's opinion, to make Las Vegas a choice destination for people who sought happiness in "sunshine and a mild, dry climate."[27]

Thus, historical context and prevailing attitudes toward the desert played an important role in the shifting the portrayal of Las Vegas to the outside world. In a society where agricultural productivity remained important to settlers, the arid, pre-tourism-oriented Las Vegas attempted to sell itself as a potential site of agriculture. While it was certainly misleading to cast Las Vegas soil as fertile, one should not be overly critical of the boosters' proclivity to play up the valley's water supply. The area had, after all, initially received attention because of its oasis-like springs. Regardless, attempts to sell Las Vegas as an agricultural wonderland took on less importance when the city's economy became more tourist oriented in the 1930s, '40s, and '50s. At that point, the desert became yet another eccentricity to sell to the vacationing American public. Thanks to almost-constant sun and lack of rain, its desolation became a commodity marketed right alongside the good times in the casino. In decades to come, however, increased environmental consciousness would lead some to question the idea of a resort city in the desert.

In recent years, Las Vegas's hyperarid climate has combined with its astonishing growth to create much anxiety over whether water limitations will ultimately constrain the city's growth. Much of this stems from the 1922 Water Pact or "law of the river," which allocates Colorado River water among southwestern states on a very unequal basis. Based on population and water needs at the time, southwestern states' portions of the 7.5 million acre-feet of Colorado River water is divided as follows: California gets 4.4 million acre-feet, Arizona gets 2.85 million, and Nevada gets 300,000.[28]

When this water allocation was drawn up, the young city of Las Vegas claimed only five thousand residents and had yet to earn its Sin City image. Yet by 1963, when the United States Supreme Court upheld southern California's primacy concerning Colorado River water allocation, Las Vegas had grown in both size and notoriety.[29] By this time, the city was known increasingly for the Rat Pack and for mob involvement in casinos. As the city grew and became more notorious, problems with its water supply became more evident. By the mid-1960s, the large springs on the city's west side that had once served as an oasis of sorts for westward travelers of the nineteenth century had dried up due to depletion of the local water table.[30] In the late 1980s, the ground in areas of Las Vegas began sinking slowly as the now-dry aquifers began to collapse and the metropolitan population approached one million. At that time, Patricia Mulroy, as head of the Las Vegas Valley Water District, laid claim to all the groundwater in the southern half of the state and proposed more than one thousand miles of pipeline to deliver it to southern Nevada. Most, if not all, ranchers and rural Nevadans balked at giving their water to the notorious self-interested city to the south. In the end, Mulroy gained her true objective of an additional allotment of almost three hundred thousand acre-feet by claiming Virgin River water, which also flowed into nearby Lake Mead.[31]

The issue of water relative to the future of Las Vegas created opposing viewpoints in the twentieth and early twenty-first centuries. Many felt that the city must eventually bow to nature's dictates. Some feel that Las Vegas is attempting to flout natural conditions as it has flouted social and cultural mores over the course of its history. A BBC story published in July 2005 offers a fine example of this viewpoint. The article portrayed Las Vegas as a "city of fantasy" that was quickly running out of water due to suburban growth, desert location, and insufficient conservation. Because of this pattern, city leaders eyed their northern neighbors' underground water. The BBC piece argued that because Vegas had been "flaunting its reputation for excess," even in the area of water use, the city was on the prowl for more water to feed its ravenous appetite. This time, as planning forecasters prophesized an increase of one million residents in the next few years, it did not seem to be a ploy to gain additional Colorado River water. Instead, the very real prospect of an Owens Valley–type water grab scared central Nevada ranchers into preparation for a water war divided along the lines of "crops versus craps."[32]

In intellectual circles, Las Vegas's water situation has combined with its image in order to create differing takes on the city's present and future environmental prospects. Well-known Las Vegas historian Hal Rothman, for example, sees Las Vegas's flamboyant use of water as merely an extension of the Las Vegas identity. Such things are what people expect from Vegas and thus contribute to the city's and the region's bottom line by giving the people what they want. Further, he argues that Las Vegas will not be the one to suffer from water scarcity. Instead, because of its cash-cow entertainment industry, Vegas will have the money to bring in the water from wherever that water might be. After all, in the American Southwest, water is a marketplace commodity, and "there is no shortage of money" in Las Vegas.[33] Rothman also points out that agriculture and ranching in central and northern Nevada are the real culprits in terms of wasting water. When looking at the return on the investment of water, for example, Rothman claims that Nevada's alfalfa farms are squandering a precious resource that could be put to more profitable use for the state. Las Vegas, after all, accounts for only 20 percent of the state's water use but produces over 90 percent of its jobs, income, and tax revenue.[34]

To an extent, Rothman's idea that water will make its way to Las Vegas as a result of economic power and efficiencies closely parallels that of Marc Reisner, a historian of water. Reisner, in his popular work *Cadillac Desert*, writes, "In the West . . . water flows uphill toward money."[35] But Reisner also cautions against the belief that wholesale reclamation and redistribution of scarce water resources is the end-all solution to maintaining the western development of arid lands. In the end, it is just too big of an undertaking, and water resources are simply too limited. Over the entire course of American settlement of the West, irrigation and reclamation have managed to "green" an area only about the size of Missouri. For the most part, nonrenewable stores of groundwater have supported most of this greening.[36] While that area of land is no pittance, to be sure, it pales in comparison to the arid West's vast geography. Las Vegas, however, is not the whole West, and as Rothman points out, it has the money and, increasingly, the political power to make things happen. Thus, although the commodity is limited and the potential demand great, those with the means will be able to obtain it. The rest of the West be damned.

This, too, is a discussion in which the image of the city plays an important role. For example, as rancher Cecil Garland sees it, the idea of Las Vegas's siphoning off rural areas' water in the name of urban development is merely as a question of "craps versus crops." His view of Las Vegas is of a city that lives beyond its environmental means and, in comparison to his rural Snake Valley community, is morally bankrupt. The choice of whether to allow Las Vegas to pump water from the Snake Valley is, in Garland's opinion, a question of whether "it is right to take water from a place that represents, is personified by cattle, children, church, and country and give it to a metropolis that is personified by glitter, gluttony, gambling, and girls."[37] Others such as Garland's wife believe that Las Vegas and its casinos should "live within their means" concerning water use.[38]

Such criticism of Las Vegas, colored both by the city's Sin City reputation and its desert locale, can also be found in more scholarly sources. Urban prognosticator Mike Davis, for example, sees much to condemn in Las Vegas's water usage as well as in most everything else about the city. Davis charges Las Vegas and cities like it with being wasteful blights on the world's landscape. He finds no redeeming value in the sprawling metropolis that was built upon the crass and overindulgent exploitation of peoples' weaknesses and scarce natural resources. Eventually, Las Vegas's flouting of very finite water resources must, in Davis's opinion, lead to the city's downfall. Because of its willful ignorance concerning the limitations of its natural environment, Las Vegas is already one of what Davis calls "dead cities." Davis goes so far in his condemnation of Las Vegas as to begin his section on the city by discussing the apt nature of Stephen King's *The Stand*, which depicts Las Vegas as the seat of an Antichrist-like figure, fit only for nuclear destruction.[39]

Perhaps Davis and other naysayers are right. Las Vegas might very well be headed for an environmental reckoning as it continues to live above its means in terms of water. It may very well be one of those societies that Ted Steinberg has identified as placing itself at increased risk of environmental disaster through its own disregard for environmental common sense.[40] Yet, in the sense of fairness, one should note Las Vegas's increased efficiency in water use and management over the last several decades. Today Las Vegas residents are among the nation's leaders in conservation of water. Nevertheless, Lake Mead's water level has continued to fall. By early 2017, the reservoir stood at a mere 40.1 percent capacity.[41]

Beyond the debate in academia over Las Vegas's future in regard to water or the lack thereof, the popular media has also frequently picked up on the extreme-desert climate of the city. Hollywood, for example, often highlights the desert setting and extreme heat of the Las Vegas valley. In one of the funnier instances, in 1997's National Lampoon's *Vegas Vacation*, Cousin Eddie (Randy Quaid), cooks a steak for Clark Griswold (Chevy Chase) by simply throwing it down on an exposed boulder outside the city limits. Later in the same film, Cousin Eddie again draws attention to the oppressive heat by telling Clark, after entering a casino, "It's a blazer out there today. Good to be in the air conditioning like God intended." Further, the desert city is consistently cast as a wayward center, distant from suburban family norms and defined by things such as gambling, stripping, and self-centered celebrities that all combine to endanger family life, albeit in hilariously entertaining ways.[42] Still, the message is that the desert locale is dangerous and deviant.

Regardless of whether Las Vegas is truly running out of water or whether its deep pockets might be able to finance the reach northward for more of the precious liquid when needed, the image of a water-starved Vegas is not what the town attempts to convey to the outside world. This is made obvious by the chamber of commerce's attempts to cast the town first as an agricultural wonderland in its earliest years and then as a climatically pleasant playground as the emphasis shifted to tourism. Yet the very fact that intellectuals, environmentalists, and popular media sources continue to debate the desert character of Las Vegas proves that the suspension of environmental reality has not been completely successful and that opposing views of desert identity remain strong in the twenty-first century.

The attempt to project Las Vegas as something other than a desert city does, however, reveal the importance that those with a stake in the town's success have placed on the intricacies of image. In a nation that is historically inclined to recoil at the mention of desert and to associate it with wasteland, one cannot doubt the motivations of those who would rather sell their city as semitropical or pleasantly sun drenched throughout most of the year. Ironically, the very desert location that boosters have shied away from has been a major contributor to the success of Las Vegas as an adult playground. While the previous examples of advertising campaigns reveal a booster-held belief that people might not want to visit or live in an uncomfortable place, the seeming remoteness of Las Vegas is what allows for its brand of fun. Las Vegas's desert location is distant enough from suburban living rooms to allow for a sense of detachment. This detachment, as David Schwartz has argued, allows for the existence of things that would not be acceptable in mainstream America.[43] Under the lights of Vegas, out over the mountains and across the desert, otherwise-upstanding people can do otherwise-unacceptable things with impunity. The idea of isolation has provided legitimacy and power to the slogan "What Happens Here, Stays Here" since its 2002 creation.[44] In turn, the distant location and the image of a place set apart provide the city with even greater continued success as an adult playground.

In this regard, Las Vegas makes use of a final characterization of the desert in American popular opinion. The desert as a place of escape has been a thread in its conceptualization in the United States throughout the latter half of the twentieth century. One can find evidence of this most obviously in the western genre of American film. The pursued, overburdened, or spurned protagonist heads into the desert to shake that which otherwise constrains or threatens to constrain him.[45] When viewed as a place in which to escape the equally overbearing norms of society, the desert becomes the perfect setting for a city such as Las Vegas.

Gambling and Sin, Las Vegas Style

Much like Birmingham and its association with the racial violence of the 1960s, seemingly abnormal events and characteristics in Las Vegas's history have influenced the national media's coverage and the public's perception of the city. The young desert city, after its initial incarnation as a railway stopover, first claimed notoriety in its early years as a divorce center. From there, it went on to be known for the mafia's involvement in its major industry, gambling, as well as its risqué sexuality, and it was ultimately known as Sin City. Recently Las Vegas has maintained its Sin City reputation while also managing to cultivate an image as a center of world-class entertainment.

Las Vegas's entrance into the divorce industry received notice early on. In 1911 the *New York Times* printed two articles dealing with the young town's arrival on the divorce scene. *Times* writers portrayed the railroad town as an impending rival to Reno's virtual monopoly on granting the nation's easy divorces.[46] Between this first mention in 1911 and the end of World War II, Las Vegas made quite a name for itself vis-á-vis the divorce and marriage industry. Most of this notoriety resulted from the matrimonial difficulties and adventures of Hollywood celebrities that were carried out in Vegas. During this period, there were no fewer than eighty feature pieces in the *Times* dealing with the marital woes of such stars as Edgar Rice Burroughs, Clark Gable, John Hearst, Lana Turner, and Mickey Rooney among others.[47]

Often the prospective divorcés would travel to Las Vegas and stay at a divorce ranch while the required six-week residency period passed. One such ranch, Twin Springs, offered the matrimonially challenged a wide array of recreational pursuits to help pass the time. If uninterested in heading the two miles into town, those awaiting divorce could spend their days horseback riding, swimming, playing their favorite games in recreational lounges, fishing, or just generally relaxing.[48] Other stars such as Oliver Hardy took the utmost advantage of Las Vegas's matrimonial industry, getting divorced one morning and getting married that same afternoon at his attorney's home.[49]

In the early 1930s the legalization of gambling in Nevada, the improvement of access roads, and the nearby construction of Hoover Dam further heightened the town's prospects. As the dam became a destination for curious travelers, Las Vegans embraced the idea of a gaming-centered economy. World War II soldiers and defense workers then reinforced the logic of this idea through their eager patronization of the town's still-small gaming emporiums.[50] City leaders and businesspeople subsequently employed various themes to draw tourists to Las Vegas hotels and legal casinos over the following decades. These ranged from the idea of America's last frontier to atomic testing to an almost-simultaneous promotion of the city as both a Sin City and a family-friendly adult Disneyland.

Examples of locals promoting the western frontier image of the city in 1930s, '40s, and '50s abound. From the inauguration of the annual Helldorado Day Parade in 1935 to the names, decor, and marketing of such early resorts as Thomas Hull's El Rancho (1941) and R. E. Griffith's New Frontier (1942), western themes seemed to be everywhere.[51] Even the menus at El Rancho's café in the 1940s highlighted the western theme. A buxom cowgirl sporting shorts and a cowboy hat graced the menu's cover. Inside, cowboy and western artwork accompanied such listings as the El Rancho prime rib dinner for two dollars and ended with "You're Welcome Podner!"[52]

The local chamber of commerce contributed heavily to the ubiquitous nature of Las Vegas's western image through its publications. Its "History of Nevada" in 1953 prominently featured the winking Vegas Vic cowboy sign on its cover, albeit missing the "Howdy Podner!" caption so often associated with it.[53] Beginning in 1947 the always-image-conscious chamber hired the West-Marquis Advertising Agency to shape the image of the city that was projected to the rest of the nation. By focusing on Los Angeles and the Pacific Coast in selective national advertisements that suggested including a stop by Las Vegas in any western trip, the agency exposed approximately fifty million readers per year to Las Vegas's

western resort characteristics in the late 1940s.[54] By 1948 the chamber's "Story
of Southern Nevada," for example, included a cowboy on horseback among
other artistic renditions of defining places such as Hoover Dam, Fremont Street
casinos, and an airplane. Inside, readers found information about the "frontier
atmosphere" of Helldorado accompanied by pictures of a cowboy on a bucking
bull and an "Indian chief" in full headdress.[55] The chamber continued with this
theme into the 1950s, as evidenced by its "Las Vegas: This Is Our City" brochure.
A cowboy on horseback and a covered wagon dominated an aerial view of the
city on this publication's cover. Inside, the chamber greeted the reader with the
slogan "Howdy Podner!" before relating how Las Vegas residents "reflect the true
hospitality and decency of the West." Prospective visitors were then welcomed
wholeheartedly to this "frontier city." In case the reader might have difficulty
finding local points of interest, the chamber also included a two-page artistic
map featuring the heading "The Las Vegas Area, Wonderland of the West" and
once again employing Vegas Vic and his "Howdy Podner!" No fewer than six
depictions of cowboys and their horses in various Old West poses graced the
map's pages. Yet, alongside this western frontier portrayal, the chamber also
provided an early characterization of Las Vegas as "the entertainment capital
of the world."[56]

Travel brochures and flyers throughout the 1950s continued to feature Vegas
Vic and the "Howdy Podner!" slogan and emphasized Las Vegas's ties to the
West.[57] Yet, in the 1960s, the city had obviously moved away from the cowboy-
and western-themed promotions. By the middle of the decade, travel brochures
promoting local motels featured only one small Vegas Vic image beside the phrase
"relax in comfort." Further deemphasizing the rugged aspects of the frontier
and the western environment, the brochures stressed "lavish accommodations,"
"gourmet" restaurants, and room service in the "world's largest" conglomeration
of motels. At decade's end, brochures promoted Las Vegas as a "motel holiday"
value where tourists could "enjoy a million dollars-worth of fun for a low, low
cost." In the place of Vegas Vic and the "Howdy Podner!" slogan, scantily clad
showgirls and a brightly burning sun beckoned visitors with claims of having
the "nation's finest motels."[58]

This focus on the West and the frontier again tapped into a deeply held belief
among Americans. Certainly since at least the 1890s, many Americans saw the
western frontier as the basis of their perceived exceptionalism. As Frederick Jackson
Turner had summed up in his famed essay "The Significance of the Frontier in
American History," many believed that the very essence of Americanness was

created by the interaction of successive generations of Americans with a frontier of free land. The so-called Frontier Thesis argued that the process of going west and its requirement of carving out an existence from the wilderness time and again had transformed Americans into an independent, individualistic, democratic-minded people.[59] The frontier was wild and dangerous, but it created freedom. Most of all, to twentieth-century Americans, the frontier was America. In this regard, Las Vegans attempted to shape their city's image to fit within Americans' expectations. At the same time, the frontier theme allowed for more rowdy and risqué behavior than could exist in more settled and refined locations.

As for the popular appeal of this center of gambling and sin on the frontier, David Schwartz and John Findlay offer insightful explanations. Schwartz argues that postwar suburban Americans did not mind gambling or a certain freedom of morality if it was safely confined to areas distant from their own communities. At a safe distance—out on the frontier—suburbanites could enjoy escapist and otherwise-deviant pleasures and then return home without endangering their communities' moral standards.[60] Findlay contends that Las Vegas offered much more than mere escapism; its gambling, even without the in-your-face frontier messaging, brought forth the American perceptions of risk and opportunity that were central to the western frontier identity. To Findlay, Las Vegas also embodied a new and innovative western society that was emanating from southern California in the postwar period. Gambling, and by association Las Vegas, offered modern Americans the thrill of chance that was so central to the westward expansion of the nineteenth century. This chance further nurtured ideas of democracy and egalitarian tendencies.[61] Social standing alone did not determine the odds of winning or losing at the tables. Yet one should note that while Americans might have been influenced by those deep-seated frontier-influenced proclivities, Las Vegas largely turned away from promoting itself as a western frontier town by the 1960s.

During the immediate post–World War II period, media representations of Las Vegas reflected this loaded identity. During the 1950s, *New York Times* reporter Gladwin Hill used his typewriter as a virtual megaphone for Las Vegas boosters. Throughout the decade, Hill offered up a steady dose of such articles as "Klondike in the Desert," "The 'Sure Thing' Boom at Las Vegas," "Las Vegas is More Than the 'Strip,'" and "Las Vegas Keeps the Wheels Turning." Each of these pieces, while acknowledging the centrality of gambling to the Las Vegas experience, cast the tourist town in an unusually favorable light. Hill consistently championed both the city's democratic opportunity and its western placement while offering up a selection of population and economic-growth statistics that any chamber of commerce publicist would proudly claim. Las Vegas, as portrayed by Hill, resembled a "cruise ship" on land where gambling and tourism served as economic motors driving a booming and surprisingly diverse urban area. In this exciting place "that could pass for Broadway," both the "man in workpants" and the "dinner dressed patron" had the same chance of realizing that "western tradition" of striking it rich. Beyond the gaming floors, a more diverse Las Vegas existed. Hill expounded the favorable influence of religion, the industrial boom of Henderson, and the windfall of defense spending. Quite simply, Hill's Las Vegas stood as a western entertainment center basking in a post–World War II boom. This Las Vegas was a place where a more democratic spirit prevailed, people had fun, and a real estate investment could never be a losing proposition. It seemed to be a place where people got it right.[62]

The attempt to sell Las Vegas as a western frontier setting had been successful. Local promoters gained attention, received favorable press, and drew in visitors. In the process, Las Vegas became well known as a tourist destination in the 1940s and '50s. By 1955 approximately eight million people visited Las Vegas each year. Even Ronald Reagan got in on the action, agreeing to headline a show at the Last Frontier Casino.[63] Although Reagan's show was a bust and closed after two weeks, the promotion was a success, selling Las Vegas as a western frontier where people could experience freedom, fun, and sun. Las Vegas had emerged as a tourist destination, and tourism had firmly entrenched itself as the foundation of the local economy.

However, as the reality of a tourist-based economy surpassed all expectations, Las Vegas began to experience problems related to its image. Soon, government officials and intellectuals were providing counterarguments to the boosters' sales pitches and Hill's articles. First, while Las Vegas's frontier freedoms attracted tourists, they also seemed to attract disreputable individuals. The city's reputation as a wide-open gambling center proved too tempting for organized crime. Second, whereas its identification with the frontier in the first half of the twentieth century was American to the core, the city's post-1950s promotion of legalized gambling, physical gratification, and vice increasingly fell outside the boundaries of America's moral norms in the second half of the century. As Las Vegas increasingly turned away from the frontier image in favor of the Sin City image, it experienced great success but also opened itself to a number of negative consequences.[64]

Tourists try their luck at one of the Sands Casino's roulette tables, 1960s.
University of Nevada, Las Vegas, Dickinson Library, Special Collections.

Gambling and organized crime became favorite topics for the national media in shaping Las Vegas's image in American minds. Between 1945 and 1949, the *New York Times* had begun placing more emphasis on Las Vegas as a tourist draw, although often only in connection to Hoover Dam. Representative titles included "Las Vegas Vacation Center: Seeing Boulder Dam by Automobile" and "Lively Las Vegas: New Vacation Wonderland is Growing Up Rapidly around the Great Lake at Hoover Dam."[65] One 1947 article, "Desert Attractions: Tourism Is Las Vegas' Major Industry and Spring Business Is Booming," marked the first instance of the national media's acknowledgment of the city as a tourist destination in its own right.[66]

Each article from this period, despite highlighting attractions other than casinos, invariably acknowledged the city's legalized gambling. *Times* reporter Ward Howe characterized the city as "the gateway to Boulder Dam" and a place where "neon signs lend a garish effect and signal invitations to try one's luck."[67] Jack Goodman used the first two paragraphs of his article to detail the growth

Showgirls at Dunes Hotel, late 1950s.
University of Nevada, Las Vegas, Dickinson Library, Special Collections.

of local gaming resorts before stipulating that "not all vacationists are heading for the gambling casinos."[68] Fellow reporter Grady Johnson introduced the city as being "known only for its legalized gambling and easy divorce laws" before noting its low rate of juvenile delinquency as well as the outdoor recreational activities at Mount Charleston and Lake Mead.[69]

Explicit ties to preexisting regional conceptions of the West also appeared in each of these early articles. Howe reaffirmed the locals' propensity to call the city "a frontier town" while he characterized it as a "gateway" and "picturesque desert town."[70] Goodman emphasized both its "desert" location and its proximity to "many noteworthy western park areas." A photograph of men dressed as cowboys and riding horses at a nearby dude ranch accompanied his article.[71] Johnson's article called attention to the West as a place of recreation with a dry climate and democratic tendencies. To him, Las Vegas resided "in the heart of some of the West's most scenic playgrounds" where visitors could "soak up sun and breathe the dry desert air." It was also a place where individuals in "dinner jackets, cowboy shirts, and jeans" mingled on the same dance floors without notice.[72] These articles conformed to a pattern of showcasing Las Vegas's exceptionalism, which was symbolized by gambling, western isolation, democratic social activities, and liberal sense of morality. Americans' perceptions of the West and the association of Las Vegas with western regional characteristics tended to soften Las Vegas's image as a gambling center at this early point.

The portrayal of Las Vegas as a bastion of organized crime began to have a more soundly negative impact during the late 1940s. Organized crime had undeniably played a role in Las Vegas's development, history, and popular image. It first reared its head in 1945 with the murder of James Ragen, who owned a race wire service, and the efforts of known gangster Bugsy Siegel to purchase the El Cortez casino. These incidents, along with the construction of the Flamingo Hotel, established a pattern in which, over the next two decades, many resorts on the Strip depended upon disreputable financing and direct mob involvement for their construction and operation.[73] In 1950 the Kefauver hearings into organized crime brought increased, albeit limited, national attention to organized crime's infiltration of the city's gaming industry. On November 16, 1950, the *New York Times* printed a small story titled "Investigation in Nevada," which was the only story to appear in the *Times* that year specifically addressing Senator Kefauver's local hearings into the influence that organized crime held over the Las Vegas gaming industry. The article did, nonetheless, tie the gaming industry to the late gangster Bugsy Siegel and to mob figures in New York.[74]

Thirteen years later, the *New York Times* made up for its subdued treatment of the Kefauver hearing. In November 1963—the same year that Birmingham became front-page news and the lead story on television networks—the *Times* ran a series of front-page stories exposing organized crime's control of the Las Vegas gaming industry. In the first of these articles, reporter Wallace Turner wrote of casinos run by convicted felons that were misusing "hundreds of millions of dollars." Further, he labeled the gambling-fueled mob as a powerful "new force in American life."[75] In the third article of the series, he credited Las Vegas with

bringing together a "greater collection of skilled law violators than exists anywhere in the country." He went on to detail the involvement of such public
personalities as Frank Sinatra and Dean Martin in gambling interests, implying their association with organized crime. Yet even Turner's indictment of Las
Vegas as a criminal haven could not resist linking the city to its isolated western placement. The "desert and mountain milieu" served as the setting for this,
the "most intensive concentration of gambling" ever to appear in the world's
history.[76]

Extensive exposure of the city's organized crime problem also appeared in
other media outlets during this period. National best sellers such as Ed Reid and
Ovis Demaris's *Green Felt Jungle* appeared along with a variety of newspaper
articles, which cast Las Vegas as a violent, greedy, immoral, and crime-infested
city.[77] Fred J. Cook, however, beat Reid and Demaris to the punch by publishing
A Two-Dollar Bet Means Murder two years earlier. In this book, based on his
1960 article "Gambling, Inc.," which ran in the *Nation*, Cook devoted a whole
chapter to the mafia's "golden paradise" of Las Vegas.[78]

Television exposés further linked the city's vice-centered gaming and entertainment industry with organized crime. David Susskind's popular television
talk show, *Open End*, aired a two-hour special on March 15, 1964, that sought
to detail "the link between a seemingly innocuous nickel bet and narcotics and
prostitution," all enterprises that were controlled by organized crime.[79] Two
years later NBC televised a three-and-a-half-hour special titled "American White
Paper: Organized Crime in the United States," which examined organized crime
in both Las Vegas and Youngstown, Ohio. In the end, it argued that while local
interests controlled the crime in Youngstown, Las Vegas's gambling industry
fostered more insidious national affiliations.[80]

One can view this dramatic upswing in media coverage of Las Vegas's ties to
organized crime as the culmination of a wider historical trend in which the United
States public sought to create an identity and national purpose for itself in the
1950s and early '60s. By the end of the 1950s, the American press, the government,
and the public had begun to question the nation's success and its direction in the
Cold War struggle with the Soviet Union. International events had seemingly
eroded the U.S. public's unquestioned confidence in world leadership in 1945.
The Soviet Union's emergence as a nuclear power in 1949, its successful launch
of Sputnik in 1957, and its economic growth rate that seemingly outstripped
that of the United States in the mid-1950s along with the disastrous Suez Crisis,
the failure to help in the Hungarian Revolution, and the U-2 spy plane incident

all combined to create uncertainty in many Americans. Occasional economic downturns during the Eisenhower years strengthened the idea that something had gone wrong. Led by the press and the government, some Americans began to look inward for the cause of this seeming deficiency. Corruption, conformism, and crass materialism were central to the conclusions they reached.[81]

As early as 1952, Dwight Eisenhower's presidential campaign revealed this uncertainty within American consciousness over the moral centering of the nation. Eisenhower constantly cast the campaign as a "crusade" to bring the nation back "to the things he thought America stood for."[82] Even his campaign slogan, K1C2 (standing for Korea, Communism, and corruption), emphasized the threats America faced and the waywardness of its culture.[83] Concerns over internal weakness, corruption, and Communist infiltration obsessed the nation. The House Un-American Activities Committee (HUAC) had been exposing imagined Communists with impunity while such popular game shows as *The $64,000 Question* proved to be dishonest. Meanwhile, consumerism had taken hold as suburbanites enjoyed their increased personal wealth and buying power during the immediate post-1945 period.[84] Some contemporaries such as John Kenneth Galbraith in his 1958 best seller *The Affluent Society* warned about the excesses of consumerism and private-sector wealth while highlighting the persistence of public-sector poverty in America.[85] Countervailing forces of traditional morality and hedonistic materialism thus fought for the American public's allegiance throughout the 1950s and early '60s.

From this cultural unease, Las Vegas emerged as an easy target for those frustrated by the nation's drift. With the media's help, as evidenced by its increased concentration on organized crime in the early 1960s, Las Vegas became a perceptual repository for the containment of widespread corruption and materialistic shortcomings in America. Obviously, such opinions have not been universal, as America is far from monolithic in culture and ideas. For example, in the 1950s and early '60s, while churchgoers in the South might have displayed a real problem with the organized crime and gambling of Las Vegas, churches in the Northeast held "Las Vegas Nights" that celebrated the exotic character of the city.[86] Yet the city, much like Birmingham, became a deviant example, at least to some portions of the nation, against which they could define their moral center.

Interestingly, Las Vegas also possessed similarities to Birmingham in terms of its deviance in race relations. Nevada had, as a result, been nicknamed the "Mississippi of the West." African Americans in Las Vegas, like their counterparts in Birmingham, certainly experienced widespread discrimination. By midcentury,

Las Vegas, Nevada, April 13, 1964. Tourists Explore "Glitter Gulch."
Photograph by John T. Bledsoe. Library of Congress, Prints and Photographs Division, U.S. News & World Report Magazine Collection, LC-DIG-ppmsca-41621.

local resorts considered hiring them only for the lowest-paying and most menial jobs. African Americans were barred from staying in hotels and at various resorts. Even famous African American performers were forced to find alternative lodging when performing at Las Vegas casinos and resorts. They also had to use segregated facilities, could live and start businesses only in a certain area of town, faced segregated services, and dealt with various other forms of discrimination.[87]

Yet Las Vegas was not ostracized because of its racism and discrimination. There are several possible reasons for this. Its association with the West rather than the South likely buffered its characterization as a racist place. In this regard, Las Vegas benefited from the fact that the West represented freedom, independence, individualistic personal advancement, and other supposedly democratic characteristics that were mythically associated with the frontier. The city's initial promotion of the frontier image along with its reputation as a place of chance and opportunity strengthened its association with the West. Birmingham, by contrast, was burdened by both its own racism and the popular historical image of the South as the most racist region of the nation. Whereas Vegas and the West offered opportunity, Birmingham and the South offered oppression.

Las Vegas also offered the opportunity to escape the stifling conformity of the 1950s and early '60s. Again, as a wild and open representative of the American West, it served as an available democratic and individualist counterbalance for the perceived tendency of suburbia and conformist society to emasculate formerly individualistic men.[88] As William Whyte observed in 1956, the conformist impulse of postwar suburban society worked to transform men from independent "inner-directed" beings into "other-directed" grey-suited clones of corporatism.[89] Las Vegas offered a convenient yet isolated escape from these consensus norms if they became too overbearing.

Media coverage of events in Las Vegas during the last three decades of the twentieth century continued to draw upon the reputation for deviance and risqué behavior that had been established at midcentury. By this time, local boosters' efforts to equate Las Vegas with the frontier West had largely disappeared, and along with such marketing campaigns went the buffering that such an association afforded the city. During the 1970s, showgirls, gambling, and organized crime, for example, were less frequently equated to frontier freedom and more often portrayed as simply unsavory, seedy, or gaudy. Las Vegas was increasingly just Sin City without the romantic illusions of the Old West.

Media accounts in the 1970s often portrayed Las Vegas as having lost much of the edgy coolness of the old gangster-controlled days. Ownership of local casinos changed markedly following a 1967 act that allowed corporations to own gambling establishments. Before this, only individuals had been allowed to own them. With this opening of ownership, corporate interests quickly rushed in. By the early 1970s, the Howard Hughes Corporation, Del Webb, Hilton, Lum's, Texas International Airlines, and Continental Airlines had all bought interests in Las Vegas casinos. With the corporate buy up, there was a change in the operation of the casinos and in the Las Vegas experience. The act of gambling became a bit more sanitized. No longer was cheating controlled by the hoodlums of the old days. Instead, the police and casino security handled matters legally. This led one casino security chief to somewhat nostalgically state that while he didn't necessarily wish to go back to the mob days, "You do find yourself thinking about how simple it would be to grab up one of these guys an beat [the cheating] out of him." Vegas, it seems, had lost a little of its swagger.[90]

In one early-seventies travel article, *New York Times* reporter Paul J. C. Friedlander set out to explore Las Vegas beyond the Strip. Over the course of several days, Friedlander spent time with a wide variety of locals ranging from churchgoers to a showgirl. He wrote of being surprised to find the latter "intelligent"

Showgirls as part of *Minsky's Follies*, 1960s.
University of Nevada, Las Vegas, Dickinson Library, Special Collections.

and, along with other Las Vegans, living an "ordinary, unexciting, simple, and sometimes happily married" life in what he knew to be a "degraded and degrading city, over devoted to the pleasures of gambling and the flesh."[91]

Such portrayals of Las Vegas could even be found in music reviews and articles about sporting events. In one particularly negative *New York Times* review, Don Heckman charged that Elvis Presley had lost his "punch" and "gutsy vitality." Heckman reasoned that perhaps Las Vegas had "gotten to" the once rocking and edgy superstar and transformed him into a "crooner." The city had, as he pointed out, been one of the singer's principal locations for the last several years.[92] Likewise, an article on George Foreman's boxing match against Ron Lyle in

1976 was less than kind to the city. The article's author, Red Smith, described the fight's location, Caesar's Palace, as merely a "gaudy gambling joint where the waitresses wear togas."[93]

Likewise, the media's continued relation of Las Vegas to organized crime during this era lost any romantic illusion that had existed in the past. Instead, such coverage relied primarily on the city's tainted reputation and organized crime's involvement in violent and costly activities. In one example of event-driven association, the front page of the February 24, 1980, *New York Times* featured an article on the federal investigation into organized crime. Through secret recordings and undercover work, the FBI had uncovered widespread racketeering, union corruption, murder, bribery of elected officials, and skimming of Las Vegas casino revenues by organized crime figures with ties to Kansas City. This article and others that followed made much of the Las Vegas connection even though, by that time, large corporations had taken over much of the gaming industry.[94] More important, the articles treated the mafia's involvement in the gaming industry as no surprise. One revealing passage stated, "In recent years . . . organized crime has infiltrated a variety of businesses in addition to gambling and pornography."[95] In other words, the only surprise was that organized crime had spread beyond the realm of Las Vegas's acknowledged vices into more seedy activities. As Hal Rothman later wrote, Las Vegas of the 1970s and early '80s faced the threat of being stigmatized as the "sleazy home of tawdry sex and mobsters."[96]

As the 1980s wore on, the national news media continued to associate Las Vegas with organized crime. Articles include 1986's "Busting the Mob" in *U.S. News & World Report*, which asserted ties between the mafia and Las Vegas merely because "racketeers" had purchased travel agencies that booked trips to the city.[97] The same issue's cover story, "Mafia, U.S.A.," listed Las Vegas as the fourth-most-active mob center in the United States. The story gave no real explanation as to why the city deserved such a high ranking.[98]

In addition to the reminders of Las Vegas's mafia associations, a fire at the MGM Grand Hotel on November 21, 1980, offers an example of how established media stereotypes of deviance often extend beyond the boundaries of events that are directly associated with perceived abnormalities. The *New York Times'* initial coverage of the fire proved straightforward and factual. A front-page article by Pamela Hollie respectfully conveyed the tragic circumstances of the fire that left more than eighty people dead and approximately thirty-five hundred trapped for several hours.[99] But the next day an article appeared that employed virtually every available stereotype of the city. Reporter John Crewdson detailed how the

greed of gambling and the desire for a good time quelled any remorse for the
fire's victims. He focused his story on individuals occupying the casinos around
the new "black gap in a brilliant neon universe." Citing individual reactions as
somehow representative of the city's values as a whole, Crewdson wrote of a man
at the Desert Inn Casino placing a ten-dollar bet with his friend over the fire's
eventual body count. The article further stated that tragedy was meaningless
to a city that experienced "a thousand tiny personal ones" on a daily basis.
The reporter ended his assault by questioning the morality of locals who had
continued gambling as the fire raged. Quite simply, he applied the time-honored
one-dimensional stereotype of the city's gambling and sinful deviance to a
horrible event that had no direct connection to gaming.[100]

Despite such observations on Las Vegas's characteristics, the city was on
the verge of a major transformation by the 1980s. Such a transformation had
been made possible by the allowance of corporate ownership of casinos over a
decade earlier. The new Las Vegas would blend the risqué gambling and sex of
the old Vegas with over-the-top extravagance. No longer just a gambling center,
it would become a premier resort center with world-class entertainment, food,
and shopping as well as a variety of activities. It would offer something for
everyone—from individual gamblers to family vacationers.

7

Mainstream Currents

Las Vegas and Respectability at the
Turn the of the Twenty-First Century

When *Time* magazine proclaimed Las Vegas the "New All-American city"
in 1994, it was not celebrated or dwelled upon by the local community
to the same degree that the "All-America City" title had been in Birmingham
twenty-four years earlier.[1] Las Vegas had, by this time, embraced a more resort-
oriented and, to a limited degree, family-friendly persona. Because of this new
image, along with rapid population growth, the city exhibited commonalities
with other American cities. This included taking part in wider demographic
patterns such as southwestern or Sunbelt population growth in the postwar
decades, expanding services, becoming corporatized, and mainstreaming business practices in regard to the dominant gambling and entertainment industries.
As a result, Las Vegas eventually became more normalized, complete with huge
master-planned suburban communities and more family-oriented residents.[2]
Yet to say that Las Vegans wholeheartedly embraced the idea of becoming Main
Street U.S.A. is far from accurate.[3] Although its suburban population boomed,
corporate gaming-backed megaresorts blossomed, and leaders of industry and
boosters sought to cast the city as encompassing more than gambling, the city
never fully relinquished its edgy, adult-themed identity.[4] Instead, by the early
2000s, Las Vegas had turned decidedly and purposefully away from "normal"
America as its boosters and advertising campaigns adopted slogans that success-

Night, aerial view, Las Vegas, Nevada, July 9, 2009.
*Photography by Carol M. Highsmith. Library of Congress, Prints and
Photographs Division, LC-DIG-highsm-04649.*

fully employed and even boasted of Las Vegas's perceptual placement outside the norms of supposed mainstream American values.[5] Las Vegas gained back its edge in a grand fashion.

The only problem was that while advertising slogans informed tourists that whatever illicit behavior they indulged in while in Vegas would "stay in Vegas," thousands of new residents who had recently flocked to the booming city had actually stayed there permanently.[6] All too often, their needs and their vision of what a home should be diverged from what the city tried to sell tourists. Yet the local economy and the residents' jobs, either directly or indirectly, depended on the successful dissemination of the Sin City image. City leaders and boosters also sought to place Las Vegas among the top tier of American cities through such means as the procurement of major-league professional sports franchises while simultaneously continuing to trumpet the city's risqué image. Initially, the Sin City reputation proved to be a significant (though not insurmountable) roadblock along the city's path to obtaining such mainstream markers of success.[7] Thus, Las Vegas's population at the turn of the twenty-first century found itself pulled in multiple directions concerning the city's reputation and the image it projected to the outside world.

As with Birmingham and its racist image after 1963, Las Vegas's image rests on small portions of the metropolis's total geography. Overwhelmingly the image of Las Vegas comes from two distinct places within the larger metropolitan area. Early on, Fremont Street, or the old "Glitter Gulch" of downtown Las Vegas, informed the nation's image of the city. Then, after this image had been established, the resorts and eventually megaresorts of the Strip, or Las Vegas Boulevard, built on the existing image and became the second major symbol of Las Vegas's visual identity. Despite being located outside the city limits, the Strip is constantly erroneously referred to as Las Vegas. South of Sahara Avenue, it is actually in unincorporated Clark County. Thus, a modern urban area of approximately two million people is identified by the narrow image of two local corridors. The perceptual geography of Las Vegas can also be said to vary chronologically. Depending upon their ages and the eras they have experienced, some people might limit their idea of authentic Las Vegas to the downtown Fremont Street area, gambling, and organized crime. To a younger set, however, the Strip and its glitzy entertainment and shopping (viewed by the proponents of the downtown image as pure artifice) might symbolize the real Las Vegas.

Local Tension over Image

The year was 1999 and *Las Vegas Review-Journal* editorial staff did not want famed defense attorney Oscar Goodman to occupy the mayor's office of the paper's storied city. An editorial with its headline proclaiming "Anybody but Oscar" warned that the election of the outspoken attorney, who was widely characterized as a mob lawyer and former legal counsel to such figures as the notorious Anthony Spilotro and bookmaker and alleged mob front man Frank "Lefty" Rosenthal, might irrevocably damage recent efforts to recast Las Vegas as a more family-friendly or entertainment-themed resort.[8] This was a new Las Vegas after all, a place where, as NBC correspondent Kelly O'Donnell exclaimed, "image matters!" It was a town where, for at least some movers and shakers, the production of a more mainstream image seemingly bore great importance.[9] To a degree, their fears were correct. Goodman's candidacy and eventual election certainly drew attention to the city's unsavory past. That is not to say, however, that they were correct in arguing that such attention hurt Las Vegas.

In his career as an attorney, Goodman had made a name for himself defending infamous clients. He was, as a result, often characterized as a mob lawyer. He had even portrayed himself as such in Martin Scorsese's classic mob film *Casino*. As his June 8, 1999, runoff election victory played out, the *New York*

Times could not resist highlighting his past and the city's history of criminal association. Storylines such as "A Colorful Lawyer Is Running for Mayor" and "Mob Lawyer Wins Race" indicated the direction of the *Times'* coverage.[10] Each of these articles and others covering the event specifically listed Goodman's past defense of Las Vegas gangsters. Reporter Todd Purdum went so far as to offer detailed descriptions of how Goodman had kept Spilotro out of Las Vegas jails "despite accusations that he had killed 22 people." Purdum also wrote of Las Vegas's stigmatized image directly, calling it a "sin-soaked city, which has worked hard in recent years to reinvent itself as a family friendly resort in which mob rule is a distant memory."[11] Neither he nor his fellow reporters displayed any qualms about playing up Goodman's relationship with that distant memory.

By the time of Goodman's election, Las Vegas's stigmatization as an abnormal city was fully formed and had been for decades. At the same time, the city had grown tremendously and displayed huge increases in visitation. Between 1970 and 2000, the city's annual visitation rate had grown from 6,787,650 to 35,849,691. Annual visitation had declined only during the national recession of 1981–82.[12] By the end of the twentieth century, tourists and new residents were flocking to Las Vegas like never before.

Las Vegas's late-century upsurge in tourism, and ultimately in population, had deep historical roots, although it was commonly attributed to Steve Wynn's opening of the Mirage. Casino interests had long attempted to make their establishments more widely appealing. The Hacienda's owners Doc and Judy Bayley, for example, had sought family tourists from the time of resort's opening in 1957. Their child-friendly resort featured multiple swimming pools and a $17,000 go-cart track to entertain the kids while mom or dad enjoyed the casino.[13] Likewise, William Bennett and William Pennington had purchased and transformed Circus Circus in 1974 to cater to family visitors. By offering carnival-like entertainment for children, Bennett and Pennington gave children something to do while their parents gambled, making the hotel more attractive to adults. As historian Eugene Moehring has pointed out, many other casinos followed Circus Circus's lead in the 1970s and '80s in acknowledging the market of family visitors. Some, like the Las Vegas Hilton, went so far as to provide a special "children's hotel."[14]

One can readily observe this gradual shift through coverage of the city in airline flight magazine advertisements. Throughout the 1970s until about 1981, advertisements for Las Vegas casinos in Western Airlines' *Western World* magazine invariably featured scantily clad women and, at times, showgirls posed

Downtown "Fremont Street Experience" light show, Las Vegas, Nevada, ca. 1980–2006.
Photograph by Carol M. Highsmith. Library of Congress, Prints and Photographs Division, LC-HS503-832.

around obvious phallic symbols. The Dunes Hotel made the most of this suggestive visual art with the frequent employment of its famed and interestingly shaped sign, which was always adorned by the most beautiful nearly naked showgirls.[15] Yet a distinct shift occurred in the early 1980s. Beginning around 1982, advertisers toned down the suggestive images and slogans they employed. In the place of buxom women and showgirls, they stressed such things as hotel amenities, values, and shopping.[16]

In 1989 Wynn turbocharged this trend with the opening of the Mirage. A spectacle complete with regularly erupting volcano, white tigers, magicians, and dolphins, the Mirage symbolized what Wynn referred to as the "New Las Vegas."[17] This version of Las Vegas was more family friendly, eventually including such special attractions as a pirate show outside Treasure Island (1993), the medieval themes of the Excalibur (1990), an amusement park at the MGM Grand (1993), thrill rides on top of the Stratosphere (1996), and a full-scale roller coaster weaving around New York, New York (1996). The news media and tourist-industry publications often characterized this trend toward resort expansion as a desire to recast the city as a family destination. Such phrases as *family theme park*, *family experience*, and *family vacationers* figured prominently in travel industry accounts of Las Vegas's 1990s transformation. Likewise, popular television news shows informed the public of Las Vegas's new "mainstream" and "family" orientation.[18] Nevertheless, this was not simply an attempt to recast Las Vegas as a family destination. Instead, as Convention and Visitor's Authority president Manny Cortez related in 1993, the "goal" was to market Las Vegas as "a multifaceted resort destination." Cortez and others such as Wynn felt that this expansion beyond a mere gambling destination would help Las Vegas compete in a world that was becoming far more populated with gambling destinations.[19]

The way to compete, it seemed, was to offer the public a broad range of resort activities in an extravagant setting in addition to the gaming that everyone expected. The $630 million Mirage—costing a full $500 million more than any previous Las Vegas hotel and casino—kicked off this over-the-top resort cycle. World-class dining, shopping, and entertainment became the norm at new and increasingly expensive Strip resorts. Within ten years, the $2.1 billion Bellagio upped the ante yet again with its spectacular man-made lake and fountain show that flouted the city's desert setting. Still, for all their size and variety, these new resorts retained the casino gambling that made Las Vegas, well, Las Vegas. The combination was successful, as the city could rightly claim the title of most-visited place on earth by 1999.[20]

In this context, the *Review-Journal*'s opposition to Goodman's mayoral candidacy and its election editorial "Anybody but Oscar" espoused the viewpoint of those seeking to move the "New Las Vegas" beyond its outcast past. The election of someone so directly tied to "Old Vegas" threatened their intentions, whether they sought to create a city with wider allure than mere gambling and other adult vices offered or one recast as a family destination. Therefore the *Review-Journal*'s scathing piece scoured Goodman as "the barrister-to-butchers," a man who had won fame and fortune defending the most despicable members of society. The editorial pondered how the public could ever take Las Vegas seriously with this high-profile mob lawyer turned politician at the helm of municipal government.[21] Surely such a situation would play up the long-standing stereotypes and stigmas associated with the city.

It is easy to see the allure of developing and maintaining a more family-friendly image for Las Vegas during the latter twentieth century. Since World War II, American settlement patterns have increasingly moved toward suburbia. The percentage of Americans living in suburban areas increased from 23 percent in

1950 to 46.8 percent in 2010.[22] Thus, by the first decade of the twenty-first century, nearly half of all Americans lived in what could be defined as a suburban setting. In this nation, the middle-class suburban ideal has promoted family and leisure-time recreational pursuits. It is not difficult to see how many could envision a more family-friendly Las Vegas profiting from such demographics and expectations.

But what many proponents of a more family-friendly Las Vegas failed to see was that Las Vegas was all about being different and pushing the limits of acceptable society. That was the established image on which the city's growth had been based. Even in the frontier-themed days of the 1950s, part of the allure of Las Vegas was escaping the confining expectations of mainstream suburban America. Others thus believed that tapping into the American mainstream suburban ideal wasn't necessarily a good fit for Las Vegas. Sure, it was beneficial to have something for the kids to do while mom and dad gambled or took in a show, but reshaping Las Vegas to meet suburban norms was not the answer. Ultimately, Las Vegas was about risk and chance and tasting the otherwise unacceptable. If it could be done with the greatest extravagance, even better. Perhaps when combined with the new trend toward extravagance, electing a so-called mob lawyer was just what Las Vegas needed—at least in terms of its continued growth as America's premier adult playground.

The mayoral election of 1999 and subsequent events in Las Vegas offer a window through which to glimpse the competition that was taking place over what Las Vegas's image would be and show how important that image ultimately was to the city. On one side of the struggle were those who were nostalgic for the town's historical identity and mindful of that identity's tie to its economic well-being; on the other side were those who sought a more "normal" existence, one isolated from the goings-on of Las Vegas Boulevard and Fremont Street.

Mayor Goodman fit squarely into the former group; he was a leader interested in selling Las Vegas as an adult destination. After he was elected on the night of June 8 with 64 percent of the vote (to Arnie Adamsen's 36 percent), the new mayor sought a return of what he saw as Las Vegas's true identity.[23] The mainstream or family-oriented approach was fine for other cities, but in his mind, Las Vegas was special. It was a town built on the allure of the showgirl, the coolness of the Rat Pack, the danger of the mafia, and the sexuality of the topless review dancer. This is what set Las Vegas apart from other cities in an age when casino gambling had become far more acceptable and widespread. If the history and image of the town were ignored, Las Vegas, in Goodman's words, "would be nothing more than El Paso with casinos."[24]

In such a mindset, Goodman used the first meeting of the Las Vegas Convention and Visitors Authority (LVCVA)—on which he now had a seat—to push the idea that Las Vegas should shift its image away from the family-safe destination and return it to the risqué promotion of Old Vegas. Soon, thanks to an ad agency hired by the LVCVA, Las Vegas advertisements would assert, "What Happens Here, Stays Here." By century's end, the wildly successful slogan would become part of the Las Vegas lure and lore. It would take root in American popular culture, often repeated and bastardized to fit new contexts.[25] By 2008 the phrase would even appear as the title of a major Hollywood motion picture starring Cameron Diaz and Ashton Kutcher.[26] Although it was unsuccessful at the box office, the film reveals how deeply the sinful Las Vegas image had seeped into American culture.

Nostalgia is a powerful force, and as such, it very much influenced the direction of late twentieth-century Las Vegas. In modern corporate Las Vegas, Goodman's promotion of the Old Vegas struck a chord with many residents. Examples of this belief in a better time, a time before Howard Hughes's buying sprees and the rise of impersonal gaming interests, are readily available whether or not such romanticized times ever truly existed. Mae Farei, for instance, who moved to Las Vegas in 1955, found midcentury Las Vegas to be a "beautiful" and "safe" place where a single woman felt comfortable walking the streets. But her happiness proved short lived as everything seemingly began to change when the city grew and "big companies" replaced early casinos.[27]

A similar theme permeated the recollections of longtime residents Suzette Cox and Phillip Cook. Cox, having moved to Las Vegas from San Diego in 1953, recalled the town of that era as being far superior to its late twentieth-century version. She found 1950s Las Vegas more personal, a place where she always ran into someone she knew and where she could easily score free tickets for shows by knowing the right people. The more modern version of Las Vegas, in her opinion, was impersonal and "not as much fun."[28]

Of course, many such laments are really about Las Vegas's growth from small town to metropolis. Similar growing pains have resulted in nostalgic longing for better times in cities across the nation, albeit in most cases without the organized crime angle. Some, however, have looked specifically to the peculiarities of Las Vegas and the days of organized crime with a sense of longing. Phillip Cook, for instance, made no attempt to conceal his reasons for preferring the Old Las Vegas. Having resided in Las Vegas since 1936, Cook witnessed what he termed a "tremendous change" in the city. One change that he did not care for was the rise of big business and the demise of mob influence. Cook recalled fondly that when the mafia held an interest in local casinos, there had been no crime in Las Vegas. The mafia, he believed, had "protected" local citizens from petty and violent crimes that might have scared off tourism. Thus, Cook remembered a time when "the mafia was good for Las Vegas." Later in his life, the conditions deteriorated as the "tight knit" Las Vegas of his youth became a "legitimate city."[29] Interestingly, such remembrances tend to overlook the more negative mob associations. The brutality, robbery, prostitution, and drugs associated with the Spilotro era of the 1970s go unremembered. Nostalgia is a selective and often-inaccurate beast.

Oscar Goodman seldom, if ever, wavered in his commitment to playing up the "cool" elements of the early Las Vegas image. By promoting the nostalgic view of the city, he tapped into a local desire for what was believed to be the less complicated past that also recognized tourists' need for escape and entertainment. It was this sense of the risqué, of a notorious past and an exciting present that had made and could continue to make Las Vegas successful. The city prospered, Goodman believed, because it sold a good time in an environment that was a little too edgy for downtown Omaha, Des Moines, or Orange County.[30] Thus, Goodman, never one to miss an opportunity, embarked on a mission to promote an image of Las Vegas that was rooted in the past and somewhat outside the mainstream. As the New York Times suggested, the former "mob lawyer" possessed the perfect baggage to reawaken the risqué image of this "sin-soaked city."[31]

Goodman accomplished this by serving as the "face of Las Vegas." In this capacity—one he considered to be his most important duty as mayor—he constructed a celebrity image tied to the expectations and stereotypes of the city that were often rooted in its past. For example, Goodman often attended important gatherings flanked by Las Vegas showgirls. This includes arriving at a meeting of Major League Baseball owners, in his constant and so far unsuccessful effort to secure a major-league sports franchise to the city, with what he called "my showgirls."[32] At other times, he appeared in print, serving as a spokesperson for Bombay Blue Sapphire gin or perhaps relishing his role as the only mayor to shoot the pictures for a Playboy.com photo spread.[33] In between, he appeared on television shows such as NBC's Las Vegas, a show that made five successful and interesting seasons out of exploiting every cliché and stereotype ever associated with the city.[34]

Because of such actions, other mayors sometimes treated Goodman as a celebrity at mayors' conventions across the nation. As he said, "When I go to places, I'm treated as though I'm royalty; I'm treated like I'm a rock star." This treatment stemmed from both Goodman's antics and from the fact that he was not just the mayor of Anytown, U.S.A. Instead, he led one of America's most infamous towns. Love it or hate it, almost everyone has an image of what Las Vegas is. And under Goodman's leadership, that image continued to revolve around vice and fun. Las Vegas maintained its role as, among other things, the capital of gambling in the United States, which had a long, widely reported and oft-portrayed history of underworld connections. As a result, Oscar Goodman or "the Mayor," as he claims his fellow mayors referred to him, provided a sense of authenticity to the city's risqué reputation.[35] Whether one approves of his methods or not, he drew attention to what Las Vegas is famous for, and he likely helped bring in tourists in the process.

Aside from New York, Chicago, Los Angeles, or maybe San Francisco, it is difficult to find a city in the early twenty-first century where a mayor has received such attention, be it adoration or disdain. Even if one can be found, such attention often stems from the mayor's actions rather than from the image of the city as is the case with Goodman. New York City's Rudolph Giuliani stands as a perfect example. If any city rivals Las Vegas for the celebrity afforded its mayor, that city must be New York. But even for that mayor, his celebrity is tied to his actions in the city. Rudolph Giuliani would likely never have been the household name that he became had the terrorist attacks of September 11 not cast the spotlight upon him.[36] Yet, in Las Vegas, Goodman built an enormous amount of celebrity by simply playing up what the public expected of the city. While celebrity can be obtained in other cities in relation to contextual issues and events, it is not usually gained by so directly acting out the established reputation of the city. Here, again, Las Vegas's established identity became a direct agent of history.

Having a mayor so intent on playing up Las Vegas's risqué identity was not, however, without its negative repercussions. Goodman's mayoralty was not always as family friendly as Las Vegas's residents might have liked. Once, for example, when asked by a classroom of fourth graders what he would most like to have with him if marooned on a desert island, he replied, simply, "a bottle of gin." Another time, he threatened to cut off the thumbs of graffiti painters. And throughout his terms as mayor, many believed that local authorities mistreated the homeless as they were pushed away from tourists' view along the Strip and banned from city parks. In these regards, Goodman arguably failed city residents and certainly failed in presenting himself as a strong role model.[37]

As a result, some of his constituents and at times the local and national media looked askance at the mayor's actions. On the local level, this stemmed in part from the changing demographics in Las Vegas. As economic opportunity drew thousands of new residents to the resort city in the 1990s and early 2000s, many newly arrived suburbanites, such as those who were displeased with the mayor promoting gin in their children's classrooms, believed the risqué image of the city to be at odds with their intentions to raise families in conditions of normalcy. In this regard, Las Vegas shared economic and political characteristics with its Sunbelt neighbors. For example, in Las Vegas—as in San Diego, San Antonio, or any number of southwestern cities—the heavy federal investment of a military presence, the closely related technology industry, and public works projects have contributed mightily to demographic growth. The city has also traveled an economic and infrastructure route very similar to other warm resort cities such as Honolulu and Miami. One must realize that Las Vegas, while widely recognized as a center of vice, is also a full-fledged metropolis complete with the characteristics and trials of other cities in its region and across the nation. These include such modern issues and problems as crime, traffic congestion, and adequate health services, to mention only a few.[38] Yet Las Vegas residents and leaders also face the challenge of balancing a profitable Sin City identity with an increasingly mainstream suburban population.

Those Nasty Billboards

One area in which this precarious balancing act can be witnessed is local advertising. Quite simply, as Las Vegas grew into a full-fledged metropolis, family-values advocates expressed discomfort with the risqué visual promotion of their city locally. Some parents preferred not to have their children exposed to advertisements promoting the adult-playground image that Goodman so enthusiastically fostered. The resultant negotiation over Las Vegas's image played a role in local events that subsequently shaped the city's physical landscape. In the early 2000s, citizen complaints about a racy billboard outside the Hard Rock Hotel and Casino just south of the city limits blew up into a significant local campaign against obscenity, complete with legal action.

The billboard that kicked off much of this action was posted during the 2003 National Rodeo Finals, which is held each year at the Thomas and Mack Center on the campus of the University of Nevada, Las Vegas. This suggestive advertisement for the Hard Rock Casino and Hotel prominently featured a discarded cowboy hat on a bedroom floor beside a shapely pair of high-heel-clad female legs with skimpy panties lowered to midcalf. In large letters, and in an obvious play on words, the caption read, "Get Ready to Buck All Night Long."[39] At least a few people failed to see the humor in it.

Residents who were put off by the advertisement responded by taking their complaints to one of the most powerful institutions in Nevada. On March 18, with help and prodding from the Nevada Concerned Citizens watchdog group, the residents gathered at a meeting of the Nevada Gaming Commission. There, they voiced their anger and concern and asked the commission to intercede on the people's behalf in response to what they considered an obscene advertisement. According to Concerned Citizens cochair Lucille Lusk, "The concern has been bubbling out there for quite some time, but it came to fruition with the ad campaign 'what happens here stays here.' The general level of acceptability has been exceeded. . . . [The casinos] have tread along the edges for a long time. . . . Now they've taken it over the edge without respect. This is indeed a family community. We still have children here."[40] This ad obviously crossed the line of what Lusk and other like-minded people in the community considered acceptable. Although there had been murmurs and complaints about the Riviera Hotel and Casino's racy *Crazy Girls* taxicab ads that featured the nearly bare bottoms of a line of women, the uproar over the Hard Rock's "Buck" billboard was unprecedented.

According to Las Vegas Advertising Federation spokesperson Patti Gerace, the racy advertising could be traced back to the opening of the Palms Casino Resort in 2001. As the Palms and Hard Rock had targeted the same twenty-one-to-forty-year-old demographic, each casino had tried to gain notoriety by issuing an ad that was a bit edgier than the other's. A sort of billboard and advertising arms race ensued, with each concept going a little further than the last. Gerace expressed surprise that it took so long for some in the community to decide that the advertisements had surpassed common decency and organize a protest in response. But even she said that the ad "kind of shocked" her when she first saw it and worried that "maybe they've gone too far."[41]

Another organization that entered the fray was the city's recently created Main Street Billboard Commission. As the commission's president, Mike Wixom joined forces with Nevada Concerned Citizens to ensure that authorities removed the "obscene" billboards and limited them to the area surrounding the Las Vegas Strip. On April 22, 2004, Wixom and the others in the antibillboard coalition won a victory of sorts when the Clark County Commission passed an ordinance prohibiting the construction of new billboards in unincorporated areas. Although the commissioners did not address the content of the billboards, most of the people pushing this ban and in attendance at the April 22 meeting had voiced concerns over sexually explicit advertising. As antibillboard activist Carolyn Edwards said after the vote, "It's great that the entire county commission is continuing to put quality of life first." Wixom was more specific in his comment regarding the victory, stating that his organization was "very pleased" with the ordinance as it would affect the racy content of billboards "because [the billboards] won't be there." He further stipulated that his organization would continue the fight against the infiltration of sexually explicit advertising into Las Vegas communities.[42]

On the same day that the county commission ruled against new billboards outside the city limits, the Nevada Gaming Commission met to discuss the issue of the Hard Rock's racy advertising. Just as they had promised they would, a little over three hundred antibillboard activists who had busied themselves lobbying the commission to punish the Hard Rock showed up for the meeting. In this April 22 meeting, the conclusion of proceedings dating back to January 21, the powerful gaming commission imposed a fine of $300,000 on the Hard Rock for three instances of "indecent" and "inappropriate" advertising that was harmful to the state's image. The other two ads that the control board referred to promoted drug use and casino cheating. The board found that the Hard Rock's advertisements had violated both a 2002 agreement that required the casino to refrain from including any "questionable elements" in advertising campaigns and state gaming laws that required gaming corporations to exercise "decency, dignity, good taste, honesty and inoffensiveness" in their public relations.[43]

The billboard battle of 2004 eventually made its way to the pages of the *New York Times*. There, in a lengthy article on the portrayal and reality of Las Vegas women, *Times* reporters Sarah Kershaw and Patricia Leigh Brown presented the city as extraordinarily exploitative of women and very much defined by the sex industry, although it was open to more mainstream professional employment by females. In an attempt to debunk the idea that all women in Las Vegas were involved in the sex trade or in hotel cleaning, Kershaw and Brown presented a blistering condemnation of Las Vegas's gender relations. This was a city, they concluded, where "the female body may be second only to the slot machine as the most visible local icon." Thus, they wondered who could be surprised when other journalists mistakenly assumed that former mayor Jan Jones had been an exotic dancer.[44] The very existence of such an article explaining that not all women in Las Vegas are maids, prostitutes, or strippers says much about the warped national image of the city in 2004. After all, the president of the University of Nevada, Las Vegas, in 2004 was a woman, Carol Harter; Patricia Mulroy headed up the Southern Nevada Water Authority; Dina Titus served as the Nevada State Senate minority leader and would go on to be a member of the U.S. House; and Shelley Berkley served as a member of the United States Congress. As in all cases, reality is not so simple; Las Vegas is not the rampant sexual exploiter of women that its reputation suggests.[45]

Yet one cannot deny that Las Vegas objectifies women. The use of women's bodies to sell products or draw in tourists has been central to the city's development as a major gaming and entertainment destination. Since at least the 1940s, the city, its casinos, and its resorts have used women and sex as enticements for would-be visitors. One can argue that over time the city and its dominant gambling and entertainment-based industries have been built on and continue to depend on the objectification of the female body.[46]

In this regard, the *Times* article accurately linked the billboard controversy to overwhelming female exploitation in Las Vegas. The writers aptly depicted the racy billboards as the literal and symbolic center of a "collision between two Las Vegases." On the one side, the hedonistic playground and economic engine of the gaming industry needed to be able to promote and play off the risqué image. On the other side, many inhabitants of the sprawling suburbs were equally determined to limit any such expression.[47]

The American Civil Liberties Union (ACLU) also took notice of the billboard controversy before its conclusion. Pitted against the city's decency-in-advertising coalition, the ACLU threw its support behind what its members saw as the First Amendment right of casino companies to advertise as they saw fit. Allen Lichtenstein of the ACLU of Nevada argued that even in the case of a privileged license agreement such as the one between the gaming board and various casinos, the government could not become the judge of "matters of taste" concerning free speech.[48] Mike Wixom disagreed, claiming that Las Vegas families were having their right to a happy life violated because they could not take their children to school or anywhere else without having the billboards' blatant sexuality forced on them. As Wixom concluded, "I can turn off the TV. I can turn off the radio. But I can't turn off a 40-foot billboard the size of a semi-truck."[49]

Regardless of whether Wixom or Lichtenstein was correct, the billboard issue did not fade away following the 2004 gaming board decision to fine the Hard Rock. On May 30, 2008, local Las Vegas television reported that citizens were once again outraged over a sexually provocative billboard. This time, members of a business association along with some residents voiced concern over a billboard promoting what they believed to be a swingers' club. In response, association president Paula Sadler contacted members of the county commission to record an official complaint. The sign's image featured three shirtless men who were closely watching as one scantily clad woman spanked another equally scantily clad woman.[50]

Several months earlier, Lichtenstein had made up for his 2004 billboard-related defeat at the hands of the Nevada Gaming Board. On July 13, 2007, he succeeded in having federal judges overturn two 1979 laws that prohibited the advertisement of brothels in Clark County. After the laws were brought to his attention by *Las Vegas City Life* editor Steve Sebelius, Lichtenstein had launched the successful legal action much to the displeasure of clean-billboard advocates. The ruling stipulated that any brothel billboard advertisement must meet the same decency standards as other local billboards. The owners of nearby Pahrump's famed Chicken Ranch brothel stated that they would advertise in the Las Vegas vicinity but would keep such advertisements "conservative." Lichtenstein saw no danger in the advertising of brothels spreading beyond Las Vegas and southern Nevada since, as everyone knows, "What Happens in Vegas, Stays in Vegas."[51]

The battle over billboards in the early 2000s reveals several things about con-temporary Las Vegas. First, it is interesting that the opposition to the billboards was cast in the language of protecting children. Certainly, families looking out for their children's well-being made up an important segment of the clean-billboard advocates. But so did other groups whose main focus resided in areas outside child or family advocacy. That is not to say that others such as feminists and conservatives without children could not have supported that case out of a shared desire to protect children from such images. That certainly could have happened. However, it is equally possible that some such groups might have jumped on the child-protection bandwagon as an available and effective avenue of protest against the actions of the city's dominant industry. In this regard, such a tack could have been more effective in bringing about change than one focused on altering local values or ending the objectification of women.

But even if it was all about the children, the antibillboard movement shows that not everyone fully supported Goodman's much-touted "adult playground" and its social side effects. Because of attempts to perpetuate this image at the local level, some citizens took action. This action ultimately influenced the type of visual advertising deemed acceptable by local authorities. Las Vegas's image and the attempt to perpetuate that image influenced citizens to act, which in turn altered the physical appearance of the city. This indicates the role of image as an agent in Las Vegas's recent history. At the same time, it reveals a drawback inherent in Las Vegas, which depends on the production and maintenance of a risqué image to drive its tourist-oriented economy. The gaming industry and, to a lesser extent, the sex industry entice visitors who support the dominant tourist trade. An argument can be made that if these industries found themselves declining as a result of oppressive advertisement regulations by the local government, the tourist industry would suffer. Thus, the debate over billboards is a debate not only about decency in the public sphere but also about economics, growth, acceptable opposition, and livelihood.

The billboard issue did not mark the first time that risqué advertisement had come under fire in Las Vegas. A similar controversy occurred in the early 1990s when the county commission attempted to end the distribution of pornographic handbills to tourists along the Strip. In this instance, however, it appears that the commission was driven by concern over the impact of such explicit materials being pushed on tourists outside major Strip resorts. Despite legal efforts to ban the handbill distribution, it was still widely encountered decades later.[52] Likewise, Las Vegas remains distinct among American cities in that distribution racks full of sex advertisements and magazines can be found on numerous street corners around town These outward indicators of the Sin City image have yet to be scrutinized on the same level as the billboards and handbills.

Mayor Oscar Goodman had his own ideas about how the local government could protect the sensibilities of concerned citizens who felt ill at ease with the proliferation of risqué advertisements. As mayor, he advocated that one way to deal with the issue while still preserving Las Vegas's all-important adult-playground and Sin City images would be to construct a district in which to house sex-themed entertainments. In many ways, this would resemble the ubiquitous red-light districts of an earlier era of urban America. Las Vegas had even once had its own red-light district, known locally as Block 16.[53] Yet, as Goodman himself pointed out, this could never happen in the current setting. Those who opposed the billboards would obviously oppose such a district's existence. These individuals, he rather dismissively believed, should just "get a life." Meanwhile, he conveniently ignored the exploitation of sex-industry workers and the increased objectification of women that would undoubtedly accompany the creation of such a district.[54]

Goodman faced criticism for his views on adult-themed districts once again when in 2007 New York Times columnist Bob Herbert harshly criticized the mayor's stance, interpreting it as support for prostitution and an array of other vices. Herbert began his "City as Predator" article by issuing the provocative statement, "There is probably no city in America where women are treated worse than in Las Vegas." Going on to quote experts who claimed that Las Vegas represented the "epicenter" of the American sex trade, Herbert further pontificated that the city's "vast and astonishingly open sex trade" ruined "tens of thousands" of girls and women. Beyond this, he specifically targeted Mayor Goodman as the "tone" setter of this "systematic, institutionalized degradation" of women. The basis of this characterization was Goodman's contention that the existence of a well-regulated red-light district, complete with legalized prostitution, should be open to discussion.[55] In an over-the-top response that many had come to expect from Goodman, the mayor publicly stated that if Herbert ever set foot back inside the limits of Las Vegas, he would personally beat him about the head with a baseball bat.[56] It is doubtful that such a hyperbolic threat intimidated the longtime New York City reporter in the least.

Many who commented on the online version of Herbert's article tended to agree with Herbert's characterization of Las Vegas. One reader, going by the name MJCIV from Massachusetts, equated the notion of legalized prostitution in Las Vegas with Emile Durkhiem's warnings about the dangers of an overload of deviance in society. He felt that the legalization of prostitution offered a great example of the normalizing of a taboo that eventually must lead to a complete reform of society. The very thought of legal prostitution in Las Vegas was "sickening" to him.[57] Reader Cory E. Friedman of Crown Point, New York, shared similar views. Friedman felt, "It's a slippery slope when society legalizes sin for profit. First gambling, then prostitution, eventually extortion and murder for hire. Each step just desensitizes society to conduct which can never be stamped out."[58] Lenora Lev, a women's and gender studies professor from Brookline, Massachusetts, felt that Herbert had done the world a great service by "standing up" to the "blustering bully and would be gangster" who was Las Vegas's mayor and arguing against the "glorifying of stripping, prostitution, and strip clubs."[59] Herbert and the commenters made valid points about the dangers of prostitution, the objectification of women, and the legalization of vice in Las Vegas.

Similar disgust with Las Vegas and its image motivated some individuals enough that they traveled to the city in an attempt to save the city's residents and tourists. The Reverend Craig Gross provides one such example. Highlighted on the ABC News program *Nightline*, Gross explained that his "Strip Church" was taking the truly Christian path by "reaching a society that a lot of us don't want to touch." *Nightline* correspondent Martin Bashir used the label *Sin City* to describe this tainted society no fewer than five times during the seven-minute span of the piece. Here, Las Vegas was cast as the "worst place as a parent to raise children," where people could not help but give in to "the temptations" that "this city has to offer." Thus, with a million-dollar yearly budget, Gross journeyed to this "metropolis in the desert where people come to escape reality." Once there, he sought to promote a new reality by handing out water bottles along the Strip as tourists ventured from casino to casino under the hot summer sun. Along with these water bottles, the tourists received invitations to the Strip Church and Gross's website, XXXChurch.com.[60]

Those lucky or unlucky enough to visit Gross's website at that time could find multiple associations between Las Vegas and pornography. In addition to soliciting donations, the site also attempted to get people to interact by sharing their "confessions" of how pornography, fornication, and Las Vegas had ruined their lives. Surprisingly, a few did just that. But of those few, it is interesting that most were not residents of Las Vegas and did not mention Las Vegas.[61] Nevertheless, Gross continued in his efforts to remove "the obvious temptation" for those who "work and live in Las Vegas" and the thirty-six to forty million who visited annually by the end of the 2000s.[62]

Las Vegas's Quest for Major-League Sports

One key marker in the modern United States that is perceived as separating big-time cities from those that have yet to make it is the presence of a major-league sports team. Be it a team from the National Basketball Association, the National Football League, Major League Baseball, or even the National Hockey League, a major-league team says that a city has arrived. Having secured one of these teams, a city's image, like that of its sports franchise, goes from minor to major league. A sports team allows equal comparisons between the city and the New Yorks, Los Angeleses and Chicagos of the nation.[63] This is one area in which Las Vegas's Sin City reputation directly harmed its ability to enter the big time. Stigmatized identities, however, are not permanent and are dependent for their power upon the cultural contexts in which they exist.

On Sunday, November 16, 2008, the Pittsburgh Steelers defeated the San Diego Chargers by a score of 11–10. In the eighty-eight-year history of the NFL, that was the first time a game had ended with that unlikely score. The problem, however, was that the score was wrong. At the game's conclusion, the Steelers had run a fumble in for a touchdown, raising the score to the more common 17–10. The officials erroneously ruled that the fumble had been a forward pass, thus negating the touchdown and returning the score to its previous margin. While this made no difference as to the game's outcome—Pittsburgh still won the game—news outlets made sure to mention that it made a huge difference to bettors, as bookmakers had favored Pittsburgh by four points. When the final score was altered, winners became losers and vice versa. Media outlets looked instantly to Las Vegas. They quickly related that in the "gambling city," the decision had caused much controversy among bettors and sports book operators alike as they struggled to figure winners and losers of the bet worth over $10 million on this single run-of-the-mill game.[64]

The amount of money at stake and the national stir arising from an otherwise-inconsequential football game early in November illustrates the scope of the sports-betting industry in modern Las Vegas. Fortunes change hands on a daily basis in such places as the sports book at the Westgate Las Vegas Resort and Casino (formerly the Las Vegas Hilton). There, in a setting that greatly resembles what one would expect from a NASA mission control in Houston or Cape Canaveral, a special form of entertainment is available in just watching and listening to the serious sports bettors. To many of these people and others at casino sports books all across the valley, sports betting is serious business. These are the Las Vegas veterans, the best in the world at forecasting the odds, setting the lines, and picking the winners. While this betting is, in a way, quaint and unique to Las Vegas, it is also a main reason that the city has struggled with successfully landing a major-league sports team. Despite the best efforts of Las Vegas boosters, politicians, and businesspeople over the years, the closest the city came prior to 2017 were with a triple-A Dodgers affiliate, a minor-league hockey team, an arena football team, the National Rodeo Finals, a NASCAR Sprint Cup race, and a onetime hosting of the NBA All-Star Game.[65]

Las Vegas first experienced rejection in the area of major-league professional sports because of its gambling culture and reputation in 1993. That year, in the midst of Las Vegas's attempted recasting as a family destination, the Disney-owned Anaheim Ducks turned down the city as a prospective location for its NHL team. In a Disney-issued statement, Disney Sports Enterprises president Tony Tavares said that Las Vegas's image and gambling industry were "incongruous" with the Disney Corporation. Tavares made no attempt to tone down the reason for the refusal, saying that the reason Las Vegas lacked a major-league sports franchise was entirely due to the city's culture and the availability of sports betting. While he claimed to harbor nothing personally against the people of Las Vegas, he just could not in good conscience associate the image of Disney with gambling.[66]

Despite Tavares's proclaimed good will toward Las Vegans, some residents obviously took offense at this snub. Among those, a Luxor Resort and Casino spokesperson, after being told of the Disney rebuke, said that Las Vegas would soon have more family-friendly destinations than Disney's entertainment capital, Orlando, Florida. Likewise, Las Vegas Chamber of Commerce president Mark Smith characterized the decision as stemming from an "unfortunate attitude" that disregarded "billion dollar" investments in family entertainment, and rested on the old-fashioned image that Las Vegas offered only gambling. Others, such as director of franchise development Dan Spellings, saw the rebuff as a real slap in the face to Las Vegans. To him, the decision ignored the million or so individuals in Las Vegas who were "hungry for well-presented family entertainment." These were the "Las Vegans who bristle at the city's pervasive image as Sin City, and proudly point to its new family attractions."[67] Reputation had interceded once again to play a major role in Las Vegas's history.

Despite the sting of Disney's slap, Las Vegas continued its efforts to make inroads into major-league sports. Ironically, these efforts increased markedly following Goodman's election and Las Vegas's public relations shift back to the Sin City, adult-playground identity. Throughout the first years of the twenty-first century, due in no small part to the mayor's efforts, there always seemed to be rumors of the possibility that some major-league franchise would either relocate or expand into the Las Vegas valley.

The first of these renewed efforts gained headlines in 2000. With the dawn of the new millennium, since the world had not succumbed to some mysterious Y2K computer glitch, Las Vegas boosters decided that if Major League Baseball was not ready to come to them, then they should go to the MLB. Quite simply, Las Vegas decided to join other gambling interests in attempting to advertise via Major League Baseball. For a fee of $1.5 million, Major League Baseball granted the Las Vegas Convention and Visitors Bureau the privilege of erecting signs in major-league parks throughout the nation. Further, in an unprecedented show of cooperation by a league that was historically paranoid regarding anything resembling sports betting—just ask Shoeless Joe Jackson or Pete Rose—owners of five teams agreed to discuss the possibility of moving their spring-training camps to Las Vegas.[68] The new century suddenly looked bright for Las Vegas's hopes of one day capturing a major-league franchise.

That goal seemed to draw a bit closer in 2001 when Major League Baseball stepped in and purchased a floundering Montreal Expos franchise. After the purchase, rumors of relocation soon became a full-fledged selection process to find a suitable new home for the team. Las Vegas, despite lobbying hard for the honor, eventually lost out to Washington, D.C. However, as financing for a proposed stadium in Washington faltered in 2004, it looked as if the newly named Washington Nationals might never take the field in that city. Las Vegas, along with other cities previously under consideration, glimpsed a spark of hope and mounted a new effort to convince the MLB to give their city a second look. Mayor Goodman, in typical form, showed up at the MLB's winter meetings in a black stretch limousine, flanked by a cadre of showgirls and an Elvis impersonator.[69]

Although he failed to convince the shareholders that Las Vegas was the best home for the team, Goodman was undaunted. He pledged that he would try again when the next opportunity presented itself through a team's relocation or the league's expansion. When asked about Las Vegas's most obvious obstacle, that of sports betting, Goodman refused to admit that it would cause a problem for any local team—even though local sports books had changed their policies and recently begun accepting bets on local teams. Instead, he argued that Las Vegas's proliferation of legal betting made the location more desirable for any league that was worried about the influence of gambling. Las Vegas was, after all, the "quintessential regulator" of such things and would always ensure against any type of shady dealing. With the perhaps-undue optimism of a local booster, he felt assured that one day Las Vegas would get its team. Goodman stated—once again playing the Old Vegas role—"We'll make them an offer they can't refuse."[70]

One cannot blame Goodman for his optimism. The stigma of gambling had decreased markedly across the nation by 2000. Gambling's increased acceptance by this time revealed itself through the national spread of casinos that now offered a majority of Americans access to gaming machines or tables within only a few-hours' drive. As the result of an ongoing process begun with the legalization of casino gambling in Atlantic City in 1978, casinos outside Las Vegas had proliferated on Native American lands and in intracoastal waterways such as the Mississippi River and the Gulf of Mexico.[71] The media took great interest in this increase, with numerous articles in national and international publications examining the "Gambling Spree across [the] Nation," "America's Gambling Craze," and "America's Gambling Fever."[72] American gambling, as the *Economist* pointed out in 1990, obviously appeared to be "on a roll."[73]

However, between the 1970s and 2000s, opposition to gambling, as well as anxiety over the nation's morals relative to the practice, continued to be a major force in American culture. In one telling article from 1975, *U.S. News & World Report* editors listed changing views on gambling as one of the many signs of declining morality in the United States.[74] Some continued to voice concerns about the supposed immorality and damnation bred by the rampant acceptance of gambling in 1999. The popular evangelist and religious broadcaster James C. Dobson saw fit to condemn gambling as one of the greatest dangers to souls and the nation's social fabric in an article posted on his Focus on the Family website. There, readers learned that Americans spent more money on gambling each year than on groceries, that addiction ran rampant even among adolescents, and that gambling directly led to increased crime and corruption. Dobson went on to "scratch the veneer" off Nevada's supposed gambling success story and focused particularly on Las Vegas. In this effort, he employed tired statistics stating that the city ranked first in the nation in suicides, listed over a hundred pages of ads for prostitution in its yellow pages (Dobson automatically transformed ads for escort services into prostitution ads), and harbored an alcoholism rate of one in ten adults. The insidious industry, according to Dobson, had further resulted in the wide and accurate recognition of Las Vegas as the most corrupt city in America.[75]

If the owners and commissioners of various sports leagues shared any of these ideas concerning Las Vegas and the influence of gambling, the city's prospects of gaining a team certainly seemed bleak. In fact, despite the upbeat talk from Goodman, Major League Baseball's decision against relocating the Expos in Las Vegas—two times, no less—was a bitter pill for many in the valley. In the weeks leading up to the initial decision in 2004, news reports had even mentioned Las Vegas as a finalist alongside the northern Virginia area, although the team ultimately ended up in Washington, D.C.[76] There are several important differences to note between this attempt to lure a major-league sports teams to Las Vegas and previous attempts to do so.

First, this time the city launched a professional and very legitimate effort to obtain the team. Headed up by Chicago businessperson Lou Weisbach, the campaign to bring the Expos to Las Vegas enjoyed widespread support in the local community and the municipal government. Most important, it had the backing of casino gaming with Steve Wynn's blessing and Caesars Incorporated willing to serve as landlord for a proposed $420 million forty-thousand-seat stadium located one block off Las Vegas Boulevard.[77] This was a new and important development in the city's quest for a major-league sports franchise. Only two years previously, Goodman had publicly stated that a major factor inLas Vegas's failure to secure a team had been opposition from the casino industry. As late as 2002 he felt that the directors of the gaming industry harbored great resistance to any form of entertainment that might lure their patrons "out of their smoke-filled casinos."[78]

The idea that casino corporations had torpedoed major-league expansion into the Las Vegas area was negated by the circumstances of the failed Expos bid in 2004, but a few other obstacles remained that could possibly explain Major League Baseball's reticence to relocate to southern Nevada. Obviously, population stood as a major concern. In 2004 the estimated population of the Las Vegas metropolitan area stood somewhere between 1.6 and 1.7 million. That provided a television market share that ranked the city fifty-first in the nation.[79]

At first glance, such population statistics do not appear promising enough to lure a professional team to the city. Yet one must also remember that by 2004, Las Vegas drew approximately thirty-two million visitors to town annually. Thus, at any one time, the number of people in the city was substantially larger than population figures provided. Further, these "extra" people were on vacation, in spending mode, and on the prowl for entertainment. It is also important to note that Las Vegas's population was rapidly growing in 2004. Experts forecast that by the time the relocated team was ready to play on opening day in 2007, the population of Vegas's metropolitan area would easily surpass the two million mark. When adding the number of visitors in town at any given time to a permanent population of two million, Las Vegas's population numbers looked much more promising. Such a combined total made the city competitive with such cities as Tampa Bay, Baltimore, Saint Louis, San Diego, and Minneapolis. Major League Baseball had granted all these cities franchises at various times, and all their metropolitan populations fell between 2.5 and 3 million at the end of 2003.[80] Thus, although it is pure speculation to think that tourists would attend baseball games, one could make an argument that Las Vegas's population in 2007 was realistically large enough to support a team.

However, other cities with relatively similar population bases did not face the obstacles that go along with gambling and the stigmatized reputation associated with that industry and its ties to organized crime. As is discussed in the previous chapter, the national public subscribed to the idea that Las Vegas was a gambling escape and sometimes a den of organized crime. The media continued to draw upon the stereotype whenever it felt warranted and just as often when not. One has to suspect that Major League Baseball—with its strict prohibition against betting on the sport—gave some thought to having a franchise play down the street from the Hilton sports book.

Although the MLB made no comments regarding the city's gambling and corrupt image, other leagues' similar stances indicated that the topic remained a concern. National Basketball Association (NBA) president David Stern, for example, blatantly refused to even consider Las Vegas as a destination for an NBA team until the city's casinos prohibited all betting on the league's games. As

Gavin Maloof, the owner of Palms Casino Resort and part-owner of the NBA's
Sacramento Kings, said, there are "certain conditions" that are highly unlikely
to ever be met for the NBA to "put a team here."[81]

The city's strange and often-contentious relationship with the National
Football League offers another indication that the movers and shakers of the
major-league sports industry looked at Las Vegas's image in a consistently
critical fashion. Although the city had never been a serious contender for an
NFL franchise by the early 2000s, that had not stopped the development of an
anxious and often-strained relationship with the league. A series of events in
2003 laid bare this animosity for the entire world to see. In the run-up to that
year's Super Bowl, the Las Vegas Convention and Visitors Authority attempted to
buy much-coveted and very expensive game-time television advertising slots. In
a very unusual move, the NFL rejected its $4 million along with its one-minute
ad. League officials based the rejection on a little-known clause in its contracts
that prohibits the advertisement of gambling on any of its networks.[82]

The ad in question neither mentioned nor depicted gambling in any manner.
Instead, it featured an attractive lady entering a limousine wearing sexy evening
attire and then exiting the same limousine at Las Vegas's McCarran Airport
dressed in a proper business suit. When confronted over the fact that the ad did
not advocate gambling, the NFL's senior vice president for broadcasting Dennis
Lewin claimed that the league would have rejected the ad regardless of its content.
Jeff Pash, an NFL executive vice president and legal counsel, clarified Lewin's
earlier statement by saying that the NFL rejected the ad because Las Vegas "is
principally associated in people's minds with one thing." This explanation came
only after Las Vegas proponents confronted Pash over the league's allowance of
a Southwest Airlines ad that urged prospective travelers to "blow" less money
by flying on the budget-conscious airline so that they could "blow" more once
they arrived in Las Vegas. To Pash and the NFL, this ad had proved acceptable
as it promoted the airline rather than the city. It is also important to note that
Southwest was a sponsor of the 2003 Super Bowl.[83]

The reaction to the NFL's snub exploded in the local Las Vegas media. In
the eleven days following the January 13 announcement that Las Vegas would
not be permitted to advertise during the Super Bowl, seven feature stories, one
editorial, and two letters to the editor appeared on the pages of the *Las Vegas
Review-Journal*.[84] To say that the NFL's opinion of the city ruffled both the local
press and residents would be an understatement. The newspapers referred to the
NFL as hypocritical, dishonest, seedy, and "anti–Las Vegas."[85] The *Review-Journal*

editor made sure to highlight the league's hypocrisy—as did virtually every other piece on the topic—by arguing that the NFL was a league built around gambling and had in fact for many years featured Jimmy "the Greek" Snyder as a regular on pregame shows and allowed Monday Night Football commentator Al Michaels to reference point spreads.[86] Columnist John L. Smith offered perhaps the most well-researched condemnation of the NFL's attitude. In his lengthy piece, Smith provided a very dirty laundry list of nine NFL team owners whose backgrounds included bookmaking, ties to organized crime, or in most instances, both.[87] An enraged Mayor Goodman echoed the same line, stating that the NFL "should get its own house in order" before attacking Las Vegas.[88]

Other arguments against the NFL's stance centered on the perception of gambling in twenty-first-century America. As several pieces pointed out, forty-seven out of fifty states allowed gambling in some form by 2003. The dissemination of gambling, although much took place on American Indian land or in international waterways, marked not the birth of the pastime in America but a return to one of the most salient of American habits. To borrow a term, the American people had always been a "people of chance."[89] By castigating Las Vegas for its gambling enterprises, the NFL was, many felt, being old fashioned and "outdated," a view evidenced by the reaction in the local press.[90] As Las Vegas Convention and Visitors Authority spokesperson Rod Powers related, "Gaming is so common in the United States . . . the stigma is largely diminished. And Las Vegas has evolved into a resort destination."[91] Ironically, it is also worth noting that the widespread press coverage of the NFL's denial of the advertisement resulted, in Mayor Goodman's opinion, in far more exposure for the city than could have ever been gained from one minute of Super Bowl airtime—and it cost nothing.[92]

In evaluating the NFL and other professional leagues' disdain for Las Vegas, one must also take into account the well-cultivated image of the city as being risqué. Prospective franchises must consider the temptations that Las Vegas would present to players in addition to gambling. In an age when every superstar's movement is tracked by paparazzi and mainstream journalists, franchise owners must question how long it would take before, as Hal Rothman put it, "a video of somebody's $50 million investment stumbling out of a strip club at 9 A.M. on game day hit the 5 o'clock news. When that happened, it would confirm every bad stereotype about Las Vegas . . . and the NBA."[93] While that is true, it should also be noted that such stereotypes are also evoked by media representations of Las Vegas, visitor and convention bureau slogans, and Mayor Goodman's actions and statements in attempting to sell Las Vegas to the vacationing public and various major-league franchises. Las Vegas, in selling itself as Sin City, delayed the real possibility of attaining a major-league sports franchise. Again, reputation played a major role in the city's historical trajectory.

This was, however, a delay and not a death sentence for those seeking a professional major-league franchise. On June 22, 2016, *Las Vegas Review-Journal* reporter Steve Carp began an article with a very simple three-word phrase: "Vegas got hockey." With the National Hockey League's decision to grant Las Vegas an expansion team, "the city skated in the major leagues." This was big news for Las Vegans, whose decades-old dream of obtaining a major-league franchise in any sport had finally become a reality. To Clark County commissioners Susan Brager and Steve Sisolak, the NHL's announcement amounted to a "game changer" for the city and its reputation. As Sisolak opined, "People will look at us differently forever. . . . We will be known for more than just gambling and entertainment. We're a major league city now."[94] Likewise, the official Clark County, Nevada, Twitter feed stated triumphantly, "It's official. We made it! #VegasgotHockey."[95]

Not only did Las Vegas's reputation not seem to hurt the city's bid to gain an expansion team, if statements by NHL commissioner Gary Bettman are to be taken at face value, it helped them. Following the unanimous vote of thirty to zero in favor of granting Las Vegas a team, Bettman characterized the "Las Vegas market" as "intriguing" and the city's "worldwide reputation" as "appealing" to league owners. He also noted the economic aspects of the decision, noting specifically the influence of a very successful drive for season-ticket deposits, which in less than two months met its goal of ten thousand deposits. By the time of the announcement, fifteen thousand deposits had been secured. This, according to Bettman, showed that the city was willing to support an NHL team.[96] Likewise, prospective team owner and billionaire Bill Foley gave the team secure financial footing. Foley, who had first suggested a Las Vegas expansion team to Bettman in 2013, backed the proposal with an agreement to pay the NHL $500 million to enter the league. Further, established NBA team owner and Palms Casino Resort owner Gavin Maloof agreed to take on 15 percent ownership.[97]

It also helped that the proposed Las Vegas team already had a state-of-the-art arena built with a major-league tenant in mind. The $375 million twenty-thousand-seat T-Mobile Arena had opened to good reviews with a concert by the Killers on April 6, 2016. Following its opening, the arena went on to become one of the most popular venues in town. By the year's end, this successful joint venture by the MGM Grand and the Los Angeles–based AEG—which developed that city's Staples Center—provided the infrastructure and again showed the local desire for major-league sports. It presented the perfect venue for the NHL's newest team, the Vegas Golden Knights.[98] It seems that through economic investment in sporting infrastructure and season tickets along with billionaire backing, Las Vegas had, in fact, offered the NHL a deal it couldn't refuse. It is also worth noting that controversial Mayor Goodman had met his term limit and left office in 2011. In his place, voters had chosen his very capable and less flamboyant wife, Carolyn Goodman.[99]

The NHL's decision to place an expansion franchise in Las Vegas seemed to open the door for other leagues to seriously consider the city. Perhaps, as proponents indicated, it lent a sense of respectability to the city. Or maybe it just showed that Las Vegas was serious about attracting and supporting major-league sports franchises. As evidenced by the T-Mobile Arena, ticket sales, and local support, Las Vegas was now a legitimate player in the market. Any doubts about Las Vegas's seriousness and attractiveness were removed in 2016 when Las Vegas emerged as the prime candidate for an NFL team whose owner wanted a new stadium that his host city refused to build.

The Oakland Raiders, one of the NFL's storied franchises with one of the league's most devoted fan bases, began play in 1960 as an original member of the American Football League. In 1970 it became part of the NFL when the two leagues merged. In 1982 the team relocated to Los Angeles before returning to Oakland in 1994, where it has remained since. Over the course of the franchise's history, the Raiders managed to win Super Bowl titles in 1976, 1980, and 1983.[100]

On January 19, 2017, Raiders owner Marc Davis—the son of original owner Al Davis—applied to the NFL to relocate the franchise to Las Vegas. Again, as with the NHL, Las Vegas simply made the Raiders a deal too good to pass up. Davis had long sought a new stadium for the team in Oakland. The Raiders' home stadium, the Oakland-Alameda County Coliseum, which had opened in 1966, was one of the oldest stadiums in the NFL. However, as Oakland's government resisted paying for a new stadium—millions were still owed on the existing stadium's renovations—Davis began looking for new locations. Southern California and San Antonio, Texas, were considered as possible relocation sites before Davis eventually chose Las Vegas as the most promising destination.[101]

As with the NHL, proponents of moving the Raiders to Las Vegas acted quickly to show support for the relocation. Such support could be seen at the state, county, and city levels and included pledges of financial support from both public and private institutions. The city and state quickly put together and approved a plan to finance a $1.9 billion stadium. The funding plan included Sheldon Adelson, chairman of the Las Vegas Sands Corporation, contributing $650 million; a hotel tax increase contributing $750 million; and the Raiders contributing the remaining $500 million. The state senate approved the funding plan and the increased room tax on October 14, 2016, and Governor Brian Sandoval signed the bill into law three days later. With his signature, Sandoval approved the largest public contribution to a professional sports stadium in the nation's history. And that did not include the $899 million in roadway improvements that would have to be fast-tracked because of the stadium's construction.[102] Las Vegas and Nevada were serious, and the Raiders' Davis was paying attention.

Following Davis's official application to move the Raiders to Las Vegas, one major obstacle stood in the way. The relocation of an NFL franchise requires the approval of three-quarters of the league's current team owners. Based on the NFL's historical aversion to being associated with Las Vegas, this step is where one would expect Las Vegas's reputation (and reality) to intervene. However, as the process played out, it seemed that the Sin City reputation and gambling were not foremost on owners' minds. Instead, many seemed to fall in line behind Cowboys owner Jerry Jones, who quickly voiced his support of Raiders' move to Las Vegas, stating, "Las Vegas is one of our country's jewels." He went on to praise Governor Sandoval and the Nevada legislature for their "impressive and persuasive" commitment.[103] Likewise, it was reported that economics, not Las Vegas's gambling or reputation, were of primary concern to NFL owners. When questioned at the NFL owners' annual fall meeting about the possibility of Las Vegas receiving an NFL franchise, Houston Texans owner Bob McNair—seemingly having missed Las Vegas's shift away from the family-oriented marketing of the 1990s—responded, "Las Vegas has changed. . . . It's a more family oriented destination now." He, along with other owners at the meeting, placed more emphasis on exploring Las Vegas's ability to support an NFL team than on the city's reputation for gambling and sin.[104]

Like the owners, NFL reporters also stressed that image would not be the main problem facing the Raiders' relocation. Instead, they indicated that the owners' concerns over market size and Las Vegas's ability to support an NFL franchise would prove to be the major hurdle. As Lance Pubmire of the *Los Angeles Times* pointed out, based on the city's population, Las Vegas would be ranked twentieth or twenty-second in market size in the league of thirty-two teams. *Washington Post* NFL writer Mark Maske echoed these concerns, quoting an anonymous "high ranking official with one NFL team" as saying, "I think in general we don't like to leave big markets for small markets." However, the unnamed official went on to say that while most owners would like to see the Raiders remain in Oakland, if "the Las Vegas deal is all there is, we'll have to consider it."[105]

By the January submission of Davis's official relocation application, owners had been seriously considering the relocation for months. On the day of the application, *Las Vegas Review-Journal* sports columnist Ed Graney opined that the smooth process and the owners' positive reception of the idea inclined him to believe that Davis would not have filed the application if he did not believe he had the necessary number of votes. It seemed that what Graney "could never imagine" happening in Las Vegas was very close to becoming a reality.[106] Three days later, the *Review-Journal*'s Jon Saraceno reported that Las Vegans could safely "start shopping for black-and-silver apparel" (the Raiders' colors).[107]

His advice proved spot-on. On March 27, 2017, NFL owners voted thirty-one to one in favor of the Raiders relocating to Las Vegas. It certainly seems that the thirty-one owners were far more inclined to do so because of Las Vegas's and Nevada's willingness to invest, recklessly or not, in building a very expensive home for the team. Quite simply, as Houston Texans owner Bob McNair opined, Las Vegas put together "a very sound plan" that "meets all our standards and financial conditions." Oakland failed to do so. The move was, therefore, seen to be in the best economic interest of the Raiders and the NFL. In the end, it was all about the money, and the vote wasn't even close.[108]

This is a league, after all, where twenty-three new stadiums have been built in the last twenty-seven years. Jerry Jones, who, as mentioned, was one of the primary supporters of the Raiders' move to Las Vegas, is credited with revolutionizing owners' perceptions of the importance of stadiums. He is regarded as having helped to create the stadium craze by showing how lucrative it was for team owners to control the cash flow generated by stadiums. This began with his 1989 lease of Texas Stadium for $70 million. Nice, shiny new stadiums with all the amenities are profitable for owners. This is particularly true when public funds finance a large part of their construction. Jones has further illustrated this with the $1.2 billion AT&T Stadium in Arlington, Texas, which was completed in 2009. Whether or not the deal is equally good for municipalities and states is debatable. In the case of AT&T, the finances seem to be working out because Arlington is on track to pay off the $300 million bond debt incurred for the stadium ten years ahead of schedule.[109]

Las Vegas could see similar results. Or this could be a case of Las Vegans being blinded by their desire for an NFL team. In either case, the result certainly could be the fleecing of major investors and citizens in order to increase an NFL owner's profits. Oakland Mayor Libby Schaaf certainly had her doubts about the process and was reluctant to lead her city down a similar path of additional public funding of infrastructure for what ultimately is a private corporation. As she told Associated Press reporter Barry Wilner, "I cannot afford for us to be thrown off our game because Nevada lawmakers have deemed it appropriate to put $750 million in public money towards a private sports facility. While I'm committed to keeping the Raiders, I will not enter into a bidding war with Nevada using public funds."[110]

It has been written that an NFL team is the "real prize" when it comes to major-league sports in postindustrial America. The NFL is now the "real marker of legitimacy" for cities when it comes to sports franchises.[111] To even have the chance of obtaining this prize, Las Vegas had to overcome its relatively small and transient population, its lack of a large hinterland population, and the stigma associated with gambling. With a metropolitan population now approaching 2.5 million, a team that has strong support in nearby California, and a remarkable lack of concern voiced by NFL owners over Las Vegas gambling, those obstacles have been scaled. Of course, $750 million of public funding helped.

Choosing a Path

The paradox that defines modern Las Vegas's relationship to its image is clear. On the one hand, as Mayor Oscar Goodman's promotions exemplified, the city seeks to play up its risqué image and reap the undeniable profits from doing so. In this regard, associating itself with the ghosts of its past and the temptations of its present means money in the bank. Las Vegas is, after all, an escape. It is a place into which the straitlaced can venture safely, commit sins away from the prying eyes of neighbors and family, then leave with those sins remaining behind and without too much worry.[112] It is, as has been said, a perceptual "sin free zone," not in the manner of being without sin, but in that sins do not seem to count against people in this stretch of desert, or so it would have tourists believe.[113]

At the same time, the promotion of this attitude as summed up in the ubiquitous "What Happens Here, Stays Here" tagline absolutely flies in the face of those who seek a more normal life than one associated with the perception of an adult playground. While the suburbanite of Des Moines might enjoy the idea of escaping for a little "eye candy" and fun in Vegas, his Las Vegas counterpart might not feel the same. This is exemplified by the locals' opposition of racy billboards promoting that risqué image. Would the Des Moines traveler want his son or daughter asking what it means to "buck all night" after passing a billboard on the way to school some morning? If he would not, then there is a good chance that the Las Vegan making the daily journey down Paradise Road might feel the same.

While many might say, as Mayor Goodman did, that it really does not matter what such people think—they chose to live in Las Vegas rather than Des Moines, after all—the city's relationship with major-league sports faces a similar conundrum. In this instance, those who promote Las Vegas's edginess to sell tourism now seek a measure of acceptance into the mainstream. By doing this, they risk denying outright the very image that they have spent their careers promoting. The result is a bipolar city that seems to be two opposing things. When its mayor showed up to sell Las Vegas to Major League Baseball owners with showgirls in tow, he should not have been surprised or offended when the league dismissed his city as too risqué.[114] In this regard, Las Vegas's reputation likely delayed its arrival as a major-league city. But without that reputation as the economic engine of Las Vegas, the city never would have been considered for a major-league team. Growth and ridiculous amounts of public funding ultimately made the arrival of major-league sports inevitable in Las Vegas. The future of major-league Sin City will be interesting indeed.

8

Stigma and Cities

Not all cities can be "All-American" all the time. Further, as this study has argued, not all segments of all cities consistently seek or benefit from such a title. Sometimes, as is the case with Las Vegas and to a lesser degree San Francisco, even a small abnormal or risqué element in a city's reputation can constitute that city's claim to fame and add to its prosperity. What might be a negative stigma for many is conversely a positive attraction for others with cash in hand. In other cases, such as Birmingham, the shift from all-American to un-American results in a deeply held negative and painful stigmatization that both inhibits the city's success and alters the mindsets and activities of local inhabitants. Thus, as the situations and characteristics of these three cities suggest, the influence of stigmatization on an urban location is relative to both the city's past and the prevalent cultural ideals and values that encapsulate its present. Quite simply, American attitudes concerning what is right and wrong, sinful and pure, and even American and un-American change over time. Occasionally a sensational event will punctuate a long process of gradual change and transform the prevailing perceptions of a place. When such a paradigm shift occurs, residents may find their city's reputation greatly altered.[1]

Such a contextual sea change or paradigm shift is exactly what happened to Birmingham's reputation in the mid-twentieth century. Although it was once the prime example of an American success story, praise of the Magic City's rapid industrial growth gave way with startling abruptness and permanence to the stigmatized Bombingham identity.[2] Ironically, the civil rights demonstrations marked the violent birth of a new, more racially inclusive Birmingham while simultaneously solidifying the city's reputation as a dangerously racist place. As the cultural context in which the city existed changed to such a great degree, the city's racist image became deeply entrenched and at odds with the nation's post–civil rights movement standard of acceptable racial beliefs and activities. Birmingham, although it made great strides regarding race relations, assumed the identity of the nation's racist pariah.

The actions of politicians provide further proof of the extent of this shift in national ideas regarding race. Before the transition to a self-reflexive awareness concerning racism, politicians could often profit from directly espousing racist views. Alabama governor George Wallace in the 1960s, for example, was not the first to be blatant and outspoken in his racism to gain, hold, and increase his political power. His rabidly racist inauguration speech on the steps of the Alabama state capitol in 1963 and his opportunistic blocking of a University of Alabama doorway that same year stand as examples of such dangerous political theater. In proclaiming "segregation today, . . . segregation tomorrow, . . . segregation forever" and making his symbolic "stand in the schoolhouse door," he knew what many white Alabamians wanted to hear in the reactionary context of the time and place.[3] One can only imagine the impact on a public servant's career in more modern times if he or she espoused racism only a fraction as virulent as Wallace's.

As an indication, look briefly to the use of racially charged language by U.S. Senator George Allen while campaigning to retain his office in 2006. Allen appeared set to win reelection easily until he directed the little-known slur *macaca* at a young man of Indian heritage during a campaign rally. Someone in the crowd captured the remark on video and uploaded it to YouTube. Within days, the news media noticed the popular and rapidly spreading video. In turn, Allen's *macaca* utterance claimed headlines nationwide. Armed with examples of more widely recognized racial slurs by long-term associates of Allen's, the media relentlessly reported on the story through Election Day. A much-damaged Allen lost his reelection bid.[4]

Senator John McCain's reaction to statements made by Congressman John Lewis during the 2008 presidential campaign similarly shows how feared and unacceptable the label of "racist" is in modern politics. Lewis, a man who faced down racial intolerance in the 1960s on Freedom Rides, at segregated lunch counters, and at the foot of Selma's Edmund Pettis Bridge with a police club splitting his skull, felt that many of the McCain campaign's rallies were coming dangerously close to inciting race-based hatred against his opponent, Barack Obama.[5] As Lewis related in an interview, much of the impassioned rhetoric at these gatherings seemed to be "sowing the seeds of hatred and division" in a manner eerily similar to the race-baiting heyday of the Wallace administration.[6] Immediately upon hearing of Lewis's rebuke, a sanctimonious McCain called the implication of racism a "character attack" against vice presidential nominee Sarah Palin and himself that went "beyond the pale."[7] Thus, where every politician from George Washington to George Wallace could speak openly—even if idiotically—about race, things changed so dramatically by the turn of the twenty-first century that even the insinuation of possible and indirect racial antagonism resulted in the loudest, quickest, and most self-righteous of retorts.

This outward political discomfort with racial division is merely one aspect of a larger societal transformation, which began in the battle against Fascism and resulted in racism being labeled distinctly un-American by the end of the twentieth century.[8] Birmingham's violent racism was exposed nationally just as the paradigm shifted away from the racial double standard that was long embraced in the United States. In fact, the scenes emanating from Birmingham no doubt helped propel this shift.[9] When Cold War–era political concerns made the alienation of Birmingham vital to United States interests abroad—particularly in contested areas of Africa—Birmingham experienced its own paradigm shift from exemplary American city to stigmatized urban outcast.[10]

The city's stigma subsequently proved extraordinarily troubling for its inhabitants and incredibly difficult to overcome. Through it, one aspect presents itself regarding the roles of perception and stigmatization in the field of urban history. Alongside planning, architecture, and political organizations and movements, perceptions and stigmas influence the trajectory of a city and the living conditions therein. In Birmingham, perceptual ties to the racial violence of 1963 bred an uncertainty and anxiety over the city's image, and the historical remembrance relative to that image has continually manifested itself. As a result, city residents have often expressed reticence concerning projects that remind people of the city's prominent place in the civil rights movement. The struggle over the construction of the Birmingham Civil Rights Institute and the unwillingness of many to rename local landmarks after individuals who played primary roles in the local movement for civil rights illustrate the enduring mark of stigmatization on the local level.

The association between Birmingham and its violently racist past has obviously resulted in a population that is, at the very least, distrustful of national publicity. Locals' reactions to the arrest and subsequent media coverage of Mayor Larry Langford in late 2008 revealed this aversion in stunning clarity. Before the media even had an opportunity to equate the arrest with race, and then race with Birmingham, locals bemoaned the coverage that was sure to follow. In reality, residents made a far greater issue of the city's past than did major media outlets. Their objections inserted race into the equation far more frequently and to a greater degree than did the national media. This example shows the hypersensitivity—and perhaps even an inferiority complex—that has developed in the city as a result of years of stigmatization.[11]

Shifting cultural and intellectual contexts have also played a central role in defining the nature of the stigmatized identities attached to San Francisco and Las Vegas. Yet, in each of these cases, the situation has lacked the abrupt and massive ideological upheaval experienced by Birmingham in regard to racism and the civil rights movement. That is not to say that San Francisco's and Las Vegas's stigmas have not influenced those cities; rather, those influences have simply taken on different and more nuanced qualities.

The stigma attached to San Francisco's association with homosexuality has been strong yet not as overwhelmingly damaging as Birmingham's racist stigmatization. One can obviously attribute this to the fact that San Francisco's stigma has been based on acceptance while Birmingham's was based on exclusion. At the same time, there is also a difference in the level of cultural acceptance of the stigmatizing characteristics. Where Birmingham became known for its racism at a time when racist attitudes were becoming unacceptable, San Francisco became known as a gay mecca at a time when gay Americans were finally gaining ground in the struggle for acceptance, albeit incomplete.

Because this acceptance of homosexuality has never been as complete in American society as has the social denunciation of racism, it has remained politically and socially acceptable for politicians and public figures to use antigay sentiment to a degree that would be taboo in regard to racist sentiment. For example, much of the rhetoric against allowing gays in the military closely resembled the earlier rhetoric and rationales against desegregating the army. However, whereas a person would have been ostracized for arguing in favor of a racially segregated military by the early 2000s, arguments in favor of military exclusion on the basis of sexual preference were still accepted and commonplace at that time. Quite simply, the perceptual lines around homosexuality and homophobia have not become as clear-cut as those around race and racism. Homophobia has subsequently remained, to some traditionalist groups, "the last acceptable prejudice."[12] As a result, San Francisco's image as the nation's gay mecca has drawn both public praise and ire. Its tolerance toward gays has also fit nicely with an intellectual tradition of casting the city as eccentric, exotic, and not quite "American" in its values.

The continued, if tempered, acceptability of gay bashing can be seen in the aftermath of Anita Bryant's and John Briggs's crusades to repeal gay rights ordinances in Florida and California. Neither the homophobic entertainer's nor the ambitious politician's career was ruined; nor were they socially ostracized in the immediate aftermath of their actions. Further, the Bryant-inspired reaction against gay rights enjoyed popular success nationwide, resulting in the repeal of gay right ordinances in communities from Florida's Dade County to Eugene, Oregon.[13] While gradual tolerance—an unfortunate but unavoidable word in and of itself that implies domination of one group over another—developed in the second half of the twentieth century, a complete paradigm shift concerning attitudes toward gay acceptance and against homophobia had not yet occurred. For that reason, politicians, pundits, and regular citizens of certain political persuasions still publicly and profitably excoriated "gay" San Francisco.

Ironically, just as the November 2008 presidential election highlighted the nation's turn away from acceptance of overt racism, it also made clear that the journey away from socially acceptable homophobia was still incomplete. By a vote of 52 percent to 48 percent, Californians approved a proposition that defined marriage as a union between a man and woman. This vote overturned a San Francisco ordinance that had allowed the recognition of gay nuptials since the previous June. It was a result of a wider Republican push to garner such anti–gay rights amendments on the state, and ultimately the national, level. More recently, the Supreme Court's decision in *Obergefell v. Hodges* asserted the U.S. Constitution's protection of same-sex marriage. Still, more than thirty years after John Briggs raised his challenge to the equality of gay Americans and almost two years after the U.S. Supreme Court's ruling, the issue of equal rights for America's gay citizens sadly remains a hotly contested political issue.[14]

San Francisco has, nevertheless, profited from its association with the gay rights movement and its reputation for gay tolerance. The growth, widespread acceptance, and profitability of gay-oriented tourism testify to this. What has stigmatized the city to some observers has made it more attractive to others. The Travel Industry Association did, after all, rank the city as the number-one gay-friendly destination 2006.[15] While that definitely helped secure its share of the $60 billion gay tourism industry, the fact that prevalent concerns still force people to travel to "gay-friendly" destinations says much about the incomplete acceptance of homosexuality in America.

As with San Francisco and its reputation as a gay mecca, Las Vegas experienced a mixed bag concerning its dominant stigma and the historical context it occupies. Gambling, like homosexuality, became more acceptable in the post–World War II United States. This is in no small part due to and represented by the proliferation of casinos across the nation as well as online gambling. The fact that residents of a majority of states now have easy access to some form of casino gambling has gone far to remove the negative stigma associated with the practice.[16]

At the same time, it is important to understand that gambling has always been an important part of the American experience. The very nature of coming to America was a gamble for all who attempted it as was the westward movement of a very mobile people during the first few centuries of settlement on the North American continent, and that westward shift of the national population still continues at the end of the first decade of the twenty-first century. Games of chance have likewise followed Americans to every corner of the nation and played an important role in socialization. As the nation became more "civilized," its citizens did not automatically lose their desire to gamble. Instead, the ultimate prohibition of gambling in "respectable" American areas allowed for the development of gambling in locations outside the mainstream United States. After experiments with gambling across the border in Tijuana, on offshore gambling boats in southern California, and in illicit back rooms around the nation, Las Vegas emerged as the nation's foremost repository for its gaming needs.[17] The remote desert identity that Las Vegas boosters sought to shed in the early twentieth century subsequently became one of the city's most valuable assets by midcentury.

Situated far away in the Mojave Desert and safely separated from the rest of the nation by canyon, mountain, and arid plain, Las Vegas played the role of the nation's distant center of vice brilliantly. It is not surprising that organized crime took root in this hard desert soil because many of the gangsters had the most experience and expertise with profiting from people's vices. Knowing that there were hefty profits in gambling, crime families certainly did not mind exercising their expertise. Thus, mid-twentieth-century Las Vegas developed a dual identity both as the nation's gambling center and as a city ruled by the mob.[18] Over subsequent years, as Vegas increasingly played up its risqué do-anything-here persona, sexual license joined gambling and the mob as a major trait of the Las Vegas image.[19]

By the late twentieth century, Las Vegas stood well established in the American imagination as an adult playground or Sin City. This idea became so prevalent that, as with Birmingham and racism, mere mentions of the city in the media often carried an accompanying reference to gambling, illicit sex, or the mob.[20] While these elements proved unacceptable to Americans in their own suburban neighborhoods, they proved perfectly wonderful as escapist pleasures. For that reason, by the early twenty-first century, tens of millions of people flocked to Vegas each year to taste a little of the forbidden fruit. Although many boarded their planes back home with knowing smiles on their faces after whatever had happened in Vegas, what stayed in Vegas most often turned out to be their money.[21] They had purchased entertainment and escaped from the mundane.

Eventually, worries over the impact of the spread of casino gambling made many nervous about Las Vegas's continued existence as the nation's gaming capital.[22] In the early and mid-1990s, some in the city even attempted to recast the destination as a more family-friendly locale before settling back on the more risqué adult playground following the election of Mayor Oscar Goodman and particularly in the aftermath of the September 11, 2001, terrorist attacks.[23] Such worries ultimately proved unwarranted as Vegas continued to draw record crowds through the beginning of the twenty-first century. Meanwhile, metropolitan Las Vegas stood as the fastest-growing major urban area in the nation, with upward of seven thousand new residents moving into Clark County per month by 2003.[24]

The key to Las Vegas's boom was that its whole was more than the sum of its casinos. To view Las Vegas as merely a place where people went to gamble is to miss the reality that is Las Vegas. If rock and roll was once the music of rebellion, then Las Vegas is the rock and roll of American cities. It is a place perceived as standing outside the box of suburban order, rules, and suffocating morality. From this perspective, Mayor Oscar Goodman was absolutely correct in pushing for a return to the promotion of the city as an adult playground. It is, after all, a place that "provided an outlet for people to live out their fantasies." All the family stuff, as he once said, is "better left to Disneyland."[25] Even the once-family-oriented pirate show outside the Strip's Treasure Island Hotel and Casino has recently transitioned into a more risqué spectacle.

Yet one of the key issues facing Las Vegas as it raced into the twenty-first century was how to accommodate the desires and needs of an ever-increasing number of resident families. The city struggled to find a way to be its glitzy and edgy self while also providing an environment suitable for the quality of life of a vastly increased suburban population. The enormously successful marketing of Sin City that increased tourism allowed for the economic opportunity that brought in those multitudes of new suburban residents. This increased population allowed Las Vegans to realistically dream of joining other major U.S. urban areas with the addition of major-league professional sports. Yet the ubiquitous nature of the Sin City label carried a double edge. As Las Vegas attempted to live up to its image in order to profit from tourism, many family-oriented residents found their values and quality of life compromised. This tension subsequently manifested itself in the battle over billboard censorship in 2004.[26] At the same time, the gambling and anything-goes identity dissuaded major-league sports leagues from locating franchises in the city for many years.[27]

Further, as economic conditions faltered in the 2000s, the Las Vegas metropolitan area (including the Strip) found itself hypersensitized to any characterization that might hurt tourism. Such was the case when President Barak Obama insinuated that convention trips to Las Vegas wasted federal bailout funds. The local outrage over this—complete with Mayor Goodman demanding an apology for the slight to his city—reveals once again the trouble of a tourism economy based on a stigmatized identity.[28] Likewise, the outrage of Mayor Goodman and other politicians who chimed in made President Obama's statements even more damaging. Knowing when and how to respond to being stigmatized is a skill that one should master when governing a stigmatized city. In sum, while cities like Las Vegas and San Francisco have found ways to profit from identities based on characteristics or actions that are stigmatized by the more conservative segments of the nation's population, the strengthening of these identities can leave those cities' tourism industries vulnerable to changes in the national context.

Unease over declining tourism proved particularly strong in the Las Vegas valley between 2008 and 2011 as the global recession and housing market collapse ended a long economic boom. Beginning late in 2007, overinflated housing prices began to fall and continued to fall through 2011. Foreclosures rocked communities as variable-interest-rate mortgages adjusted and a majority of Las Vegans with mortgages found themselves "upside down." Thousands of such individuals simply walked away from their properties or attempted cumbersome short sales because they found refinancing impossible due to a perfect storm of deflated housing prices, heavy debt, and loss of employment.[29] In the national media, the old standby characterizations of Vegas once again appeared in discussions of the economic situation. For example, on September 17, 2008, *New York Times* columnist Thomas Friedman could not help but relate the crash of the nation's financial sector with Las Vegas gambling. To him, the financiers resembled reckless patrons gathered around a Vegas blackjack table. They bet wildly and without care until "busted." This, Friedman concluded, was not supposed to happen outside the distant gambling city. In the future, he warned, "We need to make sure that what happens in Vegas stays in Vegas—and doesn't come to Main Street."[30]

But what was really happening was that Main Street had increasingly come to Las Vegas. The fabulously successful tourism industry created growth and plentiful jobs. This attracted more family-oriented residents with more mainstream values, as indicated by the billboard controversy. At the same time, the nation's cultural context seems to have shifted somewhat toward more mainstream acceptance of gaming and risqué behavior. This seems to be supported by the national proliferation of casinos as well as the city's recent successful acquisition of the NFL's Raiders and an NHL franchise. Perhaps society has changed its view of just how deviant Las Vegas really is.

Nevertheless, while undeniably more widely accepted in modern American culture than in the early to mid-twentieth century, the characteristics that make Las Vegas special have not reached the standard of an American "norm." For example, even though gambling is more widespread throughout the country, it is still typically confined to areas outside middle-class communities. Most Americans still must leave their hometowns to visit the closest casino. Possibly, as Las Vegas's ever-increasing visitation rates suggest, these trips to smaller casinos only whet their appetites for visiting Las Vegas.[31] Maybe it is more than just the gambling they are after. It could be that they have tasted gaming and now seek the overall Las Vegas experience.

Major-league sports' embrace of Las Vegas also suggests something more than just a change of heart regarding Las Vegas's image. With the city's population growth and ever-increasing tourism, the prospect of a major-league franchise's success there becomes more likely. In this scenario, the stigma remains, but it is just not as important to league officials and owners as profit is. Nevada did, after all, promise to build the second-most-expensive tax-supported stadium in history just to have the Raiders consider the city.[32] There is money to be made, and the NFL is good at making it.

Perchance it would be better for Sin City's prospects if such markers of mainstream acceptance really were misleading. Just maybe Las Vegas is better off residing outside perceived social norms. The city works because its colorful history of gambling, promiscuity, and mob ties retain a degree of resonance. In this sense, going to Las Vegas must continue to be like venturing into a foreign moral landscape, a place where one can temporarily forget the inhibitions and rules of home. Convincing the public that such is the reality has been genius of modern Vegas promotion. Las Vegas does not take a stigmatized action and tell people that there is nothing wrong with it. Neither does it try to transform the rest of America to reflect its values. To do either would mean the end of a large measure of the city's prosperity. Instead, it takes stigmatized activity and tells people, yes, it is wrong, but it is okay if you want to do it here.

It is also worth revisiting the geography in relation to each city's stigmatization. As mentioned earlier, each city's stigmatizing event or characteristic can be located historically in very limited sections of the cities' overall land areas. With Birmingham, it is a few roads and churches downtown; in San Francisco, it is a single district; and in Las Vegas, it is again only a couple of roads and their casinos. As these compact areas are magnified and projected to the world, they become the entirety of the city in the minds of a public that is unaware that it clings to easy generalizations and stereotypes. Thus, when someone thinks of Birmingham, they think of the Sixteenth Street Baptist Church; when they hear San Francisco, the Castro district emerges; and any mention of Las Vegas brings forth the Strip. These obviously incomplete images neglect the complexity of the lives and experiences making up these cities. That, in my opinion, is a great disservice.

Birmingham, San Francisco, and Las Vegas: Conclusions

If a sensational event should occur that seemingly supports the negative perception of a city, the resulting stigmatization finds a strong foundation upon which to rest. Conversely, the same may said of a sensationally good event that shows the city to be a center of progress. Yet always, the influence and staying power of the subsequent stereotype is tempered by the contemporary historical context. The wider shifting of public attitudes about the specific event or trait determines the impact of the resultant reputation. Birmingham, for example, was fortuitous enough to ride the wave of a society intrigued by industrialization in the late nineteenth and early twentieth centuries. As the industrial center of the New South, its reputation benefited from this. In contrast, in the 1950s and '60s, this progressive identity fell victim to a reactionary and violent dedication to tradition by some locals. Such attachment to racial segregation and oppression stood in total opposition to shifting cultural ideas of the time concerning racism.[33]

Birmingham's stained reputation has proven very difficult to overcome. Evidence of its existence still appears on a regular basis. Even recently, in 2017, as countless news pundits discussed the alt-right's violent demonstrations in Charlottesville, Virginia, the comparison to Birmingham proved too tempting to resist. On the night of the violence, an NAACP official appearing on MSNBC invoked Birmingham as a comparative marker for racial violence when discussing a neo-Nazi's tragic rampage in Charlottesville.[34] Whether or not Charlottesville's reputation will be damaged as a result of such violence remains to be seen. However, it is doubtful that the city will suffer damage equivalent to Birmingham. Birmingham's violent outbursts were accurately reported as driven by local violent reaction in opposition to civil rights. Also, as a result of segregation and previous violence, there was a strong reputational foundation for Birmingham's violently racist identity to build upon by 1963. Charlottesville in 2017 lacked this recent reputational foundation, and the media widely reported that the violence was visited upon the city by outsiders. Again, that was not the case in Birmingham. As the United States has never fully come to terms with the racial inequality of its history and its present, it is likely that episodes of racist violence will continue to visit the nation. It is also likely that Birmingham will continue to be held up as an example for comparison whenever this occurs.

Meanwhile, San Francisco straddles a sort of perceptual apex where it precariously balances between the praise and condemnation of the Left and Right. Because of the lessening (although not completely removed) stigma against homosexuality and the incomplete social repudiation of homophobia, San Francisco's mental placement as America's gay mecca is viewed simultaneously as a positive and negative thing. It simply depends on the perspective. For all those who, like Senator John McCain, throw up their fingers in air quotes and derisively refer to San Francisco, others are eager to experience its open culture and contribute to its emerging gay tourist industry.[35]

Yet the very existence of what is termed *gay tourism* reveals how far the nation has to go in order to see gay and lesbian people as equal citizens. On the one hand, while it is commendable that homosexual Americans can go to San Francisco in a form of pilgrimage or identity tourism to celebrate an important historical setting in their fight for equal rights, it is the fact that many go there and other places in search of greater acceptance that is troubling. It should not be necessary for people in early twenty-first-century America to travel to a certain place in order to feel comfortable about openly displaying their identity. Thus, the very existence of a gay tourism industry in San Francisco reveals a continuing stigmatization of homosexuals in the rest of society and contributes to the stigmatization of San Francisco—even if it is profitable.

It is also worth noting that San Francisco seems to be in the midst of developing a new stigma based on expense. Because of its close proximity to the lucrative high-tech industries of Silicon Valley, the city has become widely known as an unaffordable place to live. News coverage of this has been widespread in recent years with journalists reporting on the city's skyrocketing cost of living. Such reporting is certainly warranted as rent has increased 50 percent since 2010 to an average of $4,200 per month by 2017. San Francisco has subsequently gained the title of most expensive city in which to lease an apartment in the mainland United States.[36] It is now becoming known as a place where high-tech workers end up "scraping by" on six-figure incomes and "families are priced out of the market."[37]

Such a reputation shows evidence of affecting the city. In recent years, for example, some workers in high-tech industries have sought housing subsidies while others are leaving the city for lower-paying jobs in less expensive locations.[38] Still more high-tech workers are choosing not to relocate to San Francisco at all. Wade Foster, CEO of startup Zapier, chose to locate his company in Sacramento. With its lower cost of living, Sacramento proved attractive to prospective employees. As Foster put it, "A lot of folks just have a difficult time making it in the Bay Area long term" because "housing is really challenging."[39] San Francisco, along with perhaps the entire Bay Area, is quickly developing a reputation as a place where it is too expensive to live.[40]

Las Vegas, meanwhile, also faces the prospect of a shifting context and reputation. As America's Sin City, Las Vegas took a reputation for deviance and transformed it into a staggering growth rate and prosperity. Shifting social and cultural values that have embraced gambling and risqué behavior as more mainstream have, as with and San Francisco and homosexuality, alleviated the degree of stigmatization felt by Las Vegans in recent years. But local struggles between more family-oriented residents and the dominant industries over sexually themed advertising suggest growing resistance to wide-open promotion of the Sin City image as the city's demographics change. The successful relocation of the NFL's Raiders and the granting of an NHL franchise to the city also indicate a shift toward a more mainstream acceptance. How much obtaining these franchises actually signifies the mainstreaming of Las Vegas remains to be seen. They could merely indicate the profit potential offered by public financing of facilities and population growth combined with astronomical annual visitation rates. But if

Las Vegas wishes to continue its trend of profiting from being America's Sin City, its leaders need to carefully negotiate the balance between the mainstream and acceptable deviance. Attempts at maintaining this balance should make for a future that is every bit as interesting as the city's storied past.

History is not static. This is certainly true regarding historically stigmatized cities such as Birmingham, San Francisco, and Las Vegas. These cities possess reputations that are rooted in preconceived notions and heavily dependent upon a morass of shifting values, ideals, and historical actions. The influence of their reputations is determined by the beliefs and actions of locals and outsiders alike. The effects of stigmatization are thus greatly varied but always significant. Hopefully, by understanding the intricacies of this process in these three cities, we can gain insight and find commonalties with the circumstances of other stigmatized places. Because it is inevitable that such places will continue to exist as reputations remain in flux relative to time, events, and beliefs. Such is the nature of history.

■

Notes

Abbreviations

BACCP Birmingham Area Chamber of Commerce Papers, Pamphlets and Reports

BN *Birmingham News*

BP-H *Birmingham Post-Herald*

DACA Delta Airlines Corporate Archives, Atlanta, Georgia

JCH-GLC James C. Hormel Gay and Lesbian Center, San Francisco Public Library

LAT *Los Angeles Times*

LHRLA Linn Henley Research Library and Archives, Birmingham, Alabama

LVR-J *Las Vegas Review-Journal*

NYT *New York Times*

SFC *San Francisco Chronicle*

UNLVSC University of Nevada, Las Vegas, Library Special Collections, Las Vegas,

Preface

1. "Vulcan's Story," Vulcan Park and Museum, http://visitvulcan.com/about/vulcans-story/; "Fun Facts," Vulcan Park and Museum, http://visitvulcan.com/about/fun-facts/. A statue of Vulcan, the Roman god of the forge, overlooks downtown Birmingham from atop Red Mountain, which is immediately south of the city. The statue itself, at fifty-six feet tall and weighing 101,200 pounds, is the largest metal statue ever produced in the United States and the largest cast-iron statue in the world. Placed atop a 124-foot-tall pedestal, *Vulcan* reaches an overall height of 180 feet. As originally designed by sculptor Giuseppe Moretti, *Vulcan* held aloft a spear tip in his upraised right hand. In 1946 this spear was replaced with a torch that for

a brief period was used as part of a safety-awareness campaign to draw attention to traffic fatalities. Normally the light would burn green. However, if a traffic fatality occurred, it would burn red for that day. Although this practice lasted only a short time and the light permanently burned green thereafter, its lore lived on. At least it did until 1999, when the city restored the *Vulcan* to its original spear-tip-wielding form.

Chapter 1. Imagining Place

1. While I agree with geographer Rex J. Rowley's usage of the words *place* and *space* regarding Las Vegas in his book *Everyday Las Vegas: Local Life in a Tourist Town* (Reno: University of Nevada Press, 2013), I have chosen to use the term *place* generally for all references to the geographical areas under discussion. I would, however, like to call attention to how Rowley employs the word *place* when discussing locals' views of the city. When discussing outsiders' views, he uses the word *space*. To Rowley, *place* represents a deeper understanding of the location brought about by the locals' connection to the area. The local thus recognizes the intricacies of the place. The outsider, however, forms a view of an area based on visual markers and only a superficial understanding of local conditions and layers of meaning. In this regard, outsiders experience space rather than place.

2. Certainly, one should also note that some of this opposition could also be fueled by continued racism. However, it is obvious that many in opposition to such public remembrance are driven, at least to some extent, by concern for their own reputations and that of their city.

3. The "What Happens Here, Stays Here" tagline was developed by the Las Vegas Convention and Visitors Authority in 2002. The slogan, despite significant resistance from some business and industrial leaders, proved so successful that it became synonymous with Las Vegas in the early twenty-first century. See Chris Jones, "What Happens Here, Stays Here Strikes Sour Note with Some at Conference," *LVR-J*, December 18, 2003; "What Happens Here Has Been Used Elsewhere," *Las Vegas Sun*, July 22, 2005. For use of *Bombingham* as a nickname for Birmingham in the post–civil rights era, see Glenn T. Eskew, *But for Birmingham: The Local and National Movements in the Civil Rights Struggle* (Chapel Hill: University of North Carolina Press, 1997); Clarence Page, "Pro-Life until You Get in Their Way," *Chicago Tribune*, February 1, 1998; Marlon Manuel, "Birmingham Clinic Bombing: A City's Past Comes Roaring Back," *Atlanta Constitution-Journal*, February 1, 1998; Bruce Feldman, "Out of Control," *ESPN the Magazine*, June 10, 2002, http://espn.go.com/magazine/vo15no12uab.html, accessed July 7, 2008.

4. Morton White and Lucia White, *The Intellectual versus the City: From Thomas Jefferson to Frank Lloyd Wright* (New York: Mentor Books, 1964), 26; Paul Liecaster Ford, ed., *The Works of Thomas Jefferson*, vol. 4 (New York: J. P. Putnam's Sons, 1904), 86. For a more recent discussion of Americans' ambivalence toward their cities, see Steven Conn, *Americans against the City: Anti-Urbanism in the Twentieth Century* (New York: Oxford University Press, 2014).

5. Erving Goffman, *Stigma: Notes on the Management of Spoiled Identity* (New York: Simon and Schuster, 1963); Irwin Katz, *Stigma: A Social Psychological Analysis* (Hillsdale, N.J.: LEA, 1981).

6. Goffman, *Stigma*, 1–7; Katz, *Stigma*, 1–2; Robert M. Page, *Stigma* (London: Routledge, Kegan Paul, 1984), 1–3; Stephen C. Ainlay, Lerita M. Coleman, and Gaylene Becker, "Stigma Reconsidered," in *The Dilemma of Difference*, ed. Ainlay, Becker, and Coleman (New York: Plenum, 1986), 1–13.

7. Goffman, *Stigma*, 3, 5.

8. Ibid., 3.

9. Ibid., 4.

10. Ibid.; Katz, *Stigma*, 2; Page, *Stigma*, 4.

11. Sarah Kershaw and Patricia Leigh Brown, "Women's Work: They Take It Off, but They Also Put On Suits, Uniforms, and Blue Collars," *NYT*, June 2, 2004. In this article, Jones relates how, as mayor, she was often confronted with the mistaken belief that she had previously worked as a showgirl or dancer.

12. "Where I Stand: Richard Lamm Isn't a Lamb," *Las Vegas Sun*, July 10, 1996, https://lasvegassun.com/news/1996/jul/10/where-i-stand-richard-lamm-isnt-a-lamb/.

13. In numerous examples, the press has tended to place the cities in the context of regional stereotypes. A few examples of this from midcentury include "Birmingham Story," *Time*, May 16, 1960; Ward Allen Howe, "Las Vegas Vacation Center," *NYT*, March 24, 1946; Jack Goodman, "Desert Attractions: Tourism Is Las Vegas' Major Industry and Spring Business Is Booming," *NYT*, March 16, 1947; Grady Johnson, "Lively Las Vegas: New Vacationland Is Growing Up Rapidly around the Great Lake at Hoover Dam," *NYT*, November 14, 1948.

14. Daniel J. Czitrom, *Media and the American Mind: From Morse to McLuhan* (Chapel Hill: University of North Carolina Press, 1982), xii.

15. Ibid., 30–31, 35, 190–92.

16. Katz, *Stigma*, 1–11.

17. Pierre Bourdieu, *In Other Words: Essays towards a Reflexive Sociology* (Stanford, Calif.: Stanford University Press, 1990), 190.

18. For examples of this tendency, see Manuel, "Birmingham Clinic Bombing"; Benjamin Spillman, "Obama Draws Ire over Vegas Junket Criticism," *LVR-J*, February 11, 2009; Patrick Buchanan, "Why Do They Hate Anita Bryant?," *Los Angeles Herald-Examiner*, October 3, 1978; "Protect America's Children," mailer, Gary Shilts Papers, box 7, folder 1, JCH-GLC.

19. Carl Becker, "Everyman His Own Historian," *American Historical Review* 37 (January 1932): 229.

20. Walter Lippman, *Public Opinion* (New York: NuVision Books, 2007), 49–58.

21. Ibid., 79–94.

22. JBHE Foundation, "Stripping Away Myths: Improving the Lot of African Americans by Changing the American Racial Stereotype," *Journal of Black Higher Education* 11 (Spring 1996): 110.

23. "The Coolies and the Negro," *NYT*, February 17, 1878; "The Negro Point of View," *NYT*, November 17, 1903; Robert G. Jones, "The Negro Point of View," *NYT*, June 29, 1932; "Negroes Also Have Feelings," *NYT*, October 20, 1942.

24. Thomas E. Ford and George R. Tonander, "The Role of Differentiation between Groups and Social Identity in Stereotype Formation," *Social Psychology Quarterly* 61 (December 1998): 372.

25. JBHE Foundation, "Stripping Away Myths," 110. This projection of place stigmatizations on residents is a form of tribal stigmatization as discussed in Goffman, *Stigma*, 4–6.

26. Lippman, *Public Opinion*, 49–58.

27. Edward S. Herman and Noam Chomsky, *Manufacturing Consent: The Political Economy of the Mass Media* (New York: Pantheon, 1988), 2–3.

28. Media Research Center, *Special Report: An In-Depth Study, Analysis or Review Exploring the Media* (Alexandria, Va.: Media Research Center, 2007); David H. Weaver and G. Cleveland Wilhoit, "Journalists—Who Are They, Really?," *Media Studies Journal* 6 (Fall 1992): 73–76. The word *acceptable* in regard to Chomsky and Herman implies control by an outside force. The existence of that force is not necessarily a conscious entity that directs from above what stories will be covered and how they will be slanted to promote social and, more important, financial well-being for the media corporation. In some instances, this may very well be the case, but it is only necessary that market forces and professional self-interest play on journalists and the networks or publications they work for. With this in mind, one can excise both the filter of ownership and the notion of propaganda from Chomsky's theory and arrive at a model that can describe the conservative direction of news coverage.

29. Lippman, *Public Opinion*, 323–24.

30. Howard M. Solomon, "Stigma and Western Culture: A Historical Approach," in Ainlay, Becker, Coleman, *The Dilemma of Difference*, 59–76.

31. William Sharpe and Leonard Wallock, eds., *Visions of the Modern City: Essays in History, Art, and Literature* (Baltimore: Johns Hopkins University Press, 1987); Eric Avila, *Popular Culture in the Age of White Flight: Fear and Fantasy in Suburban Los Angeles* (Berkeley: University of California Press, 2006); Robert Beauregard, *Voices of Decline: The Postwar Fate of U.S. Cities* (New York: Routledge, 2002); Steve Macek, *Urban Nightmares: The Media, the Right, and the Moral Panic over the City* (Minneapolis: University of Minnesota Press, 2006).

32. Loïc Wacquant, *Urban Outcasts: A Comparative Sociology of Advanced Marginality* (Cambridge: Polity Press, 2008), 2–5, 163–98.

33. See Lynne Hancock and Gerry Mooney, "'Welfare Ghettos' and the 'Broken Society': Territorial Stigmatisation in the Contemporary U.K.," *Housing, Theory and Society* 30, no. 1 (2012): 46–64; Tom Slater and Ntsiki Anderson, "The Reputational Ghetto: Territorial Stigmatisation in St. Paul's, Bristol," *Transactions of the Institute of British Geographers* 37 (October 2012): 530–46.

Chapter 2. Not Always a Pariah

1. The most extensive coverage of Birmingham's founding can be found in Carl V. Harris, *Political Power in Birmingham, 1871–1921* (Knoxville: University of Tennessee

Press, 1977), 12–14. Two excellent studies of southern identity that examine the commonly held ideas of the lazy, laid back, or agricultural southerner can be found in James C. Cobb, *Away down South: A History of Southern Identity* (New York: Oxford University Press, 2005); Todd L. Savitt and James Harvey Young, *Disease and Distinctiveness in the American South* (Knoxville: University of Tennessee Press, 1991).

2. Justin Fuller, "Boom Towns and Blast Furnaces: Town Promotion in Alabama, 1885–1893," *Alabama Review* 29 (January 1976): 38; Harris, *Political Power in Birmingham*, 14–16. Harris reveals Birmingham's iron and industrial boom to be one of fits and starts. After the city's 1871 founding, a nationwide economic depression and a localized cholera outbreak in 1873 slowed the city's growth. Yet, by 1880, with the formation of the Pratt Coal and Coke Company and the initiation of successful coal mining four miles northwest of the city, industrial output and population began a marked expansion.

3. Harris, *Political Power in Birmingham*, 22; Martha Mitchell Bigelow, "Birmingham's Carnival of Crime, 1871–1910," *Alabama Review* 3 (April 1950): 124; U.S. Bureau of the Census, "Table 14. Population of the 100 Largest Urban Places: 1910," www.census. gov/population/www/documentation/twps0027/tab14.txt.

4. W. David Lewis, *Sloss Furnaces and the Rise of the Birmingham District: An Industrial Epic* (Tuscaloosa: University of Alabama Press, 1994), 82–91; Bobby M. Wilson, *America's Johannesburg: Industrialization and Racial Transformation in Birmingham* (Lanham, Md.: Rowman & Littlefield, 2000), 4–5, 50–51, 60–62, 65–79, 86–87, 92, 109–12.

5. Lewis, *Sloss Furnaces*, 475.

6. Robert J. Norrell, "Caste in Steel: Jim Crow Careers in Birmingham, Alabama," *Journal of American History* 73 (December 1986): 671.

7. Harris, *Political Power in Birmingham*, 45.

8. Birmingham Board of Education Minutes, June 9, 1900, LHRLA; "Advanced Grade in Colored Schools Allowed Conditionally," *BN*, June 11, 1900; Margaret E. Armbrester, *Samuel Ullman and "Youth": The Life, the Legacy* (Tuscaloosa: University of Alabama Press, 1993), 40.

9. Horace Mann Bond, *Negro Education in Alabama: A Study in Cotton and Steel* (Tuscaloosa: University of Alabama Press, 1994), 145–47.

10. Birmingham Board of Education Minutes, June 9, 1900, LHRLA; Howard N. Rabinowitz, *The First New South: 1865–1920* (Arlington Heights, Ill.: Harlan Davidson, 1992), 134–37.

11. Birmingham Board of Education Minutes, June 9, September 3, 1900, LHRLA; "High School for Negro Children," *BN*, September 4, 1900; Lynne B. Feldman, *A Sense of Place: Birmingham's Black Middle-Class Community, 1890–1930* (Tuscaloosa: University of Alabama Press, 1999), 120–21; Armbrester, *Samuel Ullman*, 42. The fact that the call for publicly supported secondary education for black children originated from the black community supports the findings of Harris's *Political Power in Birmingham*. Harris argues that multiple interest groups competed for and exercised political power in Birmingham between 1871 and 1921. While the economic

upper and middle classes wielded the greatest political power, and lower-class black residents the least, Birmingham was far from a complete dictatorship of the economic elite. Lower groups could, and often did, exert political power.

12. Arthur Harold Parker, *A Dream That Came True: Industrial High School* (Birmingham: Printing Department of Industrial High School, 1932), 86; Juliet Bradford, *The Industrial High School: A Brief History* (Birmingham: Printing Department of Industrial High School, 1925), 11–17; "Industrial High Head Is Honored," *BP-H*, May 5, 1939; Jerome Christopher Averette, "Documentation and History of Arthur Harold Parker High School," *Alabama Black in the Mirror*, May 1977, 5–8; Ambrose Caliver, "The Largest Negro High School," *School Life*, December 1931, 73–74; "Negro High School with Booker T. Washington Purpose," *Christian Science Monitor*, October 11, 1932; "Industrial School for Negroes Is 'A Dream That Came True,'" *Christian Science Monitor*, date unknown, 1930.

13. Lewis, *Sloss Furnaces*, 298.

14. "The Great South," *NYT*, August 28, 1886.

15. "The New Alabama: Recent Great Changes in the Character of Its Population," *Louisville Courier-Journal*, December 23, 1886, reprinted in *NYT*, December 26, 1886.

16. "Mad Speculation in Land," *NYT*, February 25, 1887.

17. Charles E. Connerly, *The Most Segregated City in America: City Planning and Civil Rights in Birmingham, 1920–1980* (Charlottesville: University of Virginia Press, 2005), 13; Harris, *Political Power in Birmingham*, 13–14. Harris provides biographical information on the colorful Powell, who was known as the "Duke of Birmingham."

18. "Alabama's Show City," *NYT*, December 24, 1899; "Alabama's Leading City," *NYT*, December 31, 1899; "Iron and Coal Galore," *NYT*, February 7, 1887; "New Riches Piled High," *NYT*, February 10, 1887; "A Change of Spirit," *NYT*, September 6, 1884.

19. "Iron and Coal Galore."

20. "A Change of Spirit."

21. "A Southern Incident," editorial, *NYT*, June 24, 1898.

22. "Alabama's Show City"; "Alabama's Leading City"; "Iron and Coal Galore"; "New Riches Piled High."

23. "Birmingham's Big Jump," *NYT*, September 30, 1910.

24. Charles A. Selden, "South's Giant Stride from Pawnshop to Prosperity," *NYT*, February 15, 1920.

25. Frank Bohn, "New South Throbs," *NYT*, October 25, 1925.

26. "To Disenfranchise Alabama Negroes," *NYT*, December 16, 1900.

27. "Alabama Negroes Act," *NYT*, September 25, 1901.

28. "Deporting Alabama Negroes," *NYT*, December 17, 1901.

29. J. A. MacKnight, "Levantines Driving the Negro out of Business in the Gulf States," *NYT*, April 8, 1906; Booker T. Washington, "Southern Lynchings," *NYT*, January 11, 1913; "Inciter of Negroes Held," *NYT*, April 9, 1917.

30. "Inciter of Negroes Held."

31. "New Flogging Case Bared in Alabama," *NYT*, July 14, 1927; "South Is Aroused against Flogging," *NYT*, July 17, 1927; "Flogging Inquiries Increase in Alabama,"

NYT, July 18, 1927; "Alabama Band Flogs Man, Burns His Home," *NYT*, September 11, 1927; "Alabama Floggings Charged to 18 Men," *NYT*, September 17, 1927.

32. "New Flogging Case"; "Alabama Band Flogs Man."

33. "New Flogging Case"; "South Is Aroused against Flogging"; "Flogging Inquiries Increase"; "Alabama Band Flogs Man"; "Alabama Floggings Charged."

34. "South Is Aroused against Flogging."

35. Lawrence D. McAvoy, conversation with the author, January 28, 2009.

36. Blaine A. Brownell, "Birmingham, Alabama: New South City in the 1920s," *Journal of Southern History* 38 (February 1972): 24, 28–30; Carl V. Harris, "Reforms in Governmental Control of Negroes in Birmingham, Alabama, 1890–1920," *Journal of Southern History* 38 (November 1972): 569.

37. Anne O'Hare McCormick, "The South: Its New Industrial Capitals," *NYT*, July 6, 1930.

38. Eugene R. Lyde Jr., "Ideas about the South," *NYT*, June 12, 1933.

39. John Temple Graves, "Alabama Wearies of Our Criticism," *NYT*, July 8, 1934.

40. Richard B. Sherman, "The Harding Administration and the Negro: An Opportunity Lost," *Journal of Negro History* 49 (July 1964): 157–58. Sherman argues that Harding possessed a limited knowledge of race relations in the United States and did not go far enough in pushing for equality. However, the president's public stance in favor of the antilynching law, the interstate race commission, and equality in all realms but the social indicate at least a significant acknowledgment of the nation's racial problem. Harris, *Political Power in Birmingham*, 34. Harris characterizes local reactions to Harding's comments on limited racial equality as "cold" and says audiences were "appalled."

41. Presidential scholar Alvin Felzenberg has argued that Coolidge was not nearly as silent on race as has been popularly believed. Instead, he showed disdain for the Ku Klux Klan and acknowledged the needs of black Americans. *Boston Globe*, August 2, 1998. Others such as the editors of the *Journal of Blacks in Higher Education* have taken issue with this interpretation, arguing instead that Coolidge did only the bare minimum on racial issues to keep northern blacks in the Republican corner. JBHE Foundation, "The Racial Views of American Presidents: A Look at the Record of Calvin Coolidge," *Journal of Blacks in Higher Education* 21 (Autumn 1998): 71.

42. Estimates vary widely for Klan membership during this period. Charles C. Alexander estimates Klan rolls to have included five million individuals nationwide in *The Ku Klux Klan in the Southwest* (Lexington: University of Kentucky Press, 1965), vi. Kenneth T. Jackson offers a more conservative estimate of just over two million in *The Ku Klux Klan in the City, 1915–1930* (New York: Oxford University Press, 1967), 237. Others such as Robert Goldberg place the number somewhere near six million: "Beneath the Hood and Robe: A Socioeconomic Analysis of the Ku Klux Klan Membership in Denver, Colorado, 1921–1925," *Western Historical Quarterly* 11 (April 1980): 181.

43. Alexander, *The Ku Klux Klan in the Southwest*, 55–56; Jackson, *Ku Klux Klan in the City*.

44. Harvard Sitkoff, *A New Deal for Blacks: The Emergence of Civil Rights as a National Issue* (Oxford: Oxford University Press, 1978), 47, 60–65, 72–74.

45. Ibid., 73–74.

46. "State Church Assailed," *NYT*, June 17, 1935.

47. "Jewish Author Sends Back Decorations Given Him by Italy," *Chicago Daily Tribune*, September 26, 1938.

48. "Catholics Attack Isms," *LAT*, October 20, 1938.

49. Richard H. King, *Race, Culture, and the Intellectuals* (Baltimore: Johns Hopkins University Press, 2004), 1–10. King stresses that the postwar shift toward human universality quickly gave way to particularism during the mid to latter 1960s. During this period, belief in group identification, pride, and power overtook the emphasis on universal humanity.

50. Eskew, *But for Birmingham*, 53–54. Eskew places the total number of racially motivated bombings between 1945 and 1963 at fifty. Wayne Flynt, however, states that thirty-three racially motivated bombings occurred in the city between 1940 and 1963. Wayne Flynt, *Alabama in the Twentieth Century* (Tuscaloosa: University of Alabama Press, 2004), 345.

51. Lewis, *Sloss Furnaces*, 432–33.

52. Ibid., 432–35; U.S. Bureau of the Census, "Table 18. Population of the 100 Largest Urban Places: 1950," www.census.gov/population/www/documentation/twps0027/tab18.txt.

53. For discussion of Atlanta's civil rights movement–era image, see Virginia H. Hein, "The Image of a City Too Busy to Hate: Atlanta in the 1960s," *Phylon* 33 (Fall 1972): 205–21.

54. U.S. Bureau of the Census, "Table 20: Population of the 100 Largest Urban Places: 1970," www.census.gov/population/www/documentation/twps0027/tab20.txt.

55. Lewis, *Sloss Furnaces*, 483.

56. Eskew, *But for Birmingham*, 53.

57. Connerly, *The Most Segregated City*, 70–77.

58. Ibid., 78.

59. Ibid., 90–99.

60. Ibid., 90–91; Eskew, *But for Birmingham*, 62–63.

61. Eskew, *But for Birmingham*, 62.

62. Ibid., 8, 68.

63. Andrew M. Manis, *A Fire You Can't Put Out: The Civil Rights Life of Birmingham's Reverend Fred Shuttlesworth* (Tuscaloosa: University of Alabama Press, 1999), ix.

64. Ibid., xvi.

65. Ibid., xvi–xvii.

66. Ibid., 75–76.

67. Ibid., xviii, 82–91.

68. Ibid., 92–93.

69. Ibid., 95–96.

70. Flynt, *Alabama in the Twentieth Century*, 349–50; Manis, *A Fire You Can't Put Out*, 94, 98.

71. Manis, *A Fire You Can't Put Out*, xix–xxii.
72. Henry Hampton and Steve Fayer, eds., *Voices of Freedom: An Oral History of the Civil Rights Movement from the 1950s to the 1980s* (New York: Bantam Books, 1991), 124–25.
73. Manis, *A Fire you Can't Put Out*, xix, xxi, xxvi, 108–15, 164, 328–29. The third bombing of Bethel Baptist Church occurred after Shuttlesworth had moved to Cincinnati, Ohio, to minister at Revelation Baptist Church. The home of Shuttlesworth's associate and civil rights attorney Arthur Shores was also bombed on three occasions during the same period. See Flynt, *Alabama in the Twentieth Century*, 345.
74. Harrison E. Salisbury, "Fear and Hatred Grip Birmingham: Racial Tension Smoldering after Belated Sitdowns," *NYT*, April 12, 1960.
75. Harrison E. Salisbury, "Race Issue Shakes Alabama Structure," *NYT*, April 13, 1960.
76. The following *NYT* articles directly addressed Birmingham's racially segregated structure in the decade prior to the "shocking" Salisbury exposés: "Birmingham Loses Negro Zoning Plea: Federal Appeals Court Rules City's All-White Regulation Is Unconstitutional," *NYT*, December 21, 1950; "Birmingham Firm on Law: Robinson All-Star Cannot Use White Players There," *NYT*, October 9, 1953; "Birmingham Eases Bias in Athletics," *NYT*, January 27, 1954; "Segregation Law Eased: Birmingham Permits Mixed Pro Baseball and Football," *NYT*, March 24, 1954; "Justice in Birmingham: Negro Entertainers Have Long Performed before White Southern Audiences without Challenge," *NYT*, April 22, 1956; "Segregation Foes Trail in Alabama: Vote Shows Support for Plans Aimed at High Court Rule for Schools and Parks," *NYT*, August 29, 1956; "Birmingham Defiance Ends," *NYT*, December 28, 1956; "White Foe of Bias Attacked by Mob: Sat with Negro in Alabama Station," *NYT*, March 7, 1957; "28 Negroes Fined in Bus Bias Case: Birmingham Judge Attacks Court's Integration Ruling and 14th Amendment Cites Montgomery Decision," *NYT*, March 22, 1957; "Alabama Negro Clergyman Beaten While Trying to Enroll Students," *NYT*, September 10, 1957; "Birmingham Ends Negro Job Curbs," *NYT*, July 25, 1958; "Bus Law Repealed: Birmingham Gives Companies Power on Seating," *NYT*, October 15, 1958; "Negroes Arrested in Test of Bus Law," *NYT*, October 21, 1958; "Minister Arrested in Bus Law Protest," *NYT*, October 22, 1958; "14 Negroes Jailed in Dispute on Buses," *NYT*, October 25, 1958; "2 Alabama Negroes Jailed in Bus Case," *NYT*, October 28, 1958.
77. Additional *NYT* stories featuring Birmingham's intolerant and violent race relations include "Birmingham Seeks Home Dynamiters: Police Start Hunt Following second Blasting of a Negro's Residence Within 10 Days," *NYT*, April 24, 1950; "Birmingham Bans Reds: Communists Given 48 Hours to Get out of Town," *NYT*, July 19, 1950; "Alabamians Attack King Cole on Stage," *NYT*, April 11, 1956; "Bombing in Alabama Injures 5, Wrecks Negro Minister's Home," *NYT*, December 26, 1956; "Boys in Birmingham Held as Bus Snipers," *NYT*, December 31, 1956; "Negro in Alabama to Die for Burglary," *NYT*, April 24, 1957; "3 Klansmen Held in Negro Torture," *NYT*, September 8, 1957; "Two Bomb Scares Stir Birmingham," *NYT*, September 11, 1957; "4th Klansman Guilty: Alabamian Gets 20 Years for Mutilation of Negro," *NYT*, February 21, 1958; "3 Whites Held in Blast," *NYT*, August 3, 1958.

78. David Vann, "Events Leading to the 1963 Change from Commission to the Mayor-Council Form of Government in Birmingham, Alabama" (paper presented before the University of Alabama at Birmingham Center for Urban Affairs, 1981), Birmingham City Council Papers, Pamphlets/Reports, box 9, folder 6, LHRLA.

79. "N.Y. Times Slanders Our City—Can This Be Birmingham? . . . ," *BN*, April 14, 1960. When turning to the story's page-eleven continuation, local residents were treated to the indignant headline, "New York Reporter Slanders Birmingham over Race Issue."

80. "All the News That's Fit to Print?—*N.Y. Times* Continues Attack," *BN*, April 15, 1960.

81. "Text of the *NYT* Race Hate Story," *BP-H*, April 14, 1960; "*N.Y. Times* Report Declares Race Issue Shakes Alabama," *BP-H*, April 15, 1960.

82. John Temple Graves, "Almost Total Lie from the *Times*," *BP-H*, April 16, 1960.

83. "A Grave Disservice," *BN*, April 15, 1960.

84. Vann, "Events Leading to the 1963 Change."

85. "Birmingham Story."

86. "Complaint," Civil Action no. 9634, May 6, 1960, *Theophilus Eugene Connor et al. v. NYT et al.*, trial transcript and papers, box 1, folder 1, LHRLA.

87. "Order," October 24, 1960, *Theophilus Eugene Connor et al. v. NYT et al.*, trial transcript and papers, box 1, folder 1, LHRLA.

88. "Judgment on Jury Verdict," U.S. District Court for Northern District of Alabama, Southern Division, Civil Action no. 9634, September 15, 1964, *Theophilus Eugene Connor et al. v. NYT et al.*, trial transcript and papers, box 1, folder 4, LHRLA; "Notice of Appeal," U.S. Court of Appeals for the 5th Circuit, Civil Action no. 9634, September 24, 1964, *Theophilus Eugene Connor et al. v. NYT et al.*, trial transcript and papers, box 1 folder 1, LHRLA; "Judgment," U.S. Court of Appeals for the 5th Circuit, Civil Action no. 9634, August 4, 1966, *Theophilus Eugene Connor et al. v. NYT et al.*, trial transcript and papers, box 1, folder 1, LHRLA. In regard to the intellectual background of Salisbury's passage concerning "Birmingham being like Johannesburg" and Connor's reaction to it, see also Thomas Borstelmann, *The Cold War and the Color Line: American Race Relations in the Global Arena* (Cambridge, Mass.: Harvard University Press, 2001), 4. Borstelmann examines the South's perceptual relationship to other regions of the country relative to different groups' reactions to its stance on race.

89. "Answers to Defendant's Interrogatories by Eugene Connor," U.S. District Court for Northern District of Alabama, Southern Division, Civil Action no. 9634, September 8, 1964, *Theophilus Eugene Connor et al. v. NYT et al.*, trial transcript and papers, box 1, folder 4, LHRLA.

90. "Transcript," District Court for Northern District of Alabama, Southern Division, Civil Action no. 9634, September 8, 1964, *Theophilus Eugene Connor et al. v. NYT et al.*, trial transcript and papers, 11–12, 905, box 5, folder 1, folder 9, LHRLA.

91. Ibid., 5–9, 804–6, 893–98.

92. "3 in Birmingham to Sue the *Times*: City Commissioners Base Libel Action on an Article Reporting Racial Hatred," *NYT*, April 16, 1960; "Police Head Charges Smear," *NYT*, April 16, 1960.

93. "Who Speaks for Birmingham?," *CBS Reports*, May 18, 1961, program transcript, LHRLA.

94. Richard Goldstein, "Howard K. Smith, Broadcast Newsman, Dies at 87," *NYT*, February 18, 2002.

95. Hampton and Fayer, *Voices of Freedom*, 125.

96. Ibid., 126.

97. Ibid., 129.

98. Ibid., 131.

99. Ibid., 134.

100. "Police Considers K9s One of Top '60 Achievements," *BN*, April 16, 1961. Connor bragged in this article of his numerous instruments of social control. These included police dogs, water cannons, and a specially equipped armored vehicle.

101. Foster Hailey, "Fighting Erupts at Birmingham," *NYT*, April 15, 1963; Foster Hailey, "New Birmingham Regime Sworn, Raising Hopes for Racial Peace," *NYT*, April 16, 1963; Foster Hailey, "500 Are Arrested in Negro Protest at Birmingham," *NYT*, May 3, 1963; Foster Hailey, "Dogs and Fire Hoses Repulse Negroes at Birmingham," *NYT*, May 4, 1963; Claude Sitton, "Violence Explodes at Racial Protests in Alabama," *NYT*, May 4, 1963; Foster Hailey, "U.S. Seeking a Truce in Birmingham: Hoses Again Drive Off Protestors," *NYT*, May 5, 1963; Foster Hailey, "Birmingham Talks Pushed," *NYT*, May 6, 1963; Claude Sitton, "Birmingham Jails 1,000 More Negroes," *NYT*, May 7, 1963; "Hoses and Armored Cars Used against Demonstrators," *NYT*, May 8, 1963; John D. Pomfret, "President Voices Birmingham Hope," *NYT*, May 8, 1963; Claude Sitton, "Rioting Negroes Routed by Police at Birmingham," *NYT*, May 8, 1963; Claude Sitton, "Hurdles Remain: Negroes Warn of New Protests Today If Parleys Fail," *NYT*, May 9, 1963; John D. Pomfret, "Kennedy Reacts," *NYT*, May 9, 1963; "Peace Talks Gain at Birmingham: A Day of Truce," *NYT*, May 9, 1963; Claude Sitton, "Birmingham Talks Reach an Accord on Ending Crisis," *NYT*, May 10, 1963; Claude Sitton, "Birmingham Pact Sets Timetable for Integration," *NYT*, May 11, 1963; Hedrick Smith, "Bombs Touch Off Widespread Riot at Birmingham," *NYT*, May 12, 1963; Claude Sitton, "50 Hurt in Negro Rioting after Birmingham Blasts," *NYT*, May 13, 1963; Anthony Lewis, "U.S. Sends Troops into Alabama after Riots Sweep Birmingham," *NYT*, May 13, 1963; "Wallace Decries Kennedy Action: Says Birmingham and State Can Cope with Crisis," *NYT*, May 13, 1963; Claude Sitton, "Birmingham Still Quiet," *NYT*, May 14, 1963; Tom Wicker, "Troops Won't Go into Birmingham If Peace Prevails," *NYT*, May 14, 1963; Claude Sitton, "Whites Cautious on Alabama Pact: Birmingham Leaders Balk at Giving Public Support to Accord with Negroes," *NYT*, May 15, 1963.

102. Sitton, "Violence Explodes."

103. Fred Powledge, "Alabama Bombing Protested Here," *NYT*, September 17, 1963; "Lawyer in Alabama Blames Whites, Saying 'We All Did It,'" *NYT*, September 17, 1963; John Herbers, "Parents Are Sad but Not Bitter," *NYT*, September 17, 1963; "Vatican Paper Decries Killings in Birmingham," *NYT*, September 17, 1963; "The Blame and Beyond," *NYT*, September 17, 1963; "Day of Mourning Urged," *NYT*, September 18, 1963; "Hughes Asks for Prayer for Bombing Victims," *NYT*, September 18, 1963;

"Ugandans Protest Alabama Bombing," *NYT*, September 18, 1963; John Herbers, "White Birmingham 4th Graders Back Negroes in Class Themes: All Voice Sympathy 'Sorry for Children,'" *NYT*, September 18, 1963; "Connor Holds Court to Blame in Bombing," *NYT*, September 19, 1963; "Funeral Is Held for Bomb Victims: Dr. King Delivers Tribute of Rites in Birmingham," *NYT*, September 19, 1963; "Bombing in Birmingham: Atrocities Declared No Deterrent to Negro's Fight for Equality," *NYT*, September 19, 1963; Lawrence Davies, "Negroes Protest in San Francisco: Decry Alabama Bombing," *NYT*, September 19, 1963; "Rally to Mourn 6 Slain Negroes," *NYT*, September 19, 1963; James Preston, "Birmingham: 'Look Away . . . Look Away, Look Away, Dixie Land,'" *NYT*, September 20, 1963; "1,000 in Elizabeth Attend Bomb Rites," *NYT*, September 20, 1963; "Presbyterians Ask Silence Sunday for Bomb Victims," *NYT*, September 20, 1963; George Dugan, "Birmingham Stirs Faith to Action," *NYT*, September 21, 1963; "Birmingham Bomb Planted," *NYT*, September 21, 1963; "Mayor Proclaims Day for Birmingham," *NYT*, September 21, 1963; Claude Sitton, "Birmingham: Despite Shock Caused by Bombing, Opposition to Integration Remains Firm," *NYT*, September 22, 1963; "Bombs and Rights," *NYT*, September 22, 1963; "Norwalk to Pay Tribute to Birmingham Children," *NYT*, September 22, 1963; "Prayer Being Held for Bomb Victims," *NYT*, September 22, 1963; "Churches Mourn Racial Tragedy," *NYT*, September 23, 1963; "Drive Seeks Funds to Rebuild Church Wrecked by Bomb," *NYT*, September 23, 1963; Peter Kihss, "Rallies in Nation Protest Killing of 6 in Alabama," *NYT*, September 23, 1963.

104. Mary L. Dudziak, *Cold War Civil Rights: Race and the Image of American Democracy* (Princeton, N.J.: Princeton University Press, 2000), 46, 229; Borstelmann, *The Cold War and the Color Line*, 1, 4–5.

105. Dudziak, *Cold War Civil Rights*, 46, 94, 107, 124, 130–26, 170, 186–87, 215, 229, 236–38, 240–41; Lewis, *Sloss Furnaces*, 435.

106. Former Birmingham mayor Richard Arrington mentions the small geographic area of the protests in his memoir *There's Hope for the World: The Memoir of Birmingham, Alabama's First African American Mayor* (Tuscaloosa: University of Alabama Press, 2008), 173.

Chapter 3. Remembering Bombingham

1. Mira Weinstein and Lauren Clark, "NOW Mobilizes in Wake of Deadly Clinic Bombing," *National NOW Times*, March 1998, http://archive.is/D6HaO.

2. "Congress of Racial Equality Conducts March in Memory of Negro Youngsters Killed in Birmingham Bombings, All Souls Church, 16th Street, Washington, D.C.," photograph USN&WR COLL—Job no. 10515, frame 6A [P&P], Washington, D.C., Library of Congress.

3. "Birmingham Church Bombing Anniversary," *ABC Evening News*, September 15, 1983.

4. "Kennedy: Myth and Reality, Part II," *CBS Evening News*, November 8, 1983.

5. "Birmingham, Alabama: Bombing Anniversary," *NBC Nightly News*, September 15, 1993.

6. "Birmingham, Alabama: Freedom Riders Anniversary," *ABC Evening News*, May 12, 2001.

7. "1963 Bombing: Alabama," *CBS Evening News*, February 18, 1976.

8. "Birmingham Church Bombings: Indictments," *NBC Nightly News*, September 27, 1977; "1963 Birmingham Bombings: Chambliss Charged," *ABC Evening News*, September 27, 1977; "Birmingham Church Bombings: Civil Rights Movement, Indictments," *CBS Evening News*, September 27, 1977; "Alabama Civil Rights Crimes Indictments," *ABC Evening News*, September 28, 1977; "Birmingham Bombing Trial," *NBC Nightly News*, November 14, 1977; "Alabama Church Bombing: Chambliss Trial," *ABC Evening News*, November 14, 1977; "Birmingham Bombing: Chambliss Trial," *CBS Evening News*, November 14, 1977; "Birmingham, Alabama, Bomb Trial," *NBC Nightly News*, November 15, 1977; "Birmingham Bombing: Chambliss Trial," *ABC Evening News*, November 15, 1977; "Birmingham Bombing: Chambliss Trial," *CBS Evening News*, November 15, 1977; "Birmingham Bombing: Chambliss Trial," *ABC Evening News*, November 16, 1977; "Birmingham Bombing: Chambliss Trial," *NBC Nightly News*, November 17, 1977; "Birmingham Bombing: Chambliss Trial," *CBS Evening News*, November 17, 1977; "Birmingham Bombing: Chambliss Trial," *NBC Nightly News*, November 18, 1977; "Birmingham Bombing: Chambliss Trial," *CBS Evening News*, November 18, 1977; "Birmingham Bombing: Chambliss Trial," *ABC Evening News*, November 18, 1977.

9. "Birmingham Bombing Trial," *NBC Nightly News*, November 14, 1977.

10. "Birmingham Bombing: Chambliss Trial," *NBC Nightly News*, November 18, 1977.

11. "Rick Bragg, 38 Years Later, Last of Suspects Is Convicted in Church Bombing: Ex Klansman Gets Life Sentence for Killing Four Alabama Girls," *NYT*, May 23, 2002.

12. Examples of international coverage of the trial can be found in James Doran, "Ku Klux Klan Rises from Grave to Haunt South," *Times* (London), May 25, 2002; "Klan Bomber Gets Life," *Australian*, May 5, 2002; Jay Reeves, "Defendant Wore the Crime Like a Klan Medal," *Toronto Star*, May 15, 2002.

13. Kevin Slack, "2 Charged in 1963 Church Blast That Killed 4 Birmingham Girls," *NYT*, May 18, 2000.

14. "Alabama's Long Search for Justice," *NYT*, May 18, 2000.

15. Rick Bragg, "Prosecutors Try to Recreate Birmingham's '63 Nightmare," *NYT*, May 15, 2002; Rick Bragg, "Alabama Faces Old Wound in One Last Trial: Alabama Scrutinizes the Shame of 1963," *NYT*, May 12, 2002.

16. Jane Clayson and Mark Strassmann, "Former Klansman Convicted for 1963 Birmingham Church Bombing, CBS," *Early Show*, CBS News, May 2, 2001.

17. "Analysis: Last Suspect in Birmingham Church Bombing Declared Unfit to Stand Trial," *Morning Edition*, National Public Radio, July 17, 2001.

18. "History in a Hurry: Alabama's Tops Stories of 2001," *BN*, December 31, 2001; "Judge Denies New Trial for Cherry," *BN*, September 17, 2002; "Analysis: Bobby Frank Cherry Found Guilty in Birmingham Church Bombing Trial," *All Things Considered*, National Public Radio, May 22, 2002.

19. "Analysis: Last Suspect," *Morning Edition*, National Public Radio, July 17, 2001.

20. For discussion on the use of stereotypes or generalizations in modern media, see Lippman, *Public Opinion*, 49–58.

21. For a discussion of habitus, see Bourdieu, *In Other Words*, 190; also quoted in Craig Calhoun, "Habitus, Field, and Capital: The Question of Historical Specificity," in *Bourdieu: Critical Perspectives*, ed. Craig Calhoun, Edward LiPuma, and Moishe Postone (Chicago: University of Chicago Press, 1993), 74; additional explanation of habitus can be found in Pierre Bourdieu, *Homo Academicus* (Stanford, Calif.: Stanford University Press, 1988), 3, 91, 99, 143, 149–52.

22. Carol Mason, *Killing for Life: The Apocalyptic Narrative of Pro-Life Politics* (Ithaca, N.Y.: Cornell University Press, 2002), 27; Donald P. Baker, "Blast at Alabama Abortion Clinic Kills a Policeman, Injures Nurse: Fatality Is the First from Bombing of Such a Facility," *Washington Post*, January 30, 1998.

23. Rick Bragg, "Bomb Kills Guard at an Alabama Abortion Clinic," *NYT*, January 30, 1998; Rick Bragg, "Abortion Clinic Bomb Was Intended to Kill, an Official Says," *NYT*, January 31, 1998; "The Bombing of Abortion Rights," editorial, *NYT*, January 31, 1998.

24. Kevin Slack, "Suspect in Southern Bombings Is an Enigma to Law Enforcement," *NYT*, February 28, 1998; Kevin Slack, "Southern Bombing Fugitive Is Seen in North Carolina," *NYT*, July 14, 1998.

25. Marlon Manuel, "Birmingham Clinic Bombing: A City's Past Comes Roaring Back," *Atlanta Constitution-Journal*, February 1, 1998.

26. Clarence Page, "Pro-Life Until You Get in Their Way," *Chicago Tribune*, February 1, 1998.

27. Verna Gates, "The Birmingham Civil Rights Institute," *Alabama Heritage* 66 (Fall 2002): 17; Arrington, *There's Hope for the World*, 169–71. Although Arrington makes no mention of the council's vote on the formation of a civil rights movement museum in the city, he does reveal that Vann "began to share" his ideas about the need for such an institution as early as the mid-1970s. Glenn Eskew, "The Birmingham Civil Rights Institute and the New Ideology of Tolerance," in *The Civil Rights Movement in American Memory*, ed. Renee C. Romano and Leigh Raiford (Athens: University of Georgia Press, 2006), 32.

28. Vicki Leigh Ingham, "The Birmingham Museum of Art: A Civilizing Spirit," *Alabama Heritage* 60 (Spring 2001): 6.

29. Gates, "The Birmingham Civil Rights Institute," 17–18.

30. Vann quoted in ibid., 17.

31. "Store Manager Wounded, Woman Killed in Shooting," *BN*, June 23, 1979; "Woman Killed, Man Wounded in Store Shooting," *BP-H*, June 23, 1979; Ron Casey, "The Election of Birmingham's Black Mayor," *Southern Changes: The Journal of the Southern Regional Council* 2 (Winter 1979): 11.

32. "City Seeking to Calm Kingston Area; Black Leaders Voice Concern," *BN*, July 6, 1979; Mark C. Winne, "Sniper Reported: Police Pick Up Men in Kingston," *BN*, July 8, 1979.

33. Thomas Hargrove and Greg McDonald, "Power Sweep Clears Protest Site," *BP-H*, June 25, 1979; Thomas Hargrove, "'Shoot Out Those Lights!' Sergeant Yells as Rocks Fly," *BP-H*, June 25, 1979.

34. "Store Manager Wounded, Woman Killed in Shooting"; Soloman Crenshaw and Frank Sikora, "Man Surrenders to Police Day after Store Shoot-Out," *BN*, June 24, 1979; Frank Sikora, "Bonita Was a Good Person, Recalls Mother," *BN*, June 24, 1979; Kitty Frieden, Walter Bryant, and David Kepple, "Police to Probe Death of Woman Killed by Officer," *BN*, June 25, 1979; "Protests in Shooting Move from Streets into Churches," *BN*, June 26, 1979; Peter A. Kovacs, "Police Criticize, Hope to Block Civilian Inquiry into Shooting," *BN*, June 28, 1979; Peter A. Kovacs, "'They Were Mad . . . They Went Up and Shot Her,' Miss Carter's Friend Tells Citizen Inquiry Group," *BN*, June 30, 1979; Peter Kovacs, "Witness: 'Saw a Motion' in Vehicle Just before Bonita Carter Was Killed," *BN*, July 2, 1979; "Panel Slapped At by Policemen, Ministers Give Backing," *BN*, July 4, 1979; Peter A. Kovacs, "Inquiry on Police Shooting Runs into Witness Problems," *BN*, July 4, 1979; "City Seeking to Calm Kingston Area; Black Leaders Voice Concern," *BN*, July 6, 1979; Michael Globetti and Peter A. Kovacs, "A Policeman's Wry Humor When Arrow and Bullets Fly," *BN*, July 6, 1979; Andrew Kilpatrick, "Report: Shots Fired without Enough Cause," *BN*, July 8, 1979; Mark C. Winne, "Sniper Reported: Police Pick Up Men in Kingston," *BN*, July 8, 1979; "Mayor and Chief Meet in Wake of Committee Report on Sands," *BN*, July 9, 1979; Peter A. Kovacs and Mark C. Winne, "In Response to Letter from Mayor, DA Says He'll Review Evidence in Sands-Carter Case," *BN*, July 10, 1979; Peter A. Kovacs, "Sands Removed from Street Duty; Vann Planning Changes in Policy," *BN*, July 17, 1979; "Woman Killed, Man Wounded in Store Shooting," *BP-H*, June 23, 1979; Hargrove and McDonald, "Power Sweep Clears Protest Site"; Hargrove, "'Shoot Out the Lights!'"; "Tense Sunday Afternoon," *BP-H*, June 25, 1979; Thomas Hargrove and John Northrop, "Chief Asks for Calm over Slaying," *BP-H*, June 26, 1979; John Northrop and Bruce Patterson, "Citizen Panel to Probe Police Shooting," *BP-H*, June 28, 1979; Bruce Patterson, "Officer Who Killed Woman Saved a Life Earlier," *BP-H*, June 28, 1979; John Northrop, "Hearings on Police Killing Begin Today," *BP-H*, June 29, 1979; "Dr. Blaine Brownell Fills Last Slot on Citizens' Panel," *BP-H*, June 29, 1979; John Northrop, "Shooting Hearings Begin: Hands 'On Steering Wheel,'" *BP-H*, June 30, 1979; Thomas Hargrove, "Vann Joins Bonita Carter Mourners," *BP-H*, July 2, 1979; John Northrop, "Policemen Thought Woman Had Gun, Commander Says," *BP-H*, July 3, 1979; Bruce Patterson, "Officer Resigns from CAC," *BP-H*, July 3, 1979; "New Kingston Melee; 12 Arrested," *BP-H*, July 6, 1979; John Northrop, "Major Shooting Witness Missing as Hearings End," *BP-H*, July 6, 1979; John Northrop, "Police Account of Shooting Backed by Store Manager," *BP-H*, July 7, 1979; "Armed Whites Arrested in Kingston," *BP-H*, July 7, 1979; John Northrop, "Myers to Review 'Entire Investigation,'" *BP-H*, July 9, 1979; Bruce Patterson and Greg Hill, "Vann, Myers Meet with Police," *BP-H*, July 10, 1979; Peter de Selding, "Vann Asks Prosecutor to Review Shooting Case," *BP-H*, July 11, 1979; Peter de Selding, "Vann Wanted Jury for Kingston Probe," *BP-H*, July 12, 1979; "Vann and Myers Discuss Shooting," *BP-H*, July 16, 1979; Peter de Selding and John Northrop, "Black Leaders Bitter on Sands Decision," *BP-H*, July 18, 1979; "Text on Vann's Decision," *BP-H*, July 18, 1979; "Police to Act 'Slower . . . More Logically,'" *BP-H*, July 19, 1979; "Two White Men Arrested in Kingston Incident," *BP-H*, July 20, 1979; Peter de Selding, "'I'm No Second Bull Connor,' Vann Says of Today's March,"

BP-H, July 20, 1979; Bruce Patterson, "Proposed Gun Policy Angers Officers," *BP-H*, July 20, 1979; "Blacks March to City Hall, Demand Dismissal of Sands," *BP-H*, July 21, 1979; Jim Nesbitt, "Quiet Anger: 'They Want Us to Retreat,'" *BP-H*, July 21, 1979; "The Mayor, the Crowd," *BP-H*, July 21, 1979; Peter de Selding, "SCLC Plans Store Boycott," *BP-H*, July 24, 1979. Editorials include "Shooting Tragedy," *BN*, June 27, 1979; "Blue-Ribbon Panel," *BN*, June 29, 1979; "Review of Police Shooting Death May Signal New Policy," *BN*, July 1, 1979; "Confrontations Must Stop," *BN*, July 8, 1979; "Citizens' Findings," *BN*, July 10, 1979; "City Changing Still," *BN*, July 11, 1979; "City at a Crossroads—Again," *BN*, July 15, 1979; "Vann's Decision," *BN*, July 18, 1979; "Marching—But Which Way?," *BN*, July 22, 1979; "Must Not Fester," *BP-H*, June 26, 1979; "FOP Is Wrong," *BP-H*, June 30, 1979; "Matter of Perception," *BP-H*, July 13, 1979; "Vann's Decision," *BP-H*, July 19, 1979. Letters to the editor include Rod W. Powers, "Racism, in Any Form, Is Sickening," *BN*, July 7, 1979; Don Haynes, "Police on Record as Opposed to Committee," *BN*, July 7, 1979; Roy Higginbotham, "Police Can't Really Investigate Themselves," *BN*, July 7, 1979; R. M. Howard, "Open Our Eyes before More Are Hurt," *BN*, July 7, 1979; Jack Pilley, "Kingston Confusion Has Gone Too Far," *BN*, July 7, 1979; M. L. Self, "Could Have Made Better Choice," *BN*, July 7, 1979; Joseph E. Watson, "Police Conduct Pleases 'Bull,'" *BN*, July 7, 1979; A. M. McDonald, "Thanks to Policemen and God Bless," *BN*, July 7, 1979; Cynthia S. Wallace, "Police Should Get Same, Fair Treatment," *BN*, July 7, 1979; John L. Kilner, "Let's Get behind the Policeman," *BN*, July 7, 1979; G. Gadson, "Threats by Police Only Hurt the Situation," *BN*, July 11, 1979; Catherine M. Boyd, "Why Stop Citizens Inquiry with Only Police?," *BN*, July 14, 1979; James R. Franklin, "Justice Is Same for Protester, Protested," *BN*, July 18, 1979; Karl B. Friedman, "Quality of Its People Makes a City," *BN*, July 19, 1979; David Vann, "Mayor Says No Plan to Disband Tactical Unit," *BN*, July 20, 1979; M. P. Freeman, "Insider's View of Kingston Area," *BN*, July 21, 1979; Houston Brice Jr., "Protesters Misidentify Friend as the Villain," *BP-H*, July 4, 1979; Janey L. Campbell, "Doesn't Justify," *BP-H*, July 4, 1979; John Barker, "Disagrees with Vann Remarks on Police," *BP-H*, July 25, 1979.

35. Dennis C. Morgan, letter to editor, *Birmingham World*, July 14, 1979.
36. Franklin Tate, "Klan Launches Weekend Kingston Invasion," *Birmingham Times*, July 12, 13, 14, 1979; Franklin Tate, "Bonita Is Dead . . . Mayor Does Nothing," *Birmingham Times*, July 19, 20, 21, 1979.
37. "Dr. Brownell Fills Last Slot on Citizens' Panel"; Northrop, "Hearings on Police Killing Begin Today."
38. "Hearing by the 'Blue Ribbon' Citizens' Committee," transcript, p. 3, Operation New Birmingham Papers/Testimony before the Special Ad Hoc Committee Appointed by ONB in the Matter of Inquiry and Facts Surrounding the Death of Bonita Carter, box 1, folder 1, LHRLA.
39. Kilpatrick, "Report: Shots Fired"; Franklin Tate, "Mayor's Committee Submits Report," *Birmingham Times*, July 12, 13, 14, 1979; "Sands off Job; Nerves Shot," *BP-H*, July 27, 1979; Franklin Tate, "Sands off the Police Force?," *Birmingham Times*, August, 2, 3, 4, 1979.

40. Watson, "Police Conduct Pleases 'Bull'"; de Selding, "'I'm No Second Bull Connor.'"

41. Friedman, "Quality of Its People Makes a City."

42. "Must Not Fester."

43. "Shooting Tragedy."

44. "Confrontations Must Stop."

45. "City at Crossroads—Again."

46. Operation New Birmingham, "A Report on Operation New Birmingham," BACCP, box 1, folder 4, LHRLA; Operation New Birmingham, "A Study In Progressive Productive Citizen Volunteerism," BACCP, box 5, folder 9, LHRLA.

47. Operation New Birmingham, "A Study in Progressive Productive Citizen Volunteerism."

48. Operation New Birmingham, "News Release: Ground Breaking for $17 Million 30 Story Bank Building in Birmingham," May 1, 1968, BACCP, box 1, folder 4, LHRLA; Operation New Birmingham, "News Release: Birmingham Based South Central Bell Telephone Company Begins Operation—Largest Corporation Ever Formed," July 1, 1968, BACCP, box 1, folder 4, LHRLA; Operation New Birmingham, "News Release: Birmingham Hailed by Vice President Humphrey," March 28, 1968, BACCP, box 1, folder 4, LHRLA.

49. Operation New Birmingham, "News Release: 200 Demonstrate in Birmingham Paint-In," BACCP, box 1, folder 4, LHRLA.

50. Operation New Birmingham, "A Study in Progressive Productive Citizen Volunteerism"; Gerald Astor, "All-America Cities, 1970," *Look*, March 23, 1971, 72–74.

51. Donald A. Brown, untitled introduction, *Birmingham*, March 1971, 4.

52. Donald A. Brown, "This Issue," *Birmingham*, April 1971, 3.

53. Charles Morgan Jr., "Birmingham Is Dead," news bulletin, L. C. Clark Jr. Collection, folder 1, Birmingham Civil Rights Institute Archives.

54. "We Have Come Part of the Way," *Birmingham*, April 1971, 25–27.

55. Edward LaMonte, interviewed by the author, March 13, 2009. LaMonte, Arrington's longtime chief of staff, credits the Bonita Carter incident, and Vann's handling of it, as a main factor in Vann's defeat at the polls.

56. Michele Wilson and John Lynxwiler, "The Federal Government and the Harassment of Black Leaders: A Case Study of Mayor Richard Arrington Jr. of Birmingham," *Journal of Black Studies* 28 (May 1998): 548.

57. Arrington, *There's Hope for the World*, 42–43, 58–59; Jimmie Lewis Franklin, *Back to Birmingham: Richard Arrington Jr. and His Times* (Tuscaloosa: University of Alabama Press, 1989), 169–74; Eskew, "The Birmingham Civil Rights Institute," 31–32.

58. Linda Parham, "Voters to Pick Mayor Today," *BP-H*, October 9, 1979; Richard Friedman, "Candidates Still Throwing Best Pitches as Game Ends," *BN*, October 8, 1979; "Voting Reminder," *BN*, October 9, 1979.

59. Linda Parham, "Arrington Far Ahead; Foe in Doubt," *BP-H*, October 10, 1979.

60. Richard Friedman, "Katapodis, Parsons Await Official Tally to Learn Who Faces Big-Leader Arrington," *BN*, October 10, 1979; Vicki Brown, "Voting Follows Race Pattern Except for Dents by Arrington," *BN*, October 10, 1979; "'Organization'

Brought Arrington Commanding Lead," *BN*, October 10, 1979; Olivia Barton, "For Arrington Backers, It Was an Evening to Remember," *BN*, October 10, 1979; Olivia Barton and Richard Friedman, "Vann Lost Because Blacks Deserted," *BN*, October 10, 1979; Parham, "Arrington Far Ahead"; "Foe in Doubt," *BP-H*, October 10, 1979; Ted Bryant, "Arrington Got Solid Black-Area Votes, Part of White," *BP-H*, October 10, 1979. Articles without racial focus include "'It Was a Rough Day All Over,'" *BP-H*, October 10, 1979; "KKK Leader, Socialist Not Discouraged," *BP-H*, October 10, 1979.

61. Bryant, "Arrington Got Solid Black-Area Votes"; Brown, "Voting Follows Race Pattern"; Barton and Friedman, "Vann Lost Because Blacks Deserted."

62. "Campaign Testing," *BN*, October 11, 1979.

63. "Election Questions," *BN*, October 10, 1979; "The Race for Mayor," *BP-H*, October 11, 1979.

64. Karen Robinson, "KKK Image Soils New Image," *BN*, October 13, 1979.

65. Linda Parham, "Weatherman Could Cast Big Vote Today," *BP-H*, October 30, 1979; Linda Parham, "Arrington Calls Victory Sign of Progress," *BP-H*, November 1, 1979; "Carter to Arrington: 'A Great Day,'" *BP-H*, October 31, 1979.

66. "The New Mayor," *BP-H*, November 1, 1979; "City Wins Election," *BN*, October 31, 1979.

67. Jacqueline McCarroll, "Arrington's Victory Is a Sign of Progress," *BN*, November 3, 1979.

68. James Thompson, "Must Return to Separate but Equal," *BN*, October 30, 1979.

69. Kitty Frieden, "Election's Hoopla Over; Now We'll Wait, See," *BN*, November 4, 1979.

70. Richard Arrington, "State of the City Address, 1982," BACCP, box 10, folder 6, LHRLA.

71. Richard Arrington, "State of the City Address, 1983," Birmingham, Alabama, Mayor Papers, "State of the City Addresses," box 1, folder 3, LHRLA.

72. Richard Arrington, "State of the City Address, 1984," Birmingham, Alabama, Mayor Papers, "State of the City Addresses," box 1, folder 4, LHRLA.

73. Richard Arrington, "State of the City Address, 1990," Birmingham, Alabama, Mayor Papers, "State of the City Addresses," box 1, folder 10, LHRLA.

74. Odessa Woolfolk, "Historical Overview," in *Making Connections: A Curriculum for Grades K-12* (Birmingham: Birmingham Civil Rights Institute, 2000); Gates, "The Birmingham Civil Rights Institute," 18–19.

75. Denise Stuart, "Birmingham Embraces Its Past with Eye Toward Future," *Birmingham World*, November 11, 1992; LaMonte interview; Arrington, *There's Hope for the World*, 173.

76. Susan Willoughby Anderson, "The Past on Trial: The Sixteenth Street Baptist Church Bombing, Civil Rights Memory, and the Remaking of Birmingham" (PhD diss., University of North Carolina at Chapel Hill, 2008), 146.

77. Richard Arrington, "State of the City Address, 1988," Birmingham, Alabama, Mayor Papers, "State of the City Addresses," box 1, folder 8, LHRLA; Arrington, *There's Hope for the World*, 172–73.

78. Richard Arrington, "State of the City Address, 1990," Birmingham, Alabama, Mayor Papers, "State of the City Addresses," box 1, folder 10, LHRLA.

79. Woolfolk, "Historical Overview"; Stuart, "Birmingham Embraces Its Past with and Eye toward Future"; Odessa Woolfolk, interviewed by the author, March 13, 2009; LaMonte interview. LaMonte reveals that many corporate leaders were extremely reluctant to support the institute initially. He credits the eventual support of Vulcan Materials CEO Herb Sklenar as a breakthrough moment in the funding of exhibits after which other white business leaders were willing to publicly support the institution's development.

80. "Rights Center Draws Visitors in Birmingham," *NYT*, January 17, 1997.

81. Barbara Olsen, "Civil Rights," *Birmingham*, November 1992, 26.

82. Denise Stuart, "BCRI Dedicated, Birmingham Praised for Its Vision," *Birmingham World*, November 19–25, 1992; Angela Davis, "Birmingham Civil Rights Institute Expected to Boost City's Image and Economy," *Birmingham World*, November 11, 1992; Stuart, "Birmingham Embraces Its Past with and Eye toward Future."

83. Richard Arrington, "State of the City Address, 1993," Birmingham, Alabama, Mayor Papers, "State of the City Addresses," box 1, folder 13, LHRLA.

84. Frederick Kaimann, "Dedication for Civil Rights Institute Today," *BN*, November 15, 1992.

85. Mayor Larry Langford, interviewed by the author, Birmingham, Alabama, August 18, 2008.

86. Ibid.

87. Elisabeth Noelle-Neumann, "The Contribution of Spiral of Silence Theory to an Understanding of Mass Media," in *The Mass Media in Liberal Democratic Societies*, ed. Stanley Rothman (New York: Paragon House, 1992), 5–6, 75–84.

88. Jerry Underwood, "Most Airport Board Members Back Move to Add Shuttlesworth's Name," June 25, 2008, *Birmingham News*, AL.com, http://blog.al.com/spotnews/2008/06/most_airport_board_members_bac.html, accessed July 22, 2008.

89. Chandalaro8, comment on Underwood, "Most Airport Board Members."

90. Dangriffen, comment on Underwood, "Most Airport Board Members."

91. Sjlchristian, comment on Underwood, "Most Airport Board Members."

92. Bteb, comment on Underwood, "Most Airport Board Members"; Kwn, comment on Underwood, "Most Airport Board Members."

93. Bteb, comment on Underwood, "Most Airport Board Members"; Chandalaro8, comment on Underwood, "Most Airport Board Members."

94. Kwn, comment on Underwood, "Most Airport Board Members."

95. Bamaborn1111, comment on Underwood, "Most Airport Board Members."

96. Langford interview.

97. Melanie Eversley, "Obama Designates Three Civil Rights Sites as National Monuments," *USA Today*, January 12, 2017.

98. National Trust for Historic Preservation, "Help Create a Civil Rights National Park in Birmingham," Petition, Change.org, www.change.org/p/help-create-a-civil-rights-national-park-in-birmingham-2. This petition, with over twelve thousand signatures, was delivered to President Obama and the U.S. House of Representatives.

99. GenRobELee, comment on Erin Edgemon, "President Obama Signs Proclamation Creating Birmingham Civil Rights National Monument," January 12, 2017, AL.com, www.al.com/news/birmingham/index.ssf/2017/01/birmingham_civil_rights_nation .html#comments, accessed January 24, 2015.

100. DSHornet4, comment on Edgemon, "President Obama Signs Proclamation."

101. SteelShield, comment on Edgemon, "President Obama Signs Proclamation."

Chapter 4. Never Quite American

Epigraph: Rudyard Kipling, *American Notes* (Boston: Brown, 1899), 12.

1. Astor, "All-America Cities, 1970," 72–74; "All-America City Winners," National Civic League, www.nationalcivicleague.org/america-city-award/past-winners/. The city finally won the award in 2012.

2. Kurt Anderson, "Las Vegas: The New All-American City," *Time*, January 10, 1994, 42–51.

3. An early and prominent use of the nickname *Baghdad by the Bay* in connection to San Francisco can be found in Herb Caen, *Baghdad by the Bay: The San Francisco Story* (New York: Doubleday, 1949). Herb Caen was San Francisco's leading columnist for more than forty years. The phrase *Baghdad by the Bay* continues to appear in popular culture and even in songs. A quick search on Amazon.com, for example, reveals numerous products carrying the nickname, including key chains, shirts, and coffee mugs.

4. "San Francisco: Geography and Climate," City-Data, www.city-data.com/us-cities/ The-West/San-Francisco-Geography-and-Climate.html, accessed June 9, 2009; "Birmingham: Geography and Climate," City-Data, www.city-data.com/us-cities/ The-South/Birmingham-Geography-and-Climate.html, accessed June 9, 2009; "Las Vegas: Geography and Climate," City-Data, www.city-data.com/us-cities/The-West/ Las-Vegas-Geography-and-Climate.html, accessed June 9, 2009.

5. For information on San Francisco's Barbary Coast, see Herbert Asbury, *The Barbary Coast: An Informal History of the San Francisco Underworld* (New York: Knopf, 1933). A description of the Castro district's transformation from a working-class neighborhood to the center of San Francisco's gay community can be found in Randy Shilts, *Mayor of Castro Street: The Life and Times of Harvey Milk* (New York: St. Martin's Press, 1982), 65–70.

6. Doris Muscatine, *Old San Francisco: The Biography of a City from Early Days to the Earthquake* (New York: G. P. Putnam's Sons, 1975), 31–34.

7. Asbury, *The Barbary Coast*, 3–4.

8. Alison Bing and Dominique Channell, *San Francisco City Guide* (Victoria, Australia: Lonely Planet Publications, 2008), 29–30.

9. Paul Welch and Ernest Havemann, "Homosexuality in America," *Life*, June 26, 1964, 66–74. This article was the first in a national publication to cast San Francisco as exceptionally tolerant toward homosexuals and possessive of an exceptionally large gay community. As such, it has been credited as a watershed piece in establishing the city's identity as a gay mecca. Martin Dennis Meeker has traced the first published

reference to the city as a gay mecca in the same year to William Konrad, *Someone You May Know* (Beverly Hills: Book Company of America, 1965), 114, quoted in Marin Dennis Meeker, "Come out West: Communication and the Gay and Lesbian Migration to San Francisco, 1940s to 1960s" (PhD diss., University of Southern California, 2000), 44.

10. For excellent coverage of the Manifest Destiny mindset gripping the United States in the 1840s, see David Stephen Heidler and Jeanne T. Heidler, *Manifest Destiny* (Westport, Conn.: Greenwood Press, 2003), 141–64; Henry Nash Smith, *Virgin Land: The American West as Symbol and Myth* (New York: Vintage Books, 1950), esp. 38–39, 46–48; Otis A. Singletary, *The Mexican War* (Chicago: University of Chicago Press, 1971), 14–15.

11. Singletary, *The Mexican War*, 10–11, 149–51.

12. John P. Reps, *Cities of the American West: A History of Frontier Urban Planning* (Princeton, N.J.: Princeton University Press, 1979), 194–99; Malcolm Rohrbough, "No Boy's Play: Migration and Settlement in Early Gold Rush California," in *Rooted in Barbarous Soil: People, Culture, and Community in Gold Rush California*, ed. Kevin Starr and Richard Orsi (Berkeley: University of California Press, 2000), 25–28.

13. Gray Brechin, *Imperial San Francisco: Urban Power, Earthly Ruin* (Berkeley: University of California Press, 2006), 29–30.

14. *The Pennsylvania Packet*, February 24, 1772, 2; *New York Journal*, March 5, 1772. The articles refer explicitly to "the coast of California." Yet they also reference "Senora" and "South America." One has to surmise that they are referring to modern-day Baja California.

15. "From the British Press," *Evening Post*, August 7, 1804; *New York Herald*, August 8, 1804; *Enquirer*, August 11, 1804; *Newburyport Herald*, August 14, 1804; *Columbian Courier*, August 17, 1804; *Oracle of Dauphin*, August 25, 1804; *Green Mountain Patriot*, September 4, 1804.

16. "Mexico," *Nashville Clarion*, July 27, 1819; "Mexico," *American Beacon*, August 16, 1819; "Mexico," *American Mercury*, August 24, 1819.

17. "Gold Mines," *Southern Patriot*, September 15, 1834; "Gold Mines," *New Bedford Review*, September 19, 1934.

18. *Sun*, September 22, 1842; *Madisonian for the Country*, September 24, 1842; *Berkshire County Whig*, September 29, 1842.

19. *Ohio State Journal*, October 12, 1842; *Ohio State Journal*, October 14, 1842.

20. Brechin, *Imperial San Francisco*, 29. Brechin regards the romantic myth of mining as a key element of the metallurgy, militarism, mechanization, and finance that undergird what he terms the "Pyramid of Mining." This pyramid served as the foundation upon which San Francisco emerged as the leading city of the West, both serving as the imperial spearhead of the once-unconquered region and casting and imperial eye toward the Pacific.

21. "The Effect of California Gold News in Europe," *Weekly Herald*, February 3, 1849.

22. Kevin Starr, "Rooted in Barbarous Soil: An Introduction to Gold Rush Society and Culture," in Starr and Orsi, *Rooted in Barbarous Soil*, 4.

23. Glenna Matthews, "Forging a Cosmopolitan Culture: The Regional Identity of San Francisco and Northern California," in *Many Wests: Place, Culture, and Regional Identity*, ed. David Wrobel and Michael Steiner (Lawrence: University Press of Kansas, 1997), 214–15. By relating the idea of born cosmopolitanism to San Francisco's acceptance of its image as a gay mecca, I do not intend to diminish the remarkable accomplishments of San Francisco's gay and lesbian rights activists. The idea that San Francisco's history of diversity eventually contributed to a greater local willingness to accept this national perception of it is not to say that the struggles faced by activists and gays in the city were any less daunting and dangerous than those faced in other urban areas.

24. Albert L. Hurtado, "Sex, Gender, Culture, and a Great Event: The California Gold Rush," *Pacific Historical Review* 68 (February 1999): 1–2.

25. Asbury, *The Barbary Coast*, 12.

26. Hurtado, "Sex, Gender, Culture," 4–5.

27. Asbury, *The Barbary Coast*, 18.

28. Ibid., 19.

29. "The Revolting State of Things," *Sun*, March 29, 1849.

30. "Life in San Francisco," *Daily Globe* (Washington, D.C.), January 4, 1850.

31. "Interesting from California," *Weekly Herald*, May 5, 1849; "Affairs in California," *Constitution* (Middletown, Conn.), February 6, 1850.

32. Asbury, *The Barbary Coast*, 34–35.

33. Quoted in ibid., 31.

34. "Life in California," *Weekly Eagle* (Brattleboro, Vt.), February 25, 1850.

35. "Increase in Emigration, the Gold Excitement," *New York Weekly Herald*, January 13, 1849.

36. For detailed coverage of the See America First movement and its influence on American perceptions of place, see Marguerite S. Shaffer, *See America First: Tourism and National Identity, 1880–1940* (Washington, D.C.: Smithsonian Institution Press, 2001).

37. "The Honest Miner," *San Francisco Bulletin*, September 28, 1867. The second instance of the local newspaper referring to the Barbary Coast showed a bit of ambiguity inherent in the identity process. In "A Good Precedent," *San Francisco Bulletin*, June 11, 1869, the writer referred to the entire port area of the city as the Barbary Coast without relating it to a vice district. Instead, it spoke of the political power the area had in keeping port charges exorbitantly expensive.

38. Hurtado, "Sex, Gender, Culture," 5.

39. "Chicago in San Francisco," *Trenton State Gazette*, July 13, 1869.

40. "An Arrival of Chinese: A Curious Scene in San Francisco—Opium Smuggling," *Macon Weekly Telegraph*, July 16, 1869.

41. "A Sad End," *San Francisco Bulletin*, February 20, 1872. This piece was representative of many in this genre of tragedy. It highlighted the life of Carrie Blanely, who had arrived in the city with her husband some two years earlier. Unfortunately, Blanely succumbed to the temptations of alcohol and found herself living in the Barbary

Coast district. Despite the best efforts "to turn her from her downward path," Blanely ultimately fell dead while entering into one of the very "dens" that brought about her sorrow.

42. "Victimizing and Arizona Miner," *Arizona Weekly Journal*, November 1, 1873.

43. "Jim Crutcher," *Owyhee Avalanche*, June 18, 1875.

44. Josh Sides, "Excavating the Postwar Sex District in San Francisco," *Journal of Urban History* 32 (March 2006): 359; Asbury, *The Barbary Coast*, 312–13.

45. Neil Larry Shumsky, "Tacit Acceptance: Respectable Americans and Segregated Prostitution, 1870–1900," *Journal of Social History* 19 (Summer 1986): 665.

46. Ibid.

47. Ibid., 665–66.

48. Neil Larry Shumsky, "Vice Responds to Reform: San Francisco, 1910 to 1914," *Journal of Urban History* 7 (November 1980): 31.

49. David J. Pivar, *Purity and Hygiene: Women, Prostitution, and the "American Plan," 1900–1930* (Westport, Conn.: Greenwood Press, 2002).

50. John D'Emilio and Estelle B. Freedman, *Intimate Matters: A History of Sexuality in America*, 2nd ed. (Chicago: University of Chicago Press, 1997), 211–12.

51. "Social Workers See Real Turkey Trots," *NYT*, January 27, 1912.

52. "New York's Biggest Problem, Not Police, But Girls," *NYT*, August 4, 1912.

53. "Dance Halls Here 20% Immoral," *NYT*, March 1, 1924.

54. "Dance Hall Evils Minimized in West," *NYT*, March 2, 1924.

55. "Social Workers See Real Turkey Trots."

56. Sydney J. Albright, "The Fred Kelly Story," *Journal of the American Aviation Historical Society* 13 (Fall 1968): 198; "Western Airlines Fiftieth Anniversary Program," Elma G. Leland Papers, box 1, folder 2, UNLVSC.

57. Herbert O. Fischer, "Indianapolis: The Typical American City," *Speed*, February 1931, 16–17, uncataloged, DACA.

58. Herbert O. Fischer, "Indianapolis: Crossroads of the Nation," *Speed*, January 1933, 16, DACA.

59. "Columbus: The American City," *Speed*, July 1931, 8–9, DACA.

60. Oscar Kahan, "St. Louis—Thoroughly American City," *Speed*, March 1933, 16, DACA.

61. Ibid., 17.

62. "Columbus," 8.

63. Richard M. Jones, "San Francisco: The City," *Speed*, July 1931, 16, DACA.

64. Herbert O. Warren, "Play Days in San Francisco," *Speed*, November 1931, 16, DACA.

65. Gerald D. Nash, *World War II and the West: Reshaping the Economy* (Lincoln: University of Nebraska Press, 1990). For additional discussion on the impact of World War II on the city of San Francisco and the state of California, see Roger W. Lotchin, "California Cities and the Hurricane of Change: World War II in the San Francisco, Los Angeles, and the San Diego Metropolitan Areas," *Pacific Historical Review* (August 1994): 393–420; Roger W. Lotchin, "The Metropolitan-Military Complex in Comparative Perspective: San Francisco, Los Angeles, and San Diego, 1919–1941," in *The Making of Urban America*, ed. Raymond A. Mohl (Wilmington, Del.: Scholarly

Resources, 1988), 202–13; Roger W. Lotchin, ed., *The Martial Metropolis: U.S. Cities in War and Peace* (New York: Praeger, 1984); Roger W. Lotchin, *The Bad City in the Good War: San Francisco, Los Angeles, Oakland, and San Diego* (Bloomington: Indiana University Press, 2003).

66. Nan Alamilla Boyd, *Wide Open Town: A History of Queer San Francisco to 1965* (Berkeley: University of California Press, 2003), 111–13; Allan Berube, *Coming Out under Fire: The History of Gay Men and Women in World War Two* (New York: Free Press, 1990), 113. See also Allan Berube, "Marching to a Different Drummer: Lesbian and Gay GIs in World War II," in *Hidden from History*, ed. Martin Duberman, Martha Vicinus, and George Chauncey (New York: New American Library, 1989), 383–94; John D'Emilio, "Gay Politics and Community in San Francisco in World War II," in Duberman, Vicinus, and Chauncey, *Hidden from History*.

67. Lotchin, "California Cities," 396–97.

68. In the immediate postwar decade, the idea that Americans' commonalities greatly outweighed any conflict over differences they might harbor became accepted in fields such as history. This proved a marked contrast to early schools of thought such as the Progressive historians of the twentieth century's first few decades, who based the greatest part of their interpretations on the inherent conflict between classes and ideologies within American society. For excellent discussions on Progressive and consensus historians see Peter Novick, *That Noble Dream: The Objectivity Question and the American Historical Profession* (Cambridge: Cambridge University Press, 1988), 93, 97, 320–21, 330–33, 345; Ernst Breisach, *Historiography: Ancient, Medieval, and Modern*, 3rd ed. (Chicago: University of Chicago Press, 2006), 362–69.

69. Heidi Benson, "Howl," *SFC*, October 4, 2005.

70. Bill Morgan and Nancy J. Peters, *Howl on Trial: The Battle for Free Expression* (San Francisco: City Lights Books, 2006), 1.

71. Allen Ginsberg, "Howl," in *Collected Poems, 1946 to 1980* (New York: Harper Perennial, 1988), 126–34.

72. J. W. Ehrlich, ed., *Howl of the Censor* (San Carlos, Calif.: Nourse Publishing, 1961), 127; Benson, "Howl."

73. "Beat Mystics," *Time*, February 3, 1958.

74. Ibid.

75. Stephen J. Whitfield, *The Culture of the Cold War* (Baltimore: Johns Hopkins University Press, 1996), 87–88. For a comprehensive overview of religion's growth in America from the 1930s through present, see Kevin M. Kruse, *One Nation under God: How Corporate American Invented Christian America* (New York: Basic Books, 2015).

76. See Brent Spence, "Providing That All United States Currency and Paper Money Shall Bear the Inscription 'In God We Trust,'" House Report no. 662, Committee on Banking and Currency, 82nd Congress, May 26, 1955, 11823, 82–1; Public Law 84–140, signed by the president on July 30, 1956.

77. Minxin Pei, "The Paradoxes of American Nationalism," *Foreign Policy* 136 (May/June 2003): 33.

78. Whitfield, *Culture of the Cold War*, 89–90.

79. Joe Hyams, "Good-By to the Beats," *LAT*, September 28, 1958.

80. Howard Taubman, "Spawning Ground of the Offbeat," *NYT*, May 13, 1961.

81. "The Beardniks," *NYT*, September 26, 1963.

82. Herb Lyon, "Tower Ticker," *Chicago Tribune*, January 28, 1959; Lawrence E. Davies, "Coast Bohemians Feeling Less Beat," *NYT*, June 14, 1959.

83. Steven V. Roberts, "In San Francisco's North Beach, the Many Different Worlds and Generations Never Meet," *NYT*, November 4, 1969.

84. Ibid.; "Bottomless Bars Target on Coast," *NYT*, April 1, 1973; Katherine Bishop, "The Nightclub Where It All Began Imposes an End on the Topless Era," *NYT*, January 1, 1988.

85. Loudon Wainwright, "The Strange New Love Land of the Hippies," *Life*, March 31, 1967, 14–15.

86. Hunter S. Thompson, "The 'Hashbury' Is the Capital of the Hippies," *NYT*, May 14, 1967.

87. Mark Harris, "The Flowering of the Hippies," *Atlantic*, September 1967, 63–72.

88. "Gay History Questionnaire," Len Evans Papers, box 1, folder "Gay History Questionnaire; File Responses and Related Correspondence," JCH-GLC. In this survey conducted by Evans, an equal number of respondents listed San Francisco and New York City as the gayest cities of the 1940s.

89. Martin Meeker, *Contacts Desired: Gay and Lesbian Communications and Community, 1940s–1970s* (Chicago: University of Chicago Press, 2006), 33–35.

90. John D'Emilio, *Sexual Politics, Sexual Communities: The Making of a Homosexual Minority in the United States, 1940 to 1970* (Chicago: University of Chicago Press, 1983), 58–60.

91. Ibid., 72, 89–90.

92. Marcia M. Gallo, *Different Daughters: A History of the Daughters of Bilitis and the Rise of the Lesbian Rights Movement* (New York: Carroll & Graf, 2006), 1–6; Robert B. Marks Ridinger, *The Gay and Lesbian Movement* (New York: Simon & Schuster, 1996), 21.

93. D'Emilio, *Sexual Politics, Sexual Communities*, 101–7.

94. Ridinger, *The Gay and Lesbian Movement*, 21.

95. Shilts, *Mayor of Castro Street*, 55–57.

96. Welch and Havemann, "Homosexuality in America."

97. Meeker, "Come out West," 347–48.

98. Ibid.

99. "Still Another List," *Nation*, June 22, 1964, 615.

100. Martin Duberman, *Cures: A Gay Man's Odyssey* (New York: Dutton Publications, 1991).

101. Evander C. Smith and Herbert Donaldson, "Chronology of Events Occurring in Connection with Arrest of Above Individuals on January 1, 1965," Evander Smith—California Hall Papers (GLC46), box 1, folder 4, JCH-GLC; Committee for the Mardi Gras Ball, "Here's What REALLY Happened . . . ," press statement, January 2, 1965, Evander Smith—California Hall Papers (GLC 46), box 1, folder 5, JCH-GLC.

Chapter 5. Battlefield by the Bay

1. Kenneth Labich and Michael Reese, "He Hated to Lose," *Newsweek*, December 11, 1978, 28; "San Francisco: Horror Upon Horror," *Economist*, December 2, 1978, 44; William Carlson, "Ex-Aide Held in Moscone Killing Ran as Crusader against Crime," *NYT*, November 29, 1978.

2. "Homosexual on Board Cites Role as Pioneer," *NYT*, November 10, 1977. In this piece immediately following his election, Milk compared himself to Jackie Robinson. Just as Robinson stood as a symbol to African American youths across the nation by breaking the color line in Major League Baseball, Milk hoped that his pathbreaking election could instill hope in the nation's gay population.

3. A few examples of attitudes toward homosexuals during this period can be found in Senate Committee on Expenditures in the Executive Department, *Employment of Homosexuals and Other Sexual Perverts in Government*, 81st Cong., 2nd Sess., 1950, S. Doc. 241, 2; Marshall R. McClintock, "Commie Fags: The Politicalization of Homosexuality," unpublished manuscript, Len Evens Papers, box 1, folder 7, JCH-GLC; "Perverts Called Government Peril," *NYT*, April 18, 1950; Milton E. Hahn, "The Sexually Deviate Student," *School and Society* 41 (September 17, 1955): 85–87; "What Is a Homosexual?," *Time*, June 16, 1958, 44; "Curable Disease?," *Time*, December 10, 1956, 74–75; "Homosexuals: To Punish or Pity?," *Newsweek*, July 11, 1960, 78; "The Third Sex," *Newsweek*, June 1, 1964, 76; "Psychiatry: Homosexuals Can Be Cured," *Time*, February 12, 1963, 44. An excellent scholarly study on this topic can be found in D'Emilio, *Sexual Politics, Sexual Communities*.

4. Boyd, *Wide Open Town*, 111–13; Berube, *Coming Out under Fire*, 113; D'Emilio, *Sexual Politics, Sexual Communities*, 72, 89–90; Ridinger, *The Gay and Lesbian Movement*, 21.

5. Susan Stryker and Jim Van Buskirk, *Gay by the Bay: A History of Queer Culture in the San Francisco Bay Area* (San Francisco: Chronicle Books, 1996), 18.

6. Welch and Havemann, "Homosexuality in America."

7. President Richard M. Nixon, quoted in "All the Philosopher's Men," *Harper's*, February 2000, 22–24.

8. American Psychiatric Association, press release, December 15, 1973, Randy Shilts Papers (GLC 43), box 1, folder 26, JCH-GLC; American Psychological Association, press release, January 24, 1975, Randy Shilts Papers (GLC 43), box 1, folder 26, JCH-GLC.

9. Louise Cook, "States Overhauling Laws Involving Sex," *Register-Guard* (Eugene, Ore.), May 20, 1975, Randy Shilts Papers, box 1, folder 14, JCH-GLC; Randy Shilts, "Consenting Sex Laws," unpublished manuscript, Randy Shilts Papers, box 1, folder 25, JCH-GLC; Randy Shilts, "States Rights Laws: The Big Blow Out of '75," unpublished manuscript, Randy Shilts Papers, box 1, folder 27, JCH-GLC.

10. Mervin D. Field, "The California Poll: California Sharply Divided over Homosexuals and Their Way of Life," (San Francisco: Field Institute, 1977), Randy Shilts Papers (GLC 43), box 2, folder 23, JCH-GLC.

11. Shilts, "Consenting Sex Laws."

12. Meeker, in "Come out West," argues that San Francisco's emergence as the nation's gay mecca can be traced to the 1940s. While correct in these origins, I suggest that the maturation of the city as the gay mecca and its most widespread association as such came after the 1970s.

13. Shilts, *Mayor of Castro Street*, 5–17.

14. Ibid., 21–31.

15. Ibid., 4.

16. "Psychiatry: Homosexuals Can Be Cured," 44. A very moving and detailed account of these "cures" can be found in Duberman, *Cures*.

17. Shilts, *Mayor of Castro Street*, 38.

18. Ibid., 40–46; Laura A. Belmonte, "Harvey Milk, San Francisco and the Gay Migration," in *The Human Tradition in the American West*, ed. Benson Tong and Regan A. Lutz (Wilmington, Del.: Scholarly Resources, 2002), 209, 212.

19. Shilts, *Mayor of Castro Street*, 65–70.

20. Ibid., 73–79.

21. Lacy Fosburgh, "Cheers, Then a Shot, and Crowd Screams," *NYT*, September 23, 1975; Daryl Lembke, "No Call from President: Hero in Ford Shooting Active among SF Gays," *LAT*, September 25, 1975; Daryl Lembke, "Ford to Thank S. F. Man Who Deflected Gun," *LAT*, September 26, 1975; Jesus Rangel, "O. W. Sipple, 47, Who Blocked an Attempt to Kill Ford in 1975," *NYT*, February 4, 1989.

22. Harvey Milk to Friends, February 26, 1975, Harvey Milk Papers, box 3, folder 2, JCH-GLC.

23. Shilts, *Mayor of Castro Street*, 128–49; San Francisco Mayor George Moscone to Harvey Milk, March 9, 1976, Harvey Milk Papers, box 2, folder 7, "Correspondence, 1971–1976," JCH-GLC.

24. Gay Friends of Harvey Milk, "Harvey Milk for Assembly," political campaign flyer, Harvey Milk Papers, box 3, folder 15, JCH-GLC; Harvey Milk for Assembly Committee, "Why Elect Harvey Milk?," political campaign flyer, Harvey Milk Papers, box 3, folder 15, JCH-GLC; "Harvey Milk: The Democrat for Assembly," political campaign flyer, Harvey Milk Papers, box 3, folder 15, JCH-GLC.

25. Friends of Harvey Milk, "Street Fairs, Harvey Milk, and You," political flyer, Harvey Milk Papers, box 4, folder 5, JCH-GLC; Friends of Harvey Milk, "Harvey Milk/ Supervisor 5," political flyer, Harvey Milk Papers, box 4, folder 5, JCH-GLC.

26. Shilts, *Mayor of Castro Street*, 183.

27. Herbert Gold, "A Walk on San Francisco's Gay Side," *NYT*, November 6, 1977.

28. "Homosexual on Board Cites Role as Pioneer," *NYT*, November 8, 1977.

29. D'Emilio and Freedman, *Intimate Matters*, 346.

30. Ibid.

31. Ibid., 346–47, 353; Margaret Cruikshank, *The Gay and Lesbian Liberation Movement* (New York: Routledge, 1992), 15–16.

32. "Bias against Homosexuals Is Outlawed in Miami," *NYT*, January 19, 1977.

33. "Anita Bryant Scores White House Meeting with Homosexuals," *NYT*, March 28, 1977; "Powell Defends Meeting," *NYT*, March 28, 1977.

34. "People in the News," *ABC World News Tonight*, February 15, 1977; "Special: Gay Rights," *NBC Nightly News*, June 2, 1977; "Florida: Gay Rights," *CBS Evening News*, June 3, 1977; "Miami: Gay Rights Vote," *ABC World News Tonight*, June 6, 1977; "Dade County Florida: Homosexuals," *NBC Nightly News*, June 7, 1977; "Elections," *CBS Evening News*, June 7, 1977; "Homosexual Vote: Miami," *ABC World News Tonight*, June 8, 1977; "Homosexual Equal Rights," *CBS Evening News*, June 8, 1977; "Homo-sexual Rights Referendum," *NBC Nightly News*, June 8, 1977; "Bryant: Homosexual Campaign," *NBC Nightly News*, June 9, 1977; "Bryant: Citrus Promotion Job," *ABC World News Tonight*, July 19, 1977; "Bryant, Gay Rights, and Orange Growers," *NBC Nightly News*, July 20, 1977; "Segment 3: Homosexuals," *NBC Nightly News*, September 12, 1977; "Bryant: Homosexuality," *ABC World News Tonight*, November 2, 1977; "Anita Bryant: Contract Renewed," *CBS Evening News*, November 16, 1977; "Briefly: Bryant," *NBC Nightly News*, November 16, 1977; "Briefly: Anita Bryant," *NBC Nightly News*, December 30, 1977.

35. "Easter Service," *CBS Evening News*, March 26, 1978; "St. Paul: Gay Rights," *ABC World News Tonight*, April 26, 1978; "Anti-Gay Movement: Wichita," *ABC World News Tonight*, May 8, 1978; "Gay Rights: Oregon Vote," *ABC World News Tonight*, May 22, 1978; "Gay Rights: Oregon," *CBS Evening News*, May 22, 1978; "Gay Rights: Oregon," *NBC Nightly News*, May 24, 1978; "High School Student Survey," *ABC World News Tonight*, June 22, 1978; "Campaign '78: Gay Rights in Florida and California," *NBC Nightly News*, November 5, 1978.

36. "Dr. Jerry Falwell, the Old-Time Gospel Hour Clean Up America! Crusade," mailer, July 14, 1978, Harvey Milk Papers, box 6, folder 24, JCH-GLC; Randy Shilts, "The Fundamentalists," transcript, September 20, 1978, Randy Shilts Papers, box 7, folder 1, JCH-GLC.

37. "Protect America's Children," mailer, Gary Shilts Papers, box 7, folder 1, JCH-GLC.

38. Louis Harris, "The Harris Survey: Gay Is O.K., But . . . ," (Chicago: Chicago Tribune, 1977), Randy Shilts Papers, box 2, folder 17, JCH-GLC.

39. Shilts, *Mayor of Castro Street*, 153–54.

40. Ibid. Shilts received much criticism for this article's evenhanded and at times positive portrayal of Briggs. Shilts attempted to show that Briggs was not so much antigay as politically ambitious. At the same time, he argued that the senator did not take his antigay pronouncements seriously and that comparisons between Briggs and Nazis were unfounded. One typical response to Shilts's article can be found in a leaflet, "The Human Side of Hitler," Randy Shilts Papers, box 8, folder 23, JCH-GLC. Distributed by anonymous gay rights activists signing off as "the Red Queen," the leaflet related a fictional interview of "an up-and-coming aggressive journalist" in the early years of Nazi Germany. When asked about Hitler, concentration camps, and gays, the journalist, conveniently named "Mr. Shits," claimed that Hitler was "actually quite charming when he's off stage" and "doesn't actually believe in what he says publicly." If, Mr. Shits continued, Hitler should follow through with a threat to confine gays to concentration camps, "it won't be because he dislikes us personally, which is very comforting to know." In closing, the flyer related the "moral" of the

story: "Gay opportunists in journalism are as dangerous as straight opportunists in politics."

41. California Save Our Children Committee, "Initiative Measure to Be Submitted Directly to the Voters," Randy Shilts Papers, box 7, folder 1, JCH-GLC.

42. Ibid.

43. John Balzar, "Briggs' Initiative on Gays Wins Ballot Spot," *SFC*, June 1, 1978.

44. Tom Steel, "Briggs Initiative Qualifies for Ballot," *Conspiracy*, Newsletter of the Bay Area Chapter of the National Lawyers Guild, June–July 1978, Harvey Milk Papers, box 6, folder 24, "Briggs Initiative," JCH-GLC.

45. Larry Liebert, "A Legislative Push Begins for Gay Job Rights," *SFC*, January 12, 1978.

46. United States Representative Phillip Burton to San Francisco Supervisor Harvey Milk, February 1, 1978, Harvey Milk Papers, box 7, folder 41, JCH-GLC; United States Congressman John L. Burton to San Francisco Supervisor Harvey Milk, February 5, 1978, Harvey Milk Papers, box, 7, folder 41, JCH-GLC.

47. California Speaker of the Assembly Leo T. McCarthy to San Francisco Supervisor Harvey Milk, February 1, 1978, Harvey Milk Papers, box 7, folder 41, JCH-GLC; California Assembly Majority Whip Art Agnos to San Francisco Supervisor Ella Hill Hutch, February 9, 1978, Harvey Milk Papers, box 7, folder 41, JCH-GLC; Assemblyman Willie T. Brown Jr. to San Francisco Supervisor Dan White, February 27, 1978, Harvey Milk Papers, box 7, folder 41, JCH-GLC.

48. B. Drummond Ayres Jr., "Miami Debate over Rights of Homosexuals Directs Wide Attention to a National Issue," *NYT*, May 10, 1977; Les Ledbetter, "40,000 Join Peaceful March for Homosexual Rights in San Francisco," *NYT*, June 26, 1977; Grace Lichtenstein, "Homosexuals Are Moving toward Open Way of Life as Tolerance Rises among the General Population," *NYT*, July 17, 1977; Floyd Abrams, "The Press, Privacy, and the Constitution," *NYT*, August 21, 1977; Gold, "A Walk on San Francisco's Gay Side"; "Homosexual on Board Cites Role as Pioneer"; Jean O'Leary, letter to the editor, *NYT*, December 4, 1977; Colette Holt, letter to the editor, *NYT*, December 4, 1977; L. Egan and L. Jilly, letter to the editor, *NYT*, December 4, 1977.

49. William Safire, "Big Week for Gays," *NYT*, September 29, 1975; "Support for Homosexuals," *NYT*, April 19, 1976.

50. Robert McFadden, "A. M. Rosenthal, Editor of the *Times*, Dies at 84," *NYT*, May 11, 2006; Elaine Woo, "A. M. Rosenthal, 84, Venerated Editor Recast the N.Y. Times," *LAT*, May 11, 2006; Jack Shafer, "A. M. Rosenthal (1922–2006): Ugly Genius," Slate, http://www.slate.com/articles/news_and_politics/press_box/2006/05/am_rosenthal_19222006.html; "Something Not Great about Rosenthal: How He Dealt with Gays," Observer, May 12, 2016, http://observer.com/2006/05/something-not-great-about-rosenthal-how-he-dealt-with-gays/.

51. S. Franker, "Gay Power in San Francisco," *Newsweek*, June 6, 1977, 25.

52. Harry Reasoner and Bill Wordham, "Miami Gay Rights Vote," *ABC World News Tonight*, June 6, 1977.

53. Herb Caen, "Dog Daze in San Francisco," *NYT*, March 8, 1978.

54. Les Ledbetter, "San Franciscans Mark Day," *NYT*, June 26, 1978.

55. Don Kladstrup and Walter Cronkite, "San Francisco Gay Rights Ordinance," *CBS Evening News*, March 27, 1978.

56. San Francisco Board of Supervisors, "Article 33: Gay Rights Ordinance," Harvey Milk Papers, box 8, folder 1, JCH-GLC; "Supervisor Harvey Milk," press release, April 6, 1978, Harvey Milk Papers, box 8, folder 1, JCH-GLC.

57. "The Latest Poll," *SFC*, November 3, 1978. This article listed polls relative to Proposition 6 taken in late August, late September, and on October 30–November 1.

58. Mervin D. Field, "3 Propositions Gaining Favor," unidentified newspaper clipping, Harvey Milk Papers, box 6, folder 24, JCH-GLC.

59. "The Latest Poll."

60. No on the Briggs Initiative Committee, "He's Walking the Length of California to Dispel the Lies of Briggs," flyer, Randy Shilts Papers, box 8, folder 22, JCH-GLC; Eli Setencich, "Walking Tall for Teachers," *Fresno Bee*, July 31, 1978, Randy Shilts Papers, box 8, folder 22, JCH-GLC; Shilts, *Mayor of Castro Street*, 242–43.

61. Shilts, *Mayor of Castro Street*, 243.

62. Walter Cronkite and Barry Peterson, "California, Proposition 6, and Homosexuality," *CBS Evening News*, October 26, 1978.

63. Shilts, *Mayor of Castro Street*, 244.

64. Ibid.; Tom Steel, "Briggs Initiative Qualifies for Ballot," *Conspiracy*, Newsletter of the Bay Area Chapter of the National Lawyers Guild, June–July 1978, Harvey Milk Papers, box 6, folder 24, JCH-GLC; San Francisco Board of Supervisors, "Resolution Number 511–78: Opposing the State Ballot Initiative Entitled, School Employees—Homosexuality," June 19, 1978, Harvey Milk Papers, box 6, folder 25, JCH-GLC.

65. San Francisco Chamber of Commerce, memorandum to board of directors, Harvey Milk Papers, box 6, folder 27, JCH-GLC; San Francisco Supervisor Harvey Milk to Chamber of Commerce President William E. Dauer, October 16, 1978, Harvey Milk Papers, box 6, folder 27, JCH-GLC; San Francisco Chamber of Commerce President William E. Dauer to San Francisco Supervisor Harvey Milk, October 18, 1978, Harvey Milk Papers, box 6, folder 27, JCH-GLC; San Francisco Supervisor Harvey Milk to Chamber of Commerce President William E. Dauer, October 19, 1978, Harvey Milk Papers, box 6, folder 27, JCH-GLC; San Francisco Chamber of Commerce Public Affairs Manager Gregory P. Hurst to San Francisco Supervisor Harvey Milk, October 23, 1978, Harvey Milk Papers, box 6, folder 27, JCH-GLC.

66. "Briggs Spurns Nazi Help," *Los Angeles Herald-Examiner*, September 23, 1978.

67. Shilts, *Mayor of Castro Street*, 247.

68. Caen, "Dog Daze in San Francisco."

69. Gen. 18:26–32.

70. Ralph Hinman and Bob Andrews, "Baptist Meeting in Anaheim Scolds Carter on Proposition 6," *Long Beach Independent Press-Telegram*, November 18, 1979; Kelley Tackett, letter to the editor, "Christianity and Proposition 6 Debate," *Los Angeles Herald-Examiner*, October 18, 1978; James Harrison, letter to the editor, "Christianity and Proposition 6 Debate," *Los Angeles Herald-Examiner*, October 18, 1978; Mr. and Mrs. Gerald Cleveland, letter to the editor, "Christianity and Proposition 6 Debate," *Los Angeles Herald-Examiner*, October 18, 1978.

71. Shilts, *Mayor of Castro Street*, 248.

72. Harvey Milk, "Debate Notes," Harvey Milk Archives, Scott Smith Collection, box 9, folder 45, JCH-GLC.

73. Bob Tuttle, quoted in Shilts, *Mayor of Castro Street*, 248.

74. Thomas E. Ainsworth to Harvey Milk, October 13, 1978, Harvey Milk Papers, box 9, folder 45, JCH-GLC; Oscar Villanicencio to Harvey Milk, October 14, 1978, Harvey Milk Papers, box 9, folder 45, JCH-GLC; David Held to Harvey Milk, October 12, 1978, Harvey Milk Papers, box 9, folder 45, JCH-GLC; Phillip Fay Stevenson to Harvey Milk, Harvey Milk Papers, box 9, folder 45, JCH-GLC.

75. Jerry Carroll, "Gay Happy Days Are Here Again," *SFC*, November 8, 1978.

76. "Statewide," *SFC*, November 8, 1978.

77. "S. F. Vote," *SFC*, November 9, 1978.

78. Carroll, "Gay Happy Days."

79. Anonymous to Board of Supervisors c/o Harvey Milk, May 18, 1978, Harvey Milk Papers, box 6, folder 6, "Hate Mail," JCH-GLC; Anonymous to San Francisco Board of Stupid Visors c/o *Cocksucker* Harvey Milk, May 27, 1978, Harvey Milk Papers, box 6, folder 6, "Hate Mail," JCH-GLC.

80. Anonymous to California State Senator Milton Marks, October 24, 1977, Harvey Milk Papers, box 6, folder 6, "Hate Mail," JCH-GLC; Nguen Rene Phuc Q to Harvey Milk, June 25, 1978, Harvey Milk Papers, box 6, folder 6, "Hate Mail," JCH-GLC.

81. Nguen Rene Phuc Q to Harvey Milk, June 1, 1978, Harvey Milk Papers, box 6, folder 6, "Hate Mail," JCH-GLC; Nguen Rene Phuc Q to Harvey Milk, June 25, 1978, Harvey Milk Papers, box 6, folder 6, "Hate Mail," JCH-GLC.

82. A Guy in Iowa to Harvey Milk, December 5, 1977, Harvey Milk Papers, box 6, folder 6, "Hate Mail," JCH-GLC; Nguen Rene Phuc Q to Harvey Milk, June 25, 1978, Harvey Milk Papers, box 6, folder 6, "Hate Mail," JCH-GLC.

83. Shilts, *Mayor of Castro Street*, vii, xv–xvii, 263–71; Cruikshank, *The Gay and Lesbian Liberation Movement*, 73.

84. "Day of the Assassin," *Newsweek*, December 11, 1978, 26–28; "Another Day of Death: A Former San Francisco Official Kills the Mayor and a Supervisor," *Time*, December 11, 1978, 24–26; Ben Fong Torres, "A Letter From San Francisco," *Rolling Stone*, January 24, 1979, 45–46.

85. Caen, "Dog Daze in San Francisco."

86. Extensive searches of editorials in San Francisco newspapers covering the times of particularly prominent events relative to San Francisco being cast as gay tolerant or as a gay tourist destination reveal no letters to the editor specifically voicing concern over the city's projection of a gay-friendly image to the world.

87. "Harvey Milk Sites in San Francisco: 4 Must-see Places from the Life of Gay Rights Icon," One Travel, www.onetravel.com/going-places/harvey-milk-sites-in-san-francisco-4-must-see-places-from-the-life-of-gay-rights-icon/.

88. Randy Shilts, *And the Band Played On: Politics, People, and the AIDS Epidemic* (New York: St. Martin's Press, 1987), 12–18.

89. Ibid., 15–16.

90. Michael Worobey et al., "Direct Evidence of Extensive Diversity of HIV-1 in Kinshasa by 1960," *Nature* 455 (October 2008): 661–64.

91. Dennis Altman, *AIDS in the Mind of America* (Garden City, N.Y.: Anchor Press, 1986), 1.

92. Shilts, *And the Band Played On*, 518.

93. Ibid., 490, 498–99.

94. Ira Cohen and Ann Elder, "Major Cities and Disease Crisis: A Comparative Perspective," *Social Science History* 13 (Spring 1989): 50–51.

95. Shilts, *And the Band Played On*, 121.

96. Alan Petrucelli, "The Gay Plague," *Us Magazine*, August 31, 1981.

97. Paul Jacobs, "22 More Children Contract New Immune Deficiency," *LAT*, December 17, 1982, B3. This article reveals both the shift in terminology to *AIDS* and the spread of the disease outside perceived pariah groups. Here, children had contracted the disease through blood transfusions.

98. "San Francisco Rescue Workers Wary of AIDS," *Boston Globe*, May 13, 1983, 1.

99. A few representative examples of the newspaper media linking the terms *AIDS*, *homosexuality*, and *San Francisco* include Ellen Goodman, "Gays Fighting a New Stigma," *Boston Globe*, July 7, 1983, 1; "Blood Bank Will Use Second Test in Drive to Reduce AIDS Risk," *Wall Street Journal*, March 30, 1984, 1; San Francisco Curb on Baths," *NYT*, April 10, 1984, A14; Wayne King, "Houston Voting Today on Banning Bias against Homosexuals," *NYT*, January 19, 1985, 1.

100. Tom Brokaw and Robert Brazell, "AIDS," *NBC Nightly News*, October 9, 1984; Max Robinson and Ken Kashiwahara, "San Francisco AIDS Clinic," *ABC World News Tonight*, July 25, 1983; Dan Rather and Steve Young, "AIDS," *CBS Evening News*, March 23, 1983; Dan Rather, "San Francisco, AIDS, and Gays," *CBS Evening News*, October 9, 1984; Max Robinson and Ken Kashiwahara, "AIDS Poll," *ABC World News Tonight News*, June 20, 1983.

101. "AIDS: San Francisco Recoils," *Economist*, August 23, 1986, 24.

102. King, "Houston Voting Today."

103. "AIDS Researchers: What Can They Say?," *U.S. News & World Report*, August 8, 1994, 18; Simon Robinson, "Orphans of AIDS," *Time*, December 13, 1999, 60–62; Jack E. White, "When Silence Is a Sin," *Time*, December 27, 1999; "A Devastated Continent," *Newsweek*, January 1, 2000, 41.

104. "Books and Arts: Holding up a Mirror; AIDS and Artists," *Economist*, January 1, 2005; Cynthia Reynolds, "Celebrity Chic," *MacLeans*, December 20, 2004, 51–55.

105. Alyssa Cymene Howe, "Queer Pilgrimage: The San Francisco Homeland and Identity Tourism," *Cultural Anthropology* 16 (Spring 2001): 35–39.

106. Philip Matier and Andrew Ross, "San Francisco Hopes for Big Slice of Gay Marriage Money," *SFC*, May 18, 2008; David Swansen, "Gay Tourism: The $54.1 Challenge," *Chicago Tribune*, August 4, 2002.

107. Andrew Collins, David Cashion, Constance Jones, and Robert Blake, eds., *Fodor's Gay Guide to the U.S.A.*, 3rd ed. (New York: Fodor's Travel Publications, 2001).

108. John Wilcock, ed., *Insight Guides: San Francisco* (Boston: APA, 1995), cover, 63–70.

109. Bing and Channell, *San Francisco City Guide*, 36–37, 247–55.

110. Ibid.; Ginger Adams Otis, Beth Greenfield, Robert Reid, and Regis St. Louis, *New York City: City Guide* (Victoria, Australia: Lonely Planet Publications, 2008); Mary Herczog, *Frommer's Las Vegas 2008* (New York: Wiley Publishing, 2007); Matthew R. Poole and Erika Lenkert, *Frommer's San Francisco 2008* (New York: Wiley Publishing, 2007); Matthew Richard Poole, *Frommer's Los Angeles 2008* (New York: Wiley Publishing, 2007); Brian Silverman, *Frommer's New York City 2008* (New York: Wiley Publishing, 2007).

111. Ed Salvato, "The Out Traveler Guides," www.gay.com/travel/article.html?sernum =9405, accessed December 13, 2008 (site discontinued).

112. "Articles about San Francisco Travel at Gay.com," www.gay.com/travel/destinations/ guides/?key=366, accessed December 13, 2008 (site discontinued).

113. "Travel: San Francisco: Introduction," www.gay.com/travel/premium/splash.html ?sernum=56, accessed December 13, 2008 (site discontinued).

114. Comment by exinashes on "Travel: San Francisco: Introduction."

115. "Only in San Francisco," http://exclusives.gay.com/sanfrancisco/, accessed December 13, 2008 (site discontinued).

116. "Gay and Lesbian Travel in San Francisco," San Francisco Convention and Visitors Bureau Official Website, www.onlyinsanfrancisco.com/gaytravel/, accessed December 12, 2008 (page removed).

117. Pia Sarker, "Out and About: Top Dog San Francisco Runs into Competition for Gay Tourist Dollars," *SFC*, October 24, 2004, www.sfgate.com/cgi-bin/article/comments/view?f=/c/a/2008/05/18/BANH100130.DTL, accessed November 22, 2008 (page removed); Matier and Ross, "San Francisco Hopes for Big Slice of Gay Marriage Money"; Christine Delsol and Larry Harbegger, "Gay Tourism on Dallas Wish List," *SFC*, November 19, 2006; Carol Ness, "The Magic Endures," *San Francisco Examiner*, June 18, 1995; Carol Ness, "Census 2000: San Francisco Upstaged as Gay Mecca!" *SFC*, August 8, 2001.

118. "The City and County Statement of Votes, SFC-20081104-E," (San Francisco: Department of Elections, 2008), copy in author's possession.

119. Sarker, "Out and About."

120. Folgers, comment on Sarker, "Out and About."

121. Lauravella, comment on Sarker, "Out and About."

122. Adam Liptak, "Supreme Court Ruling Makes Same-Sex Marriage a Right Nationwide," *NYT*, June 26, 2015.

Chapter 6. Sinning in the Desert

1. Hal K. Rothman, *Neon Metropolis: How Las Vegas Started the Twenty-First Century* (New York: Routledge, 2002), 63.

2. Eugene P. Moehring, *Resort City in the Sunbelt: Las Vegas 1930–2000*, 2nd ed. (Reno: University of Nevada Press, 2000).

3. Larry Gragg, *Bright Light City: Las Vegas in Popular Culture* (Lawrence: University Press of Kansas, 2013), 1–2.

4. Moehring, *Resort City in the Sunbelt*, 3; Eugene Moehring and Michael S. Green, *Las Vegas: A Centennial History* (Reno: University of Nevada Press, 2005), 9; Frank Wright, *Clark County: The Changing Face of Nevada* (Las Vegas: Nevada Historical Society, 1981), 10–13, UNLVSC.

5. Maria Barston Wheeler, "My History," unpublished manuscript, Maria Barton Wheeler Collection, ca. 1840–1933, box 1, folder 1, UNLVSC.

6. Reps, *Cities of the American West*, 327; James W. Hulse, *The Silver State: Nevada's Heritage Reinterpreted*, 3rd ed. (Reno: University of Nevada Press, 2004), 62–65; James W. Hulse, *The Nevada Adventure: A History*, rev. ed. (Reno: University of Nevada Press, 1969), 73–77; Moehring, *Resort City in the Sunbelt*, 2; Moehring and Green, *Las Vegas*, 4–5; Michael W. Bowers, *Sagebrush State: Nevada's History, Government, and Politics*, 2nd ed. (Reno: University of Nevada Press, 2002), 6–7.

7. As Moehring and Green point out in *Las Vegas: A Centennial History*, residents of these ranches were not always the best of neighbors. Helen Stewart's husband, Archibald, for example, fell victim to a shooting on the Kiel Ranch following a confrontation over a former ranch hand—recently hired by Kiel—who was gossiping about Mrs. Stewart. As she blamed Conrad Kiel for the death, Mrs. Stewart never spoke to him or his sons, Edwin and William, again. In 1900 both Edwin and William were found dead from gunshot wounds. Initially ruled a murder-suicide, it was later classified as an unsolved double murder (5–7).

8. Rothman, *Neon Metropolis*, 207.

9. The Weather Channel, "Las Vegas, NV, Monthly Weather," Weather.com, www.weather.com/weather/wxclimatology/monthly/graph/USNV0049?from=month_bottomnav_undeclared, accessed May 7, 2009; Rothman, *Neon Metropolis*. Rothman wrote that people tend not to venture out between 10 A.M. and 3 P.M. I would argue that 3 P.M. is much too early as temperatures remain well over one hundred degrees until sunset and beyond during the summer months.

10. "Jap Learning Railroading," *San Jose Mercury*, June 26, 1905.

11. "Railroad Goes to Bullfrog Camp," *Philadelphia Inquirer*, September 10, 1905.

12. "Laborers Starving in the Desert," *San Jose Mercury*, December 13, 1905.

13. "California Washout Costs $1,000,000," *Fort Worth Start-Telegram*, March 30, 1906; "Cost Clarke's Road a Million," *Kansas City Star*, March 30, 1906.

14. "Desert Trip Pleasing," *Oregonian*, June 6, 1914.

15. "12 Trains Halted at Desert Points," *Oregonian*, August 12, 1922; "Southern California Feels Impact of Railroad Strike," *San Jose Mercury News*, August 12, 1922; "Western Lines Still Suffer from Walkout," *Idaho Daily Statesman*, August 14, 1922; "Trains Move from Desert," *Duluth News-Tribune*, August 14, 1922; "Deserted Trains in Western Locations Moving On Again," *Miami Herald Record*, August 14, 1922.

16. "Trains Move from Desert."

17. Las Vegas Chamber of Commerce, "Semi-Tropical Nevada: A Region of Fertile Soils and Flowing Wells," pamphlet, UNLVSC; Las Vegas Chamber of Commerce, "Las Vegas, Nevada: Where Farming Pays," pamphlet, UNLVSC; Las Vegas Chamber of Commerce, "Las Vegas and Clark County, Nevada: A Brief Review of Climate, Resources, and Growth Opportunities," pamphlet, UNLVSC.

18. David Wrobel, *Promised Lands: Promotion, Memory, and the Creation of the American West* (Lawrence: University Press of Kansas, 2002), 2.

19. Las Vegas Chamber of Commerce, "Las Vegas, Nevada: Center and County Seat of Clark County, Nevada: Gateway of the Great Boulder Dam Project," pamphlet, UNLVSC.

20. Patricia Nelson Limerick, *Desert Passages: Encounters with the American Desert* (Albuquerque: University of New Mexico Press, 1985), 165–76; W. Eugene Hollon, *The Great American Desert: Then and Now* (New York: Oxford University Press, 1966), 1–7.

21. Num. 32:13; Matt. 4:1–11.

22. For a discussion of the significance of the "rain follows the plow" belief, see Gary D. Liebcap and Zeynep Kiocabiyik Hansen, "Rain Follows the Plow and Dryfarming Doctrine: The Climate Information Problem and Homestead Failure in the Upper Great Plains, 1890–1925," *Journal of Economic History* 62 (March 2002): 86–119.

23. Las Vegas Chamber of Commerce, "Story of Southern Nevada," 1948, Las Vegas Chamber of Commerce Collection, box 2, "History Files, Publications," UNLVSC.

24. Ibid.

25. "Las Vegas News Bureau," *Charger*, November 1970, 4–5, Chamber of Commerce Collection, box 1, Las Vegas News Bureau History, Photo Captions Folder, UNLVSC.

26. Ibid.

27. Las Vegas Chamber of Commerce, "Las Vegas, This Is Our City," booklet, 1954, Chamber of Commerce Collection, box 2, "History Files, Publications," UNLVSC.

28. Jon Christensen, "Build It and the Water Will Come," in *The Grit beneath the Glitter*, ed. Hal K. Rothman and Mike Davis (Berkeley: University of California Press, 2002), 119–20.

29. Arizona v. California, 373 U.S. 546 (1963).

30. "Urban Pressure—1952 to Present," Las Vegas Springs Preserve, www.springspreserve. org/about/history_07_urban.html, accessed July 12, 2008.

31. Christensen, "Build It," 115–20.

32. Carmen Roberts, "Vegas Heading for Dry Future," BBC News Online, July 29, 2005, http://news.bbc.co.uk/go/pr/fr/-/1/hi/sci/tech/4719473.stm, accessed July 12, 2008. The reference to an "Owens Valley–type water grab" refers to the early twentieth-century diversion of Owens River water some 250 miles to southern California for use by the city of Los Angeles. The Owens Valley and Owens Lake were subsequently left dry while Los Angeles used the water to support continued growth. See Marc Reisner, *Cadillac Desert: The American West and Its Disappearing Water* (New York: Penguin, 1993), 52–103; Erwin Cooper, *Aqueduct Empire: A Guide to Water in California, Its Turbulent History and Its Management Today* (Glendale: Arthur C. Clark, 1968), 59–68.

33. Rothman, *Neon Metropolis*, 210.

34. John Howe, dir., *Desert Wars: Water and the West*, KUED-TV, University of Utah, 2006, 25:13–25:39. In this documentary, Rothman argues that very few people benefit from the inefficient water use in the rural parts of the state. The areas continue to lack employment opportunities, and residents leave for the urban areas. He goes on

to say that it "makes no sense" to use all the water to grow alfalfa when the cities are the economic engines of the state. This certainly implies that rural water resources could subsequently benefit more people and thus accomplish greater good by being designated for the urban areas' use.

35. Reisner, *Cadillac Desert*, 13.

36. Ibid., 5–6.

37. Howe, *Desert Wars*, 23:45–24:11.

38. Ibid., 05:14–05:28.

39. Mike Davis, *Dead Cities: And Other Tales* (New York: New Press, 2003) 85–106. Stephen King, *The Stand*, expanded ed. (New York: Signet, 1991).

40. Ted Steinberg, *Acts of God: The Unnatural History of Natural Disasters* (New York: Oxford University Press, 2006), 3–5, 19, 176, 192, 201.

41. Lake Mead Water Database, http://lakemead.water-data.com/, accessed January 25, 2017.

42. Stephen Kessler, dir., *Vegas Vacation*, Warner Brothers Motion Pictures, 1997.

43. David G. Schwartz, *Suburban Xanadu: The Casino Resort on the Las Vegas Strip and Beyond* (New York: Routledge, 2003), 6–8.

44. Steve Friess, "A Firm Hits Jackpot on Las Vegas Ads: Campaign Phrase Enters the Lexicon," *Chicago Tribune*, March 17, 2004.

45. One example of the "escape into the desert" theme in feature films can be found in Sergio Leone, dir., *The Good, The Bad, and the Ugly*, Arturo Gonzalez Producciones Cinematograficas, 1966.

46. "New Rival for Reno: Las Vegas, Nev., Will Make Specialty of Winter Divorces," *NYT*, August 29, 1911; "A Rival Divorce Colony," *NYT*, August 30, 1911.

47. Between its first mention in 1911 and 1945, eighty articles appeared in the *NYT* announcing celebrity divorces or marriages in Las Vegas. A representative sampling of these includes "Nevada Divorce Aim of L. K. Rhinelander," *NYT*, June 13, 1929; "Hudson Gets Divorce to Wed Ma Kennedy," *NYT*, September 19, 1931; "Wife Sues John R. Hearst," *NYT*, March 15, 1932; "E. R. Burroughs Gets Divorce," *NYT*, December 7, 1934; "Bancroft Sues for Divorce," *NYT*, March 6, 1936; "Mrs. Gable Files Suit: Wife of Actor Nears End of Nevada's Required Residency," *NYT*, March 5, 1939; "Lana Turner Weds Crane: Actress Becomes His Wife Again after an Annulment," *NYT*, April 6, 1943; "Wife Divorces Mickey Rooney," *NYT*, September 15, 1943.

48. Mae Farei, interviewed by Martha Jane Cunningham, February 24, 1980, University of Nevada, Las Vegas Local Oral History Project, UNLVSC.

49. Betty Dokter, interviewed by Roger Jublonski, University of Nevada, Las Vegas Local Oral History Project, UNLVSC.

50. Moehring, *Resort City in the Sunbelt*, 1–21.

51. Ibid., 29, 44–46; Suzette M. Cox, interviewed by Lance Cooper, March 3, 1979, University of Nevada, Las Vegas Local Oral History Project, UNLVSC. Cox relates the magnitude of the annual Helldorado celebration in the 1950s. She recalls how it was the "biggest thing" to happen each year. People anticipated it throughout the year, and children loved it as schools all closed on the day of the parade.

52. "Menu—Hotel El Rancho Vegas," 1943, Chamber of Commerce Collection, box 2, "History Files, Publications," UNLVSC.

53. "History of Las Vegas," 1935, Las Vegas Chamber of Commerce, 1948, Chamber of Commerce Collection, box 2, "History Files, Publications," UNLVSC.

54. Perry Kaufman, "Public Relations Men, Images, and the Growth of Las Vegas" (unpublished paper presented at the Organization of American Historians Conference, Chicago, Illinois, 1973), Las Vegas Chamber of Commerce, 1948, Chamber of Commerce Collection, box 2, "History Files, Publications," UNLVSC.

55. Las Vegas Chamber of Commerce, "Story of Southern Nevada," 1948, Chamber of Commerce Collection, box 2, "History Files, Publications," UNLVSC.

56. Las Vegas Chamber of Commerce, "Las Vegas: This Is Our City," 1954, Chamber of Commerce Collection, box 2, "History Files, Publications," UNLVSC.

57. Las Vegas Chamber of Commerce, "Howdy Podner!" newsletter, May 1958, Chamber of Commerce Collection, box 2, "History Files, Publications," UNLVSC; Research and Statistical Bureau, "Las Vegas Report, 1959," 1959, Chamber of Commerce Collection, box 2, "History Files, Publications," UNLVSC; "Las Vegas, Nevada," travel brochure, ca. mid-1950s, Chamber of Commerce Collection, box 2, "History Files, Publications," UNLVSC.

58. Las Vegas Chamber of Commerce, "Las Vegas Motels: 365 Days of Sun and Fun," brochure, ca. mid-1960s, Chamber of Commerce Collection, box 2, "History Files, Publications," UNLVSC; Las Vegas Chamber of Commerce, "Las Vegas Motel Holiday," brochure, 1969, Chamber of Commerce Collection, box 2, "History Files, Publications," UNLVSC.

59. Frederick Jackson Turner, "The Significance of the Frontier in American History," in *Rereading Frederick Jackson Turner: The Significance of the Frontier in American History and Other Essays*, ed. John Mack Faragher (New York: Henry Holt, 1994), 31–60.

60. Schwartz, *Suburban Xanadu*, 6–8.

61. John M. Findlay, "Gambling, Las Vegas, and American Culture: Chance and Change in the Mid-20th Century" (paper delivered at Organization of American Historians meeting, Reno, Nevada, March 25, 1988), UNLVSC; John M. Findlay, "Suckers and Escapists? Interpreting Las Vegas and Post-War America," *Nevada Historical Society Quarterly* 33 (Spring 1990): 1–15; John M. Findlay, *People of Chance: Gambling in American Society from Jamestown to Las Vegas* (New York: Oxford University Press, 1986); additional research concerning gambling's direct link to western identity can be found in Gary L. Cunningham, "Chance, Culture, and Compulsion: The Gambling Games of the Kansas Cattle Towns," *Nevada Historical Society Quarterly* 26 (Winter 1983): 255–71.

62. Gladwin Hill, "Klondike in the Desert," *NYT*, June 7, 1953; Gladwin Hill, "The 'Sure Thing' Boom at Las Vegas," *NYT*, January 20, 1955; "Mr. Coward Dissects Las Vegas," *NYT*, June 26, 1955; Gladwin Hill, "Las Vegas Is More Than the 'Strip,'" *NYT*, March 16, 1958; Gladwin Hill, "Las Vegas Keeps the Wheels Turning," *NYT*, October 19, 1958.

63. "Timeline: 1950–59," *Las Vegas Sun*, https://lasvegassun.com/history/timeline/.

64. Hal K. Rothman, *Devil's Bargain: Tourism in the Twentieth-Century American West* (Lawrence: University Press of Kansas, 1998), 314–15; Richard O. Davies, "Only in Nevada: America's Unique Experiment with Legalized Sports Gambling," *Nevada Historical Society Quarterly* 44 (Spring 2001): 3; Peter L. Bandurraga, "Desert Mirage: Casino Gaming and the Image of Nevada," *Nevada Historical Society Quarterly* 29 (Summer 1986): 109, 114.

65. Ward Allen Howe, "Las Vegas Vacation Center: Seeing Boulder Dam by Automobile," *NYT*, March 24, 1946; Grady Johnson, "Lively Las Vegas: New Vacationland Is Growing Up Rapidly around the Great Lake at Hoover Dam," *NYT*, November 14, 1948.

66. Jack Goodman, "Desert Attractions: Tourism Is Las Vegas' Major Industry and Spring Business Is Booming," *NYT*, March 16, 1947.

67. Howe, "Las Vegas Vacation Center."

68. Goodman, "Desert Attractions."

69. Johnson, "Lively Las Vegas."

70. Howe, "Las Vegas Vacation Center."

71. Goodman, "Desert Attractions."

72. Johnson, "Lively Las Vegas."

73. Rothman, *Neon Metropolis*, 12–13.

74. "Investigation in Nevada," *NYT*, November 16, 1950.

75. Wallace Turner, "Las Vegas: Gambling Take Creates New Force in U.S.: Millions in Untaxed 'Black Money' Give Obscure Figures Power That Extends from Underworld to Government," *NYT*, November 18, 1963.

76. Wallace Turner, "Las Vegas: Casinos' Hoodlums Face a Cleanup: State Starting to Act against Shady Figures Who Run or Patronize Gambling," *NYT*, November 20, 1963.

77. Ed Reid and Ovis DeMaris, *The Green Felt Jungle* (Cutchogue, N.Y.: Buccaneer Books, 1963), 1–11, 14–29, 82–85, 92–99, 194–220; Turner, "Las Vegas: Gambling Take Creates New Force in U.S."; Turner, "Las Vegas: Casinos' Hoodlums Face a Cleanup."

78. Fred J. Cook, *A Two-Dollar Bet Means Murder* (New York: Dial Press, 1961), 172–202; Fred J. Cook, "Gambling, Inc.," *Nation*, October 22, 1960, 260.

79. "Open End Lists Crime Discussion," *NYT*, February 24, 1963.

80. George Gent, "The American Way of Crime," *NYT*, August 21, 1966.

81. John W. Jefferies, "The Quest for National Purpose of 1960," *American Quarterly* 30 (Autumn 1978): 451–70.

82. Stephen E. Ambrose, *Eisenhower: Soldier and President* (New York: Simon & Schuster, 1990), 273–77.

83. Ibid., 277.

84. William H. Chafe, *The Unfinished Journey: America since World War II* (New York: Oxford University Press, 1995), 121–23, 129–30, 145.

85. John Kenneth Galbraith, *The Affluent Society* (Boston: Houghton Mifflin, 1958).

86. Eugene Moehring conversation with the author, July 6, 2009. Moehring recalled attending "Las Vegas Nights" at Catholic churches in New York City during the

1950s and 1960s. Through these themed gatherings, the churches portrayed Las Vegas as exotic and positive. Attendees certainly were not put off by the city's ties to organized crime or gambling.

87. James P. Kraft, *Vegas at Odds: Labor Conflict in a Leisure Economy, 1960–1985* (Baltimore: Johns Hopkins University Press, 2010), 121–22.

88. Chafe, *The Unfinished Journey*, 121–23, 134. Chafe sees suburbia as having an emasculating effect on the perceived identity of the American man by bringing him more squarely into the normal routines of family life and by assaulting individualism.

89. William H. Whyte, *The Organization Man* (New York: Simon & Schuster, 1956).

90. Wallace Turner, "Cheaters Beat the New Las Vegas," *NYT*, June 26, 1972.

91. Paul J. C. Friedlander, "The Traveler's World: Inside Las Vegas: Just Folks at Home," *NYT*, December 10, 1972.

92. Don Heckman, "Presley—Has the Rocker Become a Crooner?," *NYT*, March 12, 1972.

93. Red Smith, "Ambush among the Slots," *NYT*, January 25, 1976.

94. Jeff Gerth, "U.S. to Seek Charges from a Wide Inquiry on Organized Crime: FBI Surveillance Used in Several Cities: Allegations to Focus on Union and Businesses," *NYT*, February 24, 1980; Wallace Turner, "Federal Robes Can't Disguise Local Hackles in Las Vegas," *NYT*, April 27, 1980.

95. Gerth, "U.S. to Seek Charges."

96. Rothman, *Neon Metropolis*, xiv.

97. Stewart Powell et al., "Busting the Mob," *U.S. News & World Report*, February 3, 1986, 24–28.

98. "Mafia, U.S.A.," *U.S. News & World Report*, February 3, 1986, 27.

99. Pamela G. Hollie, "Hundreds Are Injured as Blaze Traps 3,500 on the Upper Floors," *NYT*, November 22, 1980.

100. John M. Crewdson, "On Las Vegas's Strip, a Few Refused to Be Interrupted," *NYT*, November 23, 1980.

Chapter 7. Mainstream Currents

1. Anderson, "Las Vegas"; Astor, "All America Cities 1970."

2. For the best coverage of Las Vegas's participation in the Sunbelt population migration of the post–World War II period, see Moehring, *Resort City in the Sunbelt*. An excellent study of Las Vegas's late twentieth-century diversity and multiculturalism can be found in Jerry L. Simich and Thomas C. Wright, eds., *The Peoples of Las Vegas: One City, Many Faces* (Reno: University of Nevada Press, 2005); Jerry L. Simich and Thomas C. Wright, eds., *More Peoples of Las Vegas: One City, Many Faces* (Reno: University of Nevada Press, 2010).

3. The arguments that Las Vegas has become Americanized, that it has served as a pacesetter of American urban style and culture, and that America has in many ways evolved toward its example in the embrasure of the service-oriented economic base, acceptance of gambling, and boosterism are not new. Recent examples can be found in Rothman, *Neon Metropolis*; Mark Gottdiener, Claudia C. Collins, and David R.

Dickens, *Las Vegas: The Social Production of an All-American City* (Malden, Mass.: Blackwell Publishers, 1999). As Gottdiener, Collins, and Dickens point out, this line of thinking runs back decades to the publication of Tom Wolfe, *The Kandy-Kolored Tangerine-Flake Streamline Baby* (New York: Farrar, Strauss & Giroux, 1965). Wolfe referred to Las Vegas's outlandish structures as the "new landmarks of America, the new guideposts, the new way Americans get their bearings." Even in popular writing, Hunter S. Thompson tied Las Vegas to wider America in his outrageous *Fear and Loathing in Las Vegas: A Savage Journey to the Heart of the American Dream* (New York: Random House, 1971). Other examples of Las Vegas as the leading edge of urbanism can be found in Robert Venturi, Denise S. Brown, and Steven Izenour, *Learning from Las Vegas* (Cambridge, Mass.: MIT Press, 1972); Findlay, "Suckers and Escapists?," 1–16; Alan Hess, *After-Hours Architecture* (San Francisco: Chronicle Books, 1993).

4. Even in satirical popular treatments of Las Vegas during the mid to late 1990s, one can see the reluctance to embrace family-destination Vegas over Sin City Vegas. One prime example of this can be found in the Kessler film *Vegas Vacation*. Here, the Griswolds find their family ties stretched to the breaking point as Vegas's adult-themed offerings sink their claws into various family members. Only luck in the Keno parlor rescues the Griswolds from succumbing to gambling addiction, stripping, infidelity, and promiscuous partying. Another interesting version can be found in the very accurate screen adaptation of Thompson's *Fear and Loathing in Las Vegas* by Terry Gilliam (Fear and Loathing LLC, 1998) in which Raoul Duke (Johnny Depp) and Dr. Gonzo (Benicio Del Toro) experience perhaps the world's strangest acid trip while exploring the interior of the Circus Circus Hotel and Resort.

5. The most widely recognized and successful of these campaigns, as mentioned in chapter 1, is the "What Happens Here, Stays Here" tagline. See Chris Jones, "What Happens Here, Stays Here Strikes Sour Note with Some at Conference," *LVR-J*, December 18, 2003; "What Happens Here Has Been Used Elsewhere," *Las Vegas Sun*, July 22, 2005; Steve Fries, "A Firm Hits Jackpot on Las Vegas Ads: Campaign Phrase Enters the Lexicon," *Chicago Tribune*, March 17, 2004.

6. Discussion of Las Vegas's suburban growth in the post-1980 era can be found in Geoff Schumacher, *Sun, Sin and Suburbia: An Essential History of Las Vegas* (Las Vegas: Stephens Press, 2005), 17–18, 117–33, 247–48; Moehring and Green, *Las Vegas*, 225–49. The United States Census for 2000 reveals the Las Vegas metropolitan area's extraordinary growth over the last decade of the twentieth century. The metropolitan area led all others with an 83.3 percent increase between 1990 and 2000. In number of residents, that correlates to an increase from 852,737 to 1,563,282. The next-closet metropolitan areas in regard to percentage of growth were Naples, Florida, with 65.3 percent (an increase in residents from 152,099 to 251,377) and Yuma, Arizona, with an increase of 49.7 percent (from 106,895 to 160,026). U.S. Census Bureau, "Census 2000: Ranking Tables for Metropolitan Areas," Table 5, Metropolitan Areas Ranked by Percentage Population Change, 1990–2000, www.census.gov/population/www/cen2000/briefs/phc-t3/index.html.

7. Robyn Norwood, "Ducks Won't Gamble on Las Vegas Hockey," *LAT*, April 16, 1993; Benjamin Spillman, "Obama Draws Ire over Vegas Junket Criticism," *LVR-J*, February 11, 2009; Oskar Garcia, "Mayor to Obama: Your Comments Are Harmful to Las Vegas," *USA Today*, February 11, 2009.

8. "Anybody but Oscar," editorial, *LVR-J*, March 9, 1999.

9. "Las Vegas, Nevada/New Mayor," *NBC Nightly News*, June 7, 1999.

10. Todd S. Purdum, "A Colorful Lawyer Is Running for Mayor: Las Vegas Would Be His Primary Client," *NYT*, May 2, 1999; "Lawyer Faces Runoff for Las Vegas Mayor," *NYT*, May 5, 1999; "Mob Lawyer Wins Race," *NYT*, June 9, 1999.

11. Purdum, "A Colorful Lawyer."

12. Las Vegas Convention and Visitors Authority, "Historical Las Vegas Statistics (1970–2016)," www.lvcva.com/includes/content/images/media/docs/Historical-1970-to-2016.pdf. Interestingly, Las Vegas's annual visitation rates since 1970 have failed to increase each year on only four occasions. On three of these occasions, 1981–82, 2001, and 2008–09, the drop corresponded with national recessions or terror attacks. Only in 2013 was there a decline in visitation without the context of a national crisis.

13. Moehring, *Resort City in the Sunbelt*, 80–81.

14. Ibid., 271–72.

15. A limited but representative example of the risqué and sexually charged advertisements of the 1970s and early '80s includes "The Tiffany of Las Vegas," advertisement for the Tropicana Hotel and Country Club, *Western's World*, January/February 1976, In Flight Magazine Collection, uncataloged, DACA; "Everything at Your Fingertips . . . in Las Vegas," advertisement for the Landmark Hotel and Casino, *Western's World*, September/October 1976, 40, In Flight Magazine Collection, uncataloged, DACA; "Light Up Your Life . . . ," advertisement for the Dunes Hotel and Country Club, *Western's World*, May/June 1980, In Flight Magazine Collection, uncataloged, DACA; "Where the Winners Stay," advertisement for Dunes Hotel and Country Club," *Western's World*, March/April 1981, In Flight Magazine Collection, uncataloged, DACA. It is also worth mentioning that as early as the 1950s, the Las Vegas News Bureau often depicted scantily clad showgirls.

16. "The World's Best Buy," advertisement for the Las Vegas Hilton, *Western's World*, April 1983, In Flight Magazine Collection, uncataloged, DACA; "In Las Vegas, A Show Shopping Attraction," advertisement for the Fashion Show Mall, *Western's World*, March/April 1982, In Flight Magazine Collection, uncataloged, DACA; "3,174 Rooms! 3,600 Employees! & That's Just for Openers!," advertisement for Las Vegas Hilton, *Western's World*, December 1982, In Flight Magazine Collection, uncataloged, DACA.

17. Moehring, *Resort City in the Sunbelt*, 272–73.

18. N. W. Thompson, J. Kent Pinney, and J. A. Schibrowsky, "The Family That Gambles Together: Business and Social Concerns," *Journal of Travel Research* 34 (Winter 1996): 70–74; "Vegas Bets 'More Than Slots' Campaign Will Lure Baby Boomers,"

O'Dwyer's PR Services Report, August 1996; "Las Vegas, Nevada/New Mayor," *NBC Nightly News*, June 7, 1999; *48 Hours*, CBS, March 30, 1995, quoted in Thompson, Pinney, and Schibrowsky, "The Family That Gambles Together."

19. Moehring, *Resort City in the Sunbelt*, 270–71.

20. Rothman, *Neon Metropolis*, xvi–xvii.

21. "Anybody but Oscar."

22. John Rennie Short, "Metropolitan U.S.A.: Evidence from the 2010 Census," *International Journal of Population Research*, 2012, www.hindawi.com/journals/ijpr/2012/207532/.

23. Mike Zapler, "Pollster Predicts Easy Win for Goodman in Mayoral Bid," *LVR-J*, June 4, 1999; Mike Zapler, "Goodman Elected in a Landslide," *LVR-J*, June 9, 1999; Oscar Goodman, interviewed by the author, September 19, 2008.

24. Goodman interview.

25. The "What Happens Here, Stays Here" tagline was developed by the Las Vegas Convention and Visitors Authority in 2002. The slogan, despite significant resistance from some business and industrial leaders, proved so successful as to become synonymous with Las Vegas in the early twenty-first century. See Jones, "What Happens Here, Stays Here."

26. Tom Vaughan, dir., *What Happens in Vegas*, 20th Century Fox, 2008.

27. Mae Farei, interviewed by Martha Jane Cunningham, February 24, 1980, University of Las Vegas Oral History Project, UNLVSC.

28. Suzette M. Cox, interviewed by Lance Cooper, March 2, 1979, University of Las Vegas Oral History Project, UNLVSC.

29. Phillip Cook, interviewed by Richard Strahan, March 3, 1977, University of Las Vegas Oral History Project, UNLVSC.

30. Goodman interview.

31. Purdum, "A Colorful Lawyer Is Running for Mayor"; "Lawyer Faces Runoff for Las Vegas Mayor"; "Mob Lawyer Wins Race."

32. Goodman interview; "Certain Showgirls, Elvis Impersonator Often Seen with Las Vegas Mayor," *USA Today*, June 7, 2006.

33. Norm Clarke, "Luckiest Mayor Gets Even Luckier," *LVR-J*, April 24, 2005.

34. *Las Vegas*, television series, NBC Studios, 2003–2008. Detailed information available at www.imdb.com/title/tt0364828/.

35. Goodman interview.

36. An example of Giuliani's fame as a result of the September 11, 2001, terrorist attacks can be found in the headline "Giuliani: Can Hero of 9/11 Win Over His Own Party?," *USA Today*, February 1, 2007.

37. Antonio Planas and Erin Neff, "Remarks to Fourth Graders: Mayor's Talk of Gin Criticized," *LVR-J*, March 3, 2005; "Mayor Defends Praising Gin to Fourth Graders," *LAT*, March 4, 2005; Ed Koch, "The Many Colors of Mayor Oscar Goodman," *Las Vegas Sun*, May 15, 2008.

38. Moehring, *Resort City in the Sunbelt*, xi, 13–40, 107–72. For an excellent examination of the problems faced by modern metropolitan Las Vegas, see also Eugene Moehring,

"Growth, Services, and the Political Economy of Gambling in Las Vegas, 1970–2000," in Rothman and Davis, *The Grit Beneath the Glitter*, 73–98.

39. Adrienne Packer, "Racy Billboards to be Discussed," *LVR-J*, March 11, 2004.

40. Ibid.

41. Ibid.

42. Adrienne Packer, "County Bans New Signs in Unincorporated Areas," *LVR-J*, April 22, 2004.

43. Chris Jones, "Hard Rock to Pay Fine for Risqué Ads," *LVR-J*, April 23, 2004.

44. Sarah Kershaw and Patricia Leigh Brown, "Women's Work: They Take It Off but They Also Put On Suits, Uniforms, and Blue Collars," *NYT*, June 2, 2004.

45. Joanne L. Goodwin, "She Works Hard for Her Money: A Reassessment of Las Vegas Women Workers, 1945–1985," in Rothman and Davis, *The Grit Beneath the Glitter*, 243–59.

46. Michelle Irene Aiken, "Sex and Stereotyping in Sin City: A Content Analysis of Las Vegas Magazine Advertisements" (master's thesis, University of Nevada, Las Vegas, 2012), 2.

47. Kershaw and Brown, "Women's Work."

48. Jones, "Hard Rock to Pay Fine for Risqué Ads."

49. Ibid.

50. "Provocative Billboards Have Business Owners Up in Arms," KVBC Television, Las Vegas, May 30, 2008.

51. Edward Lawrence, "1979 Brothel Ad Ban Ruled Unconstitutional," KLAS Television, *Las Vegas Eyewitness News Now*, July 14, 2007.

52. Mary Hynes, "Strip 'Smut' Eyed Again," *LVR-J*, September 18, 1993.

53. Stephanie Kishi, "Home of Sin City's Original Sin," *Las Vegas Sun*, May 15, 2008.

54. Goodman interview.

55. Bob Herbert, "City as Predator," *NYT*, September 4, 2007.

56. Goodman interview; Alan Choate, "Column Mentions Book, Criticizes Las Vegas Mayor," *LVR-J*, September 6, 2007.

57. "Herbert's Heroes: Readers Comments," NYTimes.com, http://herbert.blogs.nytimes.com/, accessed March 3, 2008 (page removed).

58. Ibid.

59. Ibid.

60. Martin Bashir, "Sin City Saviors," *Nightline*, ABC News, December 6, 2008.

61. XXXChurch, http://xxxchurch.com/, accessed December 6, 2008 (website has been updated).

62. Bashir, "Sin City Saviors."

63. John Crompton, "Beyond Economic Impact: An Alternative Rationale for the Public Subsidy of Major League Sports Facilities," *Journal of Sports Management* 18 (2004): 40–58. Crompton lists "increased community visibility" and "enhanced community image" as two of the four "spillover benefits" of a city securing a major-league sports franchise.

64. "Mistake in Steelers Game Costs Some Bettors Big," Associated Press, http://sports. yahoo.com/nfl/news;_ylt=AkBN5TW1PlWdhwyVSRBclgYdsLYF?slug=ap-blowncall-gambling&prov=ap&type=lgns, accessed November 17, 2008 (page removed).

65. "NBA Visitors Loud, Rude, and Uncivil," *LVR-J*, February 20, 2007. In this collection of comments, residents related extreme displeasure with the behavior of NBA fans over the All-Star Game weekend. Complaints included shootings, fights, excessive drinking, intimidation, and generally obnoxious behavior.

66. Norwood, "Ducks Won't Gamble on Las Vegas Hockey."

67. Ibid.

68. Greg Johnson, "Baseball Allows Gambling Industry to Make Its Pitch," *LAT*, April 6, 2000.

69. Tim Brown, "Expos Sent Back to Limbo: Baseball Offers Refunds for Tickets Purchased for Washington Nationals after City Amends Stadium Agreement," *LAT*, December 16, 2004.

70. Ibid.

71. Peter William Moran, "Great Expectations: The Legitimization of Gambling in America, 1965–1995," *Journal of Popular Culture* 31 (Summer 1997): 49–65.

72. "Gambling Spree across Nation," *U.S. News & World Report*, May 29, 1978, 35; James Popkin and Katia Hetter, "America's Gambling Craze," *U.S. News & World Report*, March 14, 1994, 42; Joseph P. Shapiro, "America's Gambling Fever," *U.S. News & World Report*, January 15, 1996, 52–60.

73. "Gambling on a Roll," *Economist*, January 20, 1990, 29.

74. "What's Happening to American Morality?," *U.S. News & World Report*, October 13, 1975, 39.

75. James C. Dobson, "Gambling Fever: Gambling Is Not Harmless Entertainment; It Preys on the Vulnerable and Produces Various Forms of Social Decay," Focus on the Family, http://www2.focusonthefamily.com/docstudy/newsletters/a000000310. cfm#footnote38, accessed February 7, 2009 (page removed).

76. Brown, "Expos Sent Back to Limbo"; Hugh Dellios, "Monterrey Expos?," *Chicago Tribune*, February 7, 2004; Joe Hawk, "Las Vegas Gets Big League Attention in Bid for Expos," *LVR-J*, May 23, 2004. Las Vegas also courted the NBA's Vancouver Grizzlies. That team ended up in Memphis.

77. Hawk, "Las Vegas Gets Big League Attention."

78. Angie Wagoner, "Las Vegas Mayor Earns Respect in Spite of Himself: The Former Gangland Lawyer Is Getting Things Done in the Desert Oasis, and He's Doing It His Way," *LAT*, March 24, 2002.

79. Bureau of the Census, "Population Change in Metropolitan and Micropolitan Statistical Areas, 1990–2003," United States Census Bureau, United States Department of Commerce, Economics and Statistics Administration, September 2005. It is also important to note that Minneapolis and Seattle surpassed the three million mark by fewer than 150,000 people.

80. Ibid.

81. Mark Anderson and Dave Berns, "Major League Sports Town: Is It in the Cards?," *LVR-J*, July 4, 2004.

82. Richard Sandomir, "NFL Just Says No to a Super Bowl Ad Promoting Las Vegas," *NYT*, January 15, 2003.

83. Ibid.

84. Chris Jones, "NFL Penalizes Las Vegas, Rejects Super Bowl Ad," *LVR-J*, January 14, 2003; Chris Jones, "NFL's Rebuff of Las Vegas Could Be Challenged in Court, *LVR-J*, January 15, 2003; "NFL Ad Ban," editorial, *LVR-J*, January 15, 2003; Steve Sebelius, "A Vegas Free Super Bowl," *LVR-J*, January 16, 2003; Rod Smith, "NFL Advertising Flap," *LVR-J*, January 17, 2003; William A Shaffer, "NFL's Hypocrisy over Las Vegas Is Comical," letter to sports editor, *LVR-J*, January 19, 2003; George Fereni, "At Least Gambling in Las Vegas Is Honest," letter to sports editor, *LVR-J*, January 19, 2003; John L. Smith, "Las Vegas Risks Squeaky Clean Image by Associating with Seedy NFL," *LVR-J*, January 19, 2003; Norm Clarke, "Upon Further Review, NFL Rejection of Las Vegas Ad Still Stinks," *LVR-J*, January 20, 2003; Joe Hawk, "NFL's Gaming Stance Begs Some Answers," *LVR-J*, January 25, 2003.

85. Shaffer, "NFL's Hypocrisy over Las Vegas Is Comical"; Fereni, "At Least Gambling in Las Vegas Is Honest"; Smith, "Las Vegas Risks Squeaky Clean Image Buy Associating with Seedy NFL."

86. "NFL Ad Ban."

87. Smith, "Las Vegas Risks Squeaky Clean Image Buy Associating with Seedy NFL."

88. "NFL Ad Ban."

89. Findlay, "Gambling, Las Vegas, and American Culture"; Findlay, "Suckers and Escapists?," 1–15; Findlay, *People of Chance*, 4–8, 107–9, 122–25; David Schwartz, *Roll the Bones: The History of Gambling* (New York: Gotham Books, 2006), prologue, chaps. 15–18.

90. Sebelius, "A Vegas Free Super Bowl."

91. Sandomir, "NFL Just Says No to a Super Bowl Ad Promoting Las Vegas."

92. Goodman interview.

93. Hal Rothman, "Hal Rothman Is Skeptical of the NBA All-Star Game Leading to a Team Putting Down Roots in Las Vegas," *Las Vegas Sun*, February 26, 2006.

94. Steve Carp, "Las Vegas Awarded NHL Expansion Team," *LVR-J*, June 22, 2016.

95. Clark County (@ClarkCountyNV), "It's official. We made it! #VegasgotHockey," Twitter, June 22, 2016, https://twitter.com/ClarkCountyNV/status/745714835938127874?ref_src=twsrc%5Etfw.

96. Carp, "Las Vegas Awarded NHL Expansion Team."

97. Steve Carp, "Bill Foley to Stay Low Key as Wait for Las Vegas NHL Team Is Almost Over," *LVR-J*, June 20, 2017.

98. Spencer Patterson, "Impressions from T-Mobile Arena's Opening Night with The Killers," *Las Vegas Weekly*, April 13, 2016; "Proposed Stadium Tops List of Las Vegas Business Stories in 2016," *LVR-J*, December 31, 2016; Dave Herrera, "The Killers Did Las Vegas Proud on T-Mobile Arena's Opening Night," *LVR-J*, April 8, 2016; Case

Keener, "Golden Knights Revealed as Name of Las Vegas NHL Expansion Team," *Las Vegas Sun*, November 22, 2016.

99. Delen Goldberg, "Carolyn Goodman Easily Wins Race for Las Vegas Mayor," *Las Vegas Sun*, June 7, 2011.

100. "Timeline: Historical Highlights," Oakland Raiders, www.raiders.com/history/timeline.html.

101. Ken Belson, "Oakland Raiders Apply to Move to Las Vegas," *NYT*, January 19, 2017.

102. Ibid.; Ed Graney, "As Expected, Road to Las Vegas Stadium Passing Was Rocky," *LVR-J*, October 15, 2016; Sean Whaley and Sandrea Chereb, "Nevada Senate Passes Amended Raiders Stadium Bill; Sandoval to Sign Monday," *LVR-J*, October 14, 2016; Tom Spousta, "Gov. Brian Sandoval Signs Raiders Stadium Bill—Video," *LVR-J*, October 17, 2016, www.reviewjournal.com/business/stadium/gov-brian-sandoval-signs-raiders-stadium-bill-video. Sheldon Adelson eventually withdrew his $650 million pledge toward the stadium's construction. Adelson's contribution was replaced by Bank of America financing. See "Casino Mogul Sheldon Adelson Pulls out of Raiders-Vegas Stadium Deal," *Chicago Tribune*, January 30, 2017; John Mark Saraceno, "Raiders Las Vegas Stadium Gets Boost from Bank of America," *LVR-J*, March 6, 2017.

103. Ed Graney, "Cowboys Owner Jerry Jones Holds Sway in NFL, Helping Las Vegas' Relocation Hopes," *LVR-J*, October 18, 2016.

104. Ed Graney, "Las Vegas' Gambling Takes Backseat to Economics at NFL Meetings," *LVR-J*, October 19, 2016.

105. "What NFL Writers Are Saying about the Raiders' Possible Move to Las Vegas," *LVR-J*, October 20, 2016.

106. Ed Graney, "NFL to Las Vegas: The Reality a Sports Columnist Never Saw Coming," *LVR-J*, January 20, 2017.

107. Jon Saraceno, "NFL Will Approve Raiders Move Because Las Vegas Showed It the Money," *LVR-J*, January 21, 2017.

108. Jon Saraceno, "Oakland Raiders Get NFL's Approval to Move to Las Vegas," *LVR-J*, March 27, 2017.

109. Susan Schrock, "Arlington Blitzing through Its Stadium Debt Faster Than Expected," *Star-Telegram*, January 20, 2015.

110. "What NFL Writers Are Saying about the Raiders' Possible Move to Las Vegas."

111. Rothman, *Neon Metropolis*, 56.

112. Schwartz, *Suburban Xanadu*, 6–8.

113. Sebelius, "A Vegas Free Super Bowl."

114. Richard Sandomir, "Las Vegas's Mayor Tries to Attract a Pro Team," *NYT*, July 17, 2005.

Chapter 8. Stigma and Cities

1. Thomas Kuhn, *The Structure of Scientific Revolutions*, 3rd ed. (Chicago: University of Chicago Press, 1996), 23–34.

2. See chapter 2 for extensive listings of the media's positive portrayal of Birmingham in the late nineteenth and early twentieth centuries. A few examples of the national

press expressing the "magic" of Birmingham include "Alabama's Show City," *NYT*, December 24, 1899; "Alabama's Leading City," *NYT*, December 31, 1899. For the shift to *Bombingham*, see "Bombing in Alabama Injures 5, Wrecks Negro Minister's Home," *NYT*, December 26, 1956; "Two Bomb Scares Stir Birmingham," *NYT*, September 11, 1957; and any number of the Sixteenth Street Baptist Church bombing articles listed in chapter 2. The longevity of the Bombingham nickname is exhibited by Adam Cohen, "Back to Bombingham," *Time*, July 21, 1997.

3. For excellent coverage of George Wallace's political career, see Dan T. Carter, *The Politics of Rage: George Wallace, the Origins of the New Conservatism, and the Transformation of American Politics* (Baton Rouge: Louisiana State University Press, 2000); Daniel McCabe and Paul Strekler, dirs., *George Wallace: Setting the Woods on Fire*, PBS Home Video, 2000. Quotations taken from George Wallace, "Inaugural Address 1963," transcript in author's possession; Claude Sitton, "Gov. Wallace Vows to Defy Injunction and Block Negroes," *NYT*, June 2, 1963. See also "North Denounced by Gov. Wallace," *NYT*, January 15, 1963.

4. Tim Craig and Michael D. Shear, "Allen Quip Provokes Outrage, Apology," *Washington Post*, August 15, 2006; "George Allen's America," *Washington Post*, August 15, 2006; Mike Allen, "On Candid Camera," *Time*, August 20, 2006; Perry Bacon Jr., "Campaign '06: Down to the Wire in Virginia," *Time*, November 1, 2006; "The Un-American Senator," *LAT*, August 21, 2006; Joel Haverman, "Bush Raises Money for Senator Allen amid Uproar," *LAT*, August 24, 2006; David Stout, "Senator Says He Meant No Insult by Remark," *NYT*, August 16, 2006; David Kirkpatrick, "2 Ex-Acquaintances of Senator Allen Say He Used Slurs," *NYT*, September 25, 2006; Frank Rich, "2006: The Year of the Macaca," *NYT*, November 12, 2006.

5. John Lewis, with Michael D'Orso, *Walking with the Wind: A Memoir of the Movement* (New York: Simon & Schuster, 1998), 83–121.

6. Elisabeth Bumiller, "Congressman Rebukes McCain for Recent Rallies," *NYT*, October 12, 2008; Patrick Healy, "Race Remains Campaign Issue, But Not a Clear One," *NYT*, October 12, 2008; Russ Rymer, "The George Wallace We Forgot," *NYT*, October 24, 2008.

7. Bumiller, "Congressman Rebukes McCain."

8. George M. Frederickson, *Racism: A Short History* (Princeton, N.J.: Princeton University Press, 2002), 5.

9. The violent events in Birmingham during the late spring and early summer of 1963 helped persuade President Kennedy to take a public stance on race and civil rights issues. On the evening of June 11, 1963, after Alabama governor George Wallace famously stood in the University of Alabama door to block the enrollment of a black student, President Kennedy addressed the nation via televised speech. In this speech, the president informed the American people that civil rights for black Americans was a moral issue. He further advised Americans to follow their consciences in regard to this issue. Chafe, *The Unfinished Journey*, 212–13; Eskew, *But for Birmingham*, 310–11.

10. Richard Lentz, "Snarls Echoing 'Round the World: The 1963 Birmingham Civil Rights Campaign on the World Stage," *American Journalism* 17 (Spring 2000):

69–96; Dudziak, *Cold War Civil Rights*, 169–71, 183; see also Borstelmann, *The Cold War and the Color Line*.

11. Val Walton, "Birmingham Mayor Larry Langford Arrested on Federal Charges," *BN*, December 1, 2008, AL.com, http://blog.al.com/spotnews/2008/12/birmingham_mayor_larry_langfor_15.html, accessed December 1, 2008; "Update: Birmingham Mayor Arrested on Federal Charges," *ABC 33/40 News*, December 1, 2008; Andrea Lindenberg and Rod Carter, "Breaking News: Langford, LaPierre, Blount Face 101-Count Federal Indictment," WVTM, *NBC 13 News*, December 1, 2008; "Mayor Indicted on 101 Federal Counts, Arrested," WAIT, *CBS 42 News*, December 1, 2008; TGIF0000, comment on Walton, "Birmingham Mayor Larry Langford Arrested on Federal Charges."

12. Byrne Fone, *Homophobia: A History* (New York: Henry Holt, 2000), 3, 409.

13. D'Emilio and Freedman, *Intimate Matters*, 345–47.

14. Jessie McKinley and Laura Goodstein, "Bans in 3 States on Gay Marriage," *NYT* November 5, 2008.

15. Philip Martier and Andrew Ross, "SF Hope for Big Slice of Gay Marriage Money," *SFC*, May 18, 2008; Allyce Bess, "Rolling on Gay Tourism," *San Francisco Business Times*, October 1, 2004.

16. Schwartz, *Roll the Bones*, xviii, 443–46.

17. Ibid., xviii, 247–68; Findlay, "Gambling, Las Vegas, and American Culture"; Findlay, "Suckers and Escapists?," 1–15; Findlay, *People of Chance*, 4–8, 107–9, 122–25.

18. The relation of Las Vegas to the mafia, and of the mafia to Las Vegas, has been common in both the news media and popular entertainment media. Examples of this include "Investigation in Nevada," *NYT*, November 16, 1950; Wallace Turner, "Las Vegas: Gambling Take Creates New Force in U.S.: Millions in Untaxed Black Money Give Obscure Figures Power That Extends from Underworld to Government," *NYT*, November 18, 1963; Orr Kelly, "Corruption and Mayhem: Inside Look at the Mafia," *U.S. News & World Report*, September 29, 1980; "Mafia U.S.A."; Martin Scorsese, dir., *Casino*, Universal Pictures, 1995.

19. Steve Fries, "A Firm Hits Jackpot on Las Vegas Ads: Campaign Phrase Enters the Lexicon," *Chicago Tribune*, March 17, 2004; Chris Jones, "What Happens Here, Stays Here Strikes Sour Note with Some at Conference," *LVR-J*, December 18, 2003.

20. A few examples of the media's tendency to equate Las Vegas with vice themes include "Las Vegas Gambling," *Life*, December 21, 1942; "Las Vegas: Sin and Sun Pay Off," *Business Week*, June 17, 1950; "Wherever You Look There's Danger in Las Vegas," *Life*, November 12, 1951; "Las Vegas: Nice People Live on Divorce, Gambling," *Newsweek*, April 20, 1953; "Snake Eyes in Las Vegas," *Time*, September 19, 1955; "Gambling Town Pushes Its Luck," *Life*, June 20, 1955; Gladwin Hill, "Why They Gamble: A Las Vegas Survey," *New York Times Magazine*, August 25, 1957; William F. French, "Don't Say Las Vegas Is Short of Suckers!," *Saturday Evening Post*, November 5, 1955; Arthur Steuer, "Playground for Adults Only," *Esquire*, August 1961; Peter Wyden, "How Wicked Is Vegas?," *Saturday Evening Post*, November 11, 1961; Caskie Stinnett, "Las Vegas: Where Anything Is Forgivable Except Restraint," *Holiday*, May 1967; Cook,

"Gambling, Inc."; John S. Lang, "What Gambling Does for—and to—Las Vegas," *U.S. News & World Report*, March 9, 1981; Lester Velie, "Las Vegas: The Underworld's Secret Jackpot," *Reader's Digest*, October 1959; Lester Velie, "Underworld's Back Door to Las Vegas," *Reader's Digest*, November 1974; Karen G. Jackovich and Mark Sennet, "Wayne Newton Stars in a Real-Life Drama of Mob Extortion in Las Vegas," *People*, August 3, 1981; Kelly, "Corruption and Mayhem"; "Mafia U.S.A."

21. Goodman interview.

22. Don L. Battle, "Atlantic City: Soon to Be Las Vegas of the East," *U.S. News & World Report*, August 22, 1977; "Gambling Spree across Nation"; Pete Axthelm, "Our Man in Vegas East," *Newsweek*, June 12, 1978; K. M. Chrysler, "America's Gaming Capital: Taking Bets on Survival?," *U.S. News & World Report*, May 30, 1983; Ron Cooper, "Reinventing Las Vegas," *Investment Dealers Digest*, September 22, 1997; Dan Fost, "Fear and Marketing in Las Vegas," *American Demographics*, October 1993.

23. "Las Vegas Bets More Than Slots Will Lure Baby Boomers"; Goodman interview.

24. Joel Stein and Laura A. Locke, "The Strip Is Back!," *Time*, July 26, 2004.

25. Goodman interview.

26. Adrienne Packer, "Racy Billboards to be Discussed," *LVR-J*, March 11, 2004.

27. Robyn Norwood, "Ducks Won't Gamble on Las Vegas Hockey," *LAT*, April 16, 1993.

28. Benjamin Spillman, "Obama Draws Ire Over Vegas Junket Criticism," *LVR-J*, February 11, 2009.

29. Hubble Smith, "Las Vegas Home Prices Rising, but . . . ," *LVR-J*, December 23, 2006; Hubble Smith, "Las Vegas Home Prices Drop," *LVR-J*, January 9, 2007; Hubble Smith, "Index Sees Growth in Population Slowing," *LVR-J*, August 11, 2007; Sean Whaley, "Jobless Rate Still Climbing," *LVR-J*, August 18, 2007; Hubble Smith, "LV Foreclosure Rates Double," *LVR-J*, August 7, 2008; Hubble Smith, "Searching for Bottom," *LVR-J*, September 7, 2008; Geoff Schumacher, "Growth Interrupted," *LVR-J*, May 1, 2009.

30. Thomas Friedman, "Keep It in Vegas," *NYT*, September 17, 2008.

31. For Las Vegas's historical visitation rates, see Las Vegas Convention and Visitors Authority, "Historical Las Vegas Visitor Statistics (1970–2016)," www.lvcva.com/ includes/content/images/media/docs/Historical-1970-to-2016.pdf.

32. Adam Candee, "What's behind the $1.9 Billion Price Tag for NFL Stadium in Las Vegas," *Las Vegas Sun*, March 8, 2017; Nathan Fenno and Sam Farmer, "Los Angeles Rams Break Ground on $2.6 Billion Inglewood Stadium, 'New Era' of NFL," *LAT*, November 17, 2016. While Los Angeles's Inglewood stadium is more expensive than Las Vegas's Raiders stadium, it is important to note that the former is being privately funded whereas Las Vegas is relying on $750 million in public funding.

33. Active involvement and participation in the civil rights movement crossed racial boundaries. See Maria R. Lowe and J. Clint Morris, "Civil Rights Advocates in the Academy: White Pro-Integrationist Faculty at Millsaps College," *Journal of Mississippi History* 67 (Spring 2007): 121–45; Donald Cunnigen, "The Civil Rights Movement and Southern White Liberal Role Conflict," *Southern Studies: An Interdisciplinary Journal of the South* 3 (Winter 1992): 321–40; Andrew S. Moore, "Practicing What We Preach: White Catholics in the Civil Rights Movement in Atlanta," *Georgia*

Historical Quarterly 89 (Fall 2005): 334–67; Debra L. Shultz, *Going South: Jewish Women in the Civil Rights Movement* (New York: New York University Press, 2001); Simon Hall, *Peace and Freedom: The Civil Rights and Antiwar Movements in the 1960s* (Philadelphia: University of Pennsylvania Press, 2005).

34. *The Rachel Maddow Show*, MSNBC, August 12, 2017. This occurred on the weekend during Rachel Maddow's normal time slot. The television guide listed *The Rachel Maddow Show*, but it appeared to be more of a breaking-news segment with Joy Reid hosting.

35. McCain did this during remarks at a November 3, 2008, campaign rally in Moon Township, Pennsylvania. Looking to his coal-country crowd, he mentioned that his opponent had told a San Francisco (vocal emphasis placed on *San Francisco* and air quotes made with his hands while saying the city's name) newspaper that coal producers would go broke under an Obama administration as a result of increased environmental regulation. "Alert," FOX News Channel, November 3, 2008.

36. Jonah Engel Bromwich, "California Today: Has Silicon Valley Hit a Plateau?," *NYT*, March 31, 2017; Ester Bloom, "Google Is Spending $30 Million on Housing for Silicon Valley Employees," CNBC, www.cnbc.com/2017/06/14/google-spending-30-million-on-housing-for-silicon-valley-employees.html, accessed August 6, 2017.

37. Olivia Solon, "Scraping By on Six Figures? Tech Workers Feel Poor in Silicon Valley's Wealth Bubble," *Guardian*, February 27, 2017, www.theguardian.com/technology/2017/feb/27/silicon-aa-cost-of-living-crisis-has-americas-highest-paid-feeling-poor.

38. Ibid.

39. "Company Offers Employees $10k to Leave Bay Area," KCRA 3, March 20, 2017, www.kcra.com/article/company-offers-employees-dollar10k-to-leave-bay-area/9156877.

40. Thomas Oide, "Is Sacramento the Next Silicon Valley? Report Calls It a Market of Opportunity," *Sacramento Bee*, July 7, 2017; Solon, "Scraping by on Six Figures?"

Bibliography

Archives and Manuscript Collections

Bay Area Radio Museum, San Francisco, California
    Gene D'Accardo/KNBR Collection (1978)
Birmingham Civil Rights Institute Archives, Birmingham, Alabama
    L. C. Clark Jr. Collection
Delta Airlines Corporate Archives, Atlanta, Georgia
James C. Hormel Gay, Lesbian, and Transgender Center, San Francisco
    Evander Smith—California Hall Papers
    Harvey Milk Papers
        Scott Smith Collection
    Lee Evans Papers
    Randy Shilts Papers
Linn Henley Research Library and Archives, Birmingham, Alabama
    Birmingham, Alabama, Mayor Papers
    Birmingham Area Chamber of Commerce Papers
        Operation New Birmingham
    Birmingham Board of Education Minutes
    Birmingham City Council Papers
    Theophilus Eugene Connor et al. v. New York Times et al., Trial Transcript and Papers
University of Nevada, Las Vegas, Lied Library, Special Collections
    Chamber of Commerce Collection
    Emma G. Leland Papers

Maria Barton Wheeler Collection
University of Nevada, Las Vegas, Local Oral History Project Collection

Censuses, Polls, Surveys, and Government Documents

Bureau of the Census. "Population Change in Metropolitan and Micropolitan Statistical Areas, 1990–2003." United States Census Bureau, United States Department of Commerce, Economics and Statistics Administration, September 2005.

Bureau of the Census. *State and Metropolitan Area Data Book, 1997–1998: A Statistical Abstract Supplement.* 5th ed. Washington, D.C.: Economics and Statistics Administration, Bureau of the Census, 1998.

Committee on Homosexual Offenses and Prostitution. *The Wolfenden Report: Report of the Committee on Homosexual Offenses and Prostitution.* Authorized American ed. New York: Stein and Day, 1963.

Congressional Record. 81st Cong., 2nd Sess., 1950, 96, 4:4527–28.

Media Research Center. *Special Report: An In-Depth Study, Analysis or Review Exploring the Media.* Alexandria, Va.: Media Research Center, 2007.

Senate Committee on Expenditures in the Executive Department. *Employment of Homosexuals and Other Sexual Perverts in Government.* 81st Cong., 2nd Sess., 1950, S. Doc. 241, 2.

Feature Films, Documentaries, and Television Series

Gilliam, Terry, dir. *Fear and Loathing in Las Vegas.* Fear and Loathing LLC, 1998.

Howe, John, dir. *Desert Wars: Water and the West.* KUED-TV, University of Utah, 2006.

Kessler, Stephen, dir. *Vegas Vacation.* Warner Brothers Motion Pictures, 1997.

Las Vegas. NBC Studios, 2003–2008.

Leone, Sergio, dir. *The Good, The Bad, and the Ugly.* Arturo Gonzalez Producciones Cinematograficas, 1966.

McCabe, Daniel, and Paul Strekler, dirs. *George Wallace: Setting the Woods on Fire.* PBS Home Video, 2000.

Scorsese, Martin, dir. *Casino.* Universal Pictures, 1995.

Vaughan, Tom, dir. *What Happens in Vegas.* 20th Century Fox, 2008.

Newspapers

Atlanta Constitution Journal
Birmingham News
Birmingham Post-Herald
Birmingham Times
Birmingham World
Chicago Tribune
Christian Science Monitor
New York Times
Las Vegas Review-Journal
Las Vegas Sun

Los Angeles Times
Sacramento Bee
San Francisco Chronicle
San Francisco Examiner

Books, Articles, and Theses

"AIDS: San Francisco Recoils." *Economist*, August 23, 1986, 24.

"AIDS Researchers: What Can They Say?" *U.S. News and World Report*, August 8, 1994, 18.

Aiken, Michelle Irene. "Sex and Stereotyping in Sin City: A Content Analysis of Las Vegas Magazine Advertisements." Master's thesis, University of Nevada, Las Vegas, 2012.

Ainlay, Stephen C., Gaylene Becker, and Lerita M. Coleman, eds. *The Dilemma of Difference: A Multidisciplinary View of Stigma*. New York: Plenum, 1986.

Ainlay, Stephen C., Lerita M. Coleman, and Gaylene Becker. "Stigma Reconsidered." In Ainlay, Becker, and Coleman, *The Dilemma of Difference*, 1–13.

Albright, Sydney J. "The Fred Kelly Story." *Journal of the American Aviation Historical Society* 13 (Fall 1968): 193–215.

Alexander, Charles C. *The Ku Klux Klan in the Southwest*. Lexington: University of Kentucky Press, 1965.

"Alfred C. Kinsey: A Pioneer of Sex Research." *Journal of Public Health* 93 (June 2003): 894–98.

Allen, Mike. "On Candid Camera." *Time*, August 20, 2006.

"All the Philosopher's Men." *Harper's*, February 2000, 22–24.

Altman, Dennis. *AIDS in the Mind of America*. Garden City, N.Y.: Anchor Books, 1986.

Ambrose, Stephen E. *Eisenhower: Soldier and President*. New York: Simon & Schuster, 1990.

Anderson, Kurt. "Las Vegas: The New All-American City." *Time*, January 10, 1994, 42–51.

Anderson, Susan Willoughby. "The Past on Trial: The Sixteenth Street Baptist Church Bombing, Civil Rights Memory, and the Remaking of Birmingham." PhD diss., University of North Carolina at Chapel Hill, 2008.

"Another Day of Death: A Former San Francisco Official Kills the Mayor and a Supervisor." *Time*, December 11, 1978, 24–26.

Armbrester, Margaret E. *Samuel Ullman and "Youth": The Life, the Legacy*. Tuscaloosa: University of Alabama Press, 1993.

Arrington, Richard. *There's Hope for the World: The Memoir of Birmingham, Alabama's First African American Mayor*. Tuscaloosa: University of Alabama Press, 2008.

Asbury, Herbert. *The Barbary Coast: An Informal History of the San Francisco Underworld*. New York: Knopf, 1933.

Astor, Gerald. "All-America Cities, 1970." *Look*, March 23, 1971, 72–74.

Averette, Jerome Christopher. "Documentation and History of Arthur Harold Parker High School." *Alabama Black in the Mirror*, May 1977, 5–8.

Avila, Eric. *Popular Culture in the Age of White Flight: Fear and Fantasy in Suburban Los Angeles*. Berkeley: University of California Press, 2006.

Axthelm, Pete. "Our Man in Vegas East." *Newsweek*, June 12, 1978, 42.

Bacon, Perry, Jr. "Campaign '06: Down to the Wire in Virginia." *Time*, November 1, 2006.

Bandurraga, Peter L. "Desert Mirage: Casino Gaming and the Image of Nevada." *Nevada Historical Society Quarterly* 29 (Summer 1986): 109–14.

Barringer, Mark David. *Selling Yellowstone: Capitalism and the Construction of Nature.* Lawrence: University Press of Kansas, 2002.

Battle, Don L. "Atlantic City: Soon to Be Las Vegas of the East." *U.S. News and World Report*, August 22, 1977, 40.

"Beat Mystics." *Time*, February 3, 1958, 56.

Beauregard, Robert. *Voices of Decline: The Postwar Fate of U.S. Cities.* New York: Routledge, 2002.

Becker, Carl. "Everyman His Own Historian." *American Historical Review* 37 (January 1932): 221–36.

Belmonte, Laura A. "Harvey Milk, San Francisco and the Gay Migration" In *The Human Tradition in the American West*, edited by Benson Tong and Regan A. Lutz, 209–25. Wilmington, Del.: Scholarly Resources, 2002.

Bergler, Edmund. *Homosexuality: Disease or Way of Life?* New York: Hill and Wang, 1956.

Berube, Allan. *Coming Out under Fire: The History of Gay Men and Women in World War Two.* New York: Free Press, 1990.

———. "Marching to a Different Drummer: Lesbian and Gay GIs in World War II." In Duberman, Vicinus, and Chauncey, *Hidden from History*, 383–94.

Bigelow, Martha Mitchell. "Birmingham's Carnival of Crime, 1871–1910." *Alabama Review* 3 (April 1950): 123–33.

Bing, Alison, and Dominique Channell. *San Francisco City Guide.* Victoria, Australia: Lonely Planet Publications, 2008.

"Birmingham Story." *Time*, May 16, 1960.

Bond, Horace Mann. *Negro Education in Alabama: A Study in Cotton and Steel.* Tuscaloosa: University of Alabama Press, 1994.

"Books and Arts: Holding up a Mirror; AIDS and Artists." *Economist*, January 1, 2005.

Borstelmann, Thomas. *The Cold War and the Color Line: American Race Relations in the Global Arena.* Cambridge, Mass.: Harvard University Press, 2001.

Bourdieu, Pierre. *Homo Academicus.* Translated by Peter Collier. Stanford, Calif.: Stanford University Press, 1988.

———. *In Other Words: Essays towards a Reflexive Sociology.* Translated by Matthew Adamson. Stanford, Calif.: Stanford University Press, 1990.

Bowers, Michael W. *Sagebrush State: Nevada's History, Government, and Politics.* 2nd ed. Reno: University of Nevada Press, 2002.

Boyd, Nan Alamilla. *Wide Open Town: A History of Queer San Francisco to 1965.* Berkeley: University of California Press, 2003.

Bradford, Juliet. *The Industrial High School: A Brief History.* Birmingham: Printing Department of Industrial High School, 1925.

Brechin, Guy. *Imperial San Francisco: Urban Power, Earthly Ruin.* Berkeley: University of California Press, 2006.

Breisach, Ernst. *Historiography: Ancient, Medieval, and Modern.* 3rd ed. Chicago: University of Chicago Press, 2006.

Bristow, Joseph. *Effeminate England: Homoerotic Writing after 1885*. New York: Columbia University Press, 1995.

"Britain: Facing the Dark Facts." *Newsweek*, September 16, 1957, 50–51.

Brown, B. Katherine. "Puritan Democracy in Dedham, Massachusetts: Another Case Study." *William and Mary Quarterly* 24 (July 1967): 378–96.

Brown, Donald A. "This Issue." *Birmingham*, April 1971, 3.

———. Untitled introduction. *Birmingham*, March 1971, 4.

Brownell, Blaine A. "Birmingham, Alabama: New South City in the 1920s." *Journal of Southern History* 38 (February 1972): 21–48.

Burwell, Maria Teresa, ed. *Fodor's Los Angeles 2008*. New York: Fodor's Travel, 2008.

Buttel, Frederick H. "New Directions in Environmental Sociology." *Annual Review of Sociology* 13 (1987): 465–88.

Caen, Herb. *Baghdad by the Bay: The San Francisco Story*. New York: Doubleday, 1949.

Calhoun, Craig. "Habitus, Field, and Capital: The Question of Historical Specificity." In *Bourdieu: Critical Perspectives*, edited by Craig Calhoun, Edward LiPuma, and Moishe Postone, 61–88. Chicago: University of Chicago Press, 1993.

Caliver, Ambrose. "The Largest Negro High School." *School Life*, December 1931, 73–74.

Carter, Dan T. *The Politics of Rage: George Wallace, the Origins of the New Conservatism, and the Transformation of American Politics*. Baton Rouge: Louisiana State University Press, 2000.

Casey, Ron. "The Election of Birmingham's Black Mayor." *Southern Changes: The Journal of the Southern Regional Council* 2 (Winter 1979): 11–14.

Caton, William R., Jr., and Riley E. Dunlap, "A New Ecological Paradigm for Post-Exuberant Sociology." *Behavioral Scientist* 24 (September–October 1980): 15–47.

Chafe, William H. *The Unfinished Journey: America since World War II*. New York: Oxford University Press, 1995.

Champagne, John. "Walt Whitman, Our Great Gay Poet?" *Journal of Homosexuality* 55 (November 2008): 648–64.

Chatfield-Taylor, Hobart C. *Charmed Circles*. Boston: Houghton Mifflin, 1935.

Chauncey, George. *Gay New York: Gender, Urban Culture, and the Making of the Gay Male World, 1890–1940*. New York: Basic Books, 1994.

Christensen, Jon. "Build It and the Water Will Come." In Rothman and Davis, *The Grit beneath the Glitter*, 115–25.

Chrysler, K. M. "America's Gaming Capital: Taking Bets on Survival?" *U.S. News and World Report*, May 30, 1983, 30.

"A City Reborn." *Time*, September 27, 1976, 55.

"City Side." *Newsweek*, December 30, 1963, 43.

Cobb, James C. *Away down South: A History of Southern Identity*. Oxford: Oxford University Press, 2005.

Cohen, Adam. "Back to Bombingham." *Time*, July 21, 1997.

Cohen, Ira, and Ann Elder. "Major Cities and Disease Crisis: A Comparative Perspective." *Social Science History* 13 (Spring 1989): 50–51.

Collins, Andrew, David Cashion, Constance Jones, and Robert Blake, eds. *Fodor's Gay Guide to the U.S.A.*, 3rd ed. New York: Fodor's Travel Publications, 2001.

"Columbus: The American City." *Speed*, July 1931, 8–9.

Conn, Steven. *Americans against the City: Anti-Urbanism in the Twentieth Century*. New York: Oxford University Press, 2014.

Connerly, Charles E. *The Most Segregated City in America: City Planning and Civil Rights in Birmingham, 1920–1980*. Charlottesville: University of Virginia Press, 2005.

Cook, Fred J. "Gambling, Inc." *Nation*, October 22, 1960, 260.

———. *A Two-Dollar Bet Means Murder*. New York: Dial, 1961.

Cooper, Erwin. *Aqueduct Empire: A Guide to Water in California, Its Turbulent History and Its Management Today*. Glendale, Calif.: Arthur H. Clark, 1968.

Cooper, Ron. "Reinventing Las Vegas." *Investment Dealers Digest*, September 22, 1997, 2.

Corber, Robert J. *In the Name of National Security: Hitchcock, Homophobia, and the Political Construction of Gender in Postwar America*. Durham, N.C.: Duke University Press, 1993.

Corley, Robert Gaines. "The Quest for Racial Harmony: Race Relations in Birmingham, Alabama, 1947–1963." PhD diss., University of Virginia, 1979.

Courdileone, K. A. "Politics in an Age of Anxiety: Political Culture and Crisis in American Masculinity, 1949–1960." *Journal of American History* 87 (September 2000): 515–45.

Coyne, Michael. *The Crowded Prairie: American National Identity in the Hollywood Western*. London: I. B. Tauris, 1998.

Cromer, Gerald. "Character Assassination in the Press." In *Deviance and Mass Media*, edited by Charles Winick, 225–41. Thousand Oaks, Calif.: Sage, 1978.

Crompton, John. "Beyond Economic Impact: An Alternative Rationale for the Public Subsidy of Major League Sports Facilities." *Journal of Sports Management* 18 (2004): 40–58.

Cruikshank, Margaret. *The Gay and Lesbian Liberation Movement*. New York: Routledge, 1992.

Cullen, Tom A. "Homosexuality and British Opinion." *New Republic*, April 25, 1955, 13–15.

Cunnigen, Donald. "The Civil Rights Movement and Southern White Liberal Role Conflict." *Southern Studies: An Interdisciplinary Journal of the South* 3 (Winter 1992): 321–40.

Cunningham, Gary L. "Chance, Culture, and Compulsion: The Gambling Games of the Kansas Cattle Towns." *Nevada Historical Society Quarterly* 26 (Winter 1983): 255–71.

"Curable Disease?" *Time*, December 10, 1956, 74–75.

Czitrom, Daniel J. *Media and the American Mind: From Morse to McLuhan*. Chapel Hill: University of North Carolina Press, 1982.

"Daffy og Kalle Kanin: Trøbbel og Tryllball," *Looney Tunes*. Oslo: Schibsted Forlag, 2008.

Davies, Richard O. "Only in Nevada: America's Unique Experiment with Legalized Sports Gambling." *Nevada Historical Society Quarterly* 44 (Spring 2001): 3–19.

Davis, Jack E. *The Civil Rights Movement*. Malden, Mass.: Blackwell Publishers, 2001.

Davis, Mike. *City of Quartz: Excavating the Future in Los Angeles*. New York: Verso, 1990.

———. *Dead Cities and Other Tales*. New York: W. W. Norton, 2002.

Davis, Ronald L. *Duke: The Life and Image of John Wayne*. Norman: University of Oklahoma Press, 1998.

"Day of the Assassin." *Newsweek*, December 11, 1978, 26–28.

D'Emilio, John. "Gay Politics and Community in San Francisco since World War II." In Duberman, Vicinus, and Chauncey, *Hidden from History*, 456–73.

———. "The Homosexual Menace: The Politics of Sexuality in Cold War America." In *Making Trouble: Essays on Gay History, Politics, and the University*, 57–73. New York: Routledge, 1992.

———. *Sexual Politics, Sexual Communities: The Making of a Homosexual Minority in the United States, 1940 to 1970*. Chicago: University of Chicago Press, 1983.

D'Emilio, John, and Estelle B. Freedman. *Intimate Matters: A History of Sexuality in America*. 2nd ed. Chicago: University of Chicago Press, 1997.

Demos, John. *A Little Commonwealth: Family Life in Plymouth Colony*. New York: Oxford University Press, 1970.

"A Devastated Continent." *Newsweek*, January 1, 2000, 41.

Dowling, Linda. *Hellenism and Homosexuality in Victorian Oxford*. Ithaca, N.Y.: Cornell University Press, 1994.

Duberman, Martin. *Cures: A Gay Man's Odyssey*. New York: Dutton, 1991.

———. *Stonewall*. New York: Dutton, 1993.

Duberman, Martin, Martha Vicinus, and George Chauncey, eds. *Hidden from History: Reclaiming the Gay and Lesbian Past*. New York: New American Library, 1989.

Dudziak, Mary L. *Cold War Civil Rights: Race and the Image of American Democracy*. Princeton, N.J.: Princeton University Press, 2000.

Ehrlich, J. W., ed. *Howl of the Censor*. San Carlos, Calif.: Nourse Publishing, 1961.

Erkilla, Betsy. "Whitman and the Homosexual Republic." In *Walt Whitman: The Centennial Essays*, edited by Ed Folsum, 153–71. Iowa City: University of Iowa Press, 1994.

Eskew, Glenn. "The Birmingham Civil Rights Institute and the New Ideology of Tolerance." In *The Civil Rights Movement in American Memory*, edited by Renee C. Romano and Leigh Raiford. Athens: University of Georgia Press, 2006.

———. *But for Birmingham: The Local and National Movements in the Civil Rights Struggle*. Chapel Hill: University of North Carolina Press, 1997.

Estrada, Jose Alfredo Gomez. "Breve historia do un obscure stigma." *Yubai* (March–May 1993): 21–30.

Feldman, Lynne B. *A Sense of Place: Birmingham's Black Middle-Class Community, 1890–1930*. Tuscaloosa: University of Alabama Press, 1999.

Findlay, John. *People of Chance: Gambling in American Society from Jamestown to Las Vegas*. New York: Oxford University Press, 1986.

———. "Suckers and Escapists? Interpreting Las Vegas and Post-War America." *Nevada Historical Society Quarterly* 33 (Spring 1990): 1–15.

Fischer, Herbert O. "Indianapolis: Crossroads of the Nation." *Speed*, January 1933, 16.

———. "Indianapolis: The Typical American City." *Speed*, February 1931, 16–17.

Flynt, Wayne. *Alabama in the Twentieth Century*. Tuscaloosa: University of Alabama Press, 2004.

Fone, Bryne. *Homophobia: A History*. New York: Henry Holt, 2000.

Ford, Paul Liecaster, ed. *The Works of Thomas Jefferson*. Vol. 4. New York: G. P. Putnam's Sons, 1904.

Ford, Thomas E., and George R. Tonander. "The Role of Differentiation between Groups and Social Identity in Stereotype Formation." *Social Psychology Quarterly* 61 (December 1998): 372–82.

Fost, Dan. "Fear and Marketing in Las Vegas." *American Demographics*, October 1993, 19.

Foucault, Michel. *Discipline and Punish: The Birth of the Prison.* 2nd Vintage Books ed. New York: Vintage Books, 1995.

———. *The History of Sexuality.* Vol. 1, *An Introduction.* New York: Random House, 1990.

Franker, S. "Gay Power in San Francisco." *Newsweek*, June 6, 1977, 25.

Franklin, Jimmie Lewis. *Back to Birmingham: Richard Arrington, Jr., and His Times.* Tuscaloosa: University of Alabama Press, 1989.

Frederickson, George M. *Racism: A Short History.* Princeton, N.J.: Princeton University Press, 2002.

French, William F. "Don't Say Las Vegas Is Short of Suckers!," *Saturday Evening Post*, November 5, 1955, 12.

Fuller, Justin. "Boom Towns and Blast Furnaces: Town Promotion in Alabama, 1885–1893." *Alabama Review* 29 (January 1976): 37–48.

Galbraith, John Kenneth. *The Affluent Society.* Boston: Houghton Mifflin, 1958.

Gallo, Marcia M. *Different Daughters: A History of the Daughters of Bilitis and the Rise of the Lesbian Rights Movement.* New York: Carroll and Graf, 2006.

"Gambling on a Roll." *Economist*, January 20, 1990, 29.

"Gambling Spree across Nation." *U.S. News and World Report*, May 29, 1978, 35.

"Gambling Town Pushes Its Luck." *Life*, June 20, 1955, 20–28.

Gamin, Bryant. "Heroic Spiritual Grandfather: Whitman, Sexuality, and the American Left, 1890–1940." *American Quarterly* 52 (March 2000): 90–126.

Gates, Verna. "The Birmingham Civil Rights Institute." *Alabama Heritage* 66 (Fall 2002): 7–25.

Gillon, Steve. *Boomer Nation: The Largest and Richest Generation Ever and How It Changed America.* New York: Free Press, 2004.

Ginsberg, Allen. "Howl." In *Howl and Other Poems*, 9–26. San Francisco: City Lights Books, 1996.

Goffman, Erving. *The Presentation of Self in Everyday Life.* New York: Doubleday, 1959.

———. *Stigma: Notes on the Management of Spoiled Identity.* New York: Touchstone Books, 1986.

Goldberg, Robert. "Beneath the Hood and Robe: A Socioeconomic Analysis of the Ku Klux Klan Membership in Denver, Colorado, 1921–1925." *Western Historical Quarterly* 11 (April 1980): 181–98.

Goldfield, David R. *Region, Race, and Cities: Interpreting the Urban South.* Baton Rouge: Louisiana State University Press, 1997.

Goodwin, Joanne. "'She Works Hard for Her Money': A Reassessment of Las Vegas Women Workers, 1945–1985." In Rothman and Davis, *The Grit Beneath the Glitter*, 243–59.

Gottendiener, Mark, Claudia C. Collins, and David R. Dickens. *Las Vegas: The Social Production of an All-American City.* Malden, Mass.: Blackwell Publishers, 1999.

Gragg, Larry. *Bright Light City: Las Vegas in Popular Culture.* Lawrence: University Press of Kansas, 2013.

"Great Britain: The Wolfenden Report." *Time,* September 16, 1957, 39–40.

Hahn, Milton E. "The Sexually Deviate Student." *School and Society* 41 (September 17, 1955): 85–87.

Hall, Simon. *Peace and Freedom: The Civil Rights and Antiwar Movements in the 1960s.* Philadelphia: University of Pennsylvania Press, 2005.

Hampton, Henry, and Steve Fayer, eds. *Voices of Freedom: An Oral History of the Civil Rights Movement from the 1950s through the 1980s.* New York: Bantam Books, 1991.

Hancock, Lynne, and Gerry Mooney. "'Welfare Ghettos' and the 'Broken Society': Territorial Stigmatisation in the Contemporary U.K." *Housing, Theory and Society* 30, no. 1 (2012): 46–64.

Harris, Carl V. *Political Power in Birmingham, 1871–1921.* Knoxville: University of Tennessee Press, 1977.

———. "Reforms in Governmental Control of Negroes in Birmingham, Alabama, 1890–1920." *Journal of Southern History* 38 (November 1972): 567–600.

Harris, Mark. "The Flowering of the Hippies." *Atlantic,* September 1967, 63–72.

Heidler, David Stephen, and Jeanne T. Heidler. *Manifest Destiny.* Westport, Conn.: Greenwood Press, 2003.

Hein, Virginia H. "The Image of a City Too Busy to Hate: Atlanta in the 1960s," *Phylon* 33 (Fall 1972): 205–21.

Helmer, William J. "New York's Middle-Class Homosexuals." *Harper's,* March 1963, 85–92.

Herczog, Mary. *Frommer's Las Vegas 2008.* Hoboken, N.J.: Wiley Publishing, 2008.

Herman, Edward S., and Noam Chomsky. *Manufacturing Consent: The Political Economy of the Mass Media.* New York: Pantheon, 1988.

Hess, Alan. *After-Hours Architecture.* San Francisco: Chronicle, 1993.

———. *Viva Las Vegas.* San Francisco: Chronicle, 1993.

Hicks, Terri Lynn. "Quality of Life amidst the Lights of Las Vegas." MA thesis, University of Nevada, Las Vegas, 1999.

Hill, Gladwin. "Why They Gamble: A Las Vegas Survey." *New York Times Magazine,* August 25, 1957, 27.

Hollon, W. Eugene. *The Great American Desert: Then and Now.* New York: Oxford University Press, 1966.

"The Homosexuality Issue." *Newsweek,* November 16, 1953, 46–47.

"Homosexuals: One Soldier in 25?" *Newsweek,* May 15, 1961, 92–93.

"Homosexuals: To Punish or Pity?" *Newsweek,* July 11, 1960, 78.

Howe, Alyssa Cymene. "Queer Pilgrimage: The San Francisco Homeland and Identity Tourism." *Cultural Anthropology* 16 (Spring 2001): 35–61.

Hulse, James W. *The Nevada Adventure: A History.* Revised ed. Reno: University of Nevada Press, 1969.

———. *The Silver State: Nevada's Heritage Reinterpreted.* 3rd ed. Reno: University of Nevada Press, 2004.

Hurtado, Albert L. "Sex, Gender, Culture, and a Great Event: The California Gold Rush." *Pacific Historical Review* 68 (February 1999): 1–19.

"Idaho Underworld." *Time*, December 12, 1955, 25.

Ingham, Vicki Leigh. "The Birmingham Museum of Art: A Civilizing Spirit." *Alabama Heritage* 60 (Spring 2001): 6–19.

Jackovich, Karen G., and Mark Sennet. "Wayne Newton Stars in a Real-Life Drama of Mob Extortion in Las Vegas." *People*, August 3, 1981, 30–32.

Jackson, Kenneth T. *The Ku Klux Klan in the City, 1915–1930.* New York: Oxford University Press, 1967.

JBHE Foundation. "The Racial Views of American Presidents: A Look at the Record of Calvin Coolidge." *Journal of Blacks in Higher Education* 21 (Autumn 1998): 71.

———. "Stripping Away Myths: Improving the Lot of African Americans by Changing the American Racial Stereotype." *Journal of Blacks in Higher Education* 11 (Spring 1996): 110.

Jefferies, John W. "The Quest for National Purpose of 1960," *American Quarterly* 30 (Autumn 1978): 451–70.

Jones, Richard M. "San Francisco: The City." *Speed*, July 1931.

Kahan, Oscar. "St. Louis—Thoroughly American City." *Speed*, March 1933.

Katz, Irwin. *Stigma: A Social Psychological Analysis.* Hillsdale, N.J.: LEA, 1981.

Keller, David H. *Know Yourself: Life and Sex Facts of Man, Woman, and Youth Popularly Presented by One of the Medical Profession, Who Has Made Reproduction and Health His Special Study.* New York: Popular, 1930.

Kelly, Alexis C., ed. *Fodor's Las Vegas 2008.* New York: Fodor's Travel, 2008.

Kelly, Orr. "Corruption and Mayhem: Inside Look at the Mafia." *U.S. News and World Report*, September 29, 1980.

Kerouac, Jack. *The Dharma Bums.* New York: Penguin Books, 1986.

———. *On the Road.* New York: Penguin Books, 1976.

King, Richard H. *Race, Culture, and the Intellectuals, 1940–1970.* Baltimore: Johns Hopkins University Press, 2004.

King, Stephen. *The Stand.* Expanded ed. New York: Signet, 1991.

Kinsey, Alfred C., Wardell B. Pomeroy, and Clyde E. Martin. *Sexual Behavior in the Human Male.* Philadelphia: W. B. Saunders, 1948.

Kipling, Rudyard. *American Notes.* Boston: Brown, 1899.

Kissack, Terence. "Alfred Kinsey and Homosexuality in the '50s." *Journal of the History of Sexuality* 9 (October 2000): 474–91.

Konrad, William. *Someone You May Know.* Beverly Hills: Book Company of America, 1965.

Kraft, James P. *Vegas at Odds: Labor Conflict in a Leisure Economy, 1960–1985.* Baltimore: Johns Hopkins University Press, 2010.

Kruger, Loren. "The Drama of Country and City: Tribalization, Urbanization, and Theatre under Apartheid." *Journal of South African Studies* 23 (December 1997): 565–84.

Kruse, Kevin M. *One Nation under God: How Corporate America Invented Christian America.* New York: Basic Books, 2015.

Kuhn, Thomas. *The Structure of Scientific Revolutions.* 3rd ed. Chicago: University of Chicago Press, 1996.

Labich, Kenneth, and Michael Reese. "He Hated to Lose." *Newsweek*, December 11, 1978, 28.

Ladd, Brian. *The Ghosts of Berlin: Confronting German History in the Urban Landscape.* Chicago: University of Chicago Press, 1997.

Lang, John S. "What Gambling Does for—and to—Las Vegas." *U.S. News and World Report*, March 9, 1981, 66–67.

"Las Vegas: Nice People Live on Divorce, Gambling." *Newsweek*, April 20, 1953, 32–33.

"Las Vegas: Sin and Sun Pay Off." *Business Week*, June 17, 1950, 22–23.

"Las Vegas Bets 'More Than Slots' Campaign Will Lure Baby Boomers." *O'Dwyer's PR Services Report*, August 1996, 1.

"Las Vegas Gambling." *Life*, December 21, 1942, 91–94.

"Las Vegas News Bureau." *Charger*, November 1970, 4–5.

"Lavender and Old Blues." *Newsweek*, July 20, 1959, 82.

Lenihan, John H. *Showdown: Confronting Modern America in the Western Film.* Urbana: University of Illinois Press, 1980.

Lentz, Richard. "Snarls Echoing 'round the World: The 1963 Birmingham Civil Rights Campaign on the World Stage." *American Journalism* 17 (Spring 2000): 69–96.

Lewis, John, with Michael D'Orso. *Walking with the Wind: A Memoir of the Movement.* New York: Simon and Schuster, 1998.

Lewis, W. David. *Sloss Furnaces and the Rise of the Birmingham District.* Tuscaloosa: University of Alabama Press, 1994.

Liebcap, Gary D., and Zeynep Kiocabiyik Hansen. "Rain Follows the Plow and Dryfarming Doctrine: The Climate Information Problem and Homestead Failure in the Upper Great Plains, 1890–1925." *Journal of Economic History* 62 (March 2002): 86–119.

Limerick, Patricia Nelson. *Desert Passages: Encounters with the American Desert.* Albuquerque: University of New Mexico Press, 1985.

Lippman, Walter. *Public Opinion.* New York: NuVision Books, 2007.

Lotchin, Roger W. *The Bad City in the Good War: San Francisco, Los Angeles, Oakland, San Diego.* Bloomington: Indiana University Press, 2003.

———. "California Cities and the Hurricane of Change: World War II in the San Francisco, Los Angeles, and the San Diego Metropolitan Areas." *Pacific Historical Review* (August 1994): 393–420.

———, ed. *The Martial Metropolis: U.S. Cities in War and Peace.* New York: Praeger Publishers, 1984.

———. "The Metropolitan-Military Complex in Comparative Perspective: San Francisco, Los Angeles, and San Diego, 1919–1941." In *The Making of Urban America*, edited by Raymond A. Mohl, 202–13. Wilmington, Del.: Scholarly Resources, 1988.

Lowe, Maria R., and J. Clint Morris. "Civil Rights Advocates in the Academy: White Pro-Integrationist Faculty at Millsaps College." *Journal of Mississippi History* 67 (Spring 2007): 121–45.

Macek, Steve. *Urban Nightmares: The Media, the Right, and the Moral Panic over the City.* Minneapolis: University of Minnesota Press, 2006.

"Mafia, U.S.A." *U.S. News and World Report*, February 3, 1986, 27.

Manis, Andrew M. *A Fire You Can't Put Out: The Civil Rights Life of Birmingham's Reverend Fred Shuttlesworth.* Tuscaloosa: University of Alabama Press, 1999.

Marling, Karal Ann. *As Seen on TV: The Visual Culture of Everyday Life in the 1950s.* Cambridge, Mass.: Harvard University Press, 1994.

Mary, Gary T., and Michael Useem. "Majority Involvement in Minority Movements: Civil Rights, Abolition, Untouchability." *Journal of Social Issues* 27 (1971): 81–104.

Mason, Carol. *Killing for Life: The Apocalyptic Narrative of Pro-Life Politics.* Ithaca, N.Y.: Cornell University Press, 2002.

Matthews, Glenna. "Forging a Cosmopolitan Culture: The Regional Identity of San Francisco and Northern California." In *Many Wests: Place, Culture, and Regional Identity*, edited by David Wrobel and Michael Steiner, 211–34. Lawrence: University Press of Kansas, 1997.

Mayo, A. D. "The American City." In *The American City: Literary Sources and Documents.* Vol. 1, *The American City: Views and Debates*, edited by Graham Clarke, 391–92. East Sussex: Helm Information, 1997.

Meeker, Martin Dennis, Jr. "Come out West: Communication and the Gay and Lesbian Migration to San Francisco, 1940s–1960s." PhD diss., University of Southern California, 2000.

———. *Contacts Desired: Gay and Lesbian Communications and Community, 1940s–1970s.* Chicago: University of Chicago Press, 2006.

"Men Only." *Time*, December 26, 1955, 18.

Milbrath, Lester W. "The Context of Public Opinion: How Our Belief Systems Can Affect Poll Results." *Annals of American Academy of Political and Social Science* 472 (March 1984): 35–49.

Mitchell, Lee Clark. *Westerns: Making the Man in Fiction and Film.* Chicago: University of Chicago Press, 1996.

Moehring, Eugene. "Growth, Services, and the Political Economy of Gambling in Las Vegas, 1970–2000." In Rothman and Davis, *The Grit beneath the Glitter*, 73–98.

———. *Resort City in the Sunbelt: Las Vegas 1930–2000.* 2nd ed. Reno: University of Nevada Press, 2000.

Moehring, Eugene, and Michael S. Green. *Las Vegas: A Centennial History.* Reno: University of Nevada Press, 2005.

Moore, Andrew S. "Practicing What We Preach: White Catholics and the Civil Rights Movement in Atlanta." *Georgia Historical Quarterly* 89 (Fall 2005): 334–67.

Moran, Peter William. "Great Expectations: The Legitimization of Gambling in America, 1965–1995." *Journal of Popular Culture* 31 (Summer 1997): 49–65.

Morgan, Bill, and Nancy J. Peters. *Howl on Trial: The Battle for Free Expression.* San Francisco: City Lights Books, 2006.

Murphy, Rhoads. "City and Countryside as Ideological Issues: China and India." *Comparative Studies in Society and History* 14 (June 1972): 250–67.

Muscatine, Doris. *Old San Francisco: The Biography of a City from Early Days to the Earthquake.* New York: G. P. Putnam's Sons, 1975.

Nash, Gerald D. *World War II and the West: Reshaping the Economy.* Lincoln: University of Nebraska Press, 1990.

Noelle-Neumann, Elisabeth. "The Contribution of Spiral of Silence Theory to an Understanding of Mass Media." In *The Mass Media in Liberal Democratic Societies*, edited by Stanley Rothman, 75–84. New York: Paragon House, 1992.

Norrell, Robert J. "Caste in Steel: Jim Crow Careers in Birmingham, Alabama." *Journal of American History* 73 (December 1986): 669–94.

Novick, Peter. *That Noble Dream: The Objectivity Question and the American Historical Profession.* Cambridge: Cambridge University Press, 1988.

Olsen, Barbara. "Civil Rights." *Birmingham*, November 1992, 26.

"Orphans of AIDS." *Time*, December 13, 1999, 60–62.

Otis, Ginger Adams, Beth Greenfield, Robert Reid, and Regis St. Louis. *New York City: City Guide.* Victoria, Australia: Lonely Planet Publications, 2008.

"Out of the Briar Patch." *Time*, December 25, 1964, 54.

Page, Robert M. *Stigma.* London: Routledge; Kegan Paul, 1984.

Panter-Downes, Mollie. "Letter from London: Report of the Committee on Homosexual Offenses and Prostitution." *New Yorker*, September 28, 1957, 151–53.

Parker, Arthur Harold. *A Dream That Came True: Industrial High School.* Birmingham: Printing Department of Industrial high School, 1932.

Pei, Minxin. "The Paradoxes of American Nationalism." *Foreign Policy* 136 (May/June 2003): 30–37.

Petrucelli, Alan. "The Gay Plague." *Us Magazine*, August 31, 1981.

Pivar, David J. *Purity and Hygiene: Women, Prostitution, and the "American Plan," 1900–1930.* Westport, Conn.: Greenwood Press, 2002.

Poole, Matthew R. *Frommer's Los Angeles 2008.* Hoboken, N.J.: Wiley Publishing, 2007.

———. *Frommer's San Francisco 2008.* Hoboken, N.J.: Wiley Publishing, 2007.

Popkin, James, and Katia Hetter. "America's Gambling Craze." *U.S. News and World Report*, March 14, 1994, 42.

Powell, Stewart, Stephen Emerson, Kelly Orr, Dan Collins, and Barbara Quick. "Busting the Mob." *U.S. News and World Report*, February 3, 1986, 24–28.

Powell, Sumner. *Puritan Village: The Formation of a New England Town.* Hanover, Conn.: Wesleyan University Press, 1963.

"Psychiatry: Homosexuals Can Be Cured." *Time*, February 12, 1963, 44.

"Question of Consent." *Time*, December 16, 1957, 22–23.

Rabinowitz, Howard N. *The First New South: 1865–1920.* Arlington Heights, Ill.: Harlan Davidson, 1992.

Reid, Ed, and Ovis DeMaris. *The Green Felt Jungle.* Cutchogue, N.Y.: Buccaneer Books, 1963.

Reisner, Mark. *Cadillac Desert: The American West and Its Disappearing Water.* New York: Penguin, 1993.

Reps, John P. *Cities of the American West: A History of Frontier Urban Planning.* Princeton, N.J.: Princeton University Press, 1979.

Reynolds, Cynthia. "Celebrity Chic." *MacLeans*, December 20, 2004, 51–55.

Ridinger, Robert B. Marks. *The Gay and Lesbian Movement.* New York: Simon and Schuster, 1996.

Rohrbough, Malcolm. "No Boy's Play: Migration and Settlement in Early Gold Rush California." In Starr and Orsi, *Rooted in Barbarous Soil*, 25–43.

Rothman, Hal K. *Devil's Bargain: Tourism in the Twentieth-Century American West*. Lawrence: University Press of Kansas, 1998.

———. *Neon Metropolis: How Las Vegas Started the Twenty-First Century*. New York: Routledge, 2002.

Rothman, Hal K., and Mike Davis, eds. *The Grit beneath the Glitter: Tales from the Real Las Vegas*. Berkeley: University of California Press, 2002.

Rowley, Rex. *Everyday Las Vegas: Local Life in a Tourist Town*. Reno: University of Nevada Press, 2013.

Rubin, Gayle S. "The Miracle Mile: South of Market and Gay Male Leather, 1962–1997." In *Reclaiming San Francisco: History, Politics, Culture*, edited by James Brock, Chris Carlsson, and Nancy J. Peters, 247–72. San Francisco: City Lights Books, 1998.

"San Francisco: Horror upon Horror." *Economist*, December 2, 1978, 44.

Savitt, Todd L., and James Harvey Young. *Disease and Distinctiveness in the American South*. Knoxville: University of Tennessee Press, 1991.

Schullery, Paul. *Searching for Yellowstone: Ecology and Wonder in the Last Wilderness*. Boston: Houghton Mifflin, 1997.

Schultz, Debra L. *Going South: Jewish Women in the Civil Rights Movement*. New York: New York University Press, 2001.

Schumacher, Geoff. *Sun, Sin and Suburbia: An Essential History of Las Vegas*. Las Vegas: Stephens, 2005.

Schwartz, David G. *Roll the Bones: The History of Gambling*. New York: Gotham Books, 2006.

———. *Suburban Xanadu: The Casino Resort on the Las Vegas Strip and Beyond*. New York: Routledge, 2003.

Shaffer, Marguerite S. *See America First: Tourism and National Identity, 1880–1940*. Washington, D.C.: Smithsonian Institution Press, 2001.

Shapiro, Joseph. "America's Gambling Fever." *U.S. News and World Report*, January 15, 1996, 52–60.

Sharpe, William, and Leonard Wallock, eds. *Visions of the Modern City: Essays in History, Art, and Literature*. Baltimore: Johns Hopkins University Press, 1987.

Shayon, Robert Lewis. "TV and Radio." *Saturday Review*, December 15, 1956, 27.

Sheehan, Jack. *Skin City: Behind the Scenes of the Las Vegas Sex Industry*. New York: HarperCollins, 2006.

Sherman, Richard B. "The Harding Administration and the Negro: An Opportunity Lost." *Journal of Negro History* 49 (July 1964): 151–68.

Shilts, Randy. *And the Band Played On: Politics, People, and the AIDS Epidemic*. New York: St. Martin's, 1987.

———. *The Mayor of Castro Street: The Life and Times of Harvey Milk*. New York: St. Martin's Press, 1982.

Shumsky, Neil Larry. "Tacit Acceptance: Respectable Americans and Segregated Prostitution, 1870–1900." *Journal of Social History* 19 (Summer 1986): 665–79.

———. "Vice Responds to Reform: San Francisco, 1910 to 1914." *Journal of Urban History* 7 (November 1980): 31–47.

Sides, Josh. "Excavating the Postwar Sex District in San Francisco." *Journal of Urban History* 32 (March 2006): 355–79.

Silverman, Brian. *Frommer's New York City 2009*. Hoboken, N.J.: Wiley Publishing, 2008.

Simich, Jerry L., and Thomas C. Wright, eds. *More Peoples of Las Vegas: One City, Many Places*. Reno: University of Nevada Press, 2010.

———, eds. *The Peoples of Las Vegas: One City, Many Faces*. Reno: University of Nevada Press, 2005.

Sinfield, Alan. *The Wilde Century: Effeminacy, Oscar Wilde and the Queer Movement*. New York: Columbia University Press, 1994.

Singletary, Otis A. *The Mexican War*. Chicago: University of Chicago Press, 1971.

Sitkoff, Harvard. *A New Deal for Blacks: The Emergence of Civil Rights as a National Issue*. Oxford: Oxford University Press, 1978.

Slater, Tom, and Ntsiki Anderson. "The Reputational Ghetto: Territorial Stigmatisation in St. Paul's, Bristol." *Transactions of the Institute of British Geographers* 37 (October 2012): 530–46.

Slotkin, Richard. *Gunfighter Nation: The Myth of the Frontier in Twentieth-Century America*. Norman: University of Oklahoma Press, 1998.

Smith, Henry Nash. *Virgin Land: The American West as Symbol and Myth*. New York: Vintage Books, 1950.

"Snake Eyes in Las Vegas." *Time*, September 19, 1955, 97.

Solomon, Howard M. "Stigma and Western Culture: A Historical Approach." In Ainlay, Becker, and Coleman, *The Dilemma of Difference*, 59–76.

Spence, Mark David. *Dispossessing the Wilderness: Indian Removal and the Making of the National Parks*. New York: Oxford University Press, 1999.

Spielvogel, Jackson J. *Hitler and Nazi Germany: A History*. Upper Saddle River, N.J.: Prentice Hall, 1996.

Spigel, Lynn. *Make Room for TV: Television and the Family Ideal in Postwar America*. Chicago: University of Chicago Press, 1992.

Starr, Kevin. "Rooted in Barbarous Soil: An Introduction to Gold Rush Society and Culture." In Starr and Orsi, *Rooted in Barbarous Soil*, 1–24.

Starr, Kevin, and Richard J. Orsi, eds. *Rooted in Barbarous Soil: People, Culture, and Community in Gold Rush California*. Berkeley: University of California Press, 2000.

Stein, Joel, and Laura A. Locke. "The Strip Is Back!" *Time*, July 26, 2004.

Steinberg, Ted. *Acts of God: The Unnatural History of Natural Disasters*. New York: Oxford University Press, 2006.

———. *Down to Earth: Nature's Role in American History*. New York: Oxford University Press, 2002.

Steuer, Arthur. "Playground for Adults Only." *Esquire*, August 1961, 41–46.

"Still Another List." *Nation*, June 22, 1964, 615.

Stinnett, Caskie. "Las Vegas: Where Anything Is Forgivable Except Restraint." *Holiday*, May 1967, 32.

Stout, Janis P. *Sodoms in Eden: The City in American Fiction before 1860.* Westport, Conn.: Greenwood, 1976.

Strauss, Anselm L. *Images of the American City.* New York: Free Press, 1961.

Stryker, Susan, and Jim Van Buskirk. *Gay by the Bay: A History of Queer Culture in the San Francisco Bay Area.* San Francisco: Chronicle Books, 1996.

"Taboo on Television." *Newsweek,* December 9, 1957, 68.

Taylor, Lawrence D. "The Wild Frontier Moves South: U.S. Entrepreneurs and the Growth of Tijuana's Vice Industry, 1908–1935." *Journal of San Diego History* 48 (Summer 2002): 204–29.

Terry, Jennifer. *An American Obsession: Science, Medicine, and Homosexuality in Modern Society.* Chicago: University of Chicago Press, 1999.

"The Third Sex." *Newsweek,* June 1, 1964, 76.

Thompson, Hunter S. *Fear and Loathing in Las Vegas: A Savage Journey to the Heart of the American Dream.* 2nd Vintage Books ed. New York: Vintage Books, 1998.

Thompson, W. N., J. Kent Pinney, and J. A. Schibrowsky. "The Family That Gambles Together: Business and Social Concerns." *Journal of Travel Research* 34 (Winter 1996): 70–74.

Tompkins, Jane. *West of Everything: The Inner Life of Westerns.* New York: Oxford University Press, 1992.

Torres, Ben Fong. "A Letter from San Francisco." *Rolling Stone,* January 24, 1979, 45–46.

Towne, Alfred. "Homosexuality in American Culture: The New Taste in Literature." *American Mercury,* August 1951, 3–9.

"Treading Lightly in a Delicate Subject." *Christian Century,* September 18, 1957, 1092–94.

Turner, Frederick Jackson. "The Significance of the Frontier in American History." In *Rereading Frederick Jackson Turner: The Significance of the Frontier in American History and Other Essays,* edited by John Mack Faragher, 31–60. New York: Holt, 1994.

Velie, Lester. "Las Vegas: The Underworld's Secret Jackpot." *Reader's Digest,* October 1959, 138–44.

———. "Underworld's Back Door to Las Vegas." *Reader's Digest,* November 1974, 207–8.

Venturi, Robert, Denise S. Brown, and Steven Izenour. *Learning from Las Vegas.* Cambridge, Mass.: MIT Press, 1972.

Wacquant, Loïc. *Urban Outcasts: A Comparative Sociology of Advanced Marginality.* Cambridge, Mass.: Polity Press, 2008.

Wainwright, Loudon. "The Strange New Love Land of the Hippies." *Life,* March 31, 1967, 14–15.

Warren, Herbert O. "Play Days in San Francisco." *Speed,* November 1931.

Weaver, David H., and G. Cleveland Wilhoit. "Journalists—Who Are They, Really?" *Media Studies Journal* 6 (Fall 1992): 63–79.

"We Have Come Part of the Way." *Birmingham,* April 1971, 25–27.

Weimer, David R. *City and Country in America.* New York: Appleton-Century-Crofts, 1962.

———. *The City as Metaphor.* New York: Random House, 1966.

Welch, Paul, and Ernest Havemann. "Homosexuality in America." *Life*, June 26, 1964, 66–74.

Welles, Chris. "America's Gambling Fever." *Business Week*, April 24, 1989, 112–19.

"What Is a Homosexual?" *Time*, June 16, 1958, 44.

"What's Happening to American Morality?" *U.S. News and World Report*, October 13, 1975, 39.

"Wherever You Look There's Danger in Las Vegas." *Life*, November 12, 1951, 37.

White, Jack E. "When Silence Is a Sin." *Time*, December 27, 1999.

White, Morton, and Lucia White. *The Intellectual versus the City: From Thomas Jefferson to Frank Lloyd Wright*. New York: Mentor Books, 1964.

Whitfield, Stephen J. *The Culture of the Cold War*. Baltimore: Johns Hopkins University Press, 1996.

Whyte, William H. *The Organization Man*. New York: Simon and Schuster, 1956.

Wilcock, Brian, ed. *Insight Guides: San Francisco*. Boston: APA Publications, 1995.

Williams, Raymond. *The Country and the City*. New York: Oxford University Press, 1973.

Wilson, Bobby M. *America's Johannesburg: Industrialization and Racial Transformation in Birmingham*. Lanham, Md.: Rowman and Littlefield, 2000.

Wilson, Michele, and John Lynxwiler, "The Federal Government and the Harassment of Black Leaders: A Case Study of Mayor Richard Arrington Jr. of Birmingham." *Journal of Black Studies* 28 (May 1998): 540–60.

Wolfe, Tom. *The Kandy-Kolored Tangerine-Flake Streamline Baby*. New York: Farrar, Straus and Giroux, 1963.

Woolfolk, Odessa. "Historical Overview." In *Making Connections: A Curriculum for Grades K-12*. Birmingham: Birmingham Civil Rights Institute, 2000.

Worobey, Michael, Marlea Gemmel, Dirk E. Teuwen, Tamara Haselkorn, Kevin Kunstman, Michael Bunce, Jean-Jacques Muyembe, Jean-Marie M. Kabongo, Raphaël M. Kalengayi, Eric Van Marck, M. Thomas P. Gilbert, and Steven M. Wolinsky. "Direct Evidence of Extensive Diversity of HIV-1 in Kinshasa by 1960." *Nature* 455 (October 2008): 661–64.

Wright, Frank. *Clark County: The Changing Face of Nevada*. Las Vegas: Nevada Historical Society, 1981.

Wrobel, David. *Promised Lands: Promotion, Memory, and the Creation of the American West*. Lawrence: University of Kansas Press, 2002.

Wyden, Peter. "How Wicked Is Vegas?" *Saturday Evening Post*, November 11, 1961, 23.

Index

Page numbers in *italics* refer to illustrative matter.